Improving Energy Efficiency through Data-Driven Modeling, Simulation and Optimization

Improving Energy Efficiency through Data-Driven Modeling, Simulation and Optimization

Editor

Dirk Deschrijver

MDPI • Basel • Beijing • Wuhan • Barcelona • Belgrade • Manchester • Tokyo • Cluj • Tianjin

Editor
Dirk Deschrijver
Information Technology
Ghent University - imec
Ghent
Belgium

Editorial Office
MDPI
St. Alban-Anlage 66
4052 Basel, Switzerland

This is a reprint of articles from the Special Issue published online in the open access journal *Energies* (ISSN 1996-1073) (available at: www.mdpi.com/journal/energies/special_issues/Energy_Efficiency_Data_Driven).

For citation purposes, cite each article independently as indicated on the article page online and as indicated below:

LastName, A.A.; LastName, B.B.; LastName, C.C. Article Title. *Journal Name* **Year**, *Volume Number*, Page Range.

ISBN 978-3-0365-1207-5 (Hbk)
ISBN 978-3-0365-1206-8 (PDF)

© 2021 by the authors. Articles in this book are Open Access and distributed under the Creative Commons Attribution (CC BY) license, which allows users to download, copy and build upon published articles, as long as the author and publisher are properly credited, which ensures maximum dissemination and a wider impact of our publications.

The book as a whole is distributed by MDPI under the terms and conditions of the Creative Commons license CC BY-NC-ND.

Contents

Dirk Deschrijver
Special Issue: "Improving Energy Efficiency through Data-Driven Modeling, Simulation and Optimization"
Reprinted from: *Energies* **2021**, *14*, 1543, doi:10.3390/en14061543 1

Fang Wang, Wen-Jia Yang and Wei-Feng Sun
Heat Transfer and Energy Consumption of Passive House in a Severely Cold Area: Simulation Analyses
Reprinted from: *Energies* **2020**, *13*, 626, doi:10.3390/en13030626 5

Jessica Walther and Matthias Weigold
A Systematic Review on Predicting and Forecasting the Electrical Energy Consumption in the Manufacturing Industry
Reprinted from: *Energies* **2021**, *14*, 968, doi:10.3390/en14040968 25

Benoit G. Marinus and Antoine Hauglustaine
Data-Driven Modeling of Fuel Consumption for Turboprop-Powered Civil Airliners
Reprinted from: *Energies* **2020**, *13*, 1695, doi:10.3390/en13071695 51

Alberto V. Donati, Jette Krause, Christian Thiel, Ben White and Nikolas Hill
An Ant Colony Algorithm for Improving Energy Efficiency of Road Vehicles
Reprinted from: *Energies* **2020**, *13*, 2850, doi:10.3390/en13112850 65

Anthony Faustine and Lucas Pereira
Improved Appliance Classification in Non-Intrusive Load Monitoring Using Weighted Recurrence Graph and Convolutional Neural Networks
Reprinted from: *Energies* **2020**, *13*, 3374, doi:10.3390/en13133374 87

Chun-Wei Chen, Chun-Chang Li and Chen-Yu Lin
Combine Clustering and Machine Learning for Enhancing the Efficiency of Energy Baseline of Chiller System
Reprinted from: *Energies* **2020**, *13*, 4368, doi:10.3390/en13174368 103

Tomasz Szul, Krzysztof Necka and Thomas G. Mathia
Neural Methods Comparison for Prediction of Heating Energy Based on Few Hundreds Enhanced Buildings in Four Season's Climate
Reprinted from: *Energies* **2020**, *13*, 5453, doi:10.3390/en13205453 123

Rongjia Li, Guangya Zhu and Dalin Zhang
Investigation on the Mechanism of Heat Load Reduction for the Thermal Anti-Icing System
Reprinted from: *Energies* **2020**, *13*, 5911, doi:10.3390/en13225911 141

Giovanni Gravito de Carvalho Chrysostomo, Marco Vinicius Bhering de Aguiar Vallim, Leilton Santos da Silva, Leandro A. Silva and Arnaldo Rabello de Aguiar Vallim Filho
A Framework for Big Data Analytical Process and Mapping—BAProM: Description of an Application in an Industrial Environment
Reprinted from: *Energies* **2020**, *13*, 6014, doi:10.3390/en13226014 161

Zhibiao Guo, Weitao Li, Songyang Yin, Dongshan Yang and Zhibo Ma
An Innovative Technology for Monitoring the Distribution of Abutment Stress in Longwall Mining
Reprinted from: *Energies* **2021**, *14*, 475, doi:10.3390/en14020475 189

Editorial

Special Issue: "Improving Energy Efficiency through Data-Driven Modeling, Simulation and Optimization"

Dirk Deschrijver

Department of Information Technology, Ghent University-IMEC, Technologiepark Zwijnaarde 126, 9052 Gent, Belgium; dirk.deschrijver@ugent.be

Citation: Deschrijver, D. Special Issue: "Improving Energy Efficiency through Data-Driven Modeling, Simulation and Optimization". *Energies* **2021**, *14*, 1543. https://doi.org/10.3390/en14061543

Received: 5 March 2021
Accepted: 8 March 2021
Published: 11 March 2021

Publisher's Note: MDPI stays neutral with regard to jurisdictional claims in published maps and institutional affiliations.

Copyright: © 2021 by the author. Licensee MDPI, Basel, Switzerland. This article is an open access article distributed under the terms and conditions of the Creative Commons Attribution (CC BY) license (https://creativecommons.org/licenses/by/4.0/).

In October 2014, EU leaders agreed upon three key targets for the year 2030: a reduction of at least 40% in greenhouse gas emissions, a saving of at least a 27% share for renewable energy, and at least a 27% improvement in energy efficiency. The increase in computational power combined with advanced modeling and simulation tools makes it possible to derive new technological solutions that can enhance the energy efficiency of systems, and that can reduce the ecological footprint. This Special Issue includes 10 novel research works that are based on data-driven approaches, machine learning, or artificial intelligence for the modeling, simulation, and optimization of energy systems.

Fang et al. [1] investigated the heat transfer in the enclosure structure of passive houses in cold areas with complex climatic conditions. A three-dimensional model was established to investigate the time-by-case changes of the outdoor temperature and solar irradiation based on the principle of integral change and the method of response coefficient and harmonious wave reaction. The variations in hourly cooling and heating loads with outdoor temperature and solar irradiation were analyzed. A strategic routine was suggested to remarkably decrease the total energy consumption and the annual operation cost of passive buildings.

Walther et al. [2] presented a systematic review of the state-of-the-art of existing approaches to predicting or forecasting energy consumption in the manufacturing industry. A morphology for classifying different approaches in the field of energy prediction and forecasting was developed, based on the identified influencing factors. Seventy-two articles, based on a systematic literature search, were classified according to the defined categories: system boundary, modeling technique, modeling focus, modeling horizon, modeling perspective, modeling purpose and model output. Furthermore, based on the reviewed articles, future research activities were derived.

Marinus et al. [3] presented and validated a data-driven response-surface model of fuel consumption data for turboprop-powered civil airliners. The model coefficients were predicted from empirical correlations based solely on the operating empty weight, and validation was performed on a separate set. The model can accurately predict the fuel weights of new designs for any combination of payload and range within the current range of efficiency of the propulsion. The accuracy of the model makes it suited for the preliminary and conceptual design of near-in-kind turbo-propeller aircraft. The model can shorten the design cycle by delivering fast and accurate fuel weight estimates from the first design iteration once the operating empty weight is known.

Donati et al. [4] proposed a method to optimally combine vehicle CO_2 reduction technologies in cars and other road vehicles to improve their energy efficiency. The incompatibility of these technologies gives rise to conflicting objectives that have to be optimized in a multi-objective way. For this NP-complete (non-deterministic polynomial complete) combinatorial problem, a method based on a metaheuristic with ant colony optimization (ACO) combined with a local search (LS) algorithm was proposed and generalized as the technology packaging problem (TPP). The performance of the proposed method was compared with a genetic algorithm (GA) and the obtained improvements were shown. Computational tests were also presented to show the effectiveness of this new approach.

Faustine et al. [5] developed a new application recognition method for non-intrusive load monitoring (NILM) that utilizes the recurrence graph (RG) technique and convolutional neural networks (CNNs). A weighted recurrent graph (WRG) generation was introduced that, given one-cycle current and voltage, produces an image-like representation with more values than the binary output created by RG. Experimental results from three different sub-metered datasets showed that the proposed WRG-based image representation provides superior feature representation and, therefore, improves classification performance compared to voltage-current (V–I)-based features.

Chen at al. [6] combined clustering and machine learning for enhancing the efficiency of the energy baseline of a chiller system. First, several machine learning algorithms were reviewed to establish prediction models. Then, the concept of clustering to preprocess chiller data was adopted. Data mining, K-means clustering, and gap statistics were used to successfully identify the critical variables to cluster chiller modes. Applying these key variables effectively enhanced the quality of the chiller data, and combining the clustering results and the machine learning model effectively improved the prediction accuracy of the model and the reliability of the energy baselines.

Szul et al. [7] evaluated the efficiency of habitat thermo-modernization. Several buildings from the end of the last century, which were thermally improved at the beginning of the 21st century, were designed for a comparative analysis of the predictive modeling of heating energy consumption. A specific set of important variables was identified to characterize the examined buildings. Groups of variables were used to estimate the energy consumption in such a way as to achieve a compromise between the difficulty of obtaining them and the quality of the forecast. To predict energy consumption, several neural methods were compared. The most effective method allows one to forecast with great precision the energy consumption (after thermal improvement) of this type of residential building.

Li et al. [8] presented a study of the mechanism of heat load reduction in the thermal anti-icing system of aircraft under the evaporative mode. A GA-based optimization method was adopted to optimize the anti-icing heat load and obtain the optimal heating power distribution. An experiment carried out in an icing wind tunnel was conducted to validate the optimized results. The mechanism of the anti-icing heat load reduction was revealed by analyzing the influences of the key factors, such as the heating range, the surface temperature and the convective heat transfer coefficient. These investigations can provide valuable guidance for the design of the thermal anti-icing systems.

Chrysostomo et al. [9] presented the application of a framework for big data analytical processing and mapping. It was conceived as a decision support tool for industrial business, encompassing the whole big data analytical process. A real-world application is the implementation of a predictive maintenance decision support tool in a hydroelectric power plant. Using the analytical workbench, all variables were properly analyzed. A predictive model was implemented for the predictive maintenance of equipment, identifying critical variables that define the imminence of an equipment failure. The model was combined with a time series forecasting model, based on artificial neural networks, to project those critical variables for a future time. The effectiveness and practical feasibility of the framework were demonstrated.

Guo et al. [10] investigated the change law of side abutment pressure and the movement law of overlying strata when using the fracturing roofs to maintain entry (FRME). A new abutment pressure monitoring device, i.e., a flexible detection unit (FDU), was developed and applied in the field. The paper compared the difference in lateral abutment pressure between the tail entry and head entry by monitoring the abutment pressure of solid coal on both sides of the working face with self-developed and more reliable FDU. Then, the influence of the cutting seam on the lateral abutment pressure of solid coal was explored. On the basis of fully considering the reasons for the change in abutment pressure after cutting the roof, the change in overburden movement caused by the slit was analyzed.

The contributed papers that are included in this Special Issue offer new and valuable insights that can stimulate ongoing research activities in the field. As guest editor, I would like to thank all authors that have submitted their research work to this Special Issue.

Funding: This special issue is supported by the Flemish Government under the "Onderzoeksprogramma Artificiële Intelligentie (AI) Vlaanderen" programme.

Conflicts of Interest: The author declares no conflict of interest.

References

1. Wang, F.; Yang, W.-J.; Sun, W.-F. Heat Transfer and Energy Consumption of Passive House in a Severely Cold Area: Simulation Analyses. *Energies* **2020**, *13*, 626. [CrossRef]
2. Walther, J.; Weigold, M. A Systematic Review on Predicting and Forecasting the Electrical Energy Consumption in the Manufacturing Industry. *Energies* **2021**, *14*, 968. [CrossRef]
3. Marinus, B.G.; Hauglustaine, A. Data-Driven Modeling of Fuel Consumption for Turboprop-Powered Civil Airliners. *Energies* **2020**, *13*, 1695. [CrossRef]
4. Donati, A.V.; Krause, J.; Thiel, C.; White, B.; Hill, N. An Ant Colony Algorithm for Improving Energy Efficiency of Road Vehicles. *Energies* **2020**, *13*, 2850. [CrossRef]
5. Faustine, A.; Pereira, L. Improved Appliance Classification in Non-Intrusive Load Monitoring Using Weighted Recurrence Graph and Convolutional Neural Networks. *Energies* **2020**, *13*, 3374. [CrossRef]
6. Chen, C.-W.; Li, C.-C.; Lin, C.-Y. Combine Clustering and Machine Learning for Enhancing the Efficiency of Energy Baseline of Chiller System. *Energies* **2020**, *13*, 4368. [CrossRef]
7. Szul, T.; Nęcka, K.; Mathia, T.G. Neural Methods Comparison for Prediction of Heating Energy Based on Few Hundreds Enhanced Buildings in Four Season's Climate. *Energies* **2020**, *13*, 5453. [CrossRef]
8. Li, R.; Zhu, G.; Zhang, D. Investigation on the Mechanism of Heat Load Reduction for the Thermal Anti-Icing System. *Energies* **2020**, *13*, 5911. [CrossRef]
9. De Carvalho Chrysostomo, G.G.; de Aguiar Vallim, M.V.B.; da Silva, L.S.; Silva, L.A.; de Aguiar Vallim Filho, A.R. A Framework for Big Data Analytical Process and Mapping—BAProM: Description of an Application in an Industrial Environment. *Energies* **2020**, *13*, 6014. [CrossRef]
10. Guo, Z.; Li, W.; Yin, S.; Yang, D.; Ma, Z. An Innovative Technology for Monitoring the Distribution of Abutment Stress in Longwall Mining. *Energies* **2021**, *14*, 475. [CrossRef]

Article

Heat Transfer and Energy Consumption of Passive House in a Severely Cold Area: Simulation Analyses

Fang Wang [1], Wen-Jia Yang [1] and Wei-Feng Sun [2],*

[1] School of Mechanical and Power Engineering, Rongcheng College, Harbin University of Science and Technology, Harbin 150080, China; wangfang0228@hrbust.edu.cn (F.W.); wenjia_yang@126.com (W.-J.Y.)

[2] School of Electrical and Electronic Engineering, Harbin University of Science and Technology, Harbin 150080, China

* Correspondence: sunweifeng@hrbust.edu.cn; Tel.: +86-1584-659-2798

Received: 31 December 2019; Accepted: 30 January 2020; Published: 2 February 2020

Abstract: In order to improve the heat transfer in enclosure structure of passive houses in cold area with complex climatic conditions, a three-dimensional model is established to investigate the time-by-case changes of outdoor temperature and solar irradiation based on the principle of integral change and the method of response coefficient and harmonious wave reaction. The variations of hourly cooling and heating loads with outdoor temperature and solar irradiation are analyzed. As simulated by cloud computing technology, the passive building energy consumption meets the requirements of passive building specifications. In the present research, super-thermal insulation external wall, enclosure structure of energy-conserving doors and windows, and high efficiency heat recovery system are employed to achieve a constant temperature without active mechanical heating and cooling, which suggests a strategic routine to remarkably decrease the total energy consumption and annual operation cost of passive building.

Keywords: passive house; enclosure structure; heat transfer coefficient; energy consumption

1. Introduction

As the earth's temperature is increased by human energy consumption, great attention has been focused on high-comfort green buildings with renewable energy and near zero energy consumption, which are named "passive houses" and limit the sum of primary energy consumption to less than 120 kWh/(m^2·a). Early in 2005, Feist suggested the characteristics of combined heating and ventilation system in passive houses by investigating the energy consumption level and comfort index [1]. Passive housing and its standard were firstly proposed in Germany. After a long period of technical improvement, the standard required for passive houses gradually became more detailed and rigorous. In 2006, Schnieders tested eleven passive houses in Germany and concluded that passive houses can save 80% of space energy consumption, with the total primary energy consumption (including household electricity) being controlled lower than 50% of the traditional new buildings [2]. Based on the thermal performance of passive houses with arch roof in New Delhi, India, it is concluded by Arvind that the annual energy consumption of heating and cooling can be saved by 1481 kWh/a and 1814 kWh/a, respectively, with only 52 euros per year in carbon emission cost [3]. In 2011, Mlakar discussed the effects of different energy gains on the overheating in hot summer for a passive house in Slovenia compared with the actual heat consumption of traditional houses [4]. The construction standard of passive houses was firstly proposed by Rongen in 2012, which has become a globally recognized energy-saving building standard [5]. In 2013, Ridley reported that the total energy consumption of the first new London house certified by passive housing standard has approached to 65 kWh/(m^2·a), which is one of the lowest energy consumption for small family houses in UK [6].

Taking energy transportation cost into account and analyzing the energy consumption through the whole operation cycle, the per capita energy consumption of a typical passive house in Belgium is 19.6% lower than that of the traditional buildings before reconstructions [7,8]. Rohdin confirmed that the indoor comfort of nine passive houses in Sweden is better than that of traditional buildings without considering external shading, despite of the distinctly changed indoor temperature in summer due to cooking or other heat sources [9]. Irulegi was the first to study industrialized solar houses in which the architectural design strategy combined solar energy technology with passive design standards to achieve energy self-sufficiency and provide a high quality of life for occupants [10]. In 2016, Dan built an energy-saving house in Romania according to the design principles of passive house and proved that the total primary energy demand is less than the design goal of 120 kWh/(m^2·a) [11]. In 2019, Ilomets analyzed the indoor climate loads for dwellings in different cold climates to assess hygrothermal performance of building envelopes and put forward the suggestions for the external wall insulation [12].

The first passive house under subtropical climate in Cyprus was designed by Fokaides employing an optimized night ventilation equipment and a high efficient HVAC cooling system to reduce the average indoor temperature and significantly improve the thermal comfort, respectively [13]. A passive house in the Qivli District of Australia, which is designed using solar energy, heat, and transverse ventilation, represents a total energy consumption of 64% lower than similar households in the same city and provides excellent indoor comfort and a high air quality levels [14]. Alajmi studies the terminal energy consumption performance of double-decker villas built according to the passive house standards in Portland, Oregon, USA [15]. It is proved that passive houses achieve net zero energy consumption by using photovoltaic panels, which are suitable for the climate of northwest United States. The excellent structure, amenity, and power balance can be acquired by solar passive houses that adopt the solar energy and heating ventilation of air conditioning system as an efficient strategy to combine passive, active, and prefabricated systems [16]. Dalbem determines the thermal enclosure structure of different climates in southern Brazil according to the implementation standards of Brazilian passive houses and discusses the transformation of traditional houses into standard passive houses [17]. According to the standard of passive houses, the best scheme of Brazilian passive house has been obtained by analyzing the thermal performance index and economic feasibility with the optimized numerical model [17]. In southern Germany, the energy saving performance and CO_2 emissions of a newly built passive school implied that the passive houses have been extended to public buildings [18]. The latest version of the passive house standard was revised with new standard provisions in 2016 to be applied for all climates in the world, abating the restrictions on sub-cold and temperate climates and integrating the requirements for residential and non-residential buildings. The new standard requires that the heating or cooling demand of a passive house should be not higher than 15 kW·h/(m^2·a), the air tightness parameter should be no larger than 0.6 h^{-1}, the renewable energy demand should be no greater than 60 ± 15 kW·h/(m^2·a).

The energy saving rates of passive houses are much higher than that of traditional buildings; thus, it is of great significance to study and develop passive houses for the sustainable development of China where building energy consumption accounts for 1/3 of total energy consumption. In 2010, China built the first certified passive house of China—Hamburg House was built in Shanghai Expo Park [19]. In 2014, the first high-rise passive building in the area with hot summer and cold winter was built in Zhuzhou, Hunan Province of China [20]; and the first cold region passive house, Chenweili Bay, was built in Yingkou, Liaoning Province of China [21,22]. In 2015, the China passive Ultra-Low Energy Consumption Building Alliance organized for the China Academy of Architectural Sciences and other units to compile and issue the *Passive Ultra-Low Energy Consumption Green Building Technical Guidelines (Residential Buildings)* as the technical standard of passive houses in China [23]. According to China's sustainable development strategy, passive buildings with high energy efficiency and comfortable living are the prospective candidates for saving energy and reducing carbon emissions in the future in order to deal with climate change. By the end of 2018, more than 100 passive construction projects have been accomplished in China, 21 of which have been certified as passive houses. However, due to the vast territory, large climatic coverage, and different complexity of climatic conditions in China, passive constructions are mainly concentrated in the southern regions while the passive projects in severely cold areas are less than 10% of total passive houses. Therefore, the present study takes Senying passive office building in Harbin city of China (a typical severely cold area) as a representative to carry out theoretical investigation and practical analysis, in order to conclude the heat transfer and energy consumption of passive house with enclosure structure that are suitable for a severely cold area, and provide fundamental reference for the design and construction of passive house in a severely cold area.

2. Simulation and Analysis Methodology

2.1. Passive House Standard

The passive house requires adaptation to climate characteristics and site conditions so that the energy consumption of heating, air conditioning, and lighting can be minimized through passive architectural design. In order to improve the efficiency of energy preservation equipment and systems, renewable energy is used in all areas to provide a comfortable indoor environment with minimal energy consumption. The indoor environmental parameters and energy efficiency indexes of passive houses must conform to standards so the energy consumption without using mechanical heating and cooling is reduced to a certain level under the premise of ensuring human body comfort. In recent years, passive building standards in China have been studied and explored in a deep way. In 2019, the Heilongjiang Provincial CPC Committee published the *Passive Low Energy Consumption Residential Building Design Standard* as listed Table 1 for the relevant design standards of passive house [24]. The space heating load of passive buildings in winter should not be greater than 12 W/m^2; the cooling load in summer should be less than 20 W/m^2, and the primary energy demand (including heating, cooling, domestic hot water, and living electricity) should be less than 120 kWh/m^2 per year. The heat transfer coefficients of enclosure structure and window for passive house must be lower than 0.1 and 0.8 W/(m^2·K) respectively, with the air tightness being controlled to a ventilation number of <0.5/h under the pressure difference of 50 Pa. In summary, the enclosure structure of passive building should possess excellent heat preservation and absolute tightness while the heat recovery system has sufficient recovery rate, which can sustain high air quality without window opening in winter and summer.

Table 1. Designing standards of passive house.

Parameter	Unit	Maximum
Heating demand	kWh/m^2	18
Heating load	W/m^2	12
Cooling demand	kWh/m^2	13
Cooling load	W/m^2	20
Frequency of overheating	%	10
Air tightness (n50)	ACH	0.6
Primary energy demand	kWh/m^2	120

2.2. Climatic and Geographical Characteristics and Building Data

Harbin city is located in the south of Heilongjiang Province of Northeast China Plain, between longitude 125°42′~140°10′ east and latitude 44°04′~46°40′ north. Harbin is the capital city with the highest latitude and the lowest temperature in China with the middle temperate continental monsoon climate as: distinct four seasons, long and cold winter, and short and cool summer. The temperature in Harbin changes rapidly in the transitional seasons of spring and autumn with relatively short time. Therefore, the thermal design area of Harbin is located in the severely cold region where the annual average temperature is 4.5 °C; the lowest temperature appears in January and can reach −40 °C; the indoor heating temperature is controlled at 18–22 °C, and the average heating time is 174 days.

The Senying passive office building studied in the present paper is a double-decker structure with a building height of 9 m and a total building area of 5025.74 m^2. The first-floor area is 2683.58 m^2 and the second-floor area is 2464.37 m^2, as the photographs and ichnography shown in Figure 1, and the side view schematics shown in Figure 2. The whole building utilizes super heat preservation honeycomb wall, being equipped with special passive doors and windows, sunshade shutters, photovoltaic power generation, rainwater collection, reclaimed water treatment, waste biochemistry, waste heat exchange, and sunshine utilization. The air tightness parameter (ACH at 50 Pa) of this passive house is only 0.16/h, which is far below the international standard of 0.6/h, and the annual total saving cost of heating and cooling approaches to 1.8 million ¥ with the annual total carbon dioxide emission being reduced by 4.2×10^5 kg.

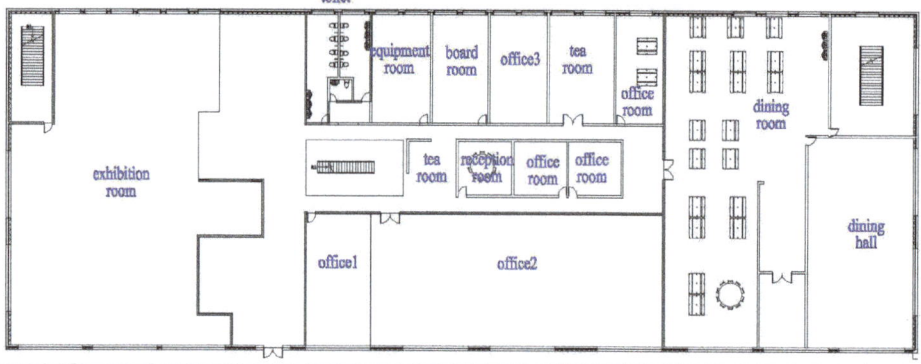

Figure 1. Senying passive office building: close and panoramic photographs (upper and middle panels), and ichnography of the first floor (bottom panel).

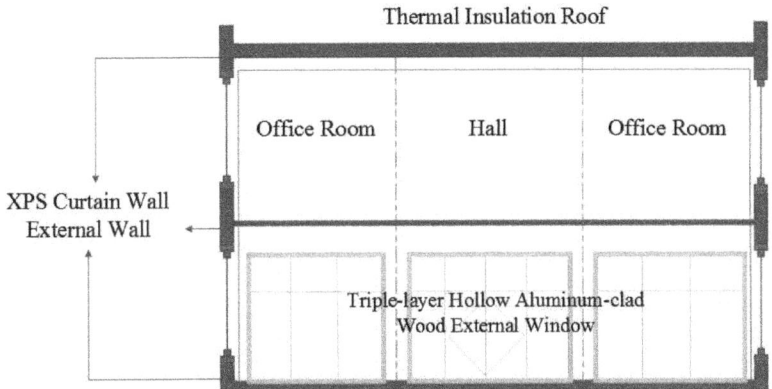

Figure 2. Side view of Senying passive office building.

2.3. Simulation Schemes and Design Parameters

The main factors of building energy consumption—envelope structure and ventilation efficiency—in the design strategy of passive buildings in a severely cold area are firstly determined to establish the building model and confirm the passive house design parameters. Then, the harmonic response method is used to calculate the thermal loads and heat transfer of wall roof, exterior window, and indoor with the various heat sources being divided into convection and radiation parts. By means of harmonic response method, the cooling load caused by the exothermic decay and delay between the different enclosure structures is specially evaluated in the radiation heat calculations, and the heat transfer caused by air penetration is included in the convection to calculate the total load. Finally, the relevant thermal loads and energy consumption are estimated and analyzed. The investigation strategy and simulation routine in the present study are schematically illustrated in Figure 3.

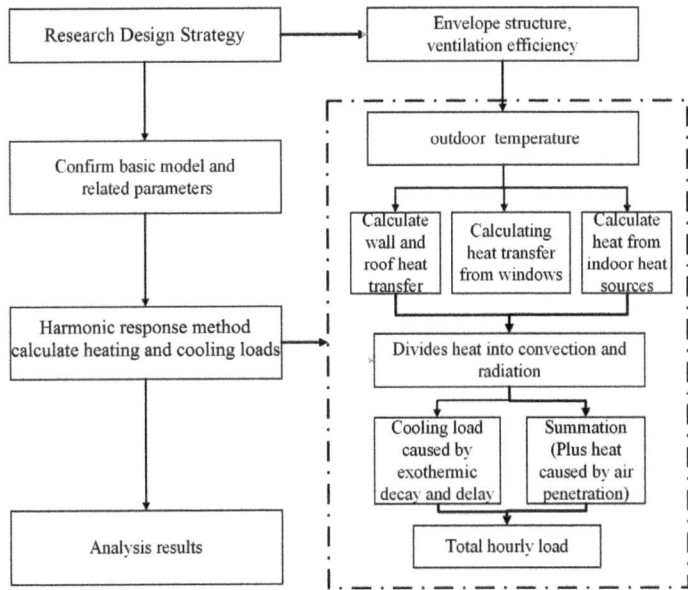

Figure 3. Schematic investigation strategy in simulation processes.

Taking Senying office building under the climate of Harbin as a paradigm, the three-dimensional model of passive house with spatial zoning and spatial tagging is established by the relevant design parameters of heat transfer environment and enclosure structure as shown in Tables 2 and 3, respectively. According to the thermal balance principle of heat transfer theory, the influences of heat transfer coefficient and thickness of different thermal insulation materials on the heat transfer performance of passive house enclosure structure are calculated and analyzed with the different structural combinations being compared. Based on the principle of integral variation, the Ecotect software is implemented to simulate the outdoor time-by-case temperature and variation of solar irradiation through a day. Employing the harmonic response method as implemented in BIM code, the hourly thermal load on the enclosure structure of passive house, which varies with outdoor temperature and solar irradiation is calculated and analyzed in the present study. Using cloud computing technology as implemented by the program Green Building Studio, we also perform energy cost analyses for the latent heat, energy, and carbon demand of passive house in severely cold area.

Table 2. Design parameters of heat transfer environment.

Parameter		Value
Summer mean temperature/°C		25
Winter mean temperature/°C		20
Outdoor mean temperature through a year/°C		4.5
Summer outdoor dry ball mean temperature/°C		30.6
Winter outdoor dry ball mean temperature/°C		−24.1
Outdoor mean air flow rate/(m/s)	Summer	2.8
	Winter	3.5
Relative humidity/%		60
Equipment power/(W/m^2)		13
Light power/(W/m^2)		11
Fresh air volume/(m^3/h)		60

Table 3. Envelope structure parameters.

Envelope Constituents	Maximum Heat Transfer Coefficient/(W·m^{-2}·K^{-1})	Envelope Delay/h	Envelope Attenuation/%
Thermal insulation wall	0.125	13.3	4
Outside window	0.65	2.5	89
Floor	0.125	11.7	2
Roof	0.125	19.7	6
Interior wall	0.1	7.0	55
Exterior door	0.65	0.6	99

Ecotect and BIM are commonly used simulation software to analyze the energy consumption and heat transfer of buildings at present. With friendly user interface, high computational compatibility, and intuitive results, Ecotect and BIM are suitable for the analysis and research of meteorological data and building environment to provide the basis for the optimization and promotion of architectural design scheme, which is beneficial to the realization of an efficient architectural scheme design [25,26]. Using harmonic response method as being implemented by BIM to calculate the thermal loads has the advantages of simple calculation and no need for repeated iteration to be effectively applied in predicting the actual engineering energy consumption [26]. By harmonic response method, the attenuation and delay of the building enclosure structure can be considered to calculate the time-by-time load and energy consumption through a year.

3. External Enclosure Structure

3.1. Thermal Insulation System of External Wall

In order to realize a passive building, a certain thickness of high-efficiency thermal insulation materials, special passive doors and windows, mechanical ventilation equipment for heat recovery, and air tightness control are inbuilt, as shown in the schematic passive house structure in Figure 4. The enclosure structure is the main constituent, being directly in contact with the external environment and thereby acting as the dominant medium through which heat transfer and energy move between the inside and outside of passive building. In the enclosure structure, the external wall as the primary constituent contributes to the major area and contacts all the other parts of thermal maintenance system. In the whole building energy consumption, the external wall accounts for >40%, so the external wall design for thermal insulation is of great significance to the enclosure structure of passive house. The external insulation structure, as a structural complex to effectively reduce the energy consumption, is set up to connect with walls through an appropriate way in the enclosure structure. The external insulation medium mainly consists of special materials with obvious capability for heat insulation, heat preservation, and energy saving. According to the practical construction features, the external wall insulation can be classified into three forms: interior thermal insulation, exterior insulation, and sandwich insulation [27], as shown in Table 4 which provides the advantages and disadvantages of three different thermal insulation structures.

In comparison for these three thermal insulation forms, the interior heat preservation occupies a larger space and lacks structural protection, and the sandwich insulation is not technologically mature and has higher construction costs, while the exterior insulation is simple in structure and easy to manufacture with developed processing technology. Therefore, considering the practical situation in Harbin, we adopt the exterior insulation system for the external wall structure of passive house to meet the standard of ultra-low energy consumption. Further, passive buildings are simultaneously required to comply with fire prevention specifications. At present, the primary four kinds of thermal insulation materials applied for passive external walls are classified as follows [28]: (1) Graphite-Molded Expanded Polystyrene Sheet (GEPS), fabricated by adding graphite particles and infrared reflector agents in the production of normal Expanded Polystyrene Sheet (EPS), which presents low thermal conductivity and high flame retardancy; (2) Extruded Foam Polystyrene Sheet (EFPS), which is obtained by uniformly extruding the molten polystyrene and appropriate additives from a pressing extruder, has smooth surfaces without pores, high tenacity, low hydrophilicity, and excellent heat preservation performance; (3) Polyurethane Foam Board (PUFB) with a small heat transfer coefficient can effectively reduce the wall thickness but at high cost; (4) Stone Wool Board (SWB) is an inorganic material with low heat transfer coefficient and high thermal resistance. The thermal insulating properties of various materials are listed in Table 5.

Due to the lower thermal resistance than that of base wall, the heat transfer coefficient of the composite wall varies with the thickness of the thermal insulation material, thus affecting the heat preservation and thermal insulation of the whole building. For the aerated concrete and reinforced concrete composite wall, the heat transfer coefficient decreases with the increasing thickness of the thermal insulation material, as the calculated results shown in Figure 5. Although the thermal insulation performance can be achieved by increasing the heat preservation material, the heat transfer coefficient of the entire composite wall will remain constant when the wall thickness rises to high values. Accordingly, the external insulation of the building's external wall is constructed with an open curtain wall system in which two layers of GEPS with a thickness of 300 mm are laid in staggered joint. The fire-proof isolation belt (A-grade non-combustible fire-proof SWB) and a sealing layer of heat-insulation are set up to reduce the heat bridge generation of external wall enclosure structure. In particular, the connection mode of the invisible curtain wall keel is employed so that the connecting firmware and the joint part are all thermally insulated, leading to a heat transfer coefficient of 0.1 W/(m^2·K) for entire external wall, as the cross-section schematics show in Figure 6.

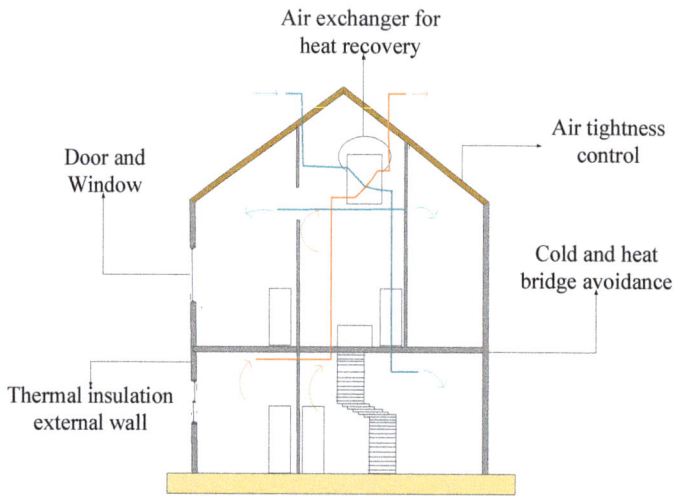

Figure 4. Schematic diagram of the passive house structure.

Table 4. Characteristics of three thermal insulation structures.

Structures	Advantages	Disadvantages
Interior insulation	1. Low requirements for insulation materials, easy to control cost; 2. Indoor construction is less dependent on environments; 3. Indoor construction is suitable for energy-saving renovation of old buildings; 4. Protecting the building facade.	1. The insulation layer inside leads to structural thermal-bridge; 2. Condensation and mildew between the insulating and structural layers; 3. Susceptible to temperature difference between day and night. 4. Difficult for secondary specialization.
Exterior insulation	1. Preventing the thermal-bridge; 2. Taking small space; 3. Extending the life space of building; 4. No requirements for wall materials; 5. Easy for secondary decoration	1. The external insulation layer has strict requirements on the fire resistance of the insulation material. 2. The construction process is increased and the quality is difficult to guarantee. 3. Easy to fall off in daily use 4. Insulation materials and structures are not comfortable.
Sandwich insulation	1. No additional requirements for insulation materials; 2. Insulation material and structure are consistent in life time; 3. Occupy small indoor space; 4. Complete construction.	1. Easy to generate thermal-bridge; 2. Complicated construction process; 3. High technical difficulty; 4. The cavity at the junction between the insulation layer and the wall affects the structural quality.

Table 5. Thermal properties of heat insulating materials.

Parameter	EPS	EFPS	PUFB	SWB
apparent density/(kg·m^{-3})	22–32	25–38	≥35	≤300
thermal conductivity/(W·m^{-1}·K^{-1})	≤0.039	≤0.035	≤0.06	≤0.04
tensile strength/MPa	≥0.1	≥0.20	≥0.15	≥0.075
dimensional stability/%	≤0.5	≤1.2	≤1.5	≤1.0
vapor permeability coefficient/(mg·Pa^{-1}·m^{-2}·s^{-1})	≤4.5	≤3.5	≤6.5	
water absorption rate/%	≤4.0	≤2.0	≤3.0	≤1.0

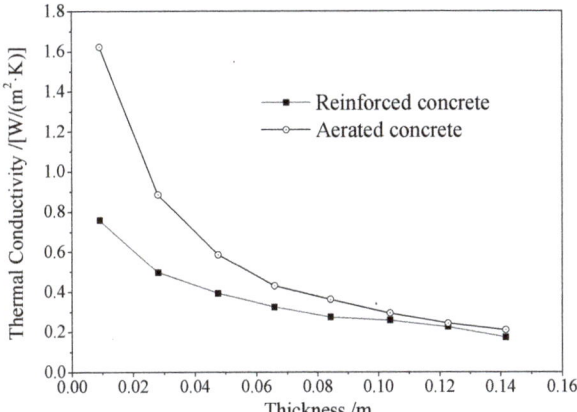

Figure 5. Heat transfer coefficients as a function of material thickness.

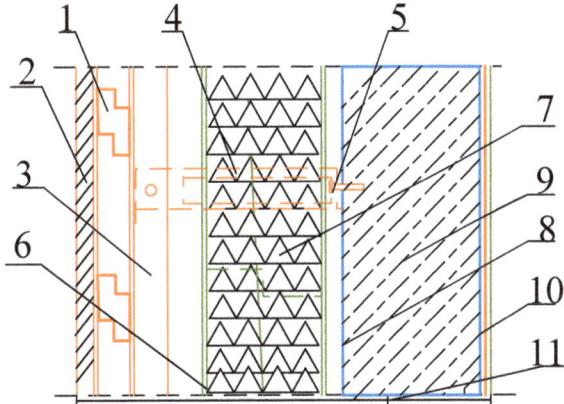

Figure 6. Schematic cross-section of external wall: (1) horizontal keel for external decoration board; (2) enhanced cement fibreboard; (3) vertical light steel keel for external decoration board; (4) thermal insulation anchorage; (5) special surface slurry; (6) composite alkali resistant glass fiber mesh cloth; (7) EPS staggered seam laying; (8) cement mortar flat layer; (9) lime mortar surface (seal layer); (10) reinforced concrete structure beam; (11) column network position axis.

3.2. Roof Insulation Structure

As a part of the non-transparent enclosure structure, building roof occupies a large area and produces serious heat loss, which dominates a majority of energy consumption. In passive buildings, the insulation layer of roof structure is specially designed thicker than that of external wall structure. Meanwhile, for maintaining an adequate humidity in room, it is necessary to add a sealing layer to the original external wall structure and lay an air-permeable waterproof layer. In order to meet the standard of ultra-low energy consumption, the external thermal insulation system comprises polymer modified surface mortar, GEPS insulation board, polymer modified surface mortar and asphalt linoleum, as shown in Figure 7 illustrating the roof thermal insulation configuration.

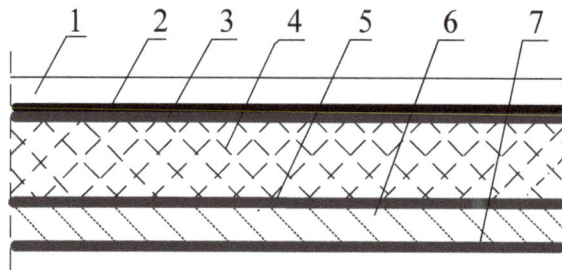

Figure 7. Thermal insulation structure of passive house roof: (1) fine stone concrete; (2) asphalt linoleum; (3) polymer plastering mortar; (4) GEPS insulation; (5) plastering mortar; (6) reinforced concrete; (7) cement plastering mortar.

3.3. Energy Conservation of Door and Window

In the whole building envelope, the house window is the weakest part with a high percentage of energy consumption approaching to 50%. Hence, improving the thermal transfer performance of window is a pivotal way to reduce the whole building's energy consumption. Senying window identified as P120, which is constituted by window frame and glass system, is the first passive window certified by German PHI in China, with the whole heat transfer coefficient being less than 0.6 W/(m^2·K). The window frame of P120 is composed of the inner aluminum-wrapped-wood frame and the outer aluminum frame which are integrated together by polymer buckle connections, as shown by the cross-sectional schematics and photograph of P120 in Figure 8. The aluminum-wrapped wood timbers are connected with Chinese traditional processes of tenon and moron to form the inner window frame, which can guarantee a moisture content of 14% and avoid the heat transfer from hardware accessories. The outer aluminum frames are welded seamlessly by patented technology to prevent joint-produced thermal bridges. The glass system is constructed in a configuration of three-glasses/two-cavities or four-glasses/three-cavities, in which the toughened low radiation glass is adopted and the air, argon, or a mixture of gas is used as thermal insulation medium.

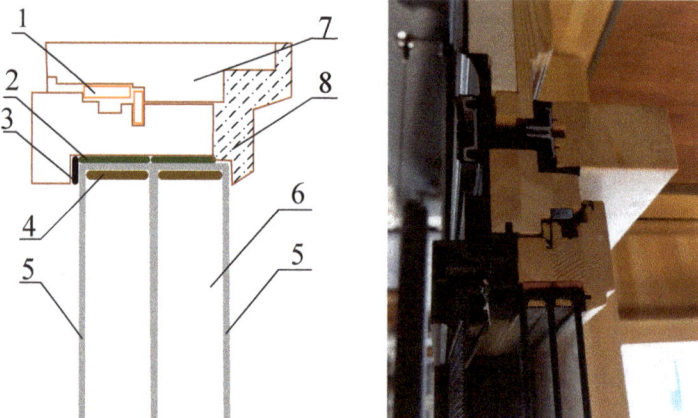

Figure 8. Window profile: (1) polymer connection clasp; (2) warm-edge interval bar; (3) seal layer; (4) dry molecular sieves; (5) tempered glass in 5 mm thickness; (6) argon in a glass cavity of 18 mm thickness; (7) window frame; (8) intensified insulation. The cross-sectional photograph of P120 window enclosure structure is also shown in the right panel.

We simulate the heat transfer of glass system by using Windows program, individually for the glass thicknesses of 12, 15, 18, and 20 mm in different window combinations, as the calculated results of thermal conductivity listed in Table 6. It is indicated that the four-glasses/three-cavities configuration represents explicitly higher performance of thermal insulation than the three-glasses/two-cavities. The heat transfer coefficient of glass system decreases with the increased thickness of argon cavity until it reaches 20 mm, while the shading coefficient (SC) and solar heat gain coefficient (SHGC) are not appreciably affected by the gas type and cavity thickness. Therefore, it is reasonably suggested that the window enclosure structure of 5GL + 15Ar + 5G + 15Ar + 5GL + 15Ar + 5GL combination can prohibit oxidization reactions of LOWE films with air and fully reduce convection and sound noise. In order to prevent joint-produced thermal bridges, the warm-edge spacers with a blending form are inserted in the connection between the glass and window frame, and the molecular sieves are used to fill internals, as shown in Figure 8 for window profile. Furthermore, the connections between window frame and the glass system are insulated with sealing tapes, and the outer side of window is intensified in insulation thickness. All these thermal insulation schemes used in passive window eventually fulfill a preferable heat transfer coefficient of <0.6 W/(m²·K) for entire window system, as listed in Table 6.

Table 6. Heat transfer coefficients of different window combinations.

Combination	Thermal Conductivity/(W·m^{-2}·K^{-1})	SC	SHGC
5GL+12Ar+5G+12Ar+5GL	0.593	0.298	0.260
5GL+15Ar+5G+15Ar+5GL	0.565	0.299	0.260
5GL+18A+5G+18A+5GL	0.590	0.300	0.261
5GL+18Ar+5G+18Ar+5GL	0.580	0.300	0.261
5GL+18M+5G+18M+5GL	0.594	0.300	0.261
5GL+20Ar+5G+20Ar+5GL	0.590	0.300	0.261
5GL+12Ar+5G+12Ar+5GL+12Ar+5GL	0.432	0.251	0.218
5GL+15Ar+5G+15Ar+5GL+15Ar+5GL	0.377	0.251	0.218
5GL+18A+5G+18A+5GL+18A+5GL	0.472	0.250	0.217
5GL+18Ar+5G+18Ar+5GL+18Ar+5GL	0.377	0.251	0.218
5GL+18M+5G+18M+5GL+18M+5GL	0.387	0.251	0.218
5GL+20Ar+5G+20Ar+5GL+20Ar+5GL	0.385	0.249	0.216

3.4. Heat Recovery Ventilation System

The passive ultra-low energy consumption building adopts an efficient heat recovery system which combines fresh air ventilation with exhaust equipment. The high efficiency heat recovery performance of fresh air ventilation system refers to preheating or pre-cooling fresh air in the heat exchange between outdoor fresh air and indoor exhaust air to achieve the purpose of energy saving. As the schematic diagram shows in Figure 9, heat recovery mode of rotary wheel is adopted in ventilation system. In winter, the indoor return air is discharged outdoors through the upper half of a heat exchanger, by which most of the heat and moisture contained in the outdoor gas are gathered in the rotary wheel so that only the polluted air is discharged outdoors, while the outdoor fresh air introduced from the lower half of the heat exchanger is preheated and humidified by the heat and moisture accumulated in rotary wheel. Similarly, in summer, the heat recovery ventilation system can pre-cool and dehumidify outdoor air and continuously supply fresh air to the room. The complete heat recovery wheel, there is an energy-saving device to recover the energy lost in ventilation. In order to ensure the safe operation of the heat recovery system, the cryogenic medium pre-heating system is adopted in fresh air ventilation with the unit treating an air volume of 5000 m³/h, which leads to a heat recovery efficiency more than 75%. The efficiency of heat recovery ventilation system can be calculated by the formula as follows:

$$\eta_s = 1 - \exp\left\{\frac{(mc_p)_{min}}{(mc_p)_{max}} NTU^{0.22} \left(\exp\left[-\frac{(mc_p)_{min}}{(mc_p)_{max}} NTU^{0.78}\right] - 1\right)\right\} \tag{1}$$

where η_s denotes the heat recovery efficiency, NTU indicates the number of heat transfer units, c_p is the fluid parameter, $(mc_p)_{min}$ represents the minimum flow rate in fresh air or exhaust air.

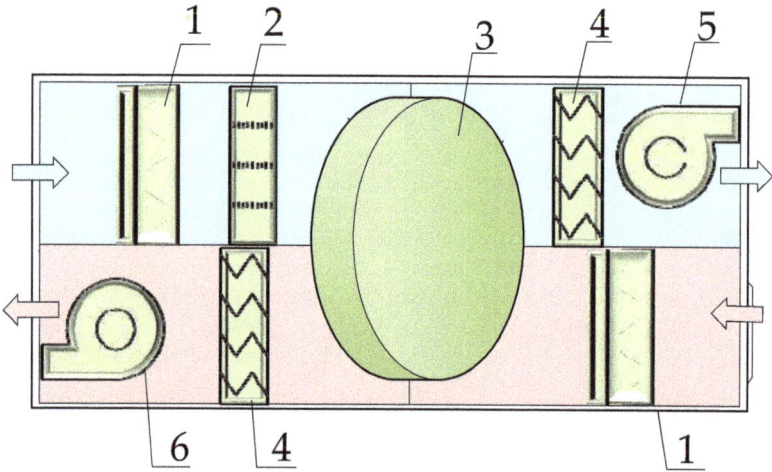

Figure 9. Schematic diagram of heat recovery ventilation system: (1) primary air filter; (2) high efficiency air filter; (3) rotary heat exchanger; (4) electrostatic precipitator; (5) air blower; (6) exhaust fan.

4. Heat Transfer and Energy Consumption Cost

4.1. Temperature and Solar Irradiation

By means of harmonic reaction method as implemented in Ecotect program, the outdoor temperature, air flow rate, and solar irradiation variation through a day are calculated to investigate the hourly thermal loads of passive building, in which the coldest and hottest days of typical weather are selected as representatives, as the results show in Figure 10. It is shown from Figure 10a that the outdoor temperature in the hottest day rises and then declines with a peak value arising at 14:00, while the coldest daily temperature fluctuates in a small magnitude with the highest and lowest values appearing at 5:00 and 13:00, respectively. As shown in Figure 10b, the hottest and coldest days represent almost identical fluctuations of air flow rate with the peak values showing at 13:00 and 14:00, respectively, although the overall air flow rate in the hottest day is distinctly lower than that in the coldest day. For the hourly solar irradiation in the hottest day, as exhibited in Figure 10c, the direct irradiation rises sharply to attain a large value at 4:00 and through a placid peak at noon and then begins to rapidly decrease at 18:00 in almost symmetrical way. The absorbed irradiation and incident irradiation peak at 10:00–12:00 with a much higher intensity than diffusive irradiation in the hottest day, while the diffusive irradiation contributes the same major part to the solar irradiation with 2 h delay of peak arising time as the absorbed irradiation and incident irradiation in the coldest day. Further for the coldest day, the direct irradiation intensity peaks at 9:00 and 12:00, with the peak value of 350 and 380 W/m^2, respectively, while the peak arising time varies similarly to the absorbed irradiation and incident irradiation.

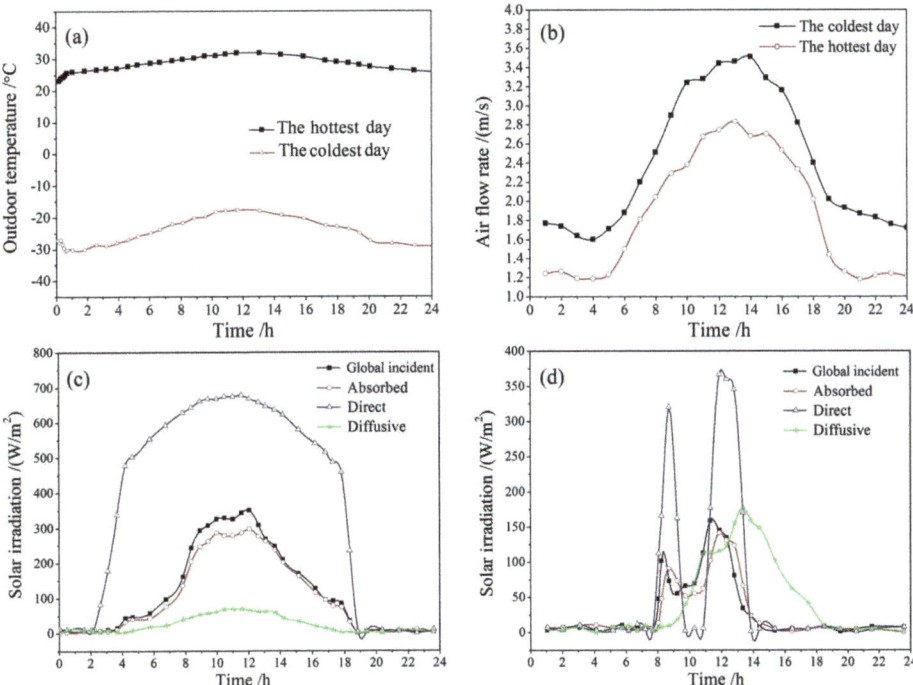

Figure 10. (**a**) Outdoor temperature and (**b**) air flow rate as a function of time; solar irradiation intensity vs. time on the (**c**) hottest day and (**d**) coldest day.

In passive building engineering, it is difficult to maintain a constant indoor temperature in severely cold area due to the greatly varying climate feature. The cooling loads in summer vary significantly through the day with the change of solar irradiation intensity, as shown in Figure 11. The total cooling load varies slightly from 0:00 to 5:00 without solar irradiation and increases intensively from 5:00 to 8:00 with the first peak of solar irradiation being reached at 8:00, after which the variation slows down until noon and then accelerates to attain the second load peak at 15:00. In comparison, the cooling load of enclosure structure is consistent with the total cooling load in summer, and the overall heating loads remain unchanged in winter. It is thus proved that the enclosure structure of passive building has acquired an excellent thermal insulation. The passive building can exploit the external enclosure structure with high thermal insulation performance to keep a constant indoor temperature, the energy consumption of which is formularized as follows:

$$Q_\tau = K \cdot F[t_z - t_n + \frac{\alpha_n}{K}\sum_1^m \frac{t_{z,n}}{v_n}\cos(\omega_n\tau - \psi_n - \varepsilon_n)] \tag{2}$$

where K and F denote the heat transfer coefficient and area of enclosure structure respectively, t_z symbolizes the average outdoor comprehensive temperature, t_n represents the real-time indoor comprehensive temperature, α_n indicates the heat transfer coefficient from inner surface of enclosure structure, $t_{z,n}$ and ω_n represent respectively the amplitude and frequency in n-order variation of outdoor comprehensive temperature, Ψ_n is the initial phase angle of n-order variation of outdoor comprehensive temperature, v_n denotes the attenuation from the n-order disturbance of comprehensive temperature in enclosure structure; v_n and ε_n respectively denote amplitude attenuation and phase delay to the n-order disturbance of comprehensive temperature, which describe the frequency-dependent response of enclosure structure to periodic external disturbance.

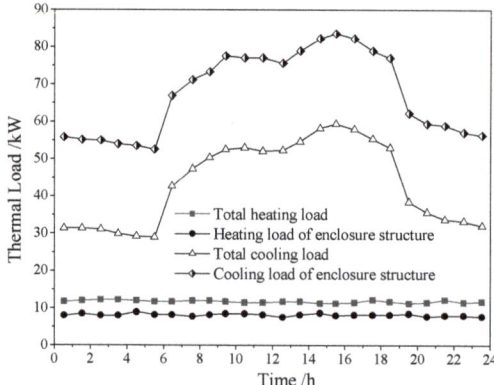

Figure 11. Thermal loads varying with time through a day in summer.

4.2. Thermal Load and Energy Demand

The three-dimensional model of passive house is established by the building information modeling method, and the harmonic response method is used to calculate the cooling and heating loads, as the simulation results listed in Table 7. In summer, the sensible cooling load of 76,759 W predominantly occupies 91% of the total cooling load of 84,154 W, while the latent and fresh air cooling loads of 7395 W and 8295 W only account for 9% and 10%, respectively. In winter, the total heating load approaches 11,450 W, which is used to compensate heat dissipation of 7622 W and 3829 W for enclosure structure and crevice permeation, respectively. The total thermal loads per unit area of 20.93 W/m² in summer and 2.82 W/m² in winter comply with the requirements of the passive building specifications. In addition, the highest thermal loads are always appearing near 14:00–15:00 whether in winter or summer.

Table 7. Simulated results of thermal load and heat dissipation.

Summer		Winter	
Cooling Load	Results	Heating Load and Dissipation	Results
Summer total cooling load/W	84,154	Winter total heating load/W	11,450
Peak load time/h	15:00	Peak load time/h	14:00
Sensible cooling load/W	76,759	Heat dissipation of enclosure structure/W	7622
Latent cooling load/W	7395	Heat dissipation of crevice penetration/W	3829
Fresh air cooling load/W	8265	Heating load per unit area/(W/m²)	2.82
Cooling load per unit area/(W/m²)	20.93		

The energy demand in passive building can be completely described by heat gain and loss of enclosure structure, the change of comprehensive temperature, the energy consumption of air penetration, the heat gain and loss of internal personnel and equipment, and the heat transfer between different local regions, as the calculated results in percentages shown in Figure 12. For cooling load, the electric power dominates energy demand in a percentage of 35.27%, while lighting and enclosure structure consume 27.13% and 20.45% of total energy, respectively, as shown in Figure 12a. For heating load, the energy demand of electric power still occupies the major part of 31.96%, which is 3.31% lower than that in cooling load, as shown in Figure 12b. In contrast to the cooling load, the 28.28% of enclosure structure is higher than the 24.58% consumed by lighting. Whether in heating or cooling loads, the proportion of personnel energy demand is about 11%, which is smaller than that of electric power, lighting and enclosure structure, while being higher than the 2.17% and 4.07% of air penetration for cooling and heating loads, respectively.

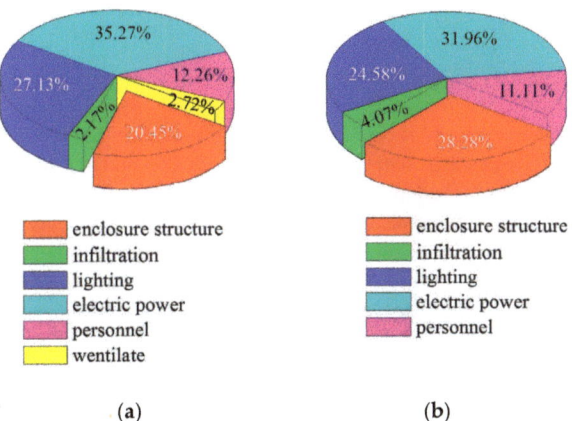

Figure 12. The energy demand percentages for (**a**) cooling load and (**b**) heating load.

The annual distribution histogram of monthly energy demand percentage in Figure 13 illustrates that the space heating accounts for more than 80% of the total energy demand from October to April of the second year, while the ventilation accounts for only about 14%. The total energy demand remarkably decreased from April to October due to the effective cooling system of natural ventilation in passive building. The energy demand of lighting, electricity, and enclosure structure accounts for the top three for both cooling and heating load through a year. Therefore, it is suggested that the EFPS be utilized for the external wall, special door, and window of passive building to improve the thermal insulation and air tightness of enclosure structure.

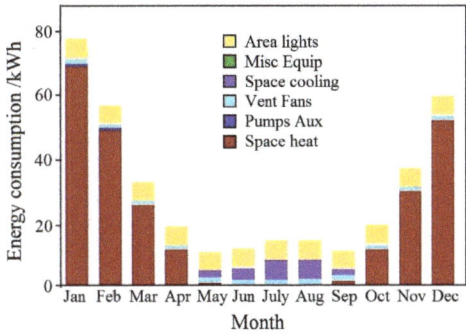

Figure 13. Total energy demand monthly through a year.

For the passive buildings with large proportion of latent heat cooling load, the energy consumption for cooling and heating of buildings is slightly different, while the energy consumption of enclosure structures still dominates the total energy consumption of buildings. In the practical project of Senying passive office building, the averaged heat transfer coefficients of external wall and window approach to 0.23 W/(m^2·K) and 1.3 W/(m^2·K), respectively, which are 50% lower than that of the external enclosure structures reported by other references [29]. Compared with other passive office buildings with similarly low energy consumption, the heating and cooling loads of Senying passive office building are reduced by 37% and 54%, respectively, with the total energy demand being saved by 36% [30], which means Senying project completely qualifies as a high standard passive house. By adopting the insulation system of thick external wall and special doors and windows, the passive building can keep warm and avert heat dissipation in severely cold area with heavy weather to reach the purpose of deliberately reducing the building energy consumption, which can also be referenced for designing the main enclosure structure of passive building in the future.

4.3. Periodic Cost

Based on the simulation results of energy demand, the annual energy and life cycle costs and the ventilation latent heat are calculated with the cloud computing technology of Green Building Studio (GBS), as the results show in Tables 8 and 9 and Figure 14. The annual energy and life cycle costs of the passive house are 17,796 ¥, and 282,388 ¥ respectively with an annual carbon dioxide emission of 8.3 SUV, in which the annual peak energy demand of 79.9 kWh/m^2 is much less than the passive house standard of 120 kWh/m^2, as listed in Table 8. The electricity source is directly delivered from electricity power transmission center by high voltage cable; hence, there is no other exhaust emission in the energy production chain except for carbon dioxide emission. For the life cycle energy, the electric power consumption of 3638.13 kWh is higher than gasoline of 2587.96 kJ in a year. Because active mechanical cooling is not used in passive room, the energy consumption of cooling room mainly originates from natural ventilation. The natural ventilation of the modeled passive building is needed to operate for 696 h, which is only 42% of the required time for mechanical cooling, and thus can save an annual electric energy of 10,780 kWh. The energy cost analyses shown in Figure 14 imply that the space heating cost dominates the total heat energy demand (except area lighting) with an average percentage of >80% from October to April of the second year. The total energy cost reaches the highest value of 1.2 ¥/m^2 in January and attains the lowest valley of 0.3 ¥/m^2 in May and September due to the high efficiency heat transfer of natural ventilation.

Although employing energy-saving schemes in buildings will increase life cycle cost or electricity-power cost, the life cycle analyses indicate that Senying passive office building will represent 15% lower of annual energy demand than the energy consumption (676 MJ/M^2) of the other similar buildings [31] and will achieve a total annual savings of 1.8 million for heating and cooling and a total annual carbon dioxide reduction of 42 million kg in comparison to the other homologous passive buildings.

Table 8. Energy carbon cost (annual).

Energy cost/¥		17,796
Life cycle cost/¥		282,388
CO_2 emissions (large SUV equivalent)		8.3 SUV
Energy intensity/(MJ/m^2)		586
Peak energy demand/(kWh/m^2)		79.9
Life cycle energy	Electricity/kWh	3638.13
	Gasoline/kJ	2587.9

Table 9. Ventilation latent heat (annual).

Natural ventilation time/h	696
Mechanical cooling time/h	1667
Electric power saving/kWh	10,780

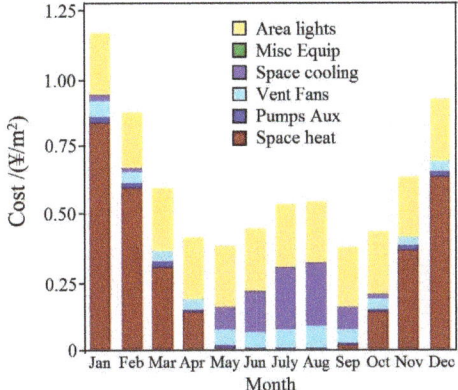

Figure 14. Total energy cost monthly through a year.

5. Conclusions

The heat transfer coefficient, cooling and heating loads, and energy demand of passive house in severely cold area are studied by heat simulations with the energy cost being analyzed to explore the widely applicable energy-saving methods. The changes of temperature and air flow rate in winter are investigated to realize preferable designs of passive building in severely cold areas, which use super thick thermal insulation structure for external wall and roof, special energy-saving window, and efficient heat recovery system. Open curtain walls are employed for the external thermal insulation system with extruded polystyrene sheets to control the heat transfer coefficient of external wall being less than 0.1 W/(m^2·K). The aluminum-coated wood window frame is combined with the four-glass/three-cavity structure to decrease heat transfer coefficient of entire window to 0.6 W/(m^2·K), in which heat-preservation interval belts are supplied to ensure sufficient air tightness. The high efficiency heat recovery system with thermal recovery rate of more than 75% can achieve a constant room temperature by recovering waste heat. The designed passive building does not need additional ground source heat pump and mechanical heating and cooling equipment in both summer and winter. The mean cooling and heating loads per area of the whole passive building are reduced to 33.58 W/m^2 and 3.79 W/m^2 respectively, with the annual energy demand decreasing to 79.9 kWh/m^2 (decreases by 33% compared with international standard), which meet and even exceed the passive specifications of buildings in Northern China.

The practical paradigm of passive building in severely cold area investigated in this paper comprises the honeycomb-type wall, the special passive doors and windows, and other super insulation enclosure structures, combining various advanced energy saving technologies of photovoltaic power generation, rainwater collection, intermediate water treatment, garbage biochemistry, and waste heat recovery. The simulation results show that it is feasible to popularize the passive office building in a severely cold area. Because of the complex factors impacting on the thermal load of passive houses, there are still some differences between the actual thermal load and energy consumption of passive houses and the simulation results from harmonic response method, which should be modified accordingly to investigate the different functional buildings with new thermal insulation materials. In the future, actual climate conditions and living habits around the world could be further combined with modern science and technology to develop more efficient HVAC systems, for example, by appropriately enlarging solar photovoltaic panels, modifying external surface colors, and optimizing geometries of roof and walls. Multi-faceted and meticulous researches are needed to further reduce building energy demand and attain the "near zero energy consumption" level in the future developments of energy-saving building and sustainable building.

Author Contributions: Conceptualization, F.W.; data curation and Formal analysis, W.-J.Y. and F.W.; investigation and writing, W.-F.S.; project administration, W.-F.S. All authors have read and agreed to the published version of the manuscript.

Funding: This research was funded by Chinese Postdoctoral Science Foundation (Grant No. 2013M531058).

Conflicts of Interest: The authors declare no conflict of interest.

References

1. Feist, W.; Schnieders, J.; Dorer, V.; Haas, A. Re-inventing air heating: Convenient and comfortable within the frame of the Passive House concept. *Energy Build.* **2005**, *37*, 1186–1203. [CrossRef]
2. Schnieders, J.; Hermelink, A. CEPHEUS results: measurements and occupants' satisfaction provide evidence for Passive Houses being an option for sustainable building. *Energy Policy* **2006**, *34*, 151–171. [CrossRef]
3. Chel, A.; Tiwari, G.N. Thermal performance and embodied energy analysis of a passive house – Case study of vault roof mud-house in India. *Appl. Energy* **2009**, *86*, 1956–1969. [CrossRef]
4. Mlakar, J.; Štrancar, J. Overheating in residential passive house: Solution strategies revealed and confirmed through data analysis and simulations. *Energy Build.* **2011**, *43*, 1443–1451. [CrossRef]
5. Kapedani, E.; Herssens, J.; Verbeeck, G. Designing for the future? Integrating energy efficiency and universal design in Belgian passive houses. *Energy Res. Soc. Sci.* **2019**, *50*, 215–223. [CrossRef]
6. Ridley, I.; Clarke, A.; Bere, J.; Altamirano, H.; Lewis, S.; Durdev, M.; Farr, A. The monitored performance of the first new London dwelling certified to the Passive House standard. *Energy Build.* **2013**, *63*, 67–78. [CrossRef]
7. Stephan, A.; Crawford, R.H.; Myttenaere, K.D. A comprehensive assessment of the life cycle energy demand of passive houses. *Appl. Energy* **2013**, *112*, 23–34. [CrossRef]
8. Stephan, A.; Crawford, R.H.; de Myttenaere, K. Multi-scale life cycle energy analysis of a low-density suburban neighbourhood in Melbourne, Australia. *Build. Environ.* **2013**, *68*, 35–49. [CrossRef]
9. Rohdin, P.; Molin, A.; Moshfegh, B. Experiences from nine passive houses in Sweden—Indoor thermal environment and energy use. *Build. Environ.* **2014**, *71*, 176–185. [CrossRef]
10. Irulegi, O.; Torres, L.; Serra, A.; Mendizabal, I.; Hernández, R. The Ekihouse: An energy self-sufficient house based on passive design strategies. *Energy Build.* **2014**, *83*, 57–69. [CrossRef]
11. Dan, D.; Tanasa, C.; Stoian, V.; Brata, S.; Stoian, D.; Nagy, G.T.; Florut, S.C. Passive house design—An efficient solution for residential buildings in Romania. *Energy Sustain. Dev.* **2016**, *32*, 99–109. [CrossRef]
12. Ilomets, S.; Kalamees, T.; Tariku, F. Indoor climate loads for dwellings in different cold climates to assess hygrothermal performance of building envelopes. *Can. J. Civ. Eng.* **2019**, *46*, 963–968. [CrossRef]
13. Fokaides, P.A.; Christoforou, E.; Ilic, M.; Papadopoulos, A. Performance of a Passive House under subtropical climatic conditions. *Energy Build.* **2016**, *133*, 14–31. [CrossRef]
14. Truong, H.; Garvie, A.M. Chifley Passive House: A Case Study in Energy Efficiency and Comfort. *Energy Procedia* **2017**, *121*, 214–221. [CrossRef]
15. Alajmi, A.; Rodríguez, S.; Sailor, D. Transforming a passive house into a net-zero energy house: a case study in the Pacific Northwest of the U.S. *Energy Conv. Manag.* **2018**, *172*, 39–49. [CrossRef]
16. Yu, Z.; Gou, Z.; Qian, F.; Fu, J.; Tao, Y. Towards an optimized zero energy solar house: A critical analysis of passive and active design strategies used in Solar Decathlon Europe in Madrid. *J. Clean. Prod.* **2019**, *236*, 117646. [CrossRef]
17. Dalbem, R.; Grala da Cunha, E.; Vicente, R.; Figueiredo, A.; Oliveira, R.; da Silva, A.C.S.B. Optimisation of a social housing for south of Brazil: From basic performance standard to passive house concept. *Energy* **2019**, *167*, 1278–1296. [CrossRef]
18. Wang, Y.; Du, J.; Kuckelkorn, J.M.; Kirschbaum, A.; Gu, X.; Li, D. Identifying the feasibility of establishing a passive house school in central Europe: An energy performance and carbon emissions monitoring study in Germany. *Renew. Sustain. Energy Rev.* **2019**, *113*, 109256. [CrossRef]
19. Zhang, S.H.; Zhuang, Z.; Hu, Y.D.; Yang, B.S.; Tan, H.W. Applicability Study on a Hybrid Renewable Energy System for Net-Zero Energy House in Shanghai. *Energy Procedia* **2016**, *88*, 768–774. [CrossRef]
20. Chen, X.; Yang, H.X. Integrated energy performance optimization of a passively designed high-rise residential building in different climatic zones of China. *Appl. Energy* **2018**, *215*, 145–158. [CrossRef]

21. Li, R.; Wang, M.; Zhu, J. Indoor Thermal Environment Monitoring and Evaluation of Double-Deck Prefabricated House in Central China—Taking Zhengzhou Area as an Example. *Energy Procedia* **2019**, *158*, 2812–2819. [CrossRef]
22. Li, C.; Zhou, D.Q.; Wang, H.; Cheng, H.B.; Li, D.D. Feasibility assessment of a hybrid PV/diesel/battery power system for a housing estate in the severe cold zone—A case study of Harbin, China. *Energy* **2019**, *185*, 671–681. [CrossRef]
23. Liu, J.Z.; Zhou, Q.X.; Tian, Z.Y.; He, B.J.; Jin, G.Y. A comprehensive analysis on definitions, development, and policies of nearly zero energy buildings in China. *Renew. Sust. Energ. Rev.* **2019**, *114*, 109314. [CrossRef]
24. Liu, J.Z.; Liu, Y.W.; He, B.J.; Xu, W.; Jin, G.Y.; Zhang, X.T. Application and suitability analysis of the key technologies in nearly zero energy buildings in China. *Renew. Sust. Energ. Rev.* **2019**, *101*, 329–345. [CrossRef]
25. Yang, L.; He, B.J.; Ye, M. Application research of Ecotect in residential estate planning. *Energy Build.* **2014**, *72*, 195–202. [CrossRef]
26. He, X.; Kong, Q.; Xiao, Z. Fast simulation methods for dynamic heat transfer though building envelope based on model-order-reduction. *Procedia Eng.* **2015**, *121*, 1764–1771. [CrossRef]
27. Yao, R.; Costanzo, V.; Li, X.; Zhang, Q.; Li, B. The effect of passive measures on thermal comfort and energy conservation. A case study of the hot summer and cold winter climate in the Yangtze River region. *J. Build. Eng.* **2018**, *15*, 298–310. [CrossRef]
28. Li, N.; Chen, Q. Experimental study on Heat Transfer Characteristics of Interior Walls under Partial-Space Heating Mode in Hot Summer and Cold Winter Zone in China. *Appl. Therm. Eng.* **2019**, *162*, 114264. [CrossRef]
29. Ballarini, I.; De Luca, G.; Paragamyan, A.; Pellegrino, A.; Corrado, V. Transformation of an office building into a nearly zero energy building (nZEB): Implications for thermal and visual comfort and energy performance. *Energies* **2019**, *12*, 895. [CrossRef]
30. Szymon, F. Cost-optimal plus energy building in a cold climate. *Energies* **2019**, *12*, 3841. [CrossRef]
31. Gustafsson, M.S.; Myhren, J.A.; Dotzauer, E.; Gustafsson, M. Life cycle cost of building energy renovation measures, considering future energy production scenarios. *Energies* **2019**, *12*, 2719. [CrossRef]

© 2020 by the authors. Licensee MDPI, Basel, Switzerland. This article is an open access article distributed under the terms and conditions of the Creative Commons Attribution (CC BY) license (http://creativecommons.org/licenses/by/4.0/).

Review

A Systematic Review on Predicting and Forecasting the Electrical Energy Consumption in the Manufacturing Industry

Jessica Walther * and Matthias Weigold

Institute of Production Management, Technology and Machine Tools (PTW), Department Mechanical Engineering, Technical University of Darmstadt, Otto-Berndt-Str. 2, 64287 Darmstadt, Germany; m.weigold@ptw.tu-darmstadt.de
* Correspondence: j.walther@ptw.tu-darmstadt.de; Tel.: +49-6151-16-20859

Abstract: In the context of the European Green Deal, the manufacturing industry faces environmental challenges due to its high demand for electrical energy. Thus, measures for improving the energy efficiency or flexibility are applied to address this problem in the manufacturing industry. In order to quantify energy efficiency or flexibility potentials, it is often necessary to predict or forecast the energy consumption. This paper presents a systematic review of state-of-the-art of existing approaches to predict or forecast the energy consumption in the manufacturing industry. Seventy-two articles are classified according to the defined categories System Boundary, Modelling Technique, Modelling Focus, Modelling Horizon, Modelling Perspective, Modelling Purpose and Model Output. Based on the reviewed articles future research activities are derived.

Keywords: energy; manufacturing; prediction; forecasting; modelling

Citation: Walther, J.; Weigold, M. A Systematic Review on Predicting and Forecasting the Electrical Energy Consumption in the Manufacturing Industry. *Energies* **2021**, *14*, 968. https://doi.org/10.3390/en14040968

Academic Editor: Vincenzo Bianco
Received: 11 January 2021
Accepted: 3 February 2021
Published: 12 February 2021

Publisher's Note: MDPI stays neutral with regard to jurisdictional claims in published maps and institutional affiliations.

Copyright: © 2021 by the authors. Licensee MDPI, Basel, Switzerland. This article is an open access article distributed under the terms and conditions of the Creative Commons Attribution (CC BY) license (https://creativecommons.org/licenses/by/4.0/).

1. Introduction

In the European Green Deal [1], the European Commission has set the goal of making Europe climate-neutral by 2050. To achieve this objective, a severe reduction in greenhouse gas emissions is necessary. Energy use has an essential part in achieving this goal, as almost three-quarters of the global emissions (measured in Carbon Dioxide Equivalents (CO_2-eq)) were caused by energy use in 2016. The industry sector accounts for about 30% of emissions, with 24.2% attributable to energy use, making it the top emission source [2]. Focusing on energy consumption, the industrial sector is the largest electricity consumer worldwide, accounting for 42% in 2018 [3]. The manufacturing sector is a subset of the industrial sector, which converts raw materials into products utilising energy while simultaneously generating waste and emissions. This sector accounts for 77% of the global end-use of energy of the industrial sector in 2018 [3]. These high levels of consumed energy during manufacturing are a great opportunity to reduce the Carbon Dioxide Equivalents (CO_2-eq) emissions, while also leading to an economic motivation for companies to increasing their energy efficiency [4].

Additionally, the utilisation of renewable energy sources are increasing. In 2019 renewable electricity generation rose 6% to a total of almost 27% share of renewable energies in global electricity generation [5]. Renewable energy sources are characterised through a volatile power generation. This volatility, and thus reduced predictability compared to conventional power generation, leads to new opportunities for savings through electricity procurement or demand response applications in the industry [6].

Thus, manifold measures to improve the energy efficiency and flexibility on different levels within a factory have gained in importance and are still increasing in the manufacturing industry. Those measures can be supported by an accurate energy prediction or forecasting model (A distinction between predicting and forecasting is made in Section 4.4) of the respective system under consideration.

On that account, a systematic literature research and classification on predicting and forecasting the energy consumption in the manufacturing industry was conducted. In the following, the related work is summarised, the methodology for the systematic literature review is presented, a classification scheme is developed and finally an analysis of the examined articles according to the developed classification scheme is performed. Eventually, a conclusion is drawn and future research fields are derived.

2. Related Work

For over 25 years models for predicting the electrical energy consumption in the manufacturing industry have been a subject of research interest. However, it is due to the increasing importance of sustainability, resource and energy efficiency that the field has gained in relevant within the last decade.

There are not only different system levels for which an energy model is created, but also different areas of application, purposes and objectives. All these factors influence the model to be developed. An overview of the different dimensions that impact the development of an energy model is only partially covered in studies so far.

Zhao et al. classify different approaches in the field of energy modelling in machining processes in the three areas cutting energy, machining process energy,and machining system energy. The category cutting energy is distinguished in the dimensions net cutting specific energy, spindle specific energy, and machine tool energy consumption during cutting. Different process stages and machine tool components are considered in the machining process energy category. In the area of machining system energy different approaches to model the energy flow at machining system level are presented. In some areas, different modelling methods are discussed in more detail. Where possible, the authors have provided the basic formulas for calculating the energy consumption of the various studies [7].

Reinhardt et al. understand the energy consumption prediction as a modelling problem and therefore derive their classification scheme from the model development input-processing-output cycle. The distinguished categories are system (consisting of the dimensions factory, multiple machines, single machine, and machine part), input (consisting of the dimensions energy, environment, process, and product) and processing (consisting of the dimensions artificial neural network, fuzzy logic, empirical expression, simulation, and theoretical expression) [8].

In this study a morphology for classifying different approaches in the field of energy prediction and forecasting is developed based on identified influencing factors. Selected articles, which are based on a systematic literature search, are then classified according to the developed scheme.

3. Methodology for Systematic Literature Review

A multi-step approach to identify articles of high scientific value was conducted as summarised in Figure 1 based on the procedures of Glock and Hochrein [9] and Reynolds et al. [10]. The process consists of eight steps. First, the search strategy was determined by conceptualising the topic. The result was a list of keywords on the subject, on which the search string is based on. Next, the data bases to be searched and the respective publication titles listed in Table 1 were selected. The meta data (title, keywords, abstract) were searched in regards to combinations of the keywords in the search string. 969 articles meet the search criteria. To identify the articles of relevance, first the title and subsequently the abstract was screened. For the resulting selection, a thorough full text analysis was performed. Additionally, the references of the analysed articles were screened to identify further articles of relevance. These articles were added to the abstract screening point in the review process. Finally, the essential characteristics in regards to the developed classification scheme were recorded and summarised for the selected articles. 72 articles were identified as relevant in this process.

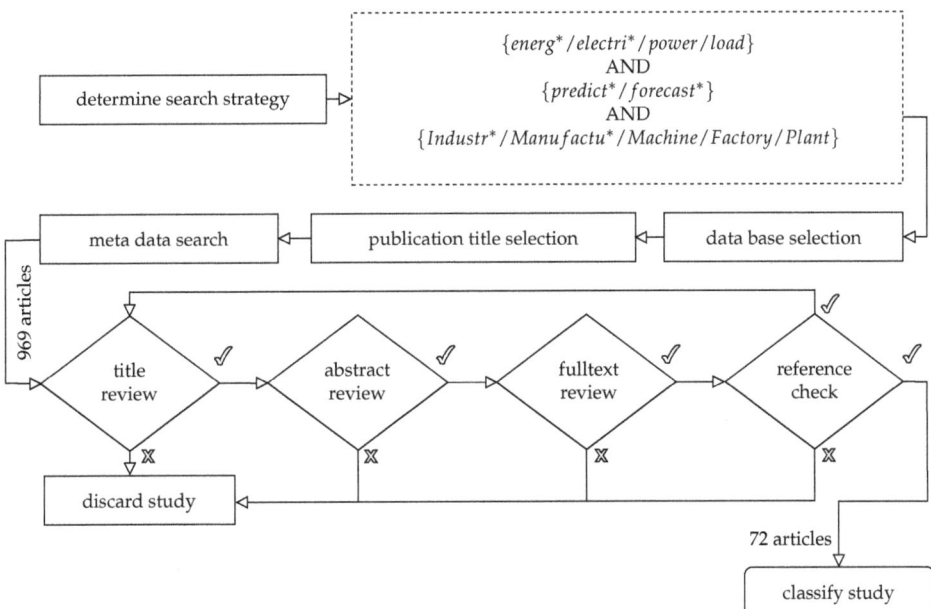

Figure 1. Methodology for systematic literature search.

Table 1. Searched data bases with respective publication titles.

Data Base	Publication Titles
Science Direct	Procedia CIRP
	Applied Energy
	Energy
	International Journal of Machine Tools and Manufacture
	International Journal of Mechanical Science
IEEE Xplore	IEEE Access
	IEEE Transactions on Sustainable Energy
	IEEE Transactions on Industry Applications
	IET Renewable Power Generation
	IEEE Transactions on Components, Packaging and Manufacturing Technology
	IEEE Transactions on Industrial Informatics
OCLC Worldcat	No journal restriction possible

4. Classification Scheme

Work in the field of energy modelling in the manufacturing industry can be classified into the categories and dimensions listed in Figure 2 based on the influencing factors of an energy model on an abstract level.

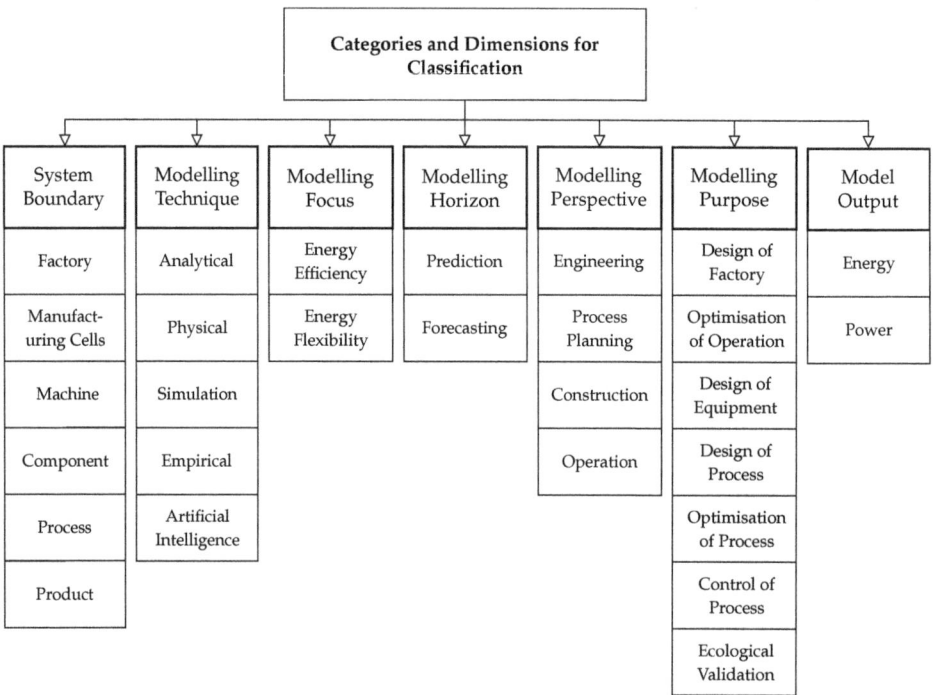

Figure 2. Dimensions for classifying work in the field of energy modelling.

4.1. System Boundary

In the context of industrial energy prediction or forecasting six dimensions can be distinguished regarding the system boundary [11].

- Factory: An energy model for factory-level demand is being developed.
- Manufacturing cell: An energy model is developed for a manufacturing cell containing several production machines.
- Machine: A machine-level energy model is developed.
- Component: An energy model of individual components of a production machine is developed.
- Process: An energy model for a specific process is developed.
- Product: An energy model is developed for the energy embedded in a product.

4.2. Modelling Technique

Generally, energy prediction or forecasting can be conducted with model-driven or data-driven approaches. Model-driven approaches include analytical, physical, simulation and empirical models, whereas Artificial Intelligence (AI) approaches are data-driven approaches.

- Analytical modelling: Theoretical analysis of the research question is conducted. In terms of energy models, the analytical procedure refers to the decomposition of the energy consumption. Different functions and areas are defined, which are usually represented by an average energy demand.
- Physical modelling: Fundamental physical relationships are described by mathematical equations.
- Simulation approaches: Physical models are solved numerically with simulation tools.

- Empirical modelling: Empirical research is performed via the systematic evaluation of experiences. Empirical models often use statistical methods, which require an explicit mathematical representation for the problem under consideration.
- Artificial Intelligence (AI) approaches: Many different approaches are summarised under the term Artificial Intelligence (AI). In general the term Artificial Intelligence (AI) encompasses three related concepts, which are illustrated in Figure 3. The broadest concept Artificial Intelligence (AI) encompasses the two sub-fields Machine Learning (ML) and Deep Learning (DL), while Deep Learning (DL) is again a sub-field of Machine Learning (ML). Artificial Intelligence (AI) is the study of "intelligent agents", which refers to any device that perceives its environment and, acting on that basis, carries out actions that maximise the chances of success for a given objective. Machine Learning (ML) is a collection of data-driven algorithms that can learn form data without being explicitly programmed. Deep Learning (DL) refers to the study of Artifical Neural Networks and related machine learning algorithms that contain more than one hidden layer, also known as deep neural networks [12].

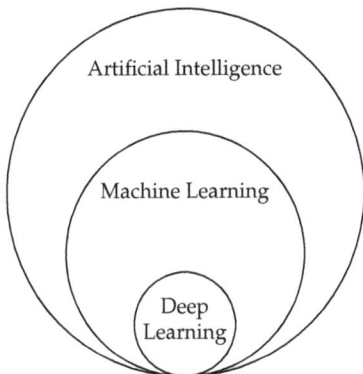

Figure 3. The relationship between Artificial Intelligence, Machine Learning, and Deep Learning [13].

4.3. Modelling Focus

Two categories can be distinguished, on which the studies in the field of energy modelling are focused.
- Energy efficiency: The "relationship between the results achieved and the resources used, where resources are limited to energy" [14]
- Energy flexibility: The "ability of a production system to adapt quickly and in a process-efficient way to changes in the energy market" [15]

4.4. Modelling Horizon

Two temporal dimensions can be distinguished regarding the modelling horizon.
- Prediction: Is the process to predict an unknown value from known inputs. In the case of energy modelling, this means that the available observations at time t of a time series are used to predict the output (energy or load) at time t.
- Forecasting: Is a procedure for making statements about the future. For energy modelling, this means that future values t + x of a time series are estimated based on current and/or past information at time t [16].

4.5. Modelling Perspective

There are different phases in the Factory Life Cycle (FLC) and Product Life Cycle (PLC) [11] in which an energy model is useful.

- Engineering (within the Factory Life Cycle (FLC)): Energy models are applied to plan the electrical energy grid of a new factory.
- Process Planning (within the Factory Life Cycle (FLC)): Designing and optimising manufacturing processes in regards to energy consumption is the objective to use energy models in this phase.
- Construction (within the Product Life Cycle (PLC)): Energy models are used to design products that are energy efficient in their production.
- Operation (within the Factory Life Cycle (FLC) and Product Life Cycle (PLC)): The operation phase is where the actual production takes place. Energy models are deployed to optimise the operation in regards to one of the two above mentioned focuses (Energy Efficiency or Flexibility). The optimisation of the operation phase can be distinguished in the operation on factory, machine and process level.

4.6. Modelling Purpose

Several reasons can be distinguished for developing an energy model.

- Design of Factory: The objective is to design the electrical grid of a new factory.
- Optimisation of operation: The operation phase is optimised with respect to different objectives.
- Design of Equipment: The objective is to configure production machines in an energy efficient way.
- Design of Process: Energy models are utilised to design energy efficient production processes.
- Optimisation of Process: The process is optimised in regards to the the most energy efficient process parameters.
- Control of Process: The objective is to control the process in regards to predictive maintenance (tool wear), anomaly detection or energy consumption allowance.
- Ecological Validation: Energy models are used for a life cycle assessment.

4.7. Model Output

Two main dimensions can be distinguished regarding the output of the energy model.

- Load: In technical usage, load is the power taken up by a plant or machine, where the power is the quotient of the work performed in a period of time and the period of time [17].
- Energy consumption or Specific Energy (SEC): "Energy consumption is the quantity of particular forms of energy consumed in order to cover energy demand under real conditions" [17] (p. 14). For the Specific Energy (SEC) the energy consumption is related to a suitable functional unit, where the functional unit may be cm^3 or kg for instance [17].

5. Analysis and Synthesis

Tables 2 and 3 provide an overview of the 72 examined articles according to the developed classification scheme. Please note that many of the articles can be assigned to more than one dimension within a category. Therefore, more than 72 articles are listed in the total column for the individual categories. Additionally, an evaluation of the time dependencies for the different categories was conducted. Figure 4 displays the total number of articles over time from 2009, as approx. 95% of the articles are in the time span from 2009. The total number of articles fluctuates around the value of five articles per year with a maximum value of 13 in 2011. Since 2017, the number of articles per year has been steadily increasing, with nine articles in 2019. For 2020, three articles have already been recorded by the time the literature search was conducted in April. The results for the different categories are displayed in the Figures 5–9 and are discussed in the following.

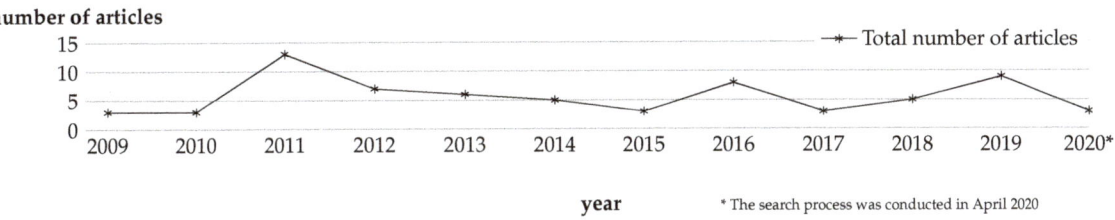

Figure 4. Total number of articles over time.

The dimension System Boundary, Modelling Technique, Focus, and Horizon (Time) are displayed in Table 2. With 50 articles in total, Machines predominate the considered System Boundary (see Figure 5). Fewer than ten articles are found in each of the remaining dimensions of the System Boundary. From the analysed articles only four develop hierarchical models (Hierarchical models decompose complex problems into simpler parts or primitives. For example 3d objects can naturally be decomposed into object parts, these parts into geometric primitives [18]. In regards to the industrial application of energy models, factories can be decomposed into manufacturing cells, which in turn into production machines, which can be be decomposed into components. A hierarchical model of a manufacturing cell for example could consists of several models of production machines.), where one model constitutes as a part of the other. In the analysed literature hierarchical models are either used at machine level, where models at component level are incorporated into the machine model or at manufacturing cell or factory level, where individual machine models are incorporated into the higher level.

Regarding the Modelling Technique, there is a more even distribution of the used methods within the examined literature. However, Analytical and Empirical models are being used most frequently with 19 and 22 articles in total. Analytical models are primarily used at Machine level. Here, the energy demand of the different operating modes—off, standby, ready for processing, and processing—and different processing steps such as handling, tool exchange or welding are usually analysed. For each operating mode and processing step an average energy consumption is calculated. The energy consumption is then predicting by combining the average consumption for the respective operating mode and process step in the form of a step function. Therefore, these models are highly simplified. The application of Analytical approaches is almost constant over time with around two articles per year (see Figure 6).

Physics-based models are mainly developed for predicting the energy consumption at Machine level. Nonetheless, Physical models are also applied at the Process or Component level. However, Physical models are often difficult to implement, because they are not lean and require a large number of parameters that are difficult to obtain. Furthermore, the incorporation of the stochastic nature of a manufacturing process is challenging [19–21] and, in addition, highly complex processes such as machining processes do not permit purely Physical modelling [21]. The development of Physical models is consistently low at between zero and two articles per year (see Figure 6).

Empirical models use experimental data and often utilise statistical methods to fit the parameters of a previously defined functional form to the problem under consideration. Empirical models are applied in all defined system boundaries. The most common statistical technique in the analysed literature to develop energy models is the Multiple Linear Regression. Empirical models prove to be very applicable and accurate in certain cases. However, formulating the right model, which requires a deep understanding of the phenomenon in question and the need for heavy experimentation are limitation factors [21,22]. Empirical models were used very frequently between 2011 and 2016 with up to six articles per year. Since 2017, the use of Empirical models has decreased sharply with a value of zero as of 2019 (see Figure 6).

As a result of the advances in machine automation and sensing, which start to overcome these limitations by allowing continuous measurements, data-driven models are gaining importance. Several energy models based on Artificial Intelligence (AI) methods have been developed recently, as they provide insights to problems that could not be addressed with a purely theoretical analysis based on physical principals [23]. Artificial Intelligence (AI) modelling techniques do not require to model the underlying physical system explicitly, as they map the input upon the output [24]. The most common Artificial Intelligence (AI) technique is the Artifical Neural Network (ANN) with 13 articles in total. Further modelling techniques are Support Vector Regression, Gaussian Process Regression, and Random Forest. When using Artifical Neural Network (ANN), ten articles used a simple Multilayer Perceptron. Only one articles applied a modelling technique from the filed of Deep Learning (DL) with the development of a Convolutional Neural Network [25]. Three of the analysed articles compared several Artificial Intelligence (AI) techniques [25–27]. Considering the time trend, Artificial Intelligence (AI) methods show a strong increase since the year 2019 with a maximum value of seven. The three articles recorded for the year 2020 are all assigned to the Artificial Intelligence (AI) modelling technique (see Figure 6).

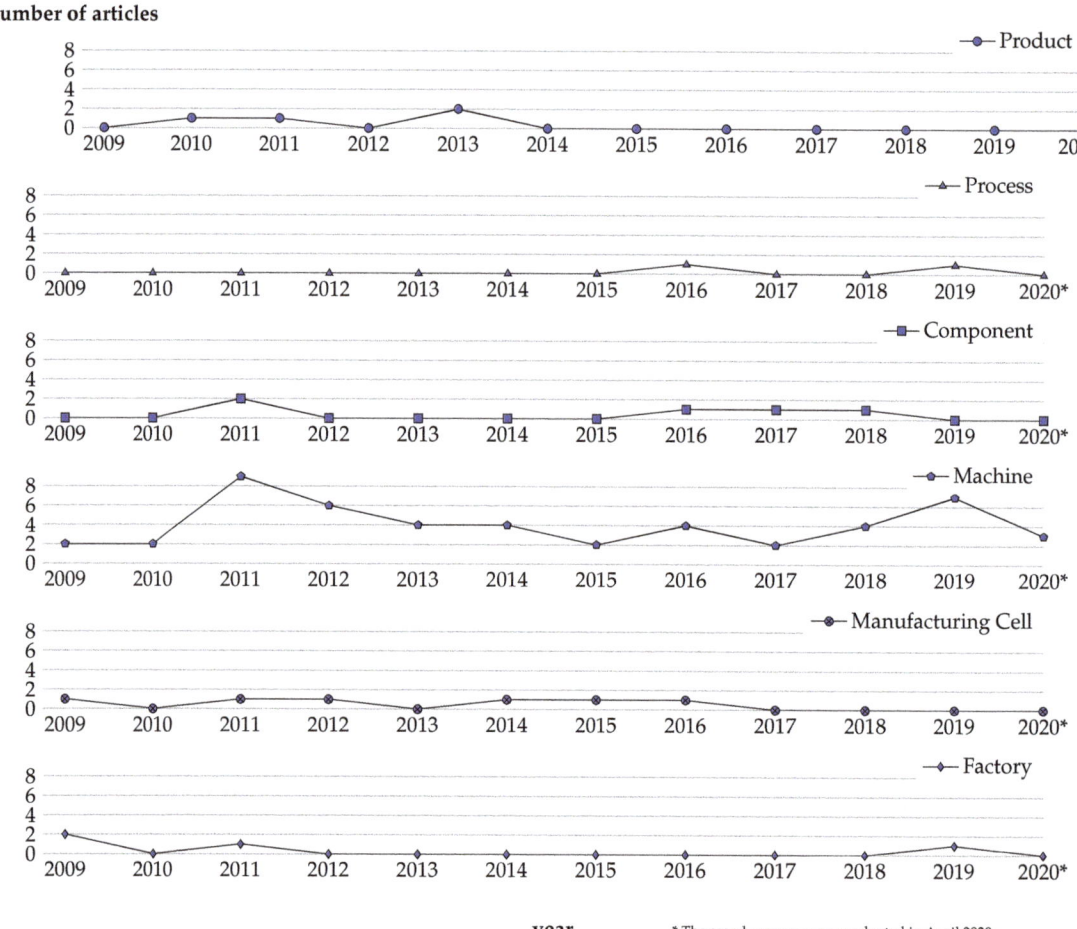

Figure 5. Number of articles over time for the category System Boundary.

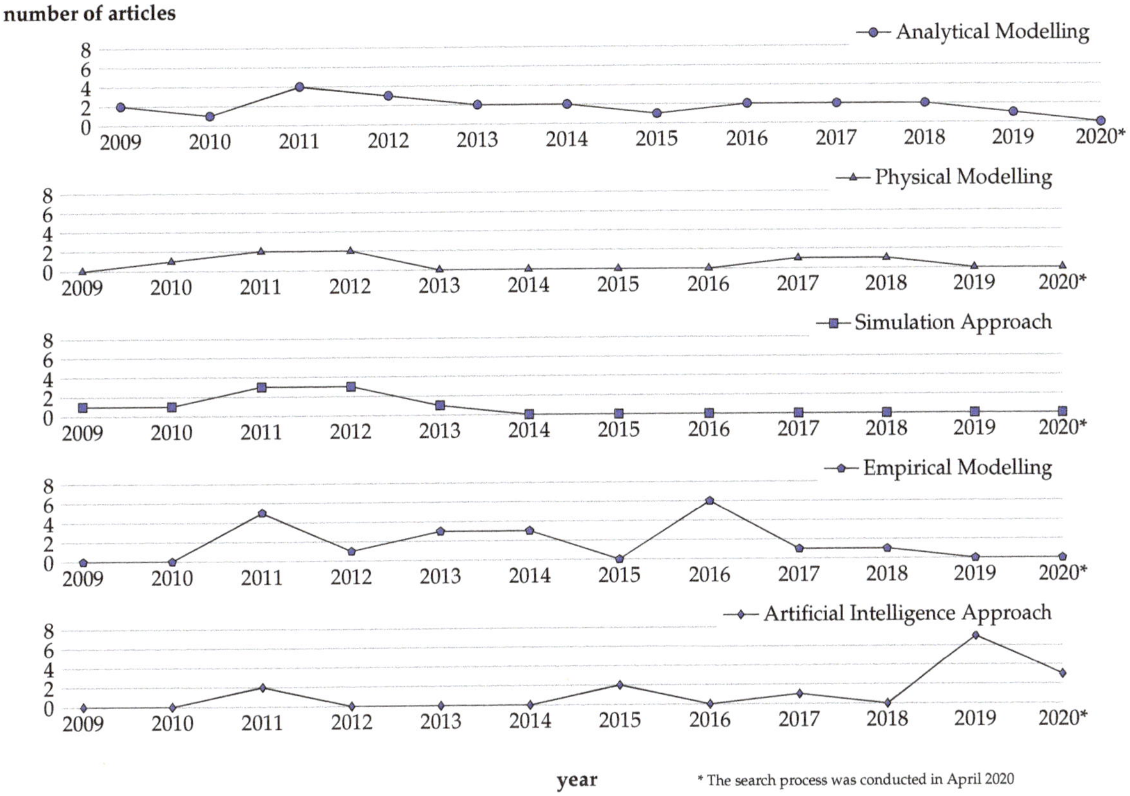

Figure 6. Number of articles over time for the category Modelling Technique.

In regards to the Focus of the studies, the field of Energy Efficiency predominates Energy Flexibility. Only three articles can be assigned to the field of Energy Flexibility. Additionally, only those three articles address the field of Forecasting in the category Horizon. The other articles are part of the field Prediction. As can be seen in Figure 7, the fields of Energy Flexibility and Forecasting are rather young research areas with zero articles before the year 2019.

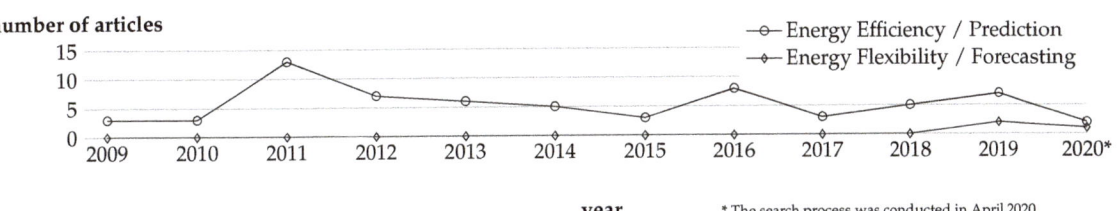

Figure 7. Number of articles over time for the categories Focus and Horizon.

Table 3 displays the categories Perspective, Modelling Purpose and Output. In regards to the Perspective, the majority of the analysed approaches focus on the Process Planning or Construction phase (see Figure 8) with 57 and 20 articles in total, of which 12 articles address both perspectives simultaneously. A predictive model within the framework of the

Engineering phase in the Factory Life Cycle (FLC) has only been developed in one study. Models for usage in the Operational phase have been developed by 10 studies.

Figure 8. Number of articles over time for the category Perspective.

With 40 articles in total the Optimisation of Processes predominates as a Modelling Purpose followed by the Design of Processes with a total of 15 articles (see Figure 9). None of these studies addresses both purposes simultaneously. Of the eight studies dealing with the Control of the Process, only three focus on it. The rest of the studies additionally address the Optimisation of the Process purpose. Furthermore, the use of models to Design Equipment seems to be a co-product in most of the approaches, as only two articles focus on this perspective. Only two of the analysed articles deal with the Design of the Factory purpose, where one addresses the Engineering phase of the Factory Life Cycle (FLC) and the other develops the model for application in Process Planning and Design phase. Of the 19 articles that undertake Ecological Validation, only 5 studies develop an energy model solely for this purpose. For the remaining studies, this is an additional purpose.

Regarding the Output of the model, 19 studies analyse the Power and thus the power curve. From the ten articles, which address the Optimisation of Operation phase, six consider the power consumption of the respective system as the Output of the model. The remaining articles develop models with the Energy or Specific Energy (SEC) as the Output with 42 and 11 articles in total.

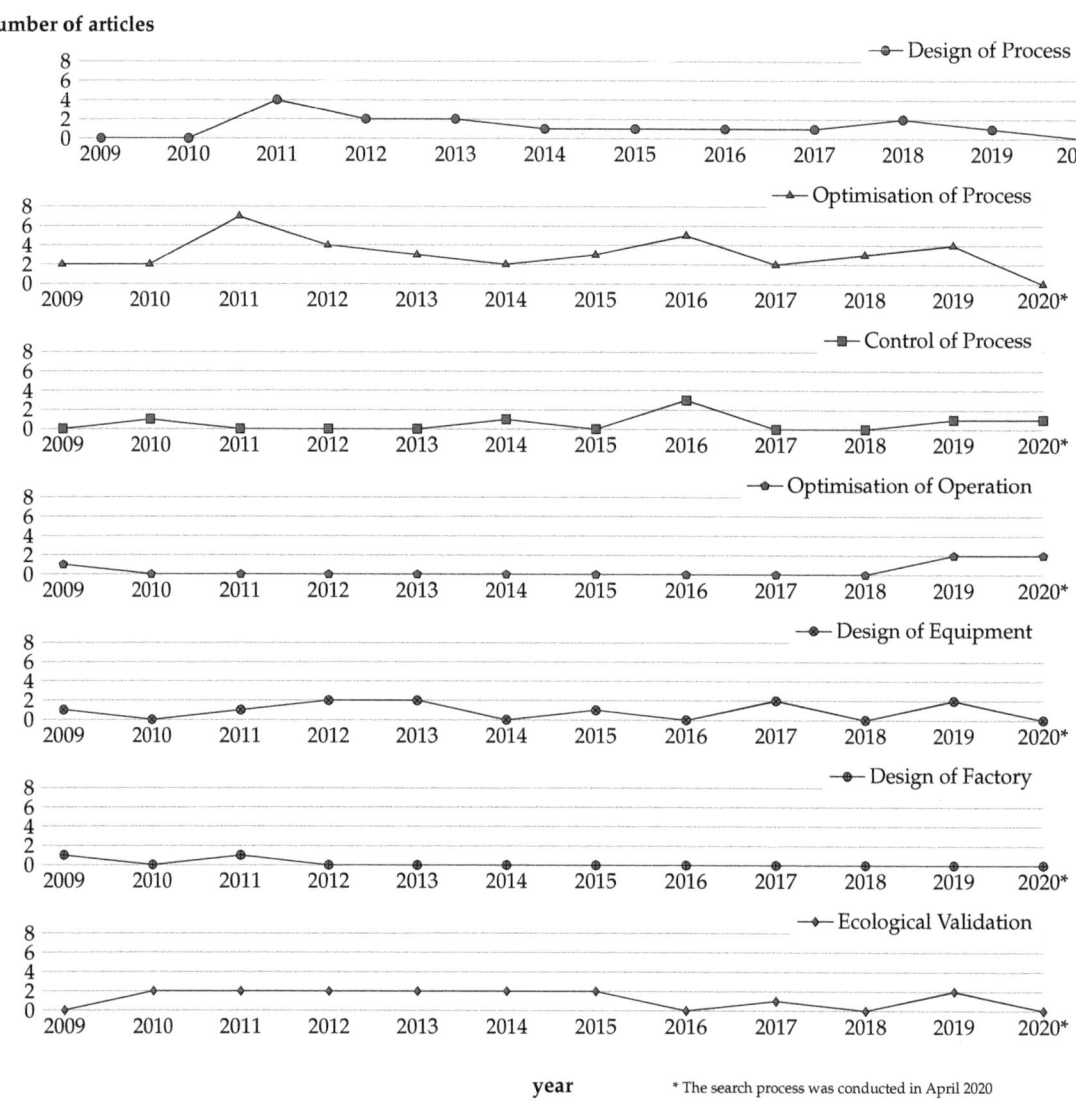

Figure 9. Number of articles over time for the category Purpose of Modelling.

Table 2. Classification for Dimensions Modelling Technique, System Boundary, Focus, and Horizon (Time).

Dimension	System Boundary						Technique					Focus		Time	
Approach from	Product	Process	Component	Machine	Manufacturing Cells	Factory	Analytical	Physical Modelling	Simulation	Empirical	Artificial Intelligence	Energy Efficiency	Energy Flexibility	Prediction	Forecast
Number of Articles	4	5	6	50	8	4	19	9	9	22	15	69	3	69	3
Abele et al. [28]				•								•		•	
Abeykoon et al. [29]				•					•	•		•		•	
Aramcharoen and Mativenga [30]				•								•		•	
Avram and Xirouchakis [31]				•								•		•	
Balogun and Mativenga [32]				•			•					•		•	
Bhinge et al. [19]				•			•				•	•		•	
Bi and Wang [33]				•				•				•		•	
Bi and Wang [34]				•				•				•		•	
Bornschlegl et al. [35]					•		•		•			•		•	
Braun and Heisel [36]				•						•		•		•	
Budinoff et al. [37]				•			•			•		•		•	
Diaz et al. [38]			•									•		•	
Diaz et al. [39]				•								•		•	
Dietmair and Verl [20]				•			•					•		•	
Dietmair and Verl [40]				•	•	•	•					•		•	
Dietrich et al. [41]				•							•	•	•		•
Doreth [26]			•									•		•	
Doreth et al. [42]										•	•	•		•	
Draganescu et al. [43]												•		•	
Feng et al. [44]				•							•	•		•	

Table 2. Cont.

Approach from	Dimension														
	System Boundary						Technique					Focus		Time	
	Product	Process	Component	Machine	Manufacturing Cells	Factory	Analytical	Physical Modelling	Simulation	Empirical	Artificial Intelligence	Energy Efficiency	Energy Flexibility	Prediction	Forecast
Number of Articles	4	5	6	50	8	4	19	9	9	22	15	69	3	69	3
Goldhahn et al. [45]				•			•					•		•	
Gutowski et al. [46]				•				•				•		•	
Al-Hazza et al. [47]				•							•	•		•	
He et al. [48]					•		•					•		•	
He et al. [49]				•					•			•		•	
He et al. [25]				•							•	•		•	
Herrmann and Thiede [50]						•			•			•		•	
Huang et al. [51]			•									•		•	
Imani Asrai et al. [52]										•		•		•	
Jia et al. [53]		•										•		•	
Kant and Sangwan [27]					•						•	•		•	
Kant and Sangwan [54]					•					•		•		•	
Kara and Li [55]				•					•			•		•	
Kong et al. [56]				•						•		•		•	
Larek et al. [57]				•								•		•	
Li et al. [58]				•						•		•		•	
Li and Kara [59]					•							•		•	
Li et al. [60]				•			•					•		•	
Li et al. [61]				•			•					•		•	
Li et al. [62]				•						•		•		•	

Table 2. Cont.

Approach from	Dimension														
	System Boundary						Technique					Focus		Time	
	Product	Process	Component	Machine	Manufacturing Cells	Factory	Analytical	Physical Modelling	Simulation	Empirical	Artificial Intelligence	Energy Efficiency	Energy Flexibility	Prediction	Forecast
Number of Articles	4	5	6	50	8	4	19	9	9	22	15	69	3	69	3
Li et al. [63]				•						•		•		•	
Li et al. [64]			•									•		•	
Mori et al. [65]				•				•				•		•	
Mose and Weinert [66]							•					•		•	
Munoz and Sheng [67]	•						•	•				•		•	
Peng and Xu [68]				•								•		•	
Quintana et al. [69]			•						•	•	•	•		•	
Rahimifard et al. [70]		•										•		•	
Rajemi et al. [71]				•				•				•		•	
Rief [72]							•					•		•	
Sato et al. [73]				•						•		•		•	
Sealy et al. [74]							•					•		•	
Seow and Rahimifard [75]		•								•		•		•	
Seow et al. [76]	•								•			•		•	
Shang et al. [77]		•								•		•		•	
Shao et al. [78]				•							•	•		•	
Shin et al. [79]				•							•	•		•	
Sossenheimer et al. [80]				•							•	•		•	
Sossenheimer et al. [81]				•						•		•		•	
Su [82]						•						•		•	

Table 2. Cont.

Approach from	Dimension														
	System Boundary						Technique					Focus		Time	
	Product	Process	Component	Machine	Manufacturing Cells	Factory	Analytical	Physical Modelling	Simulation	Empirical	Artificial Intelligence	Energy Efficiency	Energy Flexibility	Prediction	Forecast
Number of Articles	4	5	6	50	8	4	19	9	9	22	15	69	3	69	3
Teiwes et al. [83]				•			•					•		•	
Verl et al. [84]				•								•		•	
Walther et al. [85]									•		•	•	•	•	•
Walther et al. [86]				•				•			•	•	•	•	•
Wang et al. [87]		•						•							
Weinert et al. [88]					•		•					•		•	
Wu et al. [89]				•						•		•		•	
Yi et al. [90]				•				•				•		•	
Yi et al. [91]				•							•	•		•	
Yoon et al. [92]				•						•		•		•	
Yoon et al. [93]				•						•		•		•	
Zhou et al. [94]				•			•					•		•	

Table 3. Classification for Dimensions Perspective, Purpose of Modelling, and Output.

Dimension	Perspective						Modelling Purpose							Output	
Approach from	Process Planning (FLC)	Construction (PLC)	Engineering (FLC)	Operation of Factory	Operation of Machines	Operation of Process	Design of Processes	Optimisation of Processes	Control of Processes	Optimisation of Operation	Design of Equipment	Design of Factory	Ecological Validation	Energy/SEC	Power
Number of Articles	57	20	1	1	5	4	15	40	8	5	11	2	19	53	19
Abele et al. [28]		•									•			•	
Abeykoon et al. [29]	•					•		•						•	
Aramcharoen and Mativenga [30]	•	•						•						•	
Avram and Xirouchakis [31]							•		•				•	•	
Balogun and Mativenga [32]	•						•				•			•	
Bhinge et al. [19]	•							•						•	
Bi and Wang [33]	•												•	•	
Bi and Wang [34]	•	•						•					•	•	
Bornschlegl et al. [35]	•							•					•	•	
Braun and Heisel [36]	•	•					•	•			•				•
Budinoff et al. [37]	•	•						•					•	•	
Diaz et al. [38]	•							•						•	
Diaz et al. [39]	•	•			•					•				•	•
Dietmair and Verl [20]	•							•			•			•	
Dietmair and Verl [40]		•									•	•		•	
Dietrich et al. [41]	•													•	
Doreth [26]	•	•									•			•	
Doreth et al. [42]														•	
Draganescu et al. [43]	•							•							

Table 3. Cont.

Dimension	Perspective							Modelling Purpose							Output	
Approach from / Number of Articles	Process Planning (FLC)	Construction (PLC)	Engineering (FLC)	Operation of Factory	Operation of Machines	Operation of Process	Design of Processes	Optimisation of Processes	Control of Processes	Optimisation of Operation	Design of Equipment	Design of Factory	Ecological Validation	Energy/SEC	Power
(totals)	57	20	1	1	5	4	15	40	8	5	11	2	19	53	19
Feng et al. [44]	●														
Goldhahn et al. [45]	●							●						●	
Gutowski et al. [46]	●							●						●	
Al-Hazza et al. [47]	●							●						●	
He et al. [48]	●						●							●	
He et al. [49]	●							●						●	
He et al. [25]	●													●	
Herrmann and Thiede [50]	●						●			●					●
Huang et al. [51]	●									●				●	
Imani Asrai et al. [52]	●							●					●		●
Jia et al. [53]	●							●						●	
Kant and Sangwan [27]	●						●	●					●	●	
Kant and Sangwan [54]	●							●					●	●	
Kara and Li [55]	●							●						●	
Kong et al. [56]	●							●						●	
Larek et al. [57]	●	●					●				●		●		●
Li et al. [58]	●							●						●	
Li and Kara [59]	●													●	

Table 3. Cont.

Approach from	Dimension		Perspective							Modelling Purpose				Output	
	Process Planning (FLC)	Construction (PLC)	Engineering (FLC)	Operation of Factory	Operation of Machines	Operation of Process	Design of Processes	Optimisation of Processes	Control of Processes	Optimisation of Operation	Design of Equipment	Design of Factory	Ecological Validation	Energy/SEC	Power
Number of Articles	57	20	1	1	5	4	15	40	8	5	11	2	19	53	19
Li et al. [60]	•						•				•			•	
Li et al. [61]	•													•	
Li et al. [62]	•													•	
Li et al. [63]	•	•				•					•			•	•
Li et al. [64]	•							•						•	
Mori et al. [65]	•							•					•	•	
Mose and Weinert [66]	•							•						•	
Munoz and Sheng [67]	•	•					•	•					•		
Peng and Xu [68]	•	•				•		•			•		•	•	•
Quintana et al. [69]	•							•	•				•	•	•
Rahimifard et al. [70]	•	•					•						•	•	
Rajemi et al. [71]	•													•	
Rief [72]	•							•						•	
Sato et al. [73]	•							•	•					•	
Sealy et al. [74]	•							•						•	
Seow and Rahimifard [75]	•							•						•	
Seow et al. [76]	•							•						•	
Shang et al. [77]	•							•						•	
Shao et al. [78]	•	•				•		•	•						•

Table 3. Cont.

Approach from	Dimension		Perspective				Modelling Purpose							Output	
	Process Planning (FLC)	Construction (PLC)	Engineering (FLC)	Operation of Factory	Operation of Machines	Operation of Process	Design of Processes	Optimisation of Processes	Control of Processes	Optimisation of Operation	Design of Equipment	Design of Factory	Ecological Validation	Energy/SEC	Power
Number of Articles	57	20	1	1	5	4	15	40	8	5	11	2	19	53	19
Shin et al. [79]	•							•						•	
Sossenheimer et al. [80]					•				•						•
Sossenheimer et al. [81]					•				•						•
Su [82]			•									•			•
Teiwes et al. [83]	•	•													•
Verl et al. [84]				•									•	•	
Walther et al. [85]					•					•					•
Walther et al. [86]										•					•
Wang et al. [87]	•						•	•						•	
Weinert et al. [88]	•													•	
Wu et al. [89]		•					•	•						•	
Yi et al. [90]		•					•								
Yi et al. [91]	•	•											•	•	
Yoon et al. [92]	•							•							•
Yoon et al. [93]	•														•
Zhou et al. [94]					•				•					•	

6. Conclusions

In this study, a literature review on predicting and forecasting the energy consumption in the manufacturing industry is provided. The approaches are classified in seven categories with sub-dimensions, which in turn all influence the model to be developed. It can be stated that the System Boundary Machine with the Perspective Process Planing and the Purpose to Optimise the Process predominate in the examined articles. Furthermore, it can be concluded that the relevance of experiments and data increases in this field of research as Empirical studies are the Modelling Technique most likely used with a strong increase in Artificial Intelligence (AI) approaches since 2019.

In terms of the Modelling Technique, the usage of Artificial Intelligence (AI) is a rather young but promising field of research, with Artifical Neural Network (ANN) being the most used technique. A Modelling Technique from the Artificial Intelligence (AI) sub-field Deep Learning (DL) was only used by one of the examined studies [25]. However, this modelling technique seems to be promising, especially in the field of Forecasting, as Deep Learning (DL) techniques show great results for related forecasting tasks such as renewable energies forecasting [95], energy demand forecasting from the supplier perspective [96,97], and building thermal load forecasting [98]. Nevertheless, the research area of industrial Energy Forecasting, which is needed for the Focus of Energy Flexibility, is an even younger research area. From the analysed articles only three considered the temporal Horizon Forecasting. However, against the background of the increasing share of renewable energies in the power grid, it is gaining in importance.

Concluding, a qualitative comparison between the different approaches is not practicable, as different System Boundaries and different Horizons are considered with different modelling intentions. Additionally, the modelling accuracy is expressed with different metrics, such as Mean Relative Error, Coefficient of Determination or Root Mean Squared Error.

For future research, a follow-up literature search could include other databases or include other categories, such as the type of data used. In the first case, an automation of the search process would be beneficial, due to the vast amount of search results without journal restriction. Furthermore, a more profound analysis of the Artificial Intelligence (AI) based articles could be carried out. Additionally, future research could define guidelines on which Modelling Techniques are suitable for which Purposes, Perspectives and Focus for each System Boundary, as the development effort of the different modelling techniques can differ significantly. Therefore, the results and implementation efforts of the different Modelling Techniques need to be compared with a standardised procedure.

Author Contributions: Conceptualization, methodology, investigation, writing—original draft preparation, J.W.; supervision, writing—review and editing, M.W. Both authors have read and agreed to the published version of the manuscript.

Funding: We acknowledge support by the German Research Foundation and the Open Access Publishing Fund of Technical University of Darmstadt.

Conflicts of Interest: The authors declare no conflict of interest.

Abbreviations

CO_2-eq	Carbon Dioxide Equivalents
AI	Artificial Intelligence
ANN	Artifical Neural Network
DL	Deep Learning
FLC	Factory Life Cycle
ML	Machine Learning
PLC	Product Life Cycle
SEC	Specific Energy

References

1. European Commission. *The European Green Deal: Communication from the Commission to the European Parliament, the European Council, the Council, the European Economic and Social Comittee and the Committeee of the Regions*; European Commission: Brussels, Belgium, 2019.
2. Ritchie, H.; Roser, M. Emissions by Sector. Our World in Data. 2020. Available online: https://ourworldindata.org/emissions-by-sector#sector-by-sector-where-do-global-greenhouse-gas-emissions-come-from (accessed on 29 December 2020).
3. International Energy Agency (IEA). Key World Energy Statistics 2020. Paris. 2020. Available online: https://www.iea.org/reports/key-world-energy-statistics-2020 (accessed on 29 December 2020),
4. Hesselbach, J.; Herrmann, C.; Detzer, R.; Martin, L.; Thiede, S.; Ludemann, B. Energy efficiency through optimised coordination of production and technical building services. In *LCE 2008: 15th CIRP International Conference on Life Cycle Engineering: Conference Proceedings*; The University of New South Wales: Sydney, Australia, 2008; p. 624.
5. International Energy Agency (IEA). Tracking Power. Paris. 2020. Available online: https://www.iea.org/reports/tracking-power-2020 (accessed on 29 December 2020),
6. Beier, J. *Simulation Approach towards Energy Flexible Manufacturing Systems*; Sustainable Production, Life Cycle Engineering and Management, Springer International Publishing: Cham, Switzerland, 2017. doi:10.1007/978-3-319-46639-2.
7. Zhao, G.Y.; Liu, Z.Y.; He, Y.; Cao, H.J.; Guo, Y.B. Energy consumption in machining: Classification, prediction, and reduction strategy. *Energy* **2017**, *133*, 142–157. doi:10.1016/j.energy.2017.05.110.
8. Reinhardt, H.; Bergmann, J.P.; Münnich, M.; Rein, D.; Putz, M. A survey on modeling and forecasting the energy consumption in discrete manufacturing. *Procedia CIRP* **2020**, *90*, 443–448. doi:10.1016/j.procir.2020.01.078.
9. Glock, C.H.; Hochrein, S. Purchasing Organization and Design: A literature review. *Bus. Res.* **2011**, *4*, 149–191.
10. Reynolds, N.; Simintiras, A.; Vlachou, E. International business negotiations. *Int. Mark. Rev.* **2003**, *20*, 231–261.
11. Westkämper, E. Digitales Engineering von Fabriken und Prozessen. In *Schriftliche Fassung der Vorträge zum Fertigungstechnischen Kolloquium am 10 und 11 September in Stuttgart*; [Tagungsband]; Ges. für Fertigungstechnik: Stuttgart, Germany, 2008; Volume10, pp. 427–452.
12. Ongsulee, P. Artificial intelligence, machine learning and deep learning. In Proceedings of the 2017 Fifteenth International Conference on ICT and Knowledge Engineering (ICT&KE), Bangkok, Thailand, 22–24 November 2017; pp. 1–6. doi:10.1109/ICTKE.2017.8259629.
13. Goodfellow, I.; Bengio, Y.; Courville, A. *Deep Learning*; Adaptive Computation and Machine Learning, The MIT Press: Cambridge, MA, USA, 2016.
14. ISO—International Organization for Standardization. *ISO 14955-1—Machine tools—Environmental Evaluation of Machine tools—Part 1: Design Methodology for Energy-Efficient Machine Tools*; ISO: Geneva, Switzerland, 2017.
15. VDI—Verein Deutscher Ingenieure e.V. *VDI 5207 Blatt 1—Energieflexible Fabrik: Grundlagen*; VDI: Düsseldorf, Germany, 2020.
16. Box, G.E.P.; Jenkins, G.M.; Reinsel, G.C.; Ljung, G.M. *Time Series Analysis: Forecasting and Control*; John Wiley & Sons: Hoboken, NJ, USA, 2015.
17. VDI—Verein Deutscher Ingenieure e.V. *VDI 4661—Energiekenngrößen: Definitionen-Begriffe-Methodik*; VDI: Düsseldorf, Germany, 2003.
18. Spehr, J. On Hierarchical Models for Visual Recognition and Learning of Objects, Scenes, and Activities. Ph.D. Thesis, Universitätsbibliothek Braunschweig, Braunschweig, Germany, 2013. doi:10.24355/DBBS.084-201402261027-0.
19. Bhinge, R.; Park, J.; Law, K.H.; Dornfeld, D.A.; Helu, M.; Rachuri, S. Towards a generalized energy prediction model for machine tools. *J. Manuf. Sci. Eng.* **2017**, *139*. doi:10.1115/1.4034933.
20. Dietmair, A.; Verl, A. Energy consumption forecasting and optimisation for tool machines. *Energy* **2009**, pp. 62–67.
21. van Luttervelt, C.A.; Childs, T.; Jawahir, I.S.; Klocke, F.; Venuvinod, P.K.; Altintas, Y.; Armarego, E.; Dornfeld, D.; Grabec, I.; Leopold, J.; et al. Present Situation and Future Trends in Modelling of Machining Operations Progress Report of the CIRP Working Group 'Modelling of Machining Operations'. *CIRP Ann.* **1998**, *47*, 587–626. doi:10.1016/S0007-8506(07)63244-2.
22. Hahn, H.; Meyer-Nieberg, S.; Pickl, S. Electric load forecasting methods: Tools for decision making. *European journal of operational research* **2009**, *199*, 902–907.
23. Walsh, T. Empirical methods in AI. *AI Mag.* **1998**, *19*, 121–121.
24. Hong, T.; Fan, S. Probabilistic electric load forecasting: A tutorial review. *Int. J. Forecast.* **2016**, *32*, 914–938.
25. He, Y.; Wu, P.; Li, Y.; Wang, Y.; Tao, F.; Wang, Y. A generic energy prediction model of machine tools using deep learning algorithms. *Appl. Energy* **2020**, *275*. doi:10.1016/J.APENERGY.2020.115402.
26. Doreth, K. *Einsatz Maschineller Lernverfahren zur Lebenszyklusbasierten Energieprognose für Werkzeugmaschinen*; TEWISS: Garbsen, Germany, 2019.
27. Kant, G.; Sangwan, K.S. Predictive Modeling for Power Consumption in Machining Using Artificial Intelligence Techniques. *Procedia CIRP* **2015**, *26*, 403–407. doi:10.1016/j.procir.2014.07.072.
28. Abele, E.; Eisele, C.; Schrems, S. Simulation of the Energy Consumption of Machine Tools for a Specific Production Task. In *Leveraging Technology for a Sustainable World*; Dornfeld, D.A., Linke, B.S., Eds.; Springer: Berlin/Heidelberg, Germany, 2012; Volume 143, pp. 233–237. doi:10.1007/978-3-642-29069-5-40.

29. Abeykoon, C.; Kelly, A.L.; Brown, E.C.; Vera-Sorroche, J.; Coates, P.D.; Harkin-Jones, E.; Howell, K.B.; Deng, J.; Li, K.; Price, M. Investigation of the process energy demand in polymer extrusion: A brief review and an experimental study. *Appl. Energy* **2014**, *136*, 726–737. doi:10.1016/j.apenergy.2014.09.024.
30. Aramcharoen, A.; Mativenga, P.T. Critical factors in energy demand modelling for CNC milling and impact of toolpath strategy. *J. Clean. Prod.* **2014**, *78*, 63–74. doi:10.1016/j.jclepro.2014.04.065.
31. Avram, O.I.; Xirouchakis, P. Evaluating the use phase energy requirements of a machine tool system. *J. Clean. Prod.* **2011**, *19*, 699–711. doi:10.1016/j.jclepro.2010.10.010.
32. Balogun, V.A.; Mativenga, P.T. Modelling of direct energy requirements in mechanical machining processes. *J. Clean. Prod.* **2013**, *41*, 179–186. doi:10.1016/j.jclepro.2012.10.015.
33. Bi, Z.M.; Wang, L. Energy Modeling of Machine Tools for Optimization of Machine Setups. *IEEE Trans. Autom. Sci. Eng.* **2012**, *9*, 607–613. doi:10.1109/TASE.2012.2195173.
34. Bi, Z.M.; Wang, L. Optimization of machining processes from the perspective of energy consumption: A case study. *J. Manuf. Syst.* **2012**, *31*, 420–428. doi:10.1016/j.jmsy.2012.07.002.
35. Bornschlegl, M.; Bregulla, M.; Franke, J. Methods-Energy Measurement—An approach for sustainable energy planning of manufacturing technologies. *J. Clean. Prod.* **2016**, *135*, 644–656. doi:10.1016/j.jclepro.2016.06.059.
36. Braun, S.; Heisel, U. Simulation and prediction of process-oriented energy consumption of machine tools. In *Leveraging Technology for a Sustainable World*; Springer: Berlin/Heidelberg, Germany, 2012; pp. 245–250.
37. Budinoff, H.; Bhinge, R.; Dornfeld, D. A material-general energy prediction model for milling machine tools. In Proceedings of the 2016 International Symposium on Flexible Automation (ISFA), Cleveland, OH, USA, 1–3 August 2016; pp. 161–164.
38. Diaz, N.; Choi, S.; Helu, M.; Chen, Y.; Jayanathan, S.; Yasui, Y.; Kong, D.; Pavanaskar, S.; Dornfeld, D. Machine tool design and operation strategies for green manufacturing. In Proceedings of 4th CIRP International Conference on High Performance Cutting, Gifu, Japan, 24–26 October 2010.
39. Diaz, N.; Redelsheimer, E.; Dornfeld, D. Energy Consumption Characterization and Reduction Strategies for Milling Machine Tool Use. In *Glocalized solutions for sustainability in manufacturing*; Hesselbach, J.; Herrmann, C.S., Eds.; Springer: Berlin/Heidelberg, Germany; New York, NY, USA, 2011; Volume 53, pp. 263–267. doi:10.1007/978-3-642-19692-8-46.
40. Dietmair, A.; Verl, A. A generic energy consumption model for decision making and energy efficiency optimisation in manufacturing. *Int. J. Sustain. Eng.* **2009**, *2*, 123–133. doi:10.1080/19397030902947041.
41. Dietrich, B.; Walther, J.; Weigold, M.; Abele, E. Machine learning based very short term load forecasting of machine tools. *Appl. Energy* **2020**, *276*, 115440.
42. Doreth, K.; Henjes, J.; Kroening, S. Approach to Forecast Energy Consumption of Machine Tools within the Design Phase. *Adv. Mater. Res.* **2013**, *769*, 278–284. doi:10.4028/www.scientific.net/AMR.769.278.
43. Draganescu, F.; Gheorghe, M.; Doicin, C.V. Models of machine tool efficiency and specific consumed energy. *J. Mater. Process. Technol.* **2003**, *141*, 9–15. doi:10.1016/S0924-0136(02)00930-5.
44. Feng, M.; Hua, Z.; Hon, K.K.B. A Qualitative Model for Predicting Energy Consumption of Rapid Prototyping Processes—A Case of Fused Deposition Modeling Process. *IEEE Access* **2019**, *7*, 184825–184831. doi:10.1109/ACCESS.2019.2959214.
45. Goldhahn, L.; Pietschmann, C.; Eckardt, R. Process for the machine specific analysis and modeling of the technology based energetical demand forecasts. *Procedia CIRP* **2018**, *77*, 405–408. doi:10.1016/j.procir.2018.08.298.
46. Gutowski, T.; Dahmus, J.; Thiriez, A. Electrical energy requirements for manufacturing processes. In Proceedings of the 13th CIRP International Conference on Life Cycle Engineering, Leuven, Belgium, 31 May–2 June 2006; Volume 31, pp. 623–638.
47. Al-Hazza, M.H.F.; Adesta, E.Y.; Ali, A.M.; Agusman, D.; Supr, M.Y. Energy Cost Modeling for High Speed Hard Turning. *J. Appl. Sci.* **2011**, *11*, 2578–2584. doi:10.3923/jas.2011.2578.2584.
48. He, Y.; Liu, B.; Zhang, X.; Gao, H.; Liu, X. A modeling method of task-oriented energy consumption for machining manufacturing system. *J. Clean. Prod.* **2012**, *23*, 167–174. doi:10.1016/j.jclepro.2011.10.033.
49. He, Y.; Liu, F.; Wu, T.; Zhong, F.P.; Peng, B. Analysis and estimation of energy consumption for numerical control machining. *Proc. Inst. Mech. Eng. Part B J. Eng. Manuf.* **2012**, *226*, 255–266.
50. Herrmann, C.; Thiede, S. Process chain simulation to foster energy efficiency in manufacturing. *CIRP J. Manuf. Sci. Technol.* **2009**, *1*, 221–229. doi:10.1016/j.cirpj.2009.06.005.
51. Huang, J.; Liu, F.; Xie, J. A method for determining the energy consumption of machine tools in the spindle start-up process before machining. *Proc. Inst. Mech. Eng. Part B J. Eng. Manuf.* **2016**, *230*, 1639–1649. doi:10.1177/0954405415600679.
52. Imani Asrai, R.; Newman, S.T.; Nassehi, A. A mechanistic model of energy consumption in milling. *Int. J. Prod. Res.* **2018**, *56*, 642–659. doi:10.1080/00207543.2017.1404160.
53. Jia, S.; Tang, R.; Lv, J.; Zhang, Z.; Yuan, Q. Energy modeling for variable material removal rate machining process: an end face turning case. *Int. J. Adv. Manuf. Technol.* **2016**, *85*, 2805–2818. doi:10.1007/s00170-015-8133-8.
54. Kant, G.; Sangwan, K.S. Predictive Modelling for Energy Consumption in Machining Using Artificial Neural Network. *Procedia CIRP* **2015**, *37*, 205–210. doi:10.1016/j.procir.2015.08.081.
55. Kara, S.; Li, W. Unit process energy consumption models for material removal processes. *CIRP Ann.* **2011**, *60*, 37–40. doi:10.1016/j.cirp.2011.03.018.
56. Kong, D.; Choi, S.; Yasui, Y.; Pavanaskar, S.; Dornfeld, D.; Wright, P. Software-based tool path evaluation for environmental sustainability. *J. Manuf. Syst.* **2011**, *30*, 241–247. doi:10.1016/j.jmsy.2011.08.005.

57. Larek, R.; Brinksmeier, E.; Meyer, D.; Pawletta, T.; Hagendorf, O. A discrete-event simulation approach to predict power consumption in machining processes. *Prod. Eng.* **2011**, *5*, 575.
58. Li, L.; Yan, J.; Xing, Z. Energy requirements evaluation of milling machines based on thermal equilibrium and empirical modelling. *J. Clean. Prod.* **2013**, *52*, 113–121. doi:10.1016/j.jclepro.2013.02.039.
59. Li, W.; Kara, S. An empirical model for predicting energy consumption of manufacturing processes: a case of turning process. *Proc. Inst. Mech. Eng. Part B J. Eng. Manuf.* **2011**, *225*, 1636–1646.
60. Li, Y.; He, Y.; Wang, Y.; Wang, Y.; Yan, P.; Lin, S. A modeling method for hybrid energy behaviors in flexible machining systems. *Energy* **2015**, *86*, 164–174. doi:10.1016/j.energy.2015.03.121.
61. Li, Y.; He, Y.; Wang, Y.; Yan, P.; Liu, X. A framework for characterising energy consumption of machining manufacturing systems. *Int. J. Prod. Res.* **2014**, *52*, 314–325. doi:10.1080/00207543.2013.813983.
62. Liu, Z.Y.; Guo, Y.B.; Sealy, M.P.; Liu, Z.Q. Energy consumption and process sustainability of hard milling with tool wear progression. *J. Mater. Process. Technol.* **2016**, *229*, 305–312. doi:10.1016/j.jmatprotec.2015.09.032.
63. Lv, J.; Tang, R.; Jia, S. Therblig-based energy supply modeling of computer numerical control machine tools. *J. Clean. Prod.* **2014**, *65*, 168–177. doi:10.1016/j.jclepro.2013.09.055.
64. Lv, J.; Tang, R.; Tang, W.; Liu, Y.; Zhang, Y.; Jia, S. An investigation into reducing the spindle acceleration energy consumption of machine tools. *J. Clean. Prod.* **2017**, *143*, 794–803. doi:10.1016/j.jclepro.2016.12.045.
65. Mori, M.; Fujishima, M.; Inamasu, Y.; Oda, Y. A study on energy efficiency improvement for machine tools. *CIRP annals* **2011**, *60*, 145–148. doi:10.1016/j.cirp.2011.03.099.
66. Mose, C.; Weinert, N. Evaluation of Process Chains for an Overall Optimization of Manufacturing Energy Efficiency. In *Advances in Sustainable and Competitive Manufacturing Systems*; Azevedo, A., Ed.; Lecture Notes in Mechanical Engineering; Springer: Cham, Switzerland, 2013; pp. 1639–1651.
67. Munoz, A.A.; Sheng, P. An analytical approach for determining the environmental impact of machining processes. *J. Mater. Process. Technol.* **1995**, *53*, 736–758. doi:10.1016/0924-0136(94)01764-R.
68. Peng, T.; Xu, X. An interoperable energy consumption analysis system for CNC machining. *J. Clean. Prod.* **2017**, *140*, 1828–1841. doi:10.1016/j.jclepro.2016.07.083.
69. Quintana, G.; Ciurana, J.; Ribatallada, J. Modelling Power Consumption in Ball-End Milling Operations. *Mater. Manuf. Process.* **2011**, *26*, 746–756. doi:10.1080/10426910903536824.
70. Rahimifard, S.; Seow, Y.; Childs, T. Minimising Embodied Product Energy to support energy efficient manufacturing. *CIRP Ann.* **2010**, *59*, 25–28.
71. Rajemi, M.F.; Mativenga, P.T.; Aramcharoen, A. Sustainable machining: Selection of optimum turning conditions based on minimum energy considerations. *J. Clean. Prod.* **2010**, *18*, 1059–1065. doi:10.1016/j.jclepro.2010.01.025.
72. Rief, M. *Vorhersagemodell für den Energiebedarf bei der Spanenden Bearbeitung für eine Energieeffiziente Prozessgestaltung*; Shaker: Magdeburg, Germany, 2012.
73. Sato, R.; Shirase, K.; Hayashi, A. Energy Consumption of Feed Drive Systems Based on Workpiece Setting Position in Five-Axis Machining Center. *J. Manuf. Sci. Eng.* **2018**, *140*, 25. doi:10.1115/1.4037427.
74. Sealy, M.P.; Liu, Z.Y.; Zhang, D.; Guo, Y.B.; Liu, Z.Q. Energy consumption and modeling in precision hard milling. *J. Clean. Prod.* **2016**, *135*, 1591–1601. doi:10.1016/j.jclepro.2015.10.094.
75. Seow, Y.; Rahimifard, S. A framework for modelling energy consumption within manufacturing systems. *CIRP J. Manuf. Sci. Technol.* **2011**, *4*, 258–264. doi:10.1016/j.cirpj.2011.03.007.
76. Seow, Y.; Rahimifard, S.; Woolley, E. Simulation of energy consumption in the manufacture of a product. *Int. J. Comput. Integr. Manuf.* **2013**, *26*, 663–680. doi:10.1080/0951192X.2012.749533.
77. Shang, Z.; Gao, D.; Jiang, Z.; Lu, Y. Towards less energy intensive heavy-duty machine tools: Power consumption characteristics and energy-saving strategies. *Energy* **2019**, *178*, 263–276. doi:10.1016/j.energy.2019.04.133.
78. Shao, H.; Wang, H.L.; Zhao, X.M. A cutting power model for tool wear monitoring in milling. *Int. J. Mach. Tools Manuf.* **2004**, *44*, 1503–1509. doi:10.1016/j.ijmachtools.2004.05.003.
79. Shin, S.J.; Kim, Y.M.; Meilanitasari, P. A Holonic-Based Self-Learning Mechanism for Energy-Predictive Planning in Machining Processes. *Processes* **2019**, *7*, 739–766. doi:10.3390/pr7100739.
80. Sossenheimer, J.; Walther, J.; Fleddermann, J.; Abele, E. A Sensor Reduced Machine Learning Approach for Condition-based Energy Monitoring for Machine Tools. *Procedia CIRP* **2019**, *81*, 570–575. doi:10.1016/j.procir.2019.03.157.
81. Sossenheimer, J.; Vetter, O.; Abele, E.; Weigold, M. Hybrid virtual energy metering points—A low-cost energy monitoring approach for production systems based on offline trained prediction models. *Procedia CIRP* **2020**, *93*, 1269–1274. doi:10.1016/j.procir.2020.04.128.
82. Su, C.L. Load Estimation in Industrial Power Systems for Expansion Planning. *IEEE Trans. Ind. Appl.* **2011**, *47*, 2311–2323. doi:10.1109/TIA.2011.2168591.
83. Teiwes, H.; Blume, S.; Herrmann, C.; Rössinger, M.; Thiede, S. Energy load profile analysis on machine level. *Procedia CIRP* **2018**, *69*, 271–276.
84. Verl, A.; Abele, E.; Heisel, U.; Dietmair, A.; Eberspächer, P.; Rahäuser, R.; Schrems, S.; Braun, S. Modular Modeling of Energy Consumption for Monitoring and Control. In *Glocalized Solutions for Sustainability in Manufacturing*; Hesselbach, J., Herrmann, C.S., Eds.; Springer: Berlin/Heidelberg, Germany; New York, NY, USA, 2011; Volume 28, pp. 341–346. doi:10.1007/978-3-642-19692-8_59.

85. Walther, J.; Spanier, D.; Panten, N.; Abele, E. Very short-term load forecasting on factory level—A machine learning approach. *Procedia CIRP* **2019**, *80*, 705–710. doi:10.1016/j.procir.2019.01.060.
86. Walther, J.; Dietrich, B.; Abele, E. Generic Machine Learning Approach for very short term load forecasting of production machines. In Proceedings of the International Conference on Applied Energy 2019, Västerås, Sweden, 12–15 August 2019.
87. Wang, L.; He, Y.; Li, Y.; Wang, Y.; Liu, C.; Liu, X.; Wang, Y. Modeling and analysis of specific cutting energy of whirling milling process based on cutting parameters. *Procedia CIRP* **2019**, *80*, 56–61. doi:10.1016/j.procir.2019.01.028.
88. Weinert, N.; Chiotellis, S.; Seliger, G. Methodology for planning and operating energy-efficient production systems. *CIRP Ann.* **2011**, *60*, 41–44.
89. Wu, Z.; Hobgood, M.; Wolf, M. Energy Mapping and Optimization in Rough Machining of Impellers. In *International Manufacturing Science and Engineering Conference*; The American Society of Mechanical Engineers: New York, NY, USA, 2016. doi:10.1115/MSEC2016-8719.
90. Yi, L.; Krenkel, N.; Aurich, J.C. An energy model of machine tools for selective laser melting. *Procedia CIRP* **2018**, *78*, 67–72. doi:10.1016/j.procir.2018.08.302.
91. Yi, L.; Gläßner, C.; Krenkel, N.; Aurich, J.C. Energy simulation of the fused deposition modeling process using machine learning approach. *Procedia CIRP* **2019**, *86*, 216–221. doi:10.1016/j.procir.2020.01.002.
92. Yoon, H.S.; Lee, J.Y.; Kim, M.S.; Ahn, S.H. Empirical power-consumption model for material removal in three-axis milling. *J. Clean. Prod.* **2014**, *78*, 54–62. doi:10.1016/j.jclepro.2014.03.061.
93. Yoon, H.S.; Moon, J.S.; Pham, M.Q.; Lee, G.B.; Ahn, S.H. Control of machining parameters for energy and cost savings in micro-scale drilling of PCBs. *J. Clean. Prod.* **2013**, *54*, 41–48. doi:10.1016/j.jclepro.2013.04.028.
94. Zhou, X.; Liu, F.; Cai, W. An energy-consumption model for establishing energy-consumption allowance of a workpiece in a machining system. *J. Clean. Prod.* **2016**, *135*, 1580–1590. doi:10.1016/j.jclepro.2015.10.090.
95. Wang, H.; Lei, Z.; Zhang, X.; Zhou, B.; Peng, J. A review of deep learning for renewable energy forecasting. *Energy Convers. Manag.* **2019**, *198*, 111799. doi:10.1016/j.enconman.2019.111799.
96. Chen, C.; Liu, Y.; Kumar, M.; Qin, J. Energy Consumption Modelling Using Deep Learning Technique—A Case Study of EAF. *Procedia CIRP* **2018**, *72*, 1063–1068.
97. Bianchi, F.M.; Maiorino, E.; Kampffmeyer, M.C.; Rizzi, A.; Jenssen, R. *Recurrent Neural Networks for Short-Term Load Forecasting: An Overview and Comparative Analysis*; Springer: Cham, Switzerland, 2017.
98. Cheng Fan.; Fu Xiao.; Yang Zhao. A short-term building cooling load prediction method using deep learning algorithms. *Appl. Energy* **2017**, *195*, 222–233. doi:10.1016/j.apenergy.2017.03.064.

Article

Data-Driven Modeling of Fuel Consumption for Turboprop-Powered Civil Airliners

Benoit G. Marinus * and Antoine Hauglustaine

Department of Mechanical Engineering, Royal Military Academy, avenue de la Renaissance 30, 1000 Brussels, Belgium; antoine.hauglustaine@mil.be
* Correspondence: benoit.marinus@rma.ac.be

Received: 24 February 2020; Accepted: 1 April 2020; Published: 3 April 2020

Abstract: Next to empirical correlations for the specific range, fuel flow rate, and specific fuel consumption, a response surface model for estimates of the fuel consumption in early design stages is presented and validated. The response-surface's coefficients are themselves predicted from empirical correlations based solely on the operating empty weight. The model and correlations are all derived from fuel consumption data of nine current civil turbo-propeller aircraft and are validated on a separate set. The model can accurately predict fuel weights of new designs for any combination of payload and range within the current range of efficiency of the propulsion. The accuracy of the model makes it suited for preliminary and conceptual design of near-in-kind turbo-propeller aircraft. The model can shorten the design cycle by delivering fast and accurate fuel weight estimates from the first design iteration once the operating empty weight is known. Since it is based solely on the operating empty weight and it is accurate, the model is a sound variant to the Breguet range equation in order to make accurate fuel weight estimates.

Keywords: turbo-propeller; regional; fuel; weight; range; design

1. Introduction

The maximum payload of current turboprop-powered civil airliners and transports amounts to between 39% and 74% of the aircraft's operating empty weight (OEW), while the maximum fuel weight varies between 30% and 47% OEW. Therefore, an accurate estimate at early design stages of the amount of fuel required to perform the missions according to the customers' requirements—i.e., range and payload combinations—is essential to reduce the amount of iterative design work. The weight of fuel burned is also decisive in the assessment of the performance of the intended design and in benchmarking. Moreover, does the compromise between payload weight and quantity of fuel play a major role, together with structural constraints [1], in the definition of the operating boundaries of the payload-range diagram?

Several variants are available to make operating empty weight and fuel weight predictions that can be applied to diverse aircraft types: [2–19] to cite just a few. Either actual data are given about a few existing designs or the Breguet range equation [20] is invoked with the fuel fraction method to estimate the fuel burned in cruise conditions for similar designs. These spreadsheets rely on semi-empirical correlations for the approximation of the range parameter ($\eta_p C_L / (g\, SFC\, C_D)$) [2,6, 12,13,17], which translates the role of the propulsive (the propeller efficiency η_p and the equivalent Specific Fuel Consumption SFC) and aerodynamic characteristics (the lift and drag coefficients, C_L and C_D, respectively) onto the attainable distance. The range parameter is often, and rather by default, assumed to be constant along the flight due to a lack of reliable data at such early design stages. Without these parameters, the gross weight of an aircraft cannot be calculated, and without the gross weight, these parameters cannot be estimated. Therefore, the closure is brought with carefully-chosen estimates and a model, such as the Breguet range equation, is used before the next design iteration. However, the estimates of the propulsive and aerodynamic parameters as well as the weights at early design stages are difficult and lead to large discrepancies. Results differ by as much as 25% between each other [6,21]. More precise methods to estimate the parameters affecting the Breguet range equation can be found [7,22], but errors up to 10% are common [6,21].

First, a response surface model is derived and validated for civil turbo-prop aircraft to estimate, in early design stages, when detailed propulsive and aerodynamic parameters are lacking, the weight of fuel burned during any mission. The response surface coefficients are themselves deduced from an empirical correlation relying entirely on the Operating Empty Weight (OEW). This OEW,q-model is the core of the present paper. This data-driven extension of the model [23] to much lighter aircraft than the original database comes with different findings, since the distinct design requirements lead to fundamental structural differences and, thence, operating empty weights. Next, the present research paper investigates the dependency of the specific range on an aircraft's gross weight, which decreases along the flight as fuel is burned. A model is also proposed for the fuel flow rate variation with the gross weight. We formulate in a constructive way alterations and revisions to the extensive literature body found mainly in textbooks, with the aim of refining the knowledge around turboprop-powered civil airliners.

2. Database and Methods

2.1. Data Set

The database consists of 15 turboprop-powered civil airliners in current flying inventories, and is randomly split into a training set and a testing set. The training set is a representative subset covering the OEW-range at hand; it comprises nine aircraft types from eight different manufacturers. The main data are read from the performance section of the flight manual. Assembled by the authors, it comprises: the specific range SR in km/1000 kg of fuel and the fuel flow rates FF in kg/hr, together with the corresponding true air speed and gross weight combination for relevant cruise altitudes. The maximum cruise speed for each gross weight is used since most samples do not distinguish explicitly for any other cruise speed in the flight manual. Data are read for all engines operating at nominal turbine-inlet temperature ranges in standard ISA wind-free conditions. For some types, the fuel requirements depending on distance are read. The testing set comprises six samples, including one variant of a training sample. These are chosen such that their operating empty weight is distributed over the entire range present in the training set. Typical differences are of the order of 2~3% between the Base of Aircraft Data (BADA) database [24]—a comprehensive performance database and model initiated by the European authorities for operations and research—and flight manuals when available.

The gathered specific ranges are illustrated in Figure 1 for the validation set while weight characteristics and limits are given in Table 1. Since all airliner samples weight less than 30,000 kgf, no category distinction is made based on weight as is necessary for heavier transports [23].

2.2. Weights Breakdown and Weight of Fuel Burned

The total range Ra is divided into m steps (ΔRa = 1.852 km). The aircraft's Gross Weight (GW) is assumed constant for the duration of one step and given by:

$$GW_i = OEW + WP + WF_i \ (i = 1, 2, 3 \cdots m) \qquad (1)$$

where OEW is the Operating Empty Weight. This weight includes the aircrew, all fluids necessary for operation, and the required operator items and equipment. In Equation (1), WP expresses the weight of the payload (including passengers), and WF_i is the weight of usable fuel (by opposition to fuel trapped in the fuel system ducts, valves, and pumps), which is computed from the initial weight of usable fuel WF_0 and the fuel burned during all preceding steps WFB_{i-1}, so

$$WF_i = WF_0 - WFB_{i-1} \ (i = 1, 2, 3 \cdots m). \tag{2}$$

The initial weight of usable fuel includes WFRes, the weight of fuel reserves. The fuel burned prior to reaching the cruise altitude (i.e., the sum of the start-up and maneuver fuel at the departure location, the take-off fuel, and the fuel to climb), is noted WFBS. Thus, the fuel burned during all preceding steps WFB_{i-1} is now given by

$$WFB_{i-1} = WFBS + \sum_{j=0}^{i-1} WFBC_j \tag{3}$$

where $WFBC_j$ stands for the fuel consumed over the j-th range step in cruise conditions. It is calculated from the interpolated specific range SR(GW,Alt)-relationships (Figure 1):

$$WFBC_j = \frac{2 \, \Delta Ra}{SR(GW_j) + SR(GW_{j+1})}. \tag{4}$$

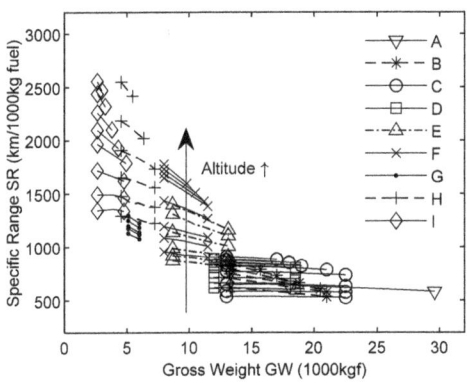

Figure 1. Specific range data with altitude variation for the aircraft from the training set of Table 1.

Table 1. Sets, samples, and aircraft weights.

Set	Sample	OEW (kgf)	OEW/MTOW	WPmax/OEW	WFmax/OEW
Training	A	17,830	0.60	0.48	0.30
	B	13,940	0.66	0.39	0.32
	C	13,610	0.60	0.53	0.37
	D	11,700	0.63	0.45	0.38
	E	8620	0.66	0.39	0.30
	F	7230	0.63	0.45	0.36
	G	4350	0.66	0.39	0.30
	H	4180	0.58	0.51	0.47
	I	2630	0.53	0.74	0.43
Testing	J	14,510	0.63	0.38	0.29
	K	13,110	0.63	0.42	0.31
	L	11,800	0.60	0.52	0.22
	M	10,440	0.67	0.39	0.25
	N	4850	0.62	0.42	0.42
	O	4322	0.63	0.31	0.38

For the preceding computations, the following hypotheses apply:

1. The Weight of Fuel Reserves (WFRes) is taken as a fixed percentage of one of the aircraft's representative masses, in the present case, the Maximum Take-Off Weight (MTOW). For civil airliners, a survey of the required reserves to satisfy the Airworthiness Authorities provisions (missed approach, hold, and diversion) among the training set led to a safe value of 3.5%. This value is less cautious than a flat 8% of the zero-fuel weight [7,25], but exceeds the 6% of the total fuel consumption taken as tolerance for reserves and trapped fuel [12].
2. After a survey through the training set, the Weight of Fuel Burned at Start (WFBS) is estimated as 2% MTOW. This conservative value corresponds to the low-end of the 1.0% to 4.4% of the take-off gross weight found in [2,4,12,13,15,21].
3. The gross weight is used for a linear interpolation of the specific range for different altitudes (6 samples), although better interpolation was obtained with a quadratic regression for 3 samples. In all cases, the goodness of fit R^2 exceeded 0.99. The maximum relative errors computed after the interpolation process did not exceed 0.8%.
4. Since the fuel that is required from the start of the descent to the arrival at the gate differs only by a small amount from the one that would be burned in cruise over the same distance, the missions end when flying atop the destination airfield, as in [17,25].

The step-wise computation of the total weight of fuel consumed for any range (Ra) and payload (WP) pair results in a matrix as illustrated in the top-right thumbnail in Figure 2. This matrix is then bracketed by the actual fuel and weight limitations to obtain the payload-range fuel-burned triplets shown in Figure 2. for an aircraft of the validation sample.

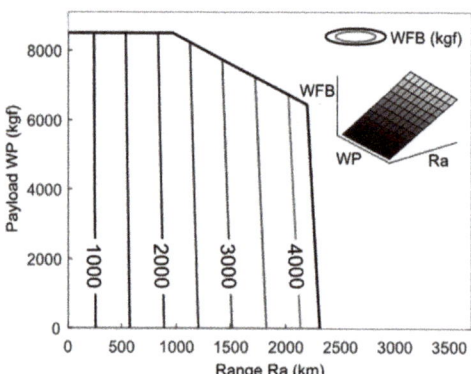

Figure 2. Contours of the Weight of Fuel Burned (WFB) bracketed by the payload-range limitations for an aircraft from the training sample. The top-right thumbnail shows the unbracketed 3D fuel consumption surface.

2.3. Fuel Estimate Model Based on OEW

The Breguet range equation reads

$$Ra = \frac{\eta_p}{g\,SFC} \frac{L}{D} \ln\left(\frac{TOW - WFBS}{OEW + WP + WFRes}\right) \qquad (5)$$

after integration over the cruise segment. In Equation (5), the take-off weight TOW is given by TOW = OEW + WP + WFRes + WFB. Since the essence of the Breguet range equation is to model how fuel is consumed to fly a distance under the implications of the propulsion and aerodynamic parameters, and given that the gross weight has a significant impact onto this consumption, we proposed in [23] a knowledge-based response surface methodology involving solely the operating empty weight OEW.

This polynomial response surface is now extended to lower OEW-values for civil turboprop-powered airliners. The response surface is based on the pair (Ra,WP) as independent variables

$$WFB = p_{00} + p_{10}\, Ra + p_{01}\, WP + p_{11}\, Ra\, WP + p_{20}\, Ra^2. \tag{6}$$

The p-coefficients are fitted to the actual data to yield the best R^2-values. Given their potential influence on the end-result, we consider two hypotheses: cruise flight at constant altitude or cruise flight with stepwise increasing altitude. The constant altitude is taken as the maximum altitude at which the maximum gross weight can be sustained with a minimum rate of climb of 300 ft/min. For the changing altitude case, jumps vary between 20 hft to 50 hft depending on the aircraft type. In any case, the knowledge-based polynomial response surface comes with excellent correspondence with the original fuel consumption surface as the coefficients of determination (R^2) are above 0.99.

As shown in Figure 3, the dominant terms of Equation (6) are the first order range term $p_{10}Ra$ and the independent term p_{00}. As is apparent in Figure 4, the last is collocated with the weight of fuel burned at start (WFBS), as expected from the fixed percentage of the MTOW hypothesis.

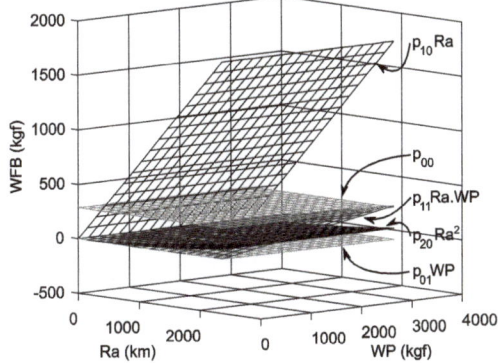

Figure 3. Relative magnitude of the p-terms for an aircraft at constant altitude.

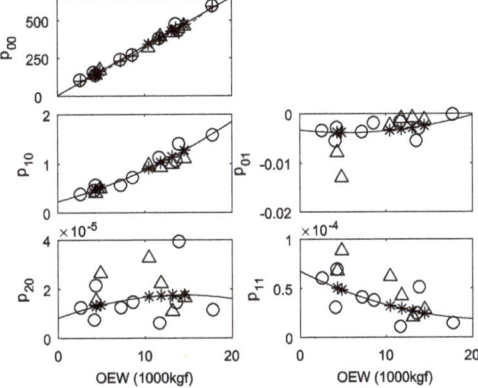

Figure 4. p-Coefficients of the fuel consumption surface (WFB) fit for the maximum constant altitude case. 'o' training samples, '△' validation samples, '*' predicted value on the validation samples, on p_{00} '- - + - -' Weight of Fuel Burned at Start WFBS = 2% of MTOW (Maximum Take-Off Weight).

In comparison with heavier military transports, the interaction term p_{11} and the range penalty term p_{20} have a more significant relative contribution but are only effective for long range and heavy missions. Since mission ranges do not exceed 2000–2500 km, the range penalty term p_{20} is not a significant contributor. That is another major difference with heavier transport aircraft. The payload represents an appreciable percentage of the operating empty weight, which typically does not exceed 39%–53% (see Table 1). These are comparatively lighter payloads than in the case of military transports. Consequently, the payload term p_{01} has only a very little influence.

Next, the model consists of expressing the response surface parameters (p-coefficients) in Equation (6) as:

$$p_{ij} = q_2 \, OEW^2 + q_1 \, OEW + q_0. \qquad (7)$$

The dependency on solely the operating empty weight is the key novel assumption. The underlying knowledgebase is that of similarity with the nearest in kind from an airframe and propulsion perspective. The strength behind the present method is that the operating empty weight is among the very first elements that are computed during the initial steps of the preliminary design process [4,12,13]. Equation (7) is shown in Figure 4 together with the original p-coefficients. The best fit for Equation (7) is detailed in Table 2. Excellent agreement is obtained on the dominant terms $p_{00}(OEW)$ and $p_{10}(OEW)$, as the respective coefficients of determination are above 0.99. For the independent term p_{00}, the linear fit yields the percentage of the operating empty weight that closely matches the postulate on the weight of fuel burned at start WFBS (see Section 3). This suggests that this assumption could also be safely expressed in other terms as 3.2% of OEW. For $p_{10}(OEW)$, the agreement confirms the main assumption behind this method namely that given OEW and WP are present in the numerator and the denominator of the logarithm in Equation (5), then it is the fuel expressed as a percentage of OEW that is the leading term next to the range parameter. As the range parameter has little variation between near-in-kind designs and the consumed fuel depends directly on how much weight is carried, the OEW plays a preponderant role.

Table 2. Response surface coefficients as a function of OEW (Operating Empty Weight): $p_{ij} = q_2 \, OEW^2 + q_1 \, OEW + q_0$.

Hypothesis	p-term	q_2	q_1	q_0
Constant Altitude	p_{00}	0	3.24×10^{-2}	4.79
	p_{10}	1.69×10^{-9}	4.74×10^{-5}	2.29×10^{-1}
	p_{01}	1.68×10^{-11}	-1.83×10^{-7}	3.33×10^{-3}
	p_{11}	9.96×10^{-14}	-4.42×10^{-9}	6.76×10^{-5}
	p_{20}	-4.54×10^{-14}	1.30×10^{-9}	8.33×10^{-6}
Variable Altitude	p_{00}	0	2.94×10^{-2}	4.36
	p_{10}	4.44×10^{-9}	2.45×10^{-6}	0.361
	p_{01}	1.37×10^{-10}	-2.89×10^{-6}	0.022
	p_{11}	8.64×10^{-13}	$-1.68e \times 10^{-8}$	1.05×10^{-4}
	p_{20}	3.84×10^{-13}	-5.93×10^{-9}	2.60×10^{-5}

Given their weak influence on Equation (6), the poor agreement on the other terms does not jeopardize the overall agreement of the model since the goodness of fit of the surface is modeled through Equations (6) and (7), and the original surface is above 0.93 for 11 samples and around 0.8 for the remaining 4.

The differences between preliminary design cycles with the Breguet range equation (Equation (5)) and the present OEW,q-model (Equations (6) and (7)) are summarized in Figure 5.

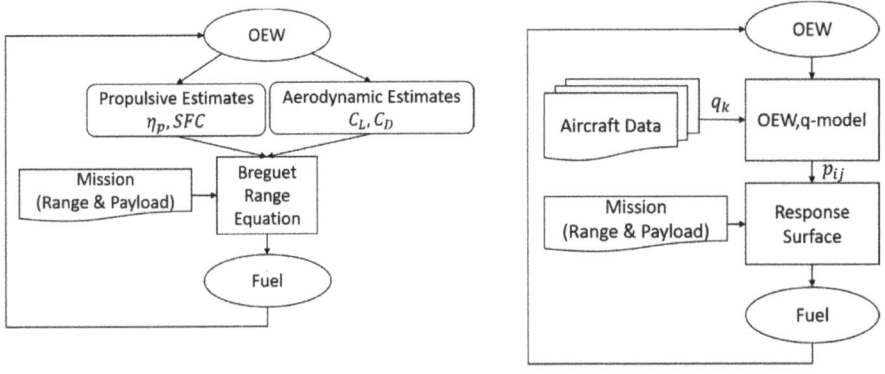

a. With Breguet range equation.   b. With OEW,q-model.

Figure 5. Preliminary design cycles (**a**) with the Breguet range equation (Equation (5)) and (**b**) the OEW,q-model (Equations (6) and (7)).

3. Results, Validation of the OEW,q-Model, and Discussion

3.1. Instantaneous Fuel Consumption Figure of Merits

The database allows us to analyze common figures of merit such as Fuel Flow Rates, Specific Range, and Specific Fuel Consumption. When looking at the fuel flow rates FF (comprising all engines) in the maximum cruising constant altitude assumption shown in Figure 6, we establish a linear relationship

$$FF = 0.0341\ GW + 105.26 \quad (8)$$

with a goodness of fit of 0.83, but the mean relative error obtained with this approach is of the order of 14%. This trend is higher than the trend established in [23] where the set consists primarily of larger, more powerful engines, which are known comparatively to consume less [5].

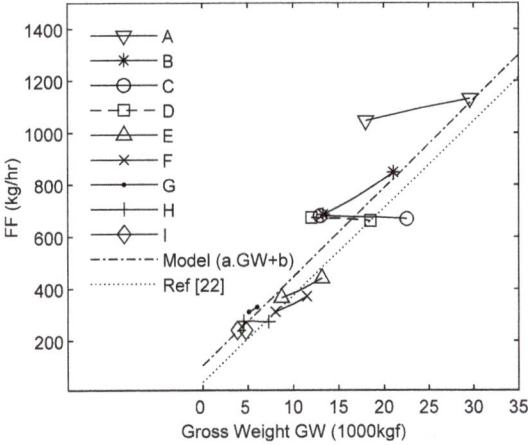

Figure 6. Hourly fuel flow and gross weight dependence at constant altitude.

Based on the data from Figure 7, the specific range is expressed as a power-fit applied to the gross weight as given in Table 3 together with R^2. The model is built either on the hypothesis of a constant altitude flight at the maximum cruise altitude (see Section 2.3), or for the minimum cruising altitude found in the flight manuals. The coefficients are given in Table 3 together with the R^2-values. Given the goodness of fit, this model should be used with care since the mean relative error for both hypotheses is of the order of 10% with actual values ranging between 0.4% and 36.1%. The largest errors occur typically for aircraft lighter than 12,500 kgf. Next to confirming the trend set for the light military transport category in [23], the present data confirm the strong dependency of specific range to gross weight and altitude and, thereby, invalidate the assumption of a constant value.

Table 3. Specific range (km/1000kg fuel) power-fit to gross weight (kgf) at the maximum constant altitude, and at the minimum cruise altitude: $SR = b\, GW^n$

Altitude	n	b	R^2
Maximum cruise	−0.57	2.070×10^5	0.70
Minimum Cruise	−0.56	1.435×10^5	0.88

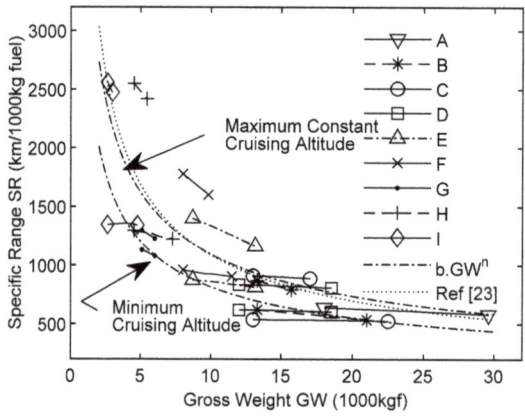

Figure 7. Specific range variation with the gross weight for the maximum constant cruise altitude, and for the minimum cruise altitude. See Table 3 for model coefficients.

We also plotted the power Specific Fuel Consumption SFC depending on the gross weight in Figure 8, since this approach is often used in conjunction with the Breguet range equation. Reported values from the literature range from 0.23–0.37 kg/kW/hr as shown in Figure 8. Current data return a mean SFC of 0.362 kg/kW/hr and a median of 0.361 kg/kW/hr, which are close to the maximum bounds found in the literature [1,6,9,12,13,15,17,26]. Figure 8 indicates that for aircraft in the present weight range, the one standard deviation interval 0.3–0.42 kg/kW/hr is better suited. Although the samples in [23] all featured a strong dependence of the Specific Fuel Consumption upon the gross weight, some samples in Figure 8 do not. This confirms the reservations made in [21–23,27] about the widely accepted assumption consisting of using a constant Specific Fuel Consumption along the integration of the Breguet range equation.

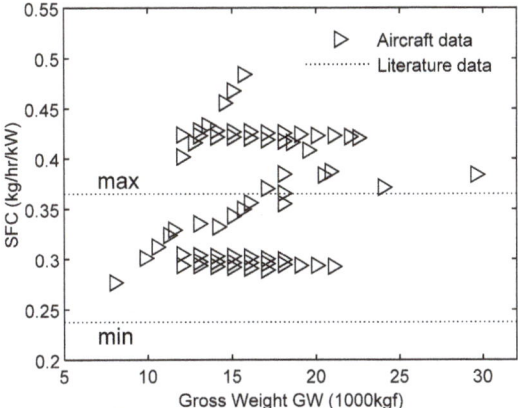

Figure 8. Power Specific Fuel Consumption in cruise at maximum constant altitude.

3.2. WFB-Predictions and Validation of the OEW,q-Model

Once an operating empty weight is given, the OEW,q-model allows us to predict the response surface coefficients through Equation (7) and in Table 2. Then the weight of fuel burned can be computed for any mission. The accuracy of the model is shown in Figure 9 for an aircraft of the validation sample. For the overall training samples, the mean error on the prediction of the weight of fuel burned $\hat{WFB}$ versus the actual weight of fuel consumed does not reach 2% of the operating empty weight. This error never exceeds 4% for the validation samples. The highest errors occur systematically for the region of the payload-range diagram that corresponds to the maximum fuel line (as in Figure 9). In comparison, the mean error when working with the Breguet range equation ($\hat{WFB}_B$) on the validation set is of 3% OEW, but the maximum error reaches 10%. This behavior is shown in Figure 10 for the same sample as in Figure 8.

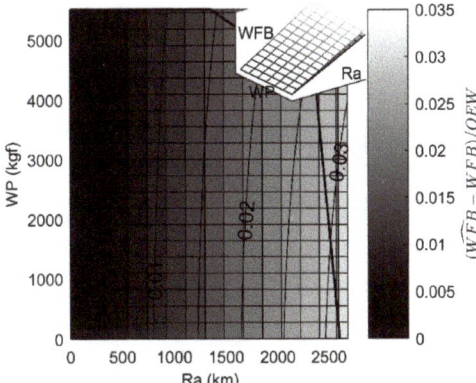

Figure 9. Relative error on the fuel consumption between the model estimate $\hat{WFB}$ and the actual value WFB in the maximum constant altitude assumption for a validation sample. The thumbnail shows the actual unbracketed WFB surface in grey tones and the estimate $\hat{WFB}$-surface in shade.

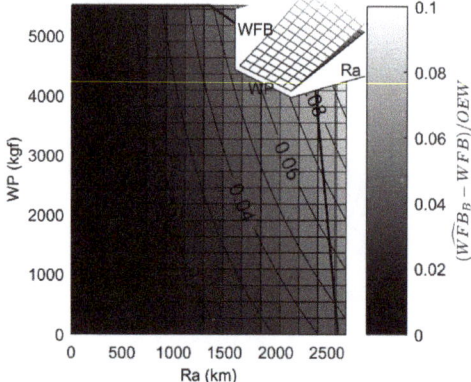

Figure 10. Relative error on the fuel consumption between the estimate with the Breguet range equation $\widehat{WFB}_B$ (Equation (5)) on the same case as in Figure 9. The thumbnail shows the actual unbracketed WFB surface in gray tones and the Breguet estimate $\widehat{WFB}_B$ -surface in shade.

Next to the analysis of the individual p-coefficients in Section 2.3 and Figure 4, the accuracy shown in Figure 9 with the OEW,q-model confirms the correctness of the principal assumption behind the model, i.e., that the fuel consumed over a distance is mainly driven by the operating empty weight.

3.3. Influence of Altitude on the OEW,q-Model

The coefficients from Table 2 are also given for the stepwise increasing altitude hypothesis, in which the flight altitude is increased concurrently as the current gross weight decreases. By doing so, the range can be further maximized. As was the case with the military transports, the change of hypothesis has no significant impact on the accuracy of the model as is illustrated in Figure 11 for a sample from the validation set. The mean error on the predicted fuel consumed $\left(\widehat{WFB} - WFB\right)$ does not exceed 3% of the operating empty weight for the whole validation set. As shown on Figure 12, the model offers significantly better accuracy than the Breguet range equation when applied to stepwise increasing altitudes.

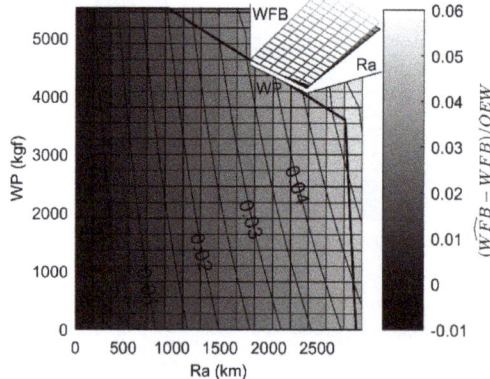

Figure 11. Relative error on the fuel consumed (WFB) between the predicted value and the actual value for the increasing altitude case on a validation sample. The thumbnail shows the actual unbracketed fuel consumption matrix in gray tones and the predicted $\widehat{WFB}$-matrix in shade.

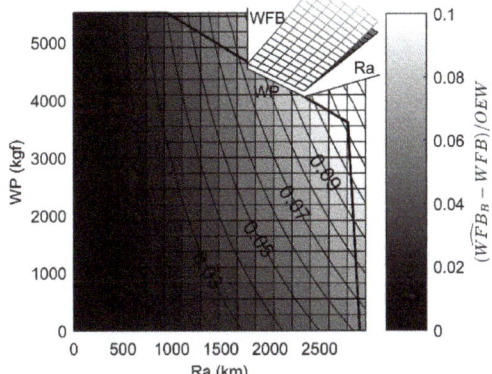

Figure 12. Relative error on the fuel consumed (WFB) between the estimate with the Breguet range equation (Equation (5)) on the same case as in Figure 11. The thumbnail shows the actual unbracketed fuel consumption matrix in gray tones and the Breguet estimate $\widehat{WFB}_B$ -matrix in shade.

3.4. Influence of Temperature on the OEW,q-Model

Since increasing the exterior temperature is known to have a negative impact on the performance of the propulsion system, the influence of a +10° deviation from cruise ISA-conditions has been assessed. The fuel flow typically increases by +2% to +7% so that the specific range is decreased for identical cruise speeds. On top of that, weight or altitude limitations could raise from higher exterior temperature, though this is out of the scope of the present method.

4. Conclusions

It is shown that the response surface describing the weight of fuel burned for every possible payload-range combination is largely determined by the first order range term (p_{10} Ra) in Equation (6). A strong correlation has been found between the range term and the operating empty weight. In other words, while fuel is burned to displace an aircraft's gross weight over a certain range, it is essentially the aircraft's operating empty weight that determines the total fuel consumption, while the payload or the deadweight fuel carried over long flights play, herein, only a minor role. Long missions (i.e., above 2000 km) come with a fuel penalty for carrying deadweight fuel over the first legs. Therefore, the OEW,q-model is proposed to make an early and reliable estimate of the mission fuel weight any range and payload pairs. The rationale behind the OEW,q-model is that comparable aircraft designs can effectively be identified through their operating empty weight within the present range of efficiency of the propulsion. It is based on actual aircraft data.

The proposed OEW,q-model is applicable to turboprop-powered civil airliners and transports since aircraft developed for military duties were dealt with in [23]. Civil and military types differ strongly in the OEW-range that is considered. Although the methodology is identical, it is not straightforward to use the response surface coefficients found on one data set for the other given the marked differences in operating empty weight. These differences come from distinct operational requirements that led to separate design solutions in terms of structure and propulsion. Because of its accuracy, which is lower than 4% of the operating empty weight, and given its dependence solely on the operating empty weight to educe a response surface, the model is particularly suited for the conceptual or preliminary design stages, or for benchmarking. Because of its accuracy and the low number of input parameters (only the OEW is required next to the present coefficients), it outperforms models, such as the Breguet range equation, which are available in the wide body of literature dedicated to aircraft design.

Additionally, empirical correlations are also established for the fuel flow rate and the specific range as functions of an aircraft's gross weight. Moreover, it is shown that the amount of fuel consumed from the engine start to the end of the climb can be safely expressed as 3.2% of *OEW* instead of a fixed percentage of the maximum take-off weight.

Author Contributions: Conceptualization, B.G.M. and A.H.; methodology, B.G.M. and A.H.; software, A.H.; validation, B.G.M. and A.H.; formal analysis, B.G.M. and A.H.; investigation, A.H.; resources, A.H.; data curation, A.H.; writing—original draft, B.G.M. All authors have read and agreed to the published version of the manuscript.

Funding: This research received no external funding.

Conflicts of Interest: The authors declare no conflict of interest.

Nomenclature

a,b	Regression coefficients
Alt	Altitude
D	Drag (N)
FF	Fuel Flow rate (kg/hr)
g	Gravitational acceleration (m/s^2)
GW	Gross Weight
L	Lift (N)
MTOW	Maximum Take-Off Weight (kgf)
n	Regression exponent
OEW	Operating Empty Weight (kgf)
p,q	Polynomial coefficients
Ra	Range (km)
SFC	Power specific fuel consumption (kg/kW/hr)
SR	Specific Range (km/1000kg of fuel)
TOW	Take-Off Weight (kgf)
WF	Weight of Fuel (kgf)
WFB	Weight of Fuel Burned (kgf)
WFBC	Weight of Fuel Burned for Cruise (kgf)
WFBS	Weight of Fuel Burned for Starting (kgf)
WFRes	Weight of Fuel Reserves (kgf)
ZFW	Zero Fuel Weight (kgf)
η_p	Propeller propulsive efficiency
$\hat{}$	Predicted value
$_B$	Breguet estimate

Note: Altitudes are expressed in hectofeet (hft) according to common aeronautical practice.
Note: Kilogram-force units (kgf) are used for weights that are otherwise expressed in mass units in standard aeronautical practice.

References

1. Babikian, R.; Lukachko, S.; Waitz, I. The historical fuel efficiency characteristics of regional aircraft from technological, operational, and cost perspectives. *J. Air Transp. Manag.* **2002**, *8*, 389–400. [CrossRef]
2. Corke, T.C. *Design of Aircraft*; Prentice Hall: Upper Saddle River, NJ, USA, 2003.
3. Filippone, A. Data and performances of selected aircraft and rotorcraft. *Prog. Aerosp. Sci.* **2000**, *36*, 629–654. [CrossRef]
4. Howe, D. *Aircraft Conceptual Design Synthesis*; Professional Engineering Publishing: London, UK, 2000.
5. Ibrahim, K. Selecting principal parameters of baseline design configuration for twin turboprop transport aircraft. In Proceedings of the 22nd Applied Aerodynamics Conference and Exhibit, Providence, RI, USA, 16–19 August 2004. Number AIAA 2004–5069. [CrossRef]
6. Kundu, A.K. *Aircraft Design*; Cambridge University Press: Cambridge, UK, 2010.
7. Lee, H.-T.; Chatterji, G.B. Closed-form takeoff weight estimation model for air transportation simulation. In Proceedings of the 10th AIAA Aviation Technology, Integration and Operations Conference, Ft. Worth, TX, USA, 13–15 September 2010; Volume 2. [CrossRef]

8. Liem, R.P.; Mader, C.A.; Martins, J.R. Surrogate models and mixtures of experts in aerodynamic performance prediction for aircraft mission analysis. *Aerosp. Sci. Technol.* **2015**, *43*, 126–151. [CrossRef]
9. Marinus, B.G.; Poppe, J. Data and design models for military turbo-propeller aircraft. *Aerosp. Sci. Technol.* **2015**, *41*, 63–80. [CrossRef]
10. Nightingale, W.I.M. Aeroplane weight analysis. *Aircr. Eng. Aerosp. Technol.* **1945**, *17*, 250–253. [CrossRef]
11. Obert, E.; Slingerland, R. *Aerodynamic Design of Transport Aircraft*; IOS Press BV: Amsterdam, The Netherlands, 2009.
12. Raymer, D.P. *Aircraft Design: A Conceptual Approach*; AIAA: Reston, VA, USA, 2006. [CrossRef]
13. Roskam, J. Part 1: Preliminary sizing of airplanes. In *Airplane Design*; DARcorporation: Lawrence, KS, USA, 2002; ISBN 9781884885556.
14. Roskam, J.; Lan, C.-T.E. *Airplane Aerodynamics and Performance*; DARcorporation: Lawrence, KS, USA, 1997.
15. Schaufele, R.D. *The Elements of Aircraft Preliminary Design*; Aries Publications: Santa Ana, CA, USA, 2000.
16. Stinton, D. *The Design of the Airplane*; BSP Professional Books: Oxford, UK, 1983.
17. Torenbeek, E. *Synthesis of Subsonic Airplane Design*; Delft University Press-Kluwer Academic Publishers: Delft, The Netherlands, 1982.
18. Torenbeek, E. Prediction of wing group weight for preliminary design. *Aircr. Eng. Aerosp. Technol.* **1971**, *43*, 16–21. [CrossRef]
19. Vouvakos, X.; Kallinderis, Y.; Menounou, P. Preliminary design correlations for twin civil turboprops and comparison with jet aircraft. *Aircr. Eng. Aerosp. Technol.* **2010**, *82*, 126–133. [CrossRef]
20. Breguet, L. Calcul du poids de combustible consommé par un avion en vol ascendant. In *Comptes Rendus Hebdomadaires des Séances de l'Académie des Sciences*; Académie des Sciences: Paris, France, 1923; pp. 870–872.
21. Randle, W.E.; Hall, C.A.; Vera-Morales, M. Improved range equation based on aircraft flight data. *J. Aircr.* **2011**, *48*, 1291–1298. [CrossRef]
22. Torenbeek, E. Cruise performance and range prediction reconsidered. *Prog. Aerosp. Sci.* **1997**, *33*, 285–321. [CrossRef]
23. Marinus, B.G.; Maison, J. Fuel weight estimates of military turbo-propeller transport aircraft. *Aerosp. Sci. Technol.* **2016**, *55*, 458–464. [CrossRef]
24. BADA v3.13. Base of Aircraft Data, March 10 2017. Available online: www.eurocontrol.int/services/bada (accessed on 15 May 2017).
25. Kroo, I. *Aircraft Design: Synthesis and Analysis*; Desktop Aeronautics, Inc.: Stanford, CA, USA, 2001.
26. Fielding, J.P. *Introduction to Aircraft Design*; Cambridge University Press: Cambridge, UK, 1999. [CrossRef]
27. Cavcar, A.; Cavcar, M. Approximate solutions of range for constant altitude-constant high subsonic speed flight of transport aircraft. *Aerosp. Sci. Technol.* **2004**, *8*, 557–567. [CrossRef]

© 2020 by the authors. Licensee MDPI, Basel, Switzerland. This article is an open access article distributed under the terms and conditions of the Creative Commons Attribution (CC BY) license (http://creativecommons.org/licenses/by/4.0/).

Article

An Ant Colony Algorithm for Improving Energy Efficiency of Road Vehicles

Alberto V. Donati [1,*], Jette Krause [1], Christian Thiel [1], Ben White [2] and Nikolas Hill [3]

[1] Joint Research Centre of the European Commission, Via Fermi 2749, 21027 Ispra (VA), Italy; jettekrause@aol.com (J.K.); christian.thiel@ec.europa.eu (C.T.)
[2] Ricardo Energy and Environment, 30 Eastbourne Terrace, Paddington, London W2 6LA, UK; b.white.1@hotmail.co.uk
[3] Ricardo Energy and Environment, Gemini Building, Fermi Avenue, Harwell, Oxon OX11 0QR, UK; nikolas.hill@ricardo.com
* Correspondence: alberto.donati@ext.jrc.ec.europa.eu

Received: 14 May 2020; Accepted: 30 May 2020; Published: 3 June 2020

Abstract: The number and interdependency of vehicle CO_2 reduction technologies, which can be employed to reduce greenhouse emissions for regulatory compliance in the European Union and other countries, has increasingly grown in the recent years. This paper proposes a method to optimally combine these technologies on cars or other road vehicles to improve their energy efficiency. The methodological difficulty is in the fact that these technologies have incompatibilities between them. Moreover, two conflicting objective functions are considered and have to be optimized to obtain Pareto optimal solutions: the CO_2 reduction versus costs. For this NP-complete combinatorial problem, a method based on a metaheuristic with Ant Colony Optimization (ACO) combined with a Local Search (LS) algorithm is proposed and generalized as the Technology Packaging Problem (TPP). It consists in finding, from a given set of technologies (each with a specific cost and CO_2 reduction potential), among all their possible combinations, the Pareto front composed by those configurations having the minimal total costs and maximum total CO_2 reduction. We compare the performance of the proposed method with a Genetic Algorithm (GA) showing the improvements achieved. Thanks to the increased computational efficiency, this technique has been deployed to solve thousands of optimization instances generated by the availability of these technologies by year, type of powertrain, segment, drive cycle, cost type and scenario (i.e., more or less optimistic technology cost for projected data) and inclusion of off-cycle technologies. The total combinations of all these parameters give rise to thousands of distinct instances to be solved and optimized. Computational tests are also presented to show the effectiveness of this new approach. The outputs have been used as basis to assess the costs of complying with different levels of new vehicle CO_2 standards, from the perspective of different manufacturer types as well as vehicle users in Europe.

Keywords: CO_2 reduction; multi-objective combinatorial optimization; meta-heuristics; ant colony optimization

1. Introduction

In recent years, the automotive industry has faced increasing pressure to reduce CO_2 emissions to meet regulatory targets set in both the EU and other legislations. Several new CO_2 reduction and energy efficiency improvement technologies have been developed to respond to these new regulatory developments. This technology proliferation increases the complexity of finding optimal combinations to achieve substantial CO_2 reductions in a cost-efficient way. The problem consists of finding feasible configurations, represented by points in the plane total CO_2 reduction versus price, and identifying the limiting subset of those, which form the Pareto front, to yield the optimal configurations for the objectives defined. The optimization problem is computationally difficult because of the size of the search space. Because of incompatibilities between certain technologies, the optimization problem cannot be solved by simple sorting according to technology efficiency (CO_2 reduction per cost) and constructing configurations starting by the most efficient technology, adding technologies based on their efficiency, from the most efficient to the least.

In the following, we discuss similar problems found in the literature and various approaches to tackle them. The Knapsack Problem (KP) and its multi-dimensional variant (MKP) are problems aimed to find an optimal subset of objects to be placed in one or more knapsacks (or limited capacity boxes/containers), maximizing the total profit or utility. These problems belong to the class of NP-complete problems and have been extensively explored as a fundamental area of discrete optimization and Operations Research (OR). Whilst the standard KP seeks to maximize the utility under a single constraint, other variations or generalizations can deal with the assignment of resources, such as in freight logistics planning, capital budgeting, allocation of tasks on processors, stock cutting problems or in distributed computing as presented in [1,2]. A well-studied extension of the MKP is the Multi-Objective Multi-dimensional Knapsack Problem (MOMKP), when taken with two objective functions and no constraints on the number or capacities of the knapsacks. A detailed survey of techniques to solve the Multi-Objective Knapsack Problem (MOKP) and MOMKP is presented in [3]; it discusses exact methods, approximation algorithms and heuristics for the MOKP, including Simulated Annealing, Tabu Search and other heuristic methods, subdivided into evolutionary algorithms and those based on local search (LS). Other methods, such as Fuzzy Logic and Kalman Filtering have been successfully applied in detecting failures of integrated sensors/systems on vehicles where high-dimensional data is present [4]. State-of-the-art genetic algorithms have been extensively applied to the multi-objective optimization like in [5,6], to the multi-criterion optimal design [7].

The Technology Packaging Problem (TPP) is introduced here since the problem differs considerably from a MOMKP, in that, if a knapsack is assimilated to a package or configuration:

(1) The same object can be placed in one or more knapsacks (or configurations), but with no repetition within the package,
(2) some objects cannot be combined in the same knapsack (or package) due to the incompatibility between them, so one or the other shall be chosen,
(3) there are no constraints on the number and capacity of knapsacks, in the sense that the number of the feasible optimal packages/configurations is not set a priori, nor its costs (or capacity) is given a priori, but rather found by the optimization.

The difference described in point (3) can be particularly noticeable if one would try to approach the problem by fixing one objective and trying to optimize the other. More specifically, this could be done by partitioning the cost (the knapsack capacity) from a minimum to a maximum cost, say in 100 slices, and solve the same number of optimization problems each with the maximum cost of the slice considered. However this would result in a loss of solutions, since the optimization would end with a pareto front with exactly the same number of solutions as slices and, further, a potential loss of efficiency in having to re-compute from scratch the solution for each slice. This would exclude for example the possibility of incrementally adding objects/technologies to already found optimal configurations. The reduction of the 2-objective problem to a sliced single objective problem has some drawbacks which will be discussed in Section 4. On the other hand, we have attempted the reduction of the current problem to other similar multi objective and constrained problems, but none brought to a satisfactory formulation without a significant loss of details or changes in the original problem. Hence, the introduction of the Technology Packaging Problem (TPP). To solve this problem with two (or more) conflicting objectives, we have devised an Ant Colony Optimization (ACO) combined with a Local Search heuristic (ACO + LS).

Bio-inspired algorithms have gained consensus as being some of the most efficient and effective to deal with complex problems and constraints in various areas of Operational Research. Examples include evolutionary algorithms, swarm intelligence, distributed systems, neural networks and similar heuristic/meta-heuristics methods for NP-complete or other computationally hard problems. In particular, the choice of ACO is motivated by the recent success of swarm intelligence approaches to solve complex and dynamical problems with a system of interacting agents, which combines exploration and learning (ACO) with simple local rules (LS). These approaches give rise to a collective and distributed intelligence through a form of system memory whereby global information is encoded locally, as presented extensively in [8,9]. ACO heuristics have proven to be particularly effective when combined with appropriate local search techniques, as evidenced in [10] and [11]. They are commonly used in operational research problems such as the classic Traveling Salesman Problem (TSP), quadratic assignment and job-shop scheduling. ACO extends to applications in problems of a dynamic nature due to the algorithm's adaptability and re-scheduling capabilities [12], for example the Vehicle Routing Problem (VRP) with variable traffic conditions [13] or with unexpected events [14]. In [15] ACO is used for the Multi-Stage Flow Shop Scheduling Problem and applied for the scheduling of real factories. The introduction of multiple colonies and different pheromones update strategies has been proved effective for multi-objective problems. An example is the application to the time and space assembly line balancing problem, presented in [16], where eight different ACO architectures are introduced and compared.

One of the first applications of ant colony inspired algorithms to the MKP and the Subset Problem (SP)—a special case of the knapsack problem—was made by [17] with an Ant System, a variation of ACO incorporating two distinct pheromone updating rules: local and global. This was followed specifically for the MKP by [18,19] (where a general ACO is introduced for multi-objective optimization) and later by [20], reporting very successful results in comparison to other evolutionary algorithms. The MKP, SP and TPP are quite different from TSP-like problems, as the ordering of objects or tasks to complete is not important: for the former the solutions are combinations, yet for the latter they are permutations (ordered sequences).

Some further considerations are therefore needed in the representation of the problem and in particular regarding the pheromone encoding. Two main approaches are present in the literature: node-based, deposited on the node or edge-based, deposited on the edges connecting nodes/objects. In this study we adopted the former, as presented in [18].

The TPP is formulated in Section 2, and the ACO + LS algorithm is discussed in Section 3. A short description of the construction of so-called cost curves for vehicle CO_2 emission reduction is also given. In Section 4, the ACO + LS results are compared with those obtained previously with a Genetic Algorithm (GA). The real world optimization problem instances, discussed in Section 5, consist of a set of specific technologies which are available and a set of initialization parameters; these include the type of vehicle, its size and powertrain, the year considered and the drive cycle over which the technology is evaluated, which together act to determine the presence or absence of a technology. Finally conclusions are drawn in Section 6.

The contribution of this study is in the following:

(a) The formulation of a novel OR problem, the TPP, which has not been seen in existing literature, which has with some crucial differences from similar problems as discussed at points (1) to (3) above this section.
(b) Since the problem is new, the development of a method for performing the optimization once the TPP is applied to the two objective optimization problem of vehicular CO_2 reduction technologies.
(c) The evaluation of the computational efficiency of this method on an extended set of problem instances.
(d) The extensive application of the method to thousands of different instances, each representing a vehicle type (size, segment, power train, etc.) to provide, for each vehicle type, its "cost curve" to

be used for each manufacturer type's fleet composition and the combined CO_2 emissions of its circulating vehicles.

With the above, once ran over the entire EU vehicle fleet typology has been used as an input for future CO_2 targets, so one of its most relevant contributions has been to the support of the EU policy making to check the feasibility of the 2025–2030 CO_2 reduction targets. The cases presented in Section 5 are just a part of a number of simulations/optimizations ran by the authors. Most of these, and their rationale, have been omitted since they are beyond the scope of this study. Thanks to its efficiency, the system has been used extensively for scenario analysis, for example to find configurations with certain technologies which are always present (such as where these technologies have already been embedded in the vehicles) or for the analysis in which different future scenarios for the price projection or CO_2 reduction potentials were to be used. Overall, the authors have run about 60,000 problem instances in the course of these analyses.

2. The Optimization Problem

The TPP with two-objectives is defined as follows. Given:

(1) A set of N technologies $T = \{t_1, \ldots, t_N\}$, each characterized by two numerical values (f_i, g_i) of their utility (or inverse utility, like cost, in the case of minimization), for every $i = 1,\ldots,N$.
(2) A matrix $E = \{e_{ij}\}$, $e_{ij} = \{0, 1\}$, defining the incompatibilities between technologies t_i, t_j of the above set (with the convention: 1=incompatible, 0=compatible). E is symmetric due to the fact that "incompatibility" is symmetric: if t_i is incompatible with t_j, t_j is incompatible with t_i.
(3) A package rule: objects can be aggregated in so-called packages or configurations, by combining any subset of compatible technologies $T_k = \{t_{k1}, \ldots, t_{kn}\}$ with $k_h \in [1,N]$, containing each technology at most once (no repetition) in each package; subscript indexes k_h are introduced just to indicate that any subset of T is possible, provided the technologies are compatible.
(4) Two analytical functions, the objectives, to aggregate the utilities of the technologies in the package $T_k = \{t_{kh}\}$: $F = F(T_k) = F(f_{k1},\ldots,f_{kn})$ and $G = G(T_k) = G(g_{k1},\ldots,g_{kn})$, with $k_h \in [1,N]$, to provide the aggregate measure of the package. The functions F and G can assume any problem-specific form, to appropriately combine the utilities of the technologies/objects composing a given configuration. They can simply be the sum of utilities or their product.

The problem is then to find, among all the possible packages/configurations, those which are Pareto optimal with respect to two objective functions chosen. Since the technologies considered here are CO_2 reduction technologies, each with a cost c_i and CO_2 reduction potential r_i (which represents the CO_2 emission reduction percentage value that can be attained with the technology in place), the objective functions F and G can be defined as the total cost of the package, C_k and its total CO_2 reduction R_k as follow:

$$C_k = \sum_{t_i \in T_k} c_i \qquad (1)$$

$$R_k = 1 - \prod_{t_i \in T_k} (1 - r_i) \qquad (2)$$

Equation (2) is obtained by considering the cumulative, interacting benefits of the technologies. For example, if technology 1 has $r_1 = 0.1$ (i.e., 10%) and technology 2 has $r_2 = 0.05$ (i.e., 5%), the total reduction of the combined technologies is obtained by applying technology 2 only after we have applied technology 1. Since technology 1 will provide a CO_2 emission of $(1-r_1)$, applying the second will result in a total CO_2 emission of $(1-r_1) \times (1-r_2)$. The total reduction of applying the two technologies is therefore $R = 1 - (1-r_1) \times (1-r_2)$ (hence the form of Equation (2)), which given r_1 and r_2 is 0.145 or 14.5%.

For this specific application, the optimization is aimed at the minimization of Equation (1) and the maximization of Equation (2). Then the Pareto optimality condition between any two configurations

T_n and T_m (independently of their size) is that: the configuration T_n is said to be dominating the configuration T_m if one of the two following conditions holds:
if:
$$C_n < C_m \text{ and } R_n \geq R_m \text{ or if } C_n = C_m \text{ and } R_n > R_m \tag{3}$$

This means that either T_n has lower total cost and same or higher total CO_2 reduction, or it has the same cost but higher total CO_2 reduction. The configuration T_n is said to be dominated by T_m if one of the following two conditions holds:
if:
$$C_n > C_m \text{ and } R_n \leq R_m \text{ or if } C_n = C_m \text{ and } R_n < R_m \tag{4}$$

If a configuration dominates another one, this cannot belong to the set of the Pareto optimal front. On the other hand, T_n is Pareto optimal with T_m if one of the two following conditions hold:
if:
$$C_n > C_m \text{ and } R_n > R_m \text{ or if } C_n < C_m \text{ and } R_n < R_m \tag{5}$$

Geometrically, these conditions are equivalent to consider in the (R,C) plane, the relative position of the two configurations: $T_m = (R_m, C_m)$ in which to center Cartesian axes, and $T_n = (R_n, C_n)$. If the latter falls in the lower-right quadrant, including the vertical and horizontal semi-axes, then T_n is dominating (condition (3)) T_m, if it falls in the upper-left quadrant, including semi-axes, it is dominated (condition (4)), while in all other cases they are pareto optimal (condition (5)), so unless other configurations are found to dominate one or both, they are both included in the Pareto optimal set. The set of all Pareto optimal configurations is also referred to as Pareto front.

The size of a configuration is the number of technologies it contains. An exhaustive exploration of solution space, in case of N distinct technologies, would imply the evaluation of (1) and (2) for all possible configurations. The number of all possible configurations of size n, is the combinations of N objects taken n at a time: $\binom{N}{n} = \frac{N!}{n!(N-n)!}$. The total search space size, or the total number of all possible configurations (without considering incompatibilities), is then given by sum of the above expression over all possible configurations' sizes:

$$S = \sum_{n=1}^{N} \binom{N}{n} = 2^N - 1 \tag{6}$$

where the second equality derives from the Binomial theorem. Even considering incompatibilities (*I*) between technologies, which tend to diminish the number of the feasible combinations, from a rough estimation of the search space with (6), is where N is usually between 50 and 80 and I is in the order of 2 or 3, is it clear that an exhaustive search is computationally impracticable.

3. The ACO Algorithm

A simple brute force approach would imply testing all possible combinations of the compatible technologies, but this is computationally infeasible, given Equation (6). Some simple heuristics were tested. Technologies were sorted by their cost efficiency (also referred to as 'technology efficiency'), defined as the CO_2 reduction divided by the cost, and to add technologies to the configuration one by one as far as they were compatible with those already present. In the construction process, when an incompatible technology is encountered, it is simply skipped, and the next is examined. This procedure is then repeated, starting each time with a different technology and adding technologies until no further technology could be added.

It was soon noticed that a procedure such as this omits some configurations, since it always starts from a pre-ordering of technologies, based on cost efficiency. Including some randomness greatly improved the number of configurations found. However, a purely random search coupled with a greedy ordering showed to use significant computational power without an efficient search strategy in the solution space. It was observed that most of the time was spent randomly exploring, rather than reinforcing good solutions and discarding certain areas.

The Ant Colony Optimization (ACO) algorithm was therefore devised. This involves the creation of an underlying graph where artificial ants can propagate and lay pheromones, a mechanism which allows the local encoding of global information, as discussed in [8–11]. The representation of the problem is the following: each node of the graph represents a technology, and two nodes are connected by an edge if, and only if, they are compatible. If an edge is present, the ant can step from a node to the next and this walk translates into a building process, where at each step, a technology is added to the configuration completed so far. Before adding a new technology, the ant must check if it is compatible with all the technologies "visited" beforehand. To this aim, the ant needs to keep an updated incompatibility list, which contains all technologies incompatible with those previously visited. To each ant step corresponds the addition of a technology to form a configuration with one more object. As the new configuration is found, it is added to the ant's set of configurations found so far, which is then composed by a collection of configurations of increasing size. The ant's walk ends when there are no more nodes to visit, that is, when no further technology can be added to the last configuration found. At this point, all the configurations found are evaluated against those stored in the best solution found so far. If they are suboptimal, some Local Search (LS) might be attempted (generally, if the configuration size is between 6 and 12). Pheromones are updated by a uniform evaporation and a deposition, for each configuration, on the edges visited by the ant, proportionally to the quality of the configuration. The quality criterion of a configuration is its overall cost efficiency, i.e., the total CO_2 reduction divided by the total cost. Otherwise, if the configuration is dominating or Pareto with respect to one or more stored in the best solution, pheromones are boosted (usually by a factor 1000) and proportionally to the quality of the configuration found. The configuration(s) of the best solution, dominated by the newly found configurations, if any, are identified and removed, and the better configuration (s) found, if any, are added to the best solution. In this way, the best solution keeps improving and stores the best configurations found so far by any ant.

3.1. Technical Description

All data pertaining to technologies and costs are fed into the system. The specific instance of the optimization problem is determined by choosing one value for each of the initialization parameters, i.e., year, powertrain, vehicle segment, drive cycle, cost scenario, cost type, and whether to include off-cycle technologies (see the list of parameter values in Section 5 for more detail). These values determine which technologies are present, their cost, their effective CO_2 reduction, and their incompatibility list. With these elements, since each technology constitutes a node, the underlying graph can be constructed at this stage.

As noted before, we denote the cost efficiency of a technology its CO_2 reduction per unit cost, briefly called technology efficiency (or node efficiency), as compared to the total CO_2 reduction R, divided by the total cost C, called the 'configuration efficiency'. Certainly, using the configuration efficiency ($CE = R/C$) instead of a Pareto selection criteria on the two objectives would have resulted in optimized configurations as well, and namely on the CE itself. However, we wanted to explicitly require an improvement in each of the two objectives separately, as in criteria in Equation (5), since the aim was to have a set of configurations to choose from with separate criteria or objectives. For example, finding which configurations can reach a certain CO_2 reduction level and the expected impact of the ambition of certain CO_2 targets on actual costs.

The ACO algorithm proceeds as follows:

3.2. Solution Construction

(1) An ant a is created and placed in the first node t_i, the first technology added to the configuration: the first node is chosen randomly in 10% of the cases and probabilistically otherwise, based on its efficiency. The ant's list of incompatible technologies is updated with the list of incompatible

technologies of this node. The node t_i to-do-list is set "done" so it will not be added again and add the configuration to the solution the ant is constructing.

(2) The next node t_j is determined by randomly selecting the decision criterion characterizing the ant's inclination of exploration versus exploitation. This is done by drawing a random number to determine one of the following 3 possible decision criteria:

(a) Greedy (usually set to 20% of cases): go to node t_j with the maximum $p\,(t_j) \propto \tau\,(t_i, t_j) \times e\,(t_j)$ where $\tau\,(t_i, t_j)$ is the pheromone on the edge (t_i, t_j), and $e\,(t_j)$ is the efficiency of t_j; this is favoring exploitation and following the colony.

(b) Probabilistic (usually set to ~80% of cases): from node t_i chose next node t_j with a probability $p\,(t_j)$ as given above; this criteria provides a mix of exploitation and exploration.

(c) Random (usually set to 1% of cases): the ant goes to the next node t_j randomly; this represents pure exploration/trial.

Then to determine t_j, a second random number is drawn in the case of criteria b. or c., while if criterion a. is selected, t_j is already determined, by argmax $(p\,(t_j))$.

(3) The step is made to node t_j, i.e., setting $t_i = t_j$, the node to-do list to "done" and updating the incompatibilities list with the technologies incompatible with t_j. The new configuration found is stored in the solution.

(4) Steps 2 and 3 are repeated until no further nodes are available to be visited (i.e., not visited yet and compatible with those already present in the configuration). With the completion of the above, a solution has been constructed. The elements of this new solution are the configurations $\{T_{1a},\ldots, T_{na}\}$ each of increasing size, where subindex a denotes the ant a. These are compared one by one with those stored in the best solution found, to check if any new best or Pareto configurations can be added to the best solution. The criteria for "new best" between 2 configurations is given by the conditions (3) and (4) described in Section 2. If any configuration is dominant or Pareto, it is added to the best solution, eliminating from the best solution those configurations that are dominated by that configuration. At this point the pheromones are updated, in the following way (update of the pheromones):

(a) Evaporation: all the pheromones on the graph undergo a uniform evaporation, i.e., all are decreased by a constant percentage (usually 20%) by multiplying by a constant ρ less than one; pheromones are never allowed to drop below a minimum level of 0.1 to avoid entering into stagnation,

(b) Deposition: first determine if a configuration is a new optimal or not (either dominating or pareto). If it is not, LS can be applied, as will be discussed shortly. Pheromones on the edges traversed by the ant are incremented proportionally to the configuration quality, as follows:

i. if not an optimal configuration: increase by $\varepsilon = S_F \times R/C$ (R and C given by Equations (1) and (2)), and with a S_F is a scale factor, depending on the problem size and costs involved.

ii. if a better or Pareto configuration is found, increase by $\varepsilon = S_F \times B \times R/C$, where B is the boosting factor, in the order of 10^3.

Note that since each configuration is a combination of technologies (e.g., the order of the technologies does not matter), a deposition will be also be performed on all edges between all technologies contained. For example, if we consider the configuration $\{t_3, t_{23}, t_{54}, t_{65}\}$ then the pheromones on edges (t_3, t_{23}), (t_3, t_{54}), (t_3, t_{65}), (t_{23}, t_{54}), (t_{23}, t_{65}), (t_{54}, t_{65}) and their reverse edges undergo i or ii above.

(5) Repeat the process of 1 to 4. For a new ant, until a predetermined computation time has been reached. If long runs are used, and no improved configuration has been found for a certain number of iterations (usually 1 million), a boost as in 4)b.ii. is induced in the system on the best solution found so far, so that the colony is repositioned to search in that neighborhood. If this is the case, the algorithm starts some boosting cycles, typically a maximum of 10^4 cycles or until an improvement has been found, by artificially enhancing the pheromones around the best solution. This value guarantees that ants would propagate around pheromone trails of the best solution; this process is reminiscent of the elitist ants, but it is much more aggressive, and proved to contribute significantly to the long-term search. The values used where tested over several runs.

(6) The run is finalized by outputting the best solution found, including a comparison if a benchmark solution for that problem is present. Various log files are also generated.

The schema of the ACO + LS algorithm is reported in pseudo code in Algorithm 1, which also calls the procedures of ant propagation, LS and pheromones update, reported in Algorithm from 2 to 4 below. The values of the ant parameters (e.g., the proportions of greedy, probabilistic and random steps, as well as the proportion of initial random step, ρ, S_F and B) given above were chosen in the algorithm tuning phase, where several tests were conducted to obtain the highest quality solutions in the shortest time.

Algorithm 1. ACO+LS algorithm

```
1    Initialize the graph G of nodes {t_i} (technologies) with the parameters given.
2    while (keepLooping)
3        • S_a = a.propagation() which provides the solution S_a={T_1_a,..., T_n_a}
4        • evaporate pheromones:  Graph.evaporatePheromones(0.8)
5        • compare S_a to S_best={T_1_best, ... T_n_best}
6          for i=1_a,...n_a,
7            for j=1_best,...,n_best
8              • if T_i dominates T_j:
9                       ○ remove T_j from S_best and add T_i (once only)
10             • else if T_i is Pareto with T_j, add T_i to S_best (def. in Equation (4))
11             • else if LS_min≤size(T_i)≤LS_max apply Local Search:
12                      ○ LocalSearch.switchTechs(T_i, 2)
13                        (LS_min,LS_max are the min and max size for LS, typically 6 and
14                   12 respectively)
15                      ○ check if T_i is better or Pareto after LS.
16               if T_i is better or Pareto, ε = S_F * B * R/C
17               else ε = S_F * R/C
18               graph.incrementPheromones(T_i, ε)
19       • if no improvement is found after N_it iterations:
20           increment pheromones on S_best={T_1best, ... T_n} for M times or till an improved
21           configuration is found (typically ε=B*R/C N_it=10^6 and M =10^4)
22       • if (time > maxComputationTime)
23              break
24          else iter++
25   Finalization:
26       • lexicographic ordering the technology IDs in each T_ib of S_best.
27       • comparison of S_best with benchmark if present
28
29   write logs, computation times, and best solution.
```

The ant algorithm, ant propagation and pheromone update mechanisms presented in this study are typical of those formulated in the ACO-related literature. It is worth noting that the pheromones are node based given that no ordering of the technologies in a configuration is needed. The ant choice criteria have been integrated here with the problem specific objectives, which drive the immediate reward. Also Local Search algorithm is bespoke, having been developed and integrated for this specific problem. The novelty is then how the ACO and LS have been applied to the specific problem.

Regarding the Local Search, three different methods of removing the technologies were attempted: removing randomly, removing the least efficient technologies and removing those with the largest incompatibility list. After a few tests, substituting technologies only on the basis of efficiency appeared to be the best criteria. Once the technologies have been removed, the same number of technologies (compatible with the reduced configuration) are randomly chosen and inserted. The modified configuration is then compared to the original and, if it is better, exchanged with the previous one in the ant's solution.

Algorithm 2. Ant propagation

```
1   (1) Create an ant a and place in the first node tᵢ:
2       a.  Generate a random number r:
3               if(r<0.1) chose tᵢ randomly
4               else chose tᵢ probabilistically as eᵢ (cost efficiency)
5       b.  Update the ant's list of incompatible nodes (technologies)
6       c.  Set the state of this node to completed
7       d.  add the configuration T₁ₐ = {tᵢ} to Sₐ:  Sₐ={T₁ₐ}
8   (2) Let ant step to the next feasible node tⱼ:
9       a.  Strategy to step: generate a random number r
10          if(r<0.2)
11              Greedy step: pick tⱼ such that:
12                  j=argmax(p(tⱼ)) where pⱼ= τᵢⱼ*eⱼ
13          else if (r<0.99)
14              Probabilistic step: pick tⱼ distributed as:
15                  pⱼ= τᵢⱼ*eⱼ
16          else
17              Random step: pick tⱼ randomly.
18  (3) Once the node tⱼ is chosen:
19      a.  Move the ant in node tⱼ, tᵢ= tⱼ
20      b.  update the ant incompatible node list with the nodes incompatible with tⱼ.
21      c.  update the to-do list for tⱼ to done.
22      d.  Store the new configuration found Tₙₐ = {T₍ₙ₋₁₎ₐ,tⱼ} in the solution,
23          Sₐ={T₁ₐ, ... ,Tₙₐ}
24  (4) Repeat 2. and 3. until no further node can be visited (added) to Tₙ (all
25      compatible nodes have been completed/visited)
```

Algorithm 3. Local Search

```
1   • Pick the ns nodes with lowest cost efficiency and remove them from Tₖ:
2     for r=1,..., ns, Tᵣ = Tₖ-{tᵣ₁, ... , tᵣ} (typically n_LS=1 or 2)
3   • Update the incompatibility list λᵣ for the reduced configuration Tᵣ
4   • repeat ns times:
5       ▪ Among the compatible nodes with λᵣ pick one randomly and insert it in Tᵣ
6       ▪ Update λᵣ
```

Algorithm 4. Pheromones update

```
1   • Evaporation: ∀ i,j, with i≠j:  τᵢⱼ=max(ρ*τᵢⱼ,0.1)
2     where ρ is the persistency constant (0<ρ<1, typically ρ=0.8)
3
4   • Deposition: for i,j such that tᵢ and tⱼ∈Tₖ:  τᵢⱼ=τᵢⱼ + ε
5     where ε is the deposition level (ε>0)
```

The Local Search is typically run for intermediate configurations sizes, usually of 6 to 12 technologies, since this is a greatly populated area in the solution space. It is performed only if the configuration is not an optimal one. It proceeds by removing one or more technologies from some chosen configuration and re-calculating the incompatibility list without the removed technologies; finally, some alternative technologies, compatible with the reduced configuration, are added. The number of technologies to switch can be chosen by the user, but as it heavily affects the efficiency, it was typically set to 2.

Finally, we note that many tests have been conducted in order to identify reasonable values for the various algorithm parameters over a wide set of problem instances which guarantee convergence to high quality solutions in timeframes on the order of 10 min. Detailed discussion of these tests is beyond the scope of this paper.

4. Results and Benchmarking

The ACO + LS algorithm presented in the previous section, was tested for a wide range of optimization scenarios and employed to calculate optimal solutions, which are the inputs for the calculation of the vehicle CO_2 emission reduction cost curves, as introduced in [21]. For cars and vans this included optimizations for all powertrains and vehicle segments, with and without off-cycle technologies, for 2025 and 2030 under the Worldwide harmonized Light vehicles Test Procedure (WLTP) test cycle (i.e., 224 optimization runs), and a number of other cases, as presented in Section 5 and in [22,23]. Moreover, the tool was employed for a number of additional computations. Each optimization was run for 10 min, yielding high quality solutions for the given algorithm parameters. By performing these runs in parallel, it was possible to complete overnight (14 h run-time) even a larger set of runs, up to 2000, taking advantage of 32 processors-threads of the Intel® Xeon® CPU E5-2687W at 3.10 GHz.

In an earlier approach, a heuristic method was applied for assessing vehicle CO_2 reduction technologies and costs as presented in [24]. In order to solve the problem, a cloud of data points (i.e., tuples of CO_2 emission reduction and cost values) was created from all possible combinations of different CO_2 reduction technologies. This method was able to generate results for problems up to about 30 technologies. However, it proved to be inefficient for larger and constrained problems, so to handle these, a more efficient heuristic was developed, at first utilising a procedure where the configurations are determined iteratively by using a set of constraints based on incompatible technologies, with a Genetic Algorithm (GA) to create and select optimized solutions.

Genetic Algorithms were proved to effectively solve a number of optimization problems and also in particular the MKP, as reported in [25]. In recent years, such algorithms have also been developed and made available in MATLAB® as a toolbox [26].

Since the current problem has two objectives, a possible approach with a GA is to divide the cost range into a certain number of 'slices' (usually a few hundred, from a minimum to maximum pre-determined cost range). In each cost slice, the algorithm seeks configurations with the maximum CO_2 reduction value, taking into account the compatibility constraints. The problem is thus reduced to a single objective optimization in each cost slice. In a preliminary study, it appeared crucial to establish an appropriate number of these slices since it heavily influences the computational time. The authors reported, after running some tests on an Intel Core i5-3340M CPU at 2.70 GHz, that a value of 200 slices yielded a reasonable computation time of 4-5 min per instance, as compared to 100 slices (about 2 min), 400 slices (about 10 min) and 1000 slices (about 30 min). This choice was also made since further increasing the number of slices, was not adding a sufficient improvement to justify the increased computational times.

The GA approach demonstrated to be able to handle problems of up to about 50 technologies. The computational work was carried out in 2015 using MATLAB® R2013a, using the function *ga* which is contained within the MATLAB® Global Optimization Toolbox to launch the optimization [27]. This function, if not specified by the user, automatically adjusts the levels of mutation and cross-over for the constrained optimization problem, as the total cost of a configuration must lie in the cost slice. The slices are created by computing, for each case, the minimum and maximum cost. The former is the minimum cost among the technologies considered in the instance problem, while the latter is the sum of the cost of all the technologies. The schema of the algorithm is given in Algorithm 5.

Although this approach is quite efficient, as the number of CO_2 reduction technologies start to increase, it becomes computationally more and more inefficient and time consuming. We recall that the search space grows very quickly, as 2^N, where N is the number of technologies.

Algorithm 5. Genetic Algorithm

```
1   Given the problem with N technologies:
2    • Create n cost slices sᵢ:  if Δ=(Cmax-Cmin)/n  sᵢ=[Cmin+i*Δ,Cmin+(i+1)*Δ]  i=0,...,n-1
3    • Repeat over each slice sᵢ the call to ga, the Genetic Algorithm, with the following
4      parameters:
5         [x, CO2 reduction]= ga(f, n, A, b, [], [], lb, ub, [], IntCon)
6
7      where f is the product of used technology cost and CO2, N is the number of unique
8      technologies, A and b form the linear constraints A*x <= b and encodes
9      technologies incompatibilities, lb and ub are vectors of lower and upper bounds;
10     ga enforces that iterations stay above lb and below ub, IntCon: vector of positive
11     integers taking values from 1 to N. Each value in IntCon represents an x component
12     that is integer-valued.
13   • Output the results: one point (a configuration) per each slide sᵢ
```

In the following section, ACO + LS outcomes have been compared against the outcomes achieved with the GA approach. The GA runs are the benchmark runs, i.e., they were not repeated for each problem instance, but rather each is the best solution found over all the runs made for that instance; for some instances different slice resolutions were ran, with different times to improve solution quality. We have reported and compared with the best solution found for a particular instance.

Figure 1 shows an example of the CO_2 reduction/cost-tuples resulting from both approaches, run for a typical case. The coloured (or grey) dots represent ACO + LS solutions, where the colours (or grey shade) indicate the size of the configuration. The black squares represent the GA benchmark solutions.

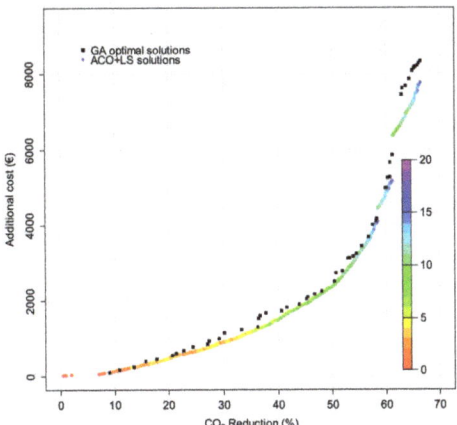

Figure 1. Comparison of CO_2 reduction and cost for optimal configurations found by GA and ACO + LS. Black squares represent GA configurations while colored (or grey) dots represent ACO + LS configurations. The color (or gray shade) represent the configuration size).

For this case, we note that there are a total of 76 Pareto optimal GA configurations (points), against the 287 optimal configurations found with ACO + LS. Moreover the GA configurations are almost always dominated by the configurations found by ACO + LS. The high number of solutions found by the ACO + LS makes the Pareto front more densely populated, which is desirable when searching differentiation or alternative configurations.

We note also a side effects of the GA slicing: the best solution found in a slice, can be dominated by solutions in other slices. In other words, dividing the 2nd objective by M slices, does not guarantee that the Pareto front will have M points. In this case, pareto-optimal configurations are not found in some slices (as their existence can be seen by the ACO + LS), therefore the GA algorithm converges to sub-optimal configurations in a number of cases.

The two noticeable discontinuities are due to two high-cost technologies, usually characterized also by a high CO_2 reduction; these, once added to a lower size optimal configuration, result in sudden increase of the additional cost and CO_2 reduction, thus appearing as a discontinuity of the pareto front.

For a more systematic comparison, ten problems were chosen, as listed in Table 1, with different initial parameters for year, powertrain, vehicle segment and test cycle, where GA benchmark solutions were available. For Problems 2, 8 and 9, the GA was run over 1000 iterations (1 h runs).

Table 1. Reference table of the benchmark problems, with typical cost scenario and total cost type. See Nomenclature for abbreviations or Section 5 for extended descriptions of the parameter values.

Problem Number	Year	Powertrain	Segment	Cycle	Include Off-Cycle
Problem 1	2015	SI ICE + HEV	Lower Medium Car	NEDC	FALSE
Problem 2	2025	SI ICE + HEV	Lower Medium Car	WLTP	FALSE
Problem 3	2015	CI ICE + HEV	Lower Medium Car	WLTP	FALSE
Problem 4	2020	CI ICE + HEV	Lower Medium Car	NEDC	FALSE
Problem 5	2025	CI ICE + HEV	Lower Medium Car	NEDC	FALSE
Problem 6	2015	CI ICE + HEV	Lower Medium Car	NEDC	FALSE
Problem 7	2015	CI ICE + HEV	Upper Medium Car	WLTP	FALSE
Problem 8	2025	CI ICE + HEV	Lower Medium Car	WLTP	TRUE
Problem 9	2025	SI ICE + HEV	Small Car	WLTP	TRUE
Problem 10	2025	BEV	Lower Medium Car	WLTP	TRUE

For each problem, ten repeated ACO + LS runs were made with a runtime of 10 min and 1 h, respectively. Then ACO + LS solutions (sets of all configurations found) were compared to GA benchmark solutions in the following way.

Accordingly, to the optimality criteria defined in Equation (3), a configuration of a solution is dominated if there is at least one configuration of the second solution that is dominating it. Therefore, to have an appropriate comparison of two Pareto optimal fronts, also called best solutions found or simply solutions, S_1 and S_2, each configuration T_k of the solution S_1 has to be compared to the set of configurations of the solution S_2. An evaluation is made to check if T_k is dominating, dominated, additional Pareto for S_2 or equal (exactly the same cost and CO_2 reduction, with 2 precision digits for costs and 8 precision digits for CO_2 reduction - these values were set considering the precision of the GA benchmark configurations at hand). If it is dominating, the number of dominated configurations of S_2 is estimated.

Then the reverse is done, to evaluate, one by one, how many configurations of S_2 are dominating, dominated, additional Pareto, or equal with respect to S_1. Since ACO + LS runs were repeated 10 times for each problem, for each run, the number of dominating, additional Pareto, equal and dominated configurations were computed for each run. Finally, their averages were estimated, along with their 95% confidence interval over the repeated runs. The runs of 10 min and 1 h are reported in Tables 2 and 3, respectively.

Table 2. Comparison of ACO + LS 10-min runs with GA Benchmark runs. Results of 10-minute ACO + LS runs, each repeated ten times for each problem, versus GA benchmark solutions. In the first part of the table, GA configurations are compared to ACO + LS, while in the second, vice-versa. The means are computed over the ten runs, and values in italics indicate the 95% confidence interval (CI) of the estimate of the mean. Boldface is used to indicate when GA has better or additional solutions than those found by ACO + LS.

Problem	N	Stat	GA Configs. Found	GA Configs. Better	ACO+LS Configs. Dominated	GA Additional Pareto	GA Configs. Equal	ACO+LS Configs. Found	ACO+LS Configs. Better	GA Configs. Dominated	ACO+LS Additional Pareto	ACO + LS Configs. Equal
1	33	mean	55	0.00	0.00	0.00	1.00	331.56	257.78	54.00	72.78	1.00
		95% CI		*0.00*	*0.00*	*0.00*	*0.00*	*6.71*	*4.27*	*0.00*	*2.73*	*0.00*
2	42	mean	76	**0.10**	**0.10**	**0.30**	4.70	271.10	228.40	70.90	37.90	4.70
		95% CI		*0.20*	*0.20*	*0.30*	*0.30*	*5.85*	*5.04*	*0.20*	*1.66*	*0.30*
3	28	mean	38	0.00	0.00	0.00	24.00	140.70	57.90	14.00	59.80	24.00
		95% CI		*0.00*	*0.00*	*0.00*	*0.00*	*0.51*	*0.46*	*0.00*	*0.26*	*0.00*
4	31	mean	47	0.00	0.00	**0.20**	4.80	256.80	169.40	42.00	82.60	4.80
		95% CI		*0.00*	*0.00*	*0.26*	*0.26*	*2.46*	*1.99*	*0.00*	*0.89*	*0.26*
5	33	mean	40	**0.20**	**0.20**	**0.10**	4.80	242.20	137.80	34.90	99.40	4.80
		95% CI		*0.26*	*0.26*	*0.20*	*0.39*	*1.05*	*1.05*	*0.20*	*0.60*	*0.39*
6	28	mean	48	0.00	0.00	**0.10**	10.10	157.40	90.10	37.80	58.20	10.10
		95% CI		*0.00*	*0.00*	*0.20*	*0.20*	*2.05*	*1.38*	*0.26*	*0.91*	*0.20*
7	28	mean	41	0.00	0.00	0.00	22.00	150.40	62.20	19.00	66.20	22.00
		95% CI		*0.00*	*0.00*	*0.00*	*0.00*	*1.25*	*1.00*	*0.00*	*0.49*	*0.00*
8	55	mean	23	0.00	0.00	0.00	0.00	407.40	345.20	23.00	62.20	0.00
		95% CI		*0.00*	*0.00*	*0.00*	*0.00*	*11.72*	*12.31*	*0.00*	*3.21*	*0.00*
9	58	mean	26	0.00	0.00	0.00	0.00	607.80	505.20	26.00	102.60	0.00
		95% CI		*0.00*	*0.00*	*0.00*	*0.00*	*24.29*	*21.35*	*0.00*	*4.07*	*0.00*
10	21	mean	51	0.00	0.00	0.00	11.00	168.00	97.00	40.00	60.00	11.00
		95% CI		*0.00*	*0.00*	*0.00*	*0.00*	*0.00*	*0.00*	*0.00*	*0.00*	*0.00*

Table 3. Comparison of ACO + LS 60-min runs with GA Benchmark runs. Similarly to Table 2 but running each of the 10 runs for 1 hour. As in Table 2, statistical quantities are in italics indicate the 95% confidence interval (CI) of the estimate of the mean, while boldface is to indicate when GA has better or additional solutions than those found by ACO+LS.

Problem	N	Stat	GA Configs. Found	GA Configs. Better	ACO + LS Configs. Dominated	GA Additional Pareto	GA Configs. Equal	ACO + LS Configs. Found	ACO + LS Configs. Better	GA Configs. Dominated	ACO+LS Additional Pareto	ACO + LS Configs. Equal
1	33	mean	55	0.00	0.00	0.00	1.00	344.00	264.80	54.00	78.20	1.00
		95% CI		0.00	0.00	0.00	0.00	1.52	0.91	0.00	1.05	0.00
2	42	mean	76	0.00	0.00	**0.20**	4.90	285.20	240.30	70.90	40.00	4.90
		95% CI		0.00	0.00	0.26	0.20	4.28	4.35	0.20	0.65	0.20
3	28	mean	38	0.00	0.00	0.00	24.00	141.00	58.00	14.00	60.00	24.00
		95% CI		0.00	0.00	0.00	0.00	0.00	0.00	0.00	0.00	0.00
4	31	mean	47	0.00	0.00	**0.10**	4.90	262.40	173.80	42.00	83.70	4.90
		95% CI		0.00	0.00	0.20	0.20	1.83	1.36	0.00	0.51	0.20
5	33	mean	40	**0.10**	**0.10**	0.00	4.90	245.90	141.20	35.00	99.70	4.90
		95% CI		0.20	0.20	0.00	0.20	0.68	0.70	0.00	0.30	0.20
6	28	mean	48	0.00	00	0.00	10.00	161.90	92.90	38.00	60.00	10.00
		95% CI		0.00	0.00	0.00	0.00	0.20	0.20	0.00	0.00	0.00
7	28	mean	41	0.00	0.00	0.00	22.00	153.60	64.00	19.00	67.60	22.00
		95% CI		0.00	0.00	0.00	0.00	0.32	0.00	0.00	0.32	0.00
8	55	mean	23	0.00	0.00	0.00	0.00	491.20	414.80	23.00	76.40	0.00
		95% CI		0.00	0.00	0.00	0.00	8.75	7.35	0.00	3.95	0.00
9	58	mean	26	0.00	0.00	0.00	0.00	618.30	511.80	26.00	106.50	0.00
		95% CI		0.00	0.00	0.00	0.00	18.75	16.33	0.00	2.67	0.00
10	21	mean	51	0.00	0.00	0.00	11.00	168.00	97.00	40.00	60.00	11.00
		95% CI		0.00	0.00	0.00	0.00	0.00	0.00	0.00	0.00	0.00

The tables contain the comparison of the GA benchmark solutions S_{GA} versus ACO + LS solutions S_{ACO+LS} (first five columns), and then the reverse (last five columns). In particular, the size of the benchmark solutions is reported (in the tables, the column "configs. found", column 1), which is measure of the search efficiency of the respective algorithm: the greater the number of configurations, the greater is their diversity and thus the possibility of combing technologies/objects in different ways. It is also reported, for each problem, the mean number of configurations of S_{GA} that are better than S_{ACO+LS}, and the mean number of configurations of S_{ACO+LS} that are dominated by the S_{GA}. Then, in the following columns 4 and 5, the mean number of additional Pareto configurations, and the mean number of equal configurations are reported (equal configurations is the only quantity which is invariant when comparing S_1 to S_2 or vice-versa). In the second part of the tables, columns 6–10, the reverse comparison is made, for the configurations of S_{ACO+LS} versus S_{GA}.

In the tables, it can be seen that the GA benchmark solutions contain additional optimal configurations in just a few cases to the optimal configurations found by ACO + LS (in the tables, these cases are marked in bold).

A value of 0.10 in column 2, means that, over 10 repeated runs, one GA configuration was better than some ACO + LS configuration (s); the value of 0.10 in column 3, tells that only one ACO + LS configuration was dominated by that GA configuration. In some other cases, a few additional Pareto configurations were found by GA. Finally a few other configurations are the same exact configurations as found by ACO + LS (the columns 5 and 10 are indeed the same). Most relevantly, in most cases ACO + LS configurations dominate the GA configurations (columns 7 and 8) or are additional Pareto (column 9) to those. The number of optimal configurations found by ACO+LS and GA is reported in columns 1 and 6 respectively, and the different order of magnitude of the two is noticeable. As computation time is increased from Table 2 to Table 3, the ACO + LS algorithm finds a slightly higher number of optimal configurations and convergence is increased over the ten repeated runs, as shown by the consistent decrease of the 95% confidence interval. Also the number of the ACO + LS dominated configurations shows a clear tendency to diminish further, as well as the GA additional Pareto solutions to ACO + LS.

It is possible to run the ACO + LS algorithm for many hours in an attempt to find even better solutions, or repeat the same runs to see how consistent is the convergence to the final solution. On an Intel Xenon at 3.10 GHz, it was found that approximately 10 min is suitable to find an optimized solution using ACO + LS. Given the high number of configurations found, a substantial improvement with respect to the GA is achieved. Depending on the number of available technologies of the problem instance, the ACO + LS algorithm typically completes between 30 and 60 million iterations (ants) in 10 min.

Besides the 10 problems discussed above, an indirect comparison was made between the fits found by the new approach for several thousand input datasets and cost scenarios. For each, the optimal configurations are fitted with a Levenberg-Marquardt non-linear regression algorithm using the *nlsLM* function of the minpack.lm library in R [28]. This provides a so-called cost function, the analytical form of the Pareto front, as documented and used in [22,23], which are then used for various other applications. This extensive exercise enhanced the authors' confidence in the efficiency and robustness of the ACO + LS algorithm.

Finally, as a further evaluation of the ACO + LS method, we examined the cloud of points in the CO_2 reduction/cost plane pertaining to the configurations the ants visited during their search. By inspecting the cloud, the ant colony's distance to the Pareto front can be evaluated. If the colony stays close enough to the optimal solution, it has a higher likelihood of finding improved configurations and avoiding stagnation in local minima. The search process is driven by the parameters which determine the ants' behavior, particularly exploitation versus exploration settings (the relative share between greedy, probabilistic and random choices during propagation). The following Figure 2 shows this cloud for Problem 1. Each of the small points relates to a configuration found by the ants during their search. The points are a random extract of 5000 points over the last part of the run; only this small number of points is extracted for visualization purposes, since the total number of points are several millions, for a typical run. Similar plots were also made for initial or intermediate intervals of the run, to monitor the activities of ants in the colony.

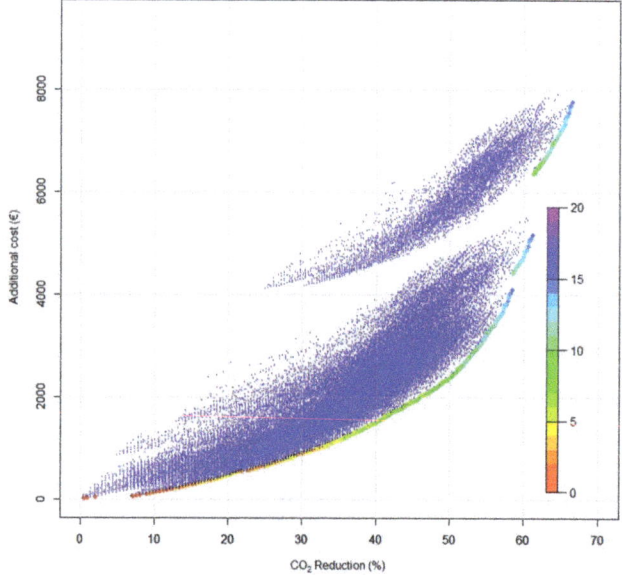

Figure 2. Randomly sampled intermediate configurations visited by the ants (small blue dots) along with optimal configurations found by ACO (colored or grey shades-bigger dots of the Pareto front).

The most significant ant parameters were varied and studied. We found that for runs of 10 min or greater, there were no significant differences in the colony behavior between the first and last fifth of iterations once the algorithm is properly tuned. This means that 10 min are sufficient for the ant colony to stabilize and indicates that it is likely that even less time would be required to find optimal solutions for the problems considered. In Figure 2 the optimal configurations (the Pareto front) found by ACO + LS are plotted indicating the number of technologies present in the particular configuration. Ideally, the cloud generated by ACO + LS should stay as close as possible to the optimal solution (which also changes during the optimization process) such that small variations in the ants' paths (explorations) can make them find new optimal configurations.

We note that configurations of intermediate size, i.e., 6 to 12 technologies, constitute the most populated area. Figure 2 visually shows why it was decided to run LS only on points in this region: to enhance exploitation in this highly populated area of the search space. Mathematically, this is due to the summation term in (6), where combinations are at their maximum when $n = N/2$.

In summary, the ACO + LS approach has been shown to be able to handle the computational complexity of the Technology Packaging Problem quite efficiently, in particular with the following benefits:

(1) It is highly efficient: it provides nearly optimal solutions within a few minutes of computation, and high-density solutions within 10 to 15 min. For the problems examined, with appropriate settings of the algorithm parameters, the ACO + LS completes roughly one million iterations in less than 10 min, reaching a considerable diversity in the configurations.
(2) It does not require reduction to a single objective function like slicing, or other ad-hoc or a priori operations, and can potentially deal with more than two objectives.

(3) It finds highly populated sets near the Pareto optimal front - that is, a large number of nearly optimal configurations which might represent an alternative when different configurations might be needed (a manufacturer might have already certain packages in place) in terms of CO_2 reduction and cost.

(4) It supports 2nd order corrections of CO_2 reduction diminishment due to technologies overlapping or interaction. This aspect has not yet been deployed.

In particular, as a consequence of (3) above, the so-called technology pathways can be identified, i.e., certain points or regions of the Pareto front can be associated with different configurations that reach them in the most cost-efficient way from sub-optimal configurations, just by adding specific technologies. In other words, it is possible to gather concrete indications as to what are the most suitable technologies to add to pre-existing packages to achieve given CO_2 reduction targets at a minimum cost, so that the transitions from these packages to new optimized ones can be done with ease and continuity.

We finally note that due to the novelty of the problem, we could not compare with other algorithms in the literature. This study aimed to present a method that could solve this problem most efficiently and with high quality solutions. This method could constitute a benchmark for future algorithms to solve this problem, and certainly provides clear indications that it is exploring extensively and efficiently the search space. The same methodology was later applied with minor changes to provide input for discussing CO_2 reduction technologies for heavy duty vehicles, which demonstrates the flexibility of the method.

5. Applications

We applied the method to identify optimal technology packages for reducing CO_2 emissions from light duty vehicles (LDVs, i.e., passenger cars and vans) [22] and later also for the heavy duty vehicles (HDVs) [23]. The approach presented in this study was employed within the analytic work supporting the impact assessments for post-2020 LDV and HDV CO_2 standards in the EU.

A dataset of more than 80 LDV CO_2 emission reduction technologies, including their reduction potentials, costs and mutual compatibilities was provided in [29]. Similarly, an extensive study was carried out for HDVs with data in [30]. For each problem, once the optimal configurations are found with the ACO + LS, a so-called cost curve can be found by fitting, and it describes the Pareto front of costs versus CO_2 reductions in a continuous analytical form.

A number of values for the initialization parameters exist, which define a specific instance of the optimization problem. For the LDVs these are namely (a list of abbreviations is also available in Nomenclature Section):

- Year, with three different values: 2020, 2025, 2030. In some cases 2015 was also used.
- Vehicle powertrain, typically with eight distinct values:

    - Spark Ignition (i.e., gasoline) Internal Combustion Engine and Hybrid (SI ICE + HEV)
    - Compression Ignition (i.e., diesel) Internal Combustion Engine and Hybrid (CI ICE + HEV)
    - Spark Ignition Plug-in Hybrid (SI PHEV)
    - Compression Ignition Plug-in Hybrid (CI PHEV)
    - Spark Ignition Range-Extended Electric Vehicle (SI REEV)
    - Compression Ignition Range-Extended Electric Vehicle (CI REEV)
    - Battery Electric Vehicle (BEV)
    - Fuel Cell Electric Vehicle (FCEV)

- Vehicle segment, with seven values: Small Car, Lower Medium Car, Upper Medium Car, Large Car, Small Van, Medium Van, Large Van.
- Drive cycle within which CO_2 emissions are determined, with three values:

- New European Drive Cycle (NEDC)
- Worldwide harmonized Light vehicles Test Procedure (WLTP)
- Real World Drive Cycle (RDC)

• Cost scenario reflecting the rate of cost reduction over time for a technology through learning, with three values: High, Low, Typical.
• Cost type: with typically two values:

    - Direct cost, i.e., manufacturing costs
    - Total costs, i.e., direct costs plus indirect costs, where indirect costs represent additional costs related to a technology such as R&D, warranties, marketing, etc.

• Off-cycle technologies: a number of CO_2 emission reduction technologies cannot be measured under a type approval drive cycle such as NEDC or WLTP, e.g., led lights, solar roofs or tire pressure monitoring. If off-cycle technologies flag is set to 'true', these are included in the set to optimize over, otherwise they are excluded.

The possible combinations of all these parameters give rise to a total combination of 6048 different instances. For the sake of most of applications, we set the cost type equal to total cost, which results in a total of 3024 possible optimization problem instances to be run for each scenario. This is quite a computational effort: if ran in sequence they correspond to about 21-day computation time for 10 min runs, or 7 days if only interested in WLTP cycle.

It is to be noted that the set of available CO_2 reduction technologies are updated infrequently, depending on the availability of new data on technologies and their costs as well as on policy needs. Therefore, the addition of new technologies doesn't constitute any computational issue, as well as the variation of their costs, having been taken into consideration via 3 technology cost scenarios in the construction of the Pareto front for modelling the Cost Curves.

Cost Curve Construction

On the basis of the optimal configurations found by the ACO optimization described in the previous sections, vehicle emission reduction cost curves can be constructed to interpolate analytically these data points. The construction of cost curves consists in the fitting of the Pareto front configurations/points. This fitting procedure was a considerable part of the work, and it is worth noticing that all the Pareto fronts were fitted with an analytical form deriving by one single generalized functional form, with at most 4 fitting parameters. The cost curves are an essential input for applications such as the evaluation of different CO_2 reduction scenarios, e.g., for calculating the costs associated with a certain desired CO_2 standard for vehicles, identifying cost-minimizing distributions of CO_2 reduction efforts across different vehicle types and segments.

A number of post-processing steps had to be applied to the raw output from the optimization procedure, to take into account some necessary adjustments. The post-processing steps, the cost curve fitting procedure and the resulting cost curves are documented in [22] for LDVs, and in [23] for HDVs.

We have conducted extensive computational campaigns to address a number of variations and hypotheses for scenario analysis, considering variations of the original problem instances where for example a certain technology is desired to be always present, or in another case, where a certain technology could be considered to be less effective (in term of CO_2 reduction) than expected or some other more costly, to derive the optimal configurations and related cost curves. These results, obtained in relative short time scales, were made possible thanks to the properties of fast convergence and efficiency of the ACO + LS methodology.

6. Conclusions

We have presented a method based on a metaheuristic with Ant Colony Optimization combined with a Local Search algorithm to efficiently solve the Technology Packaging Problem, of finding feasible configurations of CO_2 reduction technologies, maximizing the CO_2 reduction and minimizing costs.

The results presented show that this methodology provides solutions of increased quality and size versus other approaches, e.g., genetic algorithms, thus offering the possibility of finding improved configurations in a highly efficient and easily adaptable manner. This has enhanced the capability to explore optimal strategies under increasingly numerous and complex technology choices against various CO_2 reduction targets. The method can easily accommodate more technology options or perform analyses of different technology pathways. As the runtime is greatly improved, it has been employed to run multiple scenario analyses, including e.g., variations in technology impact, costs, and test cycles.

This method has been employed for supporting the impact assessments for post-2020 CO_2 standards for cars, vans and trucks in the EU, considering diverse road vehicle fleet compositions. Different scenarios for the post-2020 EU CO_2 emission standards have been evaluated by constructing vehicle emission reduction cost curves as described in the present paper, and, building on them, identifying an optimal distribution of efforts among different powertrains and segments which compose the fleet, calculating additional manufacturing costs as well as fuel savings, and computing total additional costs or savings from emission reduction. Further to applications in policy support, this methodology could also be applied by the automotive industry itself.

Author Contributions: Conceptualization: A.V.D., J.K. and C.T.; methodology: A.V.D., B.W. and N.H.; software: A.V.D., B.W. (for GA); validation: J.K. and C.T.; formal analysis: A.V.D.; investigation: N.H.; data curation: N.H. and B.W.; writing—original draft preparation: A.V.D.; writing—review and editing: all authors; visualization: A.V.D.; supervision: J.K. and C.T.; project administration: C.T.; funding acquisition: N.H. All authors have read and agreed to the published version of the manuscript.

Funding: This work was supported through the Horizon 2020 direct funding of the Joint Research Centre (JRC) of the European Commission, for the JRC authors. The work of the other authors was funded by the European Commission under the framework contract CLIMA.C.2/FRA/2012/0006. The views expressed are purely those of the authors and may not in any circumstances be regarded as stating an official position of the European Commission.

Acknowledgments: The authors wish to thank Yannis Drossinos (JRC), for the valuable comments and suggestions.

Conflicts of Interest: The authors declare no conflict of interest.

Nomenclature: List of Abbreviations

BEV	Battery Electric Vehicle
CI ICE + HEV	Compression Ignition (i.e., diesel) Internal Combustion Engine and Hybrid
CI PHEV	Compression Ignition Plug-in Hybrid
CI REEV	Compression Ignition Range-Extended Electric Vehicle
FCEV	Fuel Cell Electric Vehicle
HDV	Heavy Duty Vehicle (truck)
LDV	Light Duty Vehicle (car or van)
LS	Local Search
NEDC	New European Drive Cycle
RDC	Real World Drive Cycle
SI ICE + HEV	Spark Ignition (i.e., gasoline) Internal Combustion Engine and Hybrid
SI PHEV	Spark Ignition Plug-in Hybrid
SI REEV	Spark Ignition Range-Extended Electric Vehicle
WLTP	Worldwide harmonized Light vehicles Test Procedure

References

1. Martello, S.; Toth, P. *Knapsack Problems: Algorithms and Computer Implementations*; Wiley: New York, NY, USA, 1990.
2. Kellerer, H.; Pferschy, U.; Pisinger, D. *Knapsack Problems*; Springer: Berlin, Germany, 2004.
3. Lust, T.; Teghem, J. Multiobjective Multidimensional Knapsack Problem: A survey and a new approach. *Int. Trans. Oper. Res.* **2012**, *19*, 495–520. [CrossRef]
4. Rodger, J.A. Toward reducing failure risk in an integrated vehicle health maintenance system: A fuzzy multi-sensor data fusion Kalman filter approach for IVHMS. *Expert Syst. Appl.* **2012**, *39*, 9821–9836. [CrossRef]
5. Fonseca, C.M.; Fleming, P.J. Genetic algorithms for multi-objective optimization: Formulation, discussion, generalization. In Proceedings of the Fifth International Conference on Genetic Algorithms, Urbana-Champaign, IL, USA, 17–21 July 1993; pp. 416–423.
6. Srinivas, N.; Deb, K. Multi-objective optimization using non dominated sorting in genetic algorithms. *Evol. Comput.* **1994**, *2*, 221–248. [CrossRef]
7. Hajela, P.; Lin, C.-Y. Genetic search strategies in multicriterion optimal design. *Struct. Optim.* **1992**, *4*, 99–107. [CrossRef]
8. Bonabeau, E.; Dorigo, M.; Theraulaz, G. *Swarm Intelligence: From Natural to Artificial Systems*; Oxford University Press: New York, NY, USA, 1999.
9. Dorigo, M.; Di Caro, G.A. Ant colony optimization: A new meta-heuristic. In Proceedings of the Congress on Evolutionary Computation, Washington, DC, USA, 6–9 July 1999; pp. 1470–1477.
10. Dorigo, M.; Maniezzo, V.; Colorni, A. Ant system: Optimization by a colony of cooperating agents. *IEEE Trans. Syst. Man Cybern. Part B Cybern.* **1996**, *26*, 29–41. [CrossRef] [PubMed]
11. Dorigo, M.; Gambardella, L.M. Ant Colony System: A cooperative learning approach to the Traveling Salesman Problem. *IEEE Trans. Evol. Comput.* **1997**, *1*, 53–66. [CrossRef]
12. Dorigo, M.; Brittari, M.; Blum, C.; Clerc, M.; Winfield, T.S.A. *Ant Colony Optimization and Swarm Intelligence*; Springer: Berlin/Heidelberg, Germany, 2008.
13. Donati, A.V.; Montemanni, R.; Casagrande, N.; Rizzoli, A.E.; Gambardella, L.M. Time dependent vehicle routing problem with a multi ant colony system. *Eur. J. Oper. Res.* **2006**, *185*, 1174–1191. [CrossRef]
14. Montemanni, R.; Gambardella, L.M.; Rizzoli, A.E.; Donati, A.V. Ant colony system for a dynamic vehicle routing problem. *J. Comb. Optim.* **2005**, *10*, 327–343. [CrossRef]
15. Donati, A.V.; Darley, V.; Ramachandran, B. An ant-bidding algorithm for generalized flow shop scheduling problem: Optimization and Phase Transitions. In *Advances in Metaheuristics for Hard Optimization*; Springer: Berlin/Heidelberg, Germany; New York, NY, USA, 2008; pp. 111–138.
16. Rada-Vilela, J.; Chica, M.; Cordón, O.; Damas, S. A comparative study of multi-objective ant colony optimization algorithms for the time and space assembly line balancing problem. *Appl. Soft Comput.* **2013**, *13*, 4370–4382. [CrossRef]
17. Leguizamon, G.; Michalewicz, Z. A new version of ant system for subset problem. In Proceedings of the 1999 Congress on Evolutionary Computation (CEC99), Washington, DC, USA, 6–9 July 1999.
18. Fidanova, S. Ant colony optimization and multiple knapsack problem. In *Handbook of Research on Nature Inspired Computing for Economics and Management*; Rennard, J.-P., Ed.; IGR Global: Hershey, PA, USA, 2006; Volume 2, pp. 498–509.
19. Alaya, I.; Solnon, C.; Ghéira, K. Ant colony optimization for multi-objective optimization prblems. In Proceedings of the 19th IEEE International Conference on Tools with Artificial Intelligence, Patras, Greece, 29–31 October 2007; pp. 450–457.
20. Kong, M.; Tian, P.; Kao, Y. A new ant colony optimization algorithm for the multidimensional Knapsack problem. *Comput. Oper. Res.* **2008**, *35*, 2672–2683. [CrossRef]
21. Hill, N.; Windisch, E.; Kirsch, F.; Horton, G.; Dun, C.; Hausberger, S.; Matzer, C.; Skinner, I.; Donati, A.V.; Krause, J.; et al. *Improving Understanding of Technology and Costs for CO_2 Reductions from Cars and LCVs in the Period to 2030 and Development of Cost Curves*; Service Request 4 to LDV Emissions Framework Contract; Final Report for DG Climate Action, Ref. CLIMA C.2/FRA/2012/0006; Ricardo Energy & Environment ref.: ED59621; Ricardo: Shoreham-by-Sea, UK, 2016.

22. Krause, J.; Donati, A.V.; Thiel, C. *Light Duty Vehicle CO_2 Emission Reduction Cost Curves and Cost Assessment—the DIONE Model*; EUR 28821 EN; Publications Office of the European Union: Luxembourg, 2017; ISBN 978-92-79-74136-4.
23. Krause, J.; Donati, A.V. *Heavy Duty Vehicle CO_2 Emission Reduction Cost Curves and Cost Assessment enhancement of the DIONE Model*; EUR 29284 EN; Publications Office of the European Union: Luxembourg, 2018; ISBN 978-92-79-88812-0.
24. Smokers, R.; Vermeulen, R.; Van Mieghem, R.; Gense, R.; Skinner, I.; Fergusson, M.; MacKay, E.; Brink, P.T.; Fontaras, G.; Samaras, Z. *Review and Analysis of the Reduction Potential and Costs of Technological and Other Measures to Reduce CO_2-Emissions from Passenger Cars*; TNO Final Report; TNO: Delft, The Netherlands, 2011.
25. Chu, C.; Beasley, J.E. A genetic algorithm for the multidimensional knapsack problem. *J. Heuristic* **1998**, *4*, 63–86. [CrossRef]
26. Chipperfield, J.; Fleming, P.J.; Pohlheim, H.; Fonseca, C.M. A genetic algorithm toolbox for MatLab. In Proceedings of the International Conference on Systems Engineering, Coventry, UK, 6–8 September 1994; pp. 200–207.
27. MatLab Documentation on Genetic Algorithms and ga Function. Available online: http://it.mathworks.com/help/gads/ga.html (accessed on 31 May 2020).
28. Elzhov, V.; Mullen, K.M.; Spiess, A.N.; Bolker, B. R Interface to the Levenberg-Marquardt Nonlinear Least-Squares Algorithm Found in MINPACK, Plus Support for Bounds. R Package 'minpack.lm', Version 1.2–1. November 2016. Available online: https://cran.r-project.org/web/packages/minpack.lm/minpack.lm.pdf (accessed on 31 May 2020).
29. The Dataset of CO_2 Reduction Technologies. Available online: https://ec.europa.eu/clima/sites/clima/files/transport/vehicles/docs/technology_results_web.xlsx (accessed on 31 May 2020).
30. TNO; Graz University of Technology; CE Delft; ICCT. Support for Preparation of the Impact Assessment for CO_2 Emissions Standards for Heavy Duty Vehicles. Service Request 9 under Framework Contract no CLIMA.C.2./FRA/2013/0007. Available online: https://ec.europa.eu/clima/sites/clima/files/transport/vehicles/heavy/docs/support_impact_assessment_hdv_en.pdf (accessed on 31 May 2020).

© 2020 by the authors. Licensee MDPI, Basel, Switzerland. This article is an open access article distributed under the terms and conditions of the Creative Commons Attribution (CC BY) license (http://creativecommons.org/licenses/by/4.0/).

Article

Improved Appliance Classification in Non-Intrusive Load Monitoring Using Weighted Recurrence Graph and Convolutional Neural Networks

Anthony Faustine [1,2,*] and Lucas Pereira [2]

1. Ireland's National Centre for Applied Data Analytics (CeADER), University College Dublin, Dublin 4, Ireland
2. ITI, LARSyS, Técnico Lisboa, 1049-001 Lisboa, Portugal; lucas.pereira@tecnico.ulisboa.pt
* Correspondence: sambaiga@gmail.com; Tel.: +32-49-397-2982

Received: 13 May 2020; Accepted: 19 June 2020; Published: 1 July 2020

Abstract: Appliance recognition is one of the vital sub-tasks of NILM in which a machine learning classier is used to detect and recognize active appliances from power measurements. The performance of the appliance classifier highly depends on the signal features used to characterize the loads. Recently, different appliance features derived from the voltage–current (V–I) waveforms have been extensively used to describe appliances. However, the performance of V–I-based approaches is still unsatisfactory as it is still not distinctive enough to recognize devices that fall into the same category. Instead, we propose an appliance recognition method utilizing the recurrence graph (RG) technique and convolutional neural networks (CNNs). We introduce the weighted recurrent graph (WRG) generation that, given one-cycle current and voltage, produces an image-like representation with more values than the binary output created by RG. Experimental results on three different sub-metered datasets show that the proposed WRG-based image representation provides superior feature representation and, therefore, improves classification performance compared to V–I-based features.

Keywords: non-intrusive load monitoring; appliance classification; appliance feature; recurrence graph; weighted recurrence graph; V–I trajectory; convolutional neural network

1. Introduction

The introduction of smart meters as part of smart grids will produce quantities of data energy consumption data at very fast rates. Analysis of these data streams offers a lot of exciting opportunities for understanding energy consumption patterns. Understanding the consumption pattern of individual loads at consumer premises plays an essential role in the design of customized energy efficiency and energy demand management strategies [1]. It is also useful for improving energy consumption awareness to households, which is likely to stimulate energy-saving behavior and engage energy users towards sustainable energy consumption [2,3]. Non-intrusive Load Monitoring (NILM), also known as energy disaggregation, is a useful technique for analyzing energy consumption data, monitored from a single-point source such as a smart meter. This is because the method can be easily integrated with buildings. The operation of NILM relies on signal processing and machine learning techniques to extract individual load profile from aggregate signal [4,5]. Considerable research attention has been lately devoted to deep neural networks (DNN) to solve energy disaggregation problems [6–12]. The presented approaches can be classified into event-based and non-event based methods [13]. The former approaches seek to disaggregate appliances through detecting and classifying their transitions in the aggregated signal [9,10,12,14]. In contrast, the non-event-based methods attempt to match each sample of the aggregated signal to the consumption of one or more appliances [6–8,11]. This paper falls under the event-based approach.

A typical event-based NILM system often involves four main steps, data acquisition, event detection, appliance classification, and energy estimation [15]. Appliance classification, also known as load identification, is an essential sub-task for identifying the type and status of an unknown load from appliance features extracted from the aggregate power signal. [10]. Therefore, it is imperative to build robust classification models for effective NILM [14]. On the other hand, the performance of classification models highly depends on the appliance features used to characterize appliances [16]. Henceforth, there is a need to develop appliance features that best characterize appliances and improve classification performance.

Appliance features are electrical characteristics of the appliance collected after the state-transition of the device has been detected. In practice, appliance features are obtained from high-frequency or low-frequency measurements, depending on what electrical characteristics are required for NILM. Compared to low-sampling measurements, high-sampling data offer the possibility to consider fine-grained features from steady-state and transient behavior. Typical appliance features at the high frequency used in the literature include transient and harmonics, harmonic contents of current or power waveforms, spectral envelope, wavelet-based feature, and voltage–current (V–I) trajectories [17]. Several recent studies have explored the use of V–I trajectory to characterize appliances [9,10,12,14,16,18–21]. A V–I-trajectory is obtained by plotting one-cycle steady-state voltage and current. The use of V–I-based features for appliance classification was first introduced in [18], where wave-shape features were hand-engineered the from a V–I trajectory (e.g., number of self-interceptions), and used as input to supervised machine learning classifiers. A review and performance evaluation of seven load wave-shape is presented in [22]. The wave-based features were found to have a direct correspondence to operating characteristics of appliances, and several other features such as peak of middle segment and asymmetry were later developed and evaluated in [20].

However, this approach compresses the information in the V–I-trajectory into a limited amount of hand-engineering feature space. Other studies have shown that transforming the V–I trajectory into a visual representation is computationally efficient and improves classification performance [16,21] by allowing that advanced machine learning algorithms extract features that would be otherwise unobserved.

In [16,21], the V–I trajectory is transformed into a 2D image representation by meshing the V–I trajectory where each cell of the mesh is assigned a binary value and denotes whether or not the trajectory traverses it. The work by [16] extracted several other features, such as the number of continuums of occupied cells, the binary value of the left horizontal cell, and a central cell, from the 2D V–I images. In [9,10,21], the V–I image is used as a direct input to a machine learning classifier such as random forest and convolutional neural networks (CNNs). A hardware implementation of the appliance recognition system based on V–I curves and convolutional neural network (CNN) classier is proposed in [14]. Recently, it has been demonstrated that the visual representation of V–I trajectory can be used effectively with transfer learning [12].

Even though V–I image representation has been successfully used for appliance classification in NILM, its performance is still unsatisfactory since this representation is still not distinctive enough to recognize appliances that fall into the same category. This is because the V–Is have the same shape independently of the current magnitude, which substantially reduces their discerning ability.

Motivated by the quest to create strong feature representation and improve classification performance, in this study, we propose new feature representation for appliance classification which relies on the recurrence graph (RG), also known as the recurrence plot. The RG analyses signal dynamics in phase–space to reveal the repeating and non-linear patterns [23] and has been used extensively for feature representation in time-series classification problems [23–25]. Unlike the V–I image, the RG feature representation uses a distance-similarity matrix to represent and visualize structural patterns in the signal. As a consequence, RG feature representation also depends on the magnitude of the current and voltage signals.

RG's use for the characterization of appliances features was introduced in [26], and later Rajabi and Estebsari [27] applied RG for estimating power consumption of individual loads. However, similar to other RG methods for time-series classification, the proposed RG uses a compressed distance function that represents all recurrences in the form of a binary matrix. Binarizing the recurrence plot through thresholding is likely to cause information loss and degrade classification performance. To avoid information loss by binarization, we propose the generation of RG that gives a few more values instead of binary output. To classify the generated RG, we follow the approach used in [10] and apply CNN for this task. Experimental evaluation in the three sub-metered datasets shows that the proposed WRG feature representation offers superior performance when compared to the V–I-based image feature. The source code used in our experiments can be found on a GitHub repository (https://github.com/sambaiga/WRG-NILM).

The main contributions of this paper are listed as follows:

1. We present a recurrence graph feature representation that gives a few more values (WRG) instead of the binary output, which improves the robustness of appliance recognition. The WRG representation for activation current and voltage not only enhances appliance classification performance but also guarantees the appliance feature's uniqueness, which is highly desirable for generalization purposes.
2. We present a novel pre-processing procedure for extracting steady-state cycle activation current from current and voltage measurements. The pre-processing method ensures that the selected activation current is not a transient signal.
3. We conduct evaluations on three sub-metered public datasets and comparing with the V–I image, which is its most direct competitor. We also conduct an empirical investigation on how different parameters of the proposed WRG influence classification performance.

2. Proposed Methods

Recognizing the appliance from the aggregate power signal is a vital sub-task of NILM. The goal of appliance classifier in NILM is to identify active appliances $k \in \{i = 1, 2, \ldots M\}$ from aggregate signal x_t where M indicates the number of appliances. This is a multi-class classification problem. The aggregate signal x_t at any time t is assumed to be

$$x_t = \sum_{k}^{M} y_t^{(k)} \cdot s_t^{(k)} + \sigma_t \qquad (1)$$

where $y_t^{(k)}$ is the contribution of appliance k, $s_t^{(k)} \in \{0, 1\}$ is its state and σ_t represents both any contribution from appliances not accounted for and measurement noise. The proposed approach is summarized Figure 1 and consist of the following main building blocks; Feature extraction and pre-processing, WRG generation and the CNN classifier.

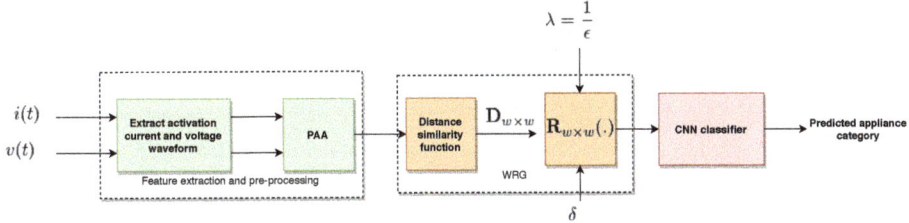

Figure 1. Block diagram of the proposed approach. It consist of the Feature extraction and pre-processing, WRG generation and the CNN classifier blocks.

2.1. Feature Extraction and Pre-Processing

Appliance features used for appliance recognition can be categorized into snapshot-form or delta-form features [22]. Snapshot form refers to the appliance feature extracted from aggregate power measurements as the results of more than one appliance being activated. Delta-form, on the other hand, expresses load characteristics in brief windows of time containing the only single event. In this work, we consider delta-form appliance features and define an activation signal as a one-cycle steady-state signal extracted from current or voltage waveform in a brief time after state transition.

To obtain an activation signal from monitored power signals; we measure $N_s = 20$ cycles of v and i before and after state-transitions of appliance has been detected as shown in Figure 2a,c. The N_s cycles correspond to steady-state behavior and is equivalent to $T_s \times N_s$ samples where $T_s = \frac{f_s}{f}$, f_s is sampling frequency and f is mains frequency. Since in this work, we only consider sub-metered data, the activation current i and voltage v from current-voltage signals is obtained as follows: $i = i^{(a)}$ and $v = v^{(a)}$ if the event is caused by activation of appliance and $i = i^b$ and $v = v^b$ if the event is caused by de-activation of appliance as illustrated in Figure 2b,d.

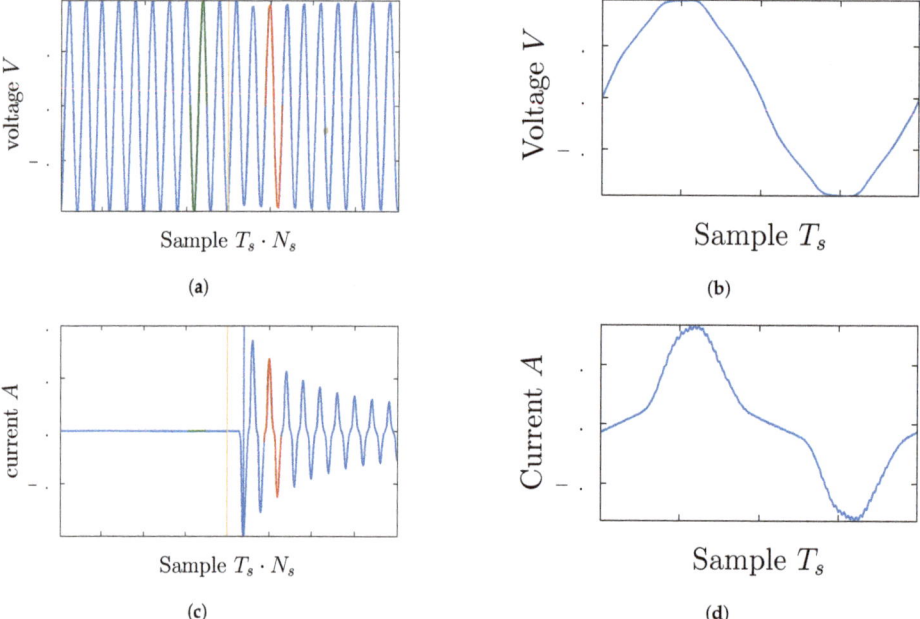

Figure 2. Extraction of an activation signal from current and voltage measurements. The green color is the steady-state signal before the event where the steady-state signal after the event is shown in red: (**a**) Voltage waveforms before and after an event; (**b**) Activation voltage; (**c**) Current waveforms before and after events; (**d**) Activation current.

To remove noise and ensure that the obtained activation signal is a complete cycle with size T_s, we propose a pre-processing procedure summarized in Algorithm 1. This is an empirical method and is based on the engineering knowledge that steady-state activation current should have at least two zero-crossings.

Algorithm 1: Feature pre-processing

Result: i^j, v^j
Data: i_1^N, v_1^N
Get voltage zero crossings: zc_v;
for $j = 2$ to $len(zc_v) - 2$ **do**
$\quad T_s^j = zc_v[-(j+2)] - zc_v[-j]$;
$\quad i^j = i[zc_v[-(j+2)] : zc_v[-j]]$;
$\quad v^j = v[zc_v[-(j+2)] : zc_v[-j]]$;
$\quad$Get current zero crossing: zc_i;
$\quad$**if** $T_s^j = T_s$ **and** $zc_i \geq 2$ **and** $len(i^j) = T_s$ **then**
$\quad\quad$| break;
$\quad$**end**
end

Once activation-waveforms have been extracted, the piece-wise aggregate approximation (PAA) is used to reduce the dimensional of the signal from T_s to a predefined size w with minimal information loss. The PAA algorithm reduces the dimensionality of i and v from T_s to embedding size w before generating the $D_{w \times w}$ distance matrix. It works by dividing the data into n segments of equal size, then the approximation is a vector of the median values of the data readings per segment. The embedding size w is the hyper-parameter that needs to be selected in advance. Empirically, it was found that the choice of w does not significantly influence the classification performance. However, large values of w impact the learning speed, and small values of w will most likely lead to larger information loss, as depicted in Figure 3. Note that for Figure 3b the embedding size of $w = 50$ does not change the shape of the input signal, whereas in Figure 3c an embedding size of $w = 10$ deforms the input shape.

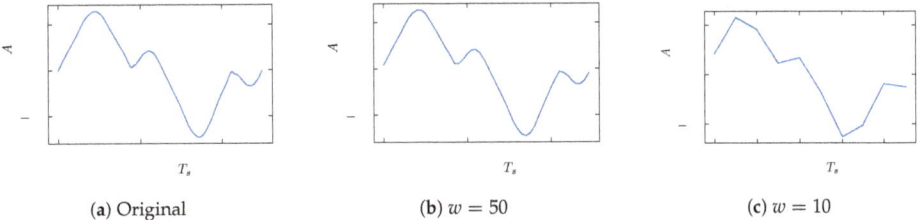

(a) Original   (b) $w = 50$ (c) $w = 10$

Figure 3. Illustration of dimension reduction with PAA for different embedding w: (**a**) The original activation current before dimension reduction; (**b**) The activation current after PAA with $w = 50$. The generated signal resembles the original activation current before PAA; (**c**) The activation current after PAA with $w = 10$. There is a loss of information on the generated signal.

2.2. Weighted Recurrence Plot (WRG)

The RG feature representation uses a distance similarity matrix $D_{w \times w}$ to represent and visualize structural patterns in the signal. The distance similarity matrix provides a relationship metric between each element in the time-series signal [28]. It has been recommended as a pre-processing step for many of the machine learning approaches such as K-means clustering and K-nearest neighbor algorithms. Consider T_s points of activation signal $\mathbf{x} = \{x_1, x_2 \ldots x_{T_s}\}$. The distance similarity between x_k and x_j is given as $d_{k,j} = ||x_k - x_j||^2$ where $||.||$ denotes the Euclidean norm. The distance similarity matrix $D_{w \times w} = [d_{k,j}]$ is the similarity matrix such that:

$$D_{w \times w} = \begin{bmatrix} d_{1,1} & \cdots & \cdots & \cdots & d_{1,j} \\ \vdots & \ddots & \cdots & \cdots & \vdots \\ \vdots & \cdots & \ddots & \cdots & \vdots \\ d_{k,1} & \cdots & \cdots & \ddots & d_{k,j} \end{bmatrix} \qquad (2)$$

For a classification problem, the compressed distance similarity matrix that represents all recurrences in the form of a binary matrix $RG_{w \times w} = [r_{k,j}]$ is usually used. The $r_{k,j}$ function is defined as follows:

$$r_{k,j} = \begin{cases} 1 & \text{if } d_{k,j} \geq \epsilon \\ 0 & \text{otherwise} \end{cases} \qquad (3)$$

where $\epsilon \in (0, 1]$ is the recurrence threshold. Equation (3) implies that, a dot will be drawn on a $w \times w$ grid if two values within a signal $\mathbf{x} = \{x_1, x_2, \ldots x_w\}$ are closer than ϵ.

This can be interpreted as unweighed graph G with vertex set N and edge E where $RG_{w \times w} = [r_{k,j}]$ is the adjacency matrix that depicts the graph between the data points. It should be noted that the structural representation of RG provides the similarity between two adjacent points in time series which is necessary for classification [29]. However, binarizing the distance matrix $D_{w \times w}$ through thresholding can lead to information loss and therefore degrade classification performance. Thus in this work, we propose the generation of $WRG_{w \times w}$ that goes beyond the traditional binary output. More precisely, we introduce the parameter $\delta \geq 1$ that enforce $r_{k,j}$ to have values between 0 and δ such that:

$$r_{k,j} = \begin{cases} \delta & \text{if } \tau > \delta \\ \tau & \text{otherwise} \end{cases} \qquad (4)$$

where $\tau = \left\lfloor \frac{d_{k,j}}{\epsilon} \right\rfloor$. $\lfloor . \rfloor$ is the floor function such $\lfloor x \rfloor = n \leq x \leq (n+1), 0 \leq n \leq \delta, \epsilon \geq 0$.

For computational stability, we apply the parametrization on the value of ϵ such that $\lambda = \frac{1}{\epsilon}$. The matrix $WRG_{w \times w}$ can be interpreted as a weighted graph $G = (V, E)$ where each value represents the edge weights. Since $d_{k,j} > 0$ Equation (4) reduces to RG for $\delta \leq 1$. The recurrence threshold ϵ and δ are the hyper-parameters that need to be optimized. Figure 4 illustrates the process of generating the WRG and RG from distance similarity matrix D. We see that the RG image representation in Figure 4c has more limited information compared to the WRG image representation in Figure 4b.

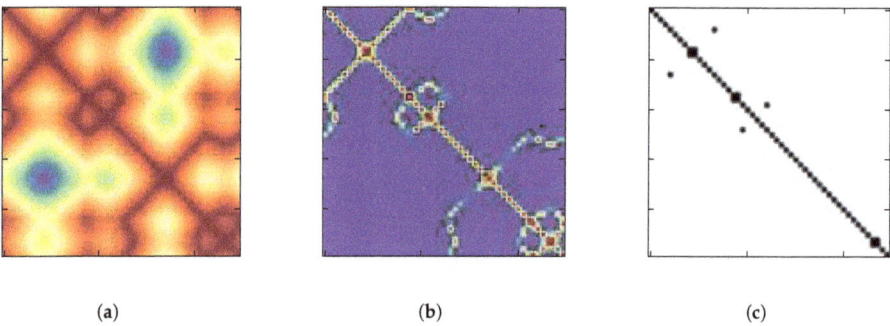

(a)   (b)   (c)

Figure 4. Generation of distance similarity matrix and RGs for a vacuum cleaner activation current in PLAID dataset: (**a**) Distance similarity matrix $D_{w \times w}$; (**b**) WRG matrix $WRG_{w \times w}$; (**c**) RG matrix $RG_{w \times w}$.

2.3. Classifier and Training Procedure

Once the appliance features are extracted, a generic machine learning classifier can be used to learn the pattern from labeled data. We consider a convolution neural network (CNN) for this task. CNNs are specific kinds of neural networks for processing visual data. They leverage local connectivity and equivariant representations that make CNN useful for computer vision tasks. Each hidden unit of a CNN layer is connected only to the subregion of the input image. This allows CNNs to exploit spatially local correlation between neurons of adjacent layers while reducing the number of parameters. Thus, at each CNN layer, the classifier learns several small filters (feature maps). These feature maps are then applied to the entire layer, allowing features to be detected regardless of their position in the image.

The CNN network applied in this work consists of three-stages 2D CNN layers each with 16, 32 and 64 feature maps, 3×3 filter, 2×1 stride and padding of 1. Each CNN layer is followed by batch normalization (BN) block and Leaky relu activation functions. The final layer consists of one flatten layer and two Fully connected layers (FC) layers. The FC layers have a hidden size of 1024 and K, respectively, where the number of appliances available determines the number of classes (K). The final predicted class is obtained by applying softmax activation function. To learn the model parameters, a standard back propagation is used to optimize the cross-entropy objective function defined in Equation (5):

$$\mathcal{L}_\theta(y, p) = -\sum_{i=1}^{M} y_i \cdot \log p_i \qquad (5)$$

Specifically the mini-batch Stochastic Gradient Descent (SDG) with a momentum of 0.9, a learning rate of 0.001, and a batch size of 16 is used to train the model for 100 iterations. To avoid over-fitting, early stopping with patience is used where the traing is terminated once the validation performance does not change after 20 iterations.

3. Experimental Design

3.1. Datasets

The proposed method is tested on the three publicly accessible datasets; Plug Load Appliance Identification Dataset (PLAID v1) [30], Worldwide Household and Industry Transient Energy Data Set (WHITED v1.1) [31], and Controlled On/Off Loads Library (COOLL) datasets [32]. The PLAID v1 contains 1074 instances of current and voltage measurements sampled at 30 kHz from 11 different appliance types in Pittsburgh, Pennsylvania, USA. Each appliance type is represented by various samples of varying make/models. The WHITED consists of sub-metered current and voltage measurements recorded in households and small industry settings at 44.1 KHz sampling frequency. In this work, we use the WHITED v1.1 that comprises 11259 instances for 110 various appliances, which can be grouped into 47 different types (classes).

The COOLL dataset, on the other hand, consists of d 840 current and voltage measurements for 42 controllable appliances sampled at a 100 kHz sampling frequency. Unlike PLAID and WHITED datasets, the COOLL dataset provides twenty turn-on transient signals corresponding to a different turn-on instant (with a controlled delay to the zero-crossing of the mains voltage) for each appliance. The appliances are of 12 different types with a certain number of examples each [32].

3.2. Evaluation Metrics

Several performance metrics have been proposed in the NILM literature [13]. This work uses macro averaged F_1 score, zero-loss score (ZL) and Matthews correlation coefficient (MCC), as these are known for being less sensitive to class imbalance [33]. We also use the confusion matrix which shows the correct predictions (the diagonal) and provide a clear view on which appliances are confused with each other.

The F_1 (%) score is defined as $F_{macro} = 100 \cdot \frac{1}{M} \sum_{i=1}^{M} F_1^{(i)}$ where M is the number of appliances and F_1 is the harmonic mean of precision and recall.

The zero-loss give the number of miss-classifications with the best performance being 0 and is defined as $ZL = \sum_{i=1}^{M} I(y_i \neq \hat{y}_i)$ The Matthews correlation coefficient, MCC, provides a balanced performance measure of the quality of classification algorithm. It takes into account true and false positives and negatives. Given confusion matrix C for M different classes, the MCC can be defined as

$$MCC = \frac{c \times s - \sum_i^M p_i \times t_i}{\sqrt{(s^2 - \sum_i^M p_i^2) \times (s^2 - \sum_i^M t_i^2)}} \quad (6)$$

where $t_i = \sum_k^M C_{ki}$, $p_i = \sum_k^M C_{ik}$, $c = \sum_k^M C_{kk}$, and $s = \sum_i^M \sum_j^M C_{ij}$. The maximum MCC score is +1 and the minimum value can be between -1 and 0. A score of +1 represents a perfect prediction.

3.3. Experimental Description

We are interested in answering the following two research questions: (1) how to pick a suitable set of WRG hyper-parameters? And, (2) how do the graph features extracted by WRG compare against V–I based approach concerning classification performance? We investigate the first objective by altering the WRG hyper-parameters w, δ, and $\lambda = 1/\epsilon$ on the PLAID, and COOLL sub-metered datasets. We first investigate how do the λ and δ parameters influence performance measure when the embedding size is set to 50 ($w = 50$). We then analyze the impact of the embedding size w on classification performance for given values of λ and δ. We further compare the general performance between the binary RP and WRG.

In the second experiment, we establish a baseline in which the V–I binary image is used as the appliance feature. The baseline is then compared with the WRG feature representation. The V–I image of size $w \times w$, is obtained by first resizing the activation current i and voltage v into corresponding scale d_i and d_v respectively where: $d_c = \max(|\min(i)|, \max(i))$ and $d_v = \max(|\min(v)|, \max(v))$ and transformed into $w \times w$ scale. The scaled current and voltage are then converted into $w \times w$ image by meshing the V–I trajectory and assigned a binary value that denotes whether it is traversed by trajectory as described in De Baets et al. [10]. Figure 5 illustrate the generation of V–I image from microwave activation current and voltage in the PLAID dataset.

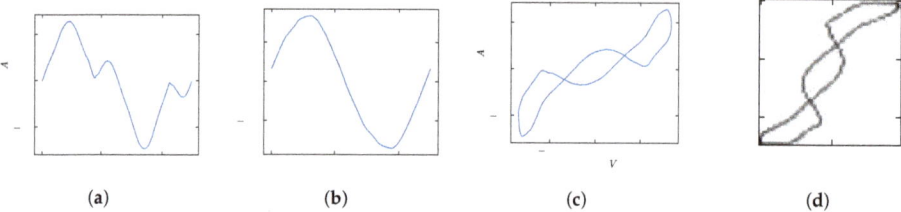

Figure 5. Generation of V–I image from Microwave activation current and voltage in the PLAID dataset: (**a**) Activation current; (**b**) Activation voltage; (**c**) V–I trajectory; (**d**) Generated V–I image.

The objective of this experiment is to compare the generalization performance of the proposed approach with that of VI across buildings. To achieve this, we employ leave-one-house-out cross-validation as presented in [21]. A classifier is trained on a dataset in $N_b - 1$ houses and then tested using the unseen house in the same dataset. However, unlike PLAID, the WHITED and COOLL datasets do not have household annotations. Therefore, we adopt the method used in [10], which consists of assigning appliances randomly to artificial homes. The total number of houses is set to 9 for the WHITED dataset and 8 for the COOLL dataset, corresponding to the minimum number of appliance types in each dataset.

The parameters used in this experiment are presented in Table 1.

Table 1. Parameters used in experiment two.

Parameter	COOLL	WHITED	PLAID
$\lambda = \frac{1}{\epsilon}$	10^3	10^3	10^1
δ	50	50	20
w	50	50	50

4. Results and Discussion

This section presents and discusses the results obtained with respect to the two research objectives of this paper.

4.1. Objective 1: WRG Analysis

In the first objective, we investigate how do WRG parameters w, λ and δ influence performance measure. Figure 6a,b shows the relationship between λ and MCC score for different value δ on COOLL and PLAID datasets.

From Figure 6b, we observe that in PLAID a maximum score of 0.981 MCC is reached, when $\lambda = 10^1$ and $\delta = 20$. It can be also observed from Figure 6a, that in COOLL, a maximum score of 1.0 MCC is reached for $\lambda = 10^3$ and $\delta = 50$. We further see that the binary RG (when $\delta = 1$) achieves a maximum score of 0.97 MCC (when $\lambda = 10$) in COOLL, and 0.90 MCC (when $\lambda = 5$) in PLAID. However, the performance drops rapidly as λ increases and eventually become zero in PLAID. We also observe that the influence of δ on performance score depends on the selected value of λ. For larger values of λ, the performance increases as δ increases. In contrast, for small values of λ, δ does not significantly impact the performance score.

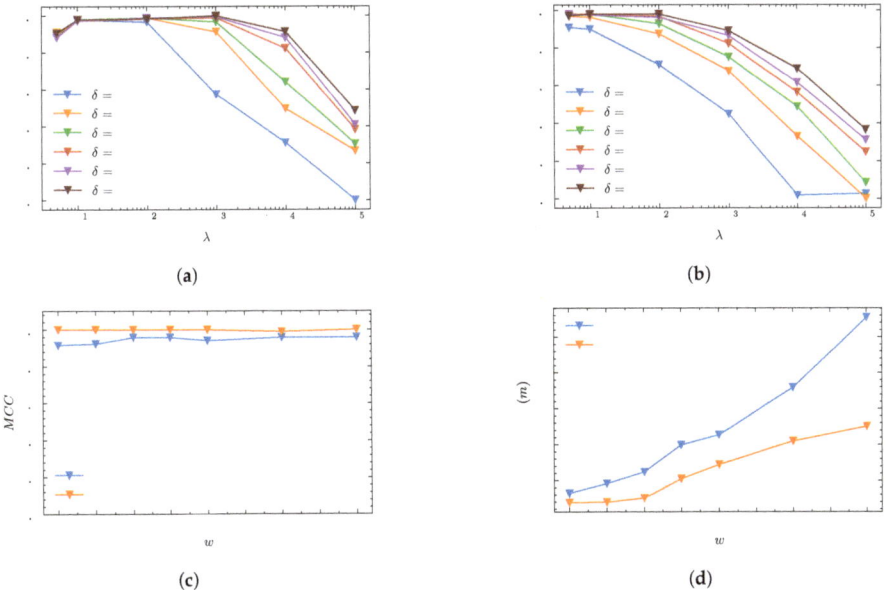

Figure 6. Impact of WRG parameters in the measured performance: (a) Impact of λ for different value of δ on the COOLL dataset; (b) Impact of λ for different value of δ on the PLAID dataset; (c) The relationship between w and MCC score for COOLL and PLAID dataset; (d) The relationship between w and training time on the PLAID and COOLL dataset.

We also investigate the influence of embedding size w in the classification performance as depicted in Figure 6c. We see that the higher value of w does not significantly improve classification performance. This result is in line with the one obtained in [9] for the V–I image, which concluded that, once a particular resolution is obtained, adding information by increasing the embedding size does not improve performance. Nevertheless, a significantly high value of w impacts the learning speed as shown in Figure 6d. Also as discussed in the feature extraction and pre-processing subsection, a low value of w might lead to information loss, thereby degrading the performance score. Finally, we compare the general performance between the binary RG and WRG, as tabulated in Table 2. We see that compared to binary RG, the proposed WRG improves classification performance from 98.96% to 99.86% F_1 score for the COOLL dataset and 88.18% to 94.35% F_1 score for the PLAID dataset.

Table 2. Results comparision between WRG and RG on PLAID and COOLL dataset.

Data	Method	Metrics		
		MCC	F1	ZL
COOLL	RG	0.98	98.99	1.90
	WRG	1.00	99.86	0.12
PLAID	RG	0.91	88.18	8.18
	WRG	0.97	94.35	2.98

4.2. Objective 2: Comparison against V–I Image Method

In this experiment, we compare the generalization performance of the WRG and V–I image representation across multiple buildings. We first present and discuss the overall performance of the three sub-metered datasets, as listed in Table 3. From the results presented in Table 3, we see that WRG out-performs the V–I image in all three datasets with 0.92%, 8.5%, and 4.5% percentage points increase in F_1 macro for COOLL, WHITED and PLAID dataset respectively.

For benchmarking purposes, the results presented in this paper are compared with the ones presented in [10] for WHITED and PLAID datasets. We see an increase in F_1 macro score from 77% to 88.53% on PLAID and from 75.46% to 97.23 on the WHITED dataset. Ultimately, these results demonstrate the effectiveness of the WRG feature in characterizing appliances across multiple buildings. We also see the improved performance on the presented V–I based CNN. Yet, the increase in F_1 macro score is attributed to the improved pre-prepossessing procedure and developed CNN model architecture.

Table 3. Generalisation performance between WRG and VI on PLAID, COOLL and WHITED datasets.

Data	Method	Metrics		
		MCC	F1	ZL
COOLL	V-I	0.99	98.95	1.174
	WRG	1.0	99.86	0.17
WHITED	De Baets et al. [10] V-I		75.46	
	Presented work V-I	0.9	89.63	9.29
	WRG	0.98	97.23	2.29
PLAID	De Baets et al. [10] V-I		77.60	
	Presented work V-I	0.88	84.75	10.71
	WRG	0.92	88.53	7.26

We also present and discuss the per-appliance performance on the three datasets. Figure 7 shows the F_1 macro (%) per appliance for the COOLL dataset. It can be observed in Figure 7a that except for two appliances (Saw and Hedge), the F_1 macro (%) is above 99.0% for WRG. Examining the confusion matrix for the V–I image in Figure 7b, we see that the V–I makes four confusions between Vacuum and Drill (all having rotating components), one confusion between Vaccum and Grinder, Drill and Lamp and between Drill and Lamp. The use of WRG reduces these confusions to only one confusion, between Saw and Drilling machine (all having rotating components) as depicted in Figure 7c.

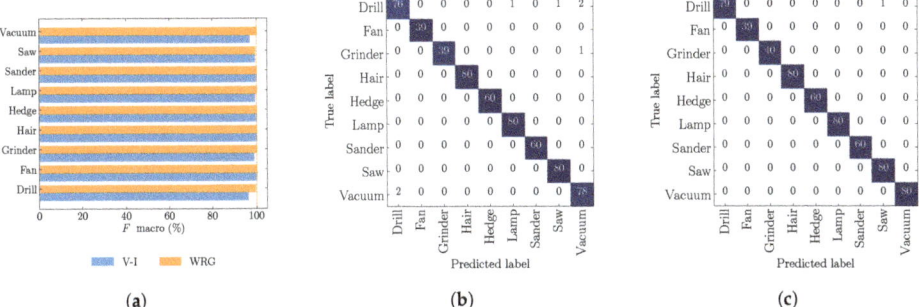

Figure 7. The F_1 macro (%) matrix per appliance and confusion matrix for the COOLL dataset: (a) F_1 macro (%) for V–I and WRG; (b) V–I confusion matrix; (c) WRG confusion matrix.

Figure 8a presents the per appliance F_1 macro (%) for the PLAID dataset. From Figure 8a, we see that with exception to Washer, Heater, Fridge, AC, and Fan, the WRG reaches at least 88% F_1 macro score for all other appliances. Observing the confusion matrix for WRG in Figure 8c and V–I image in Figure 8c, we see WRG reduces most of the confusions. More precisely, between Fan and Hairdryer (from 19 to 0), Fan and Bulb (from 19 to 6), Fridge and Washer (from 6 to 1) and between AC and other appliances (from 25 to 23). However, despite the increase performance, the WRG makes four confusions between Washer and AC, and five confusions between Fan and Vacuum (both having motor).

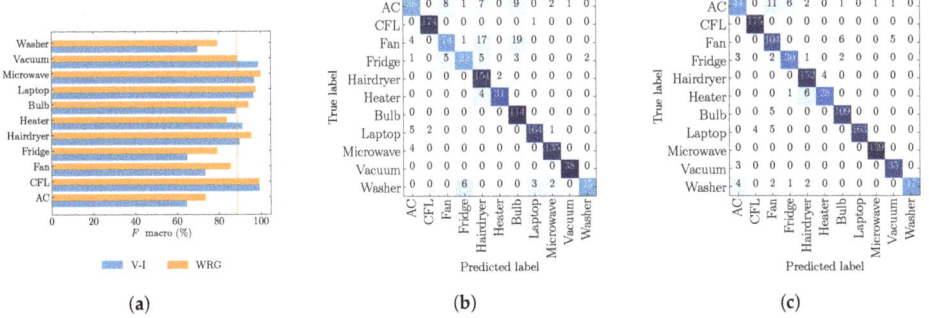

Figure 8. The F_1 macro (%) matrix per appliance and confusion matrix for the PLAID dataset: (a) F_1 macro (%) for VI and WRG; (b) V–I confusion matrix; (c) WRG confusion matrix; AC = air conditioning, CFL = compact fluorescent lamp, ILB = incandescent light bulb

Finally, Figure 9a presents results for the WHITED dataset. We see that for the WRG, most appliances achieve 97.0 F_1 macro and above. The exceptions are the PowerSupply, Shredder, Hairdryer, Flat Iron, and CFL. From the confusion matrix Figure 9b, we observe that for V–I image representation, the HairDryer is confused with the Iron (9) and kettle (6) (both having heating elements); however, the WRG reduces these confusions to 5 as shown in Figure 9c.

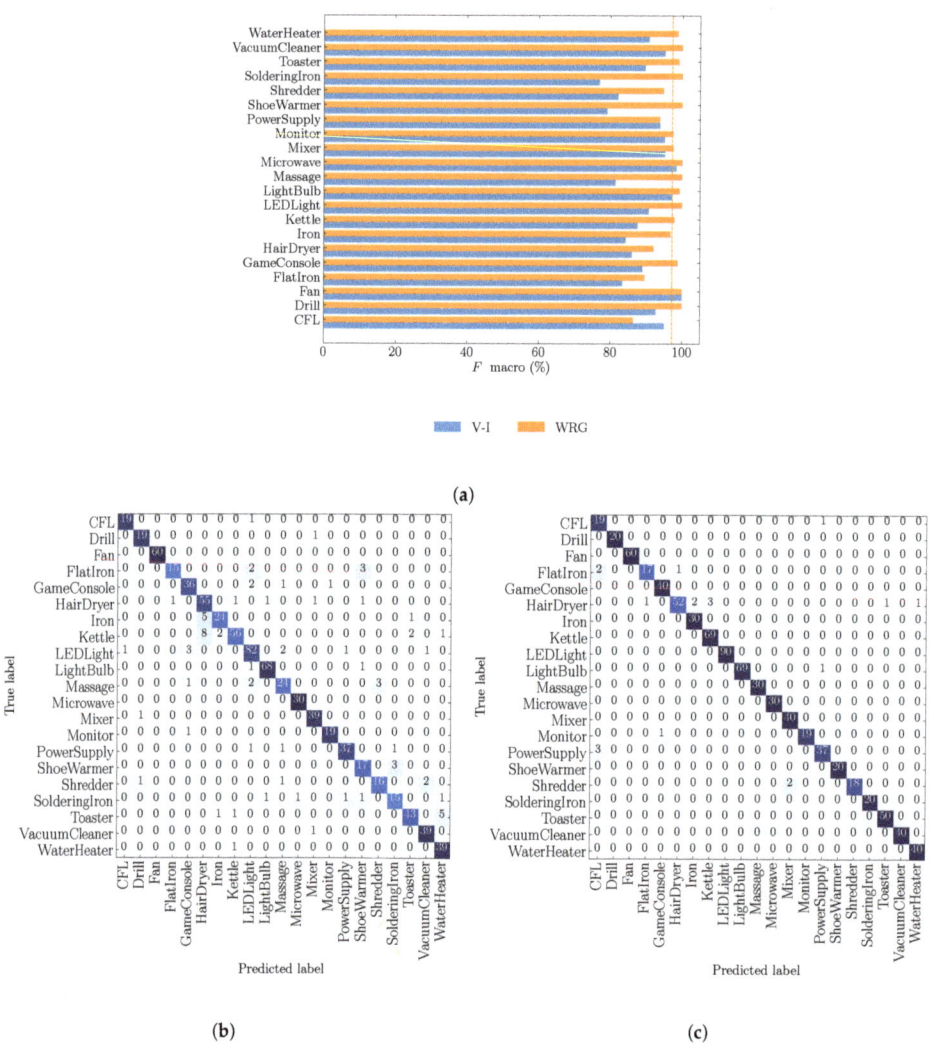

Figure 9. The The F_1 macro and confusion matrix for the WHITED dataset: (**a**) The F_1 macro (%) for the WHITED dataset with V–I and WRG feature representation; (**b**) WRG confusion matrix.

5. Conclusion and Future Work Directions

In this paper, we presented a WRG-based feature representation for appliance classification in NILM. Specifically, we propose a variation of the RG plot that goes beyond the traditional binary outputs. By following this non-binary approach, the proposed method ensures that more information is preserved in the RG, thus improving its discriminant power.

Extensive evaluations using CNNs for classification, and three public sub-metered datasets show that the proposed WRG feature consistently improves the appliance classification performance compared to the commonly used V–I image representation.

We further assessed how WRG's hyper-parameters influence classification performance. We found that the hyper-parameters are dataset dependent, which raises another fundamental research question: how these parameters can be selected and if they are related to data characteristics like sampling frequency. In future work, we will investigate appropriate methods for choosing these parameters. Precisely, we will investigate whether the WRG hyper-parameters could be treated as learn-able parameters like standard neural network weights.

Finally, even though the proposed approach was evaluated against three public datasets, it is essential to remark that these are all sub-metered. Therefore, future work should also assess the WRG on aggregated datasets. Furthermore, when considering aggregated data, it is also essential to determine the impact of the event detection algorithms (e.g., [34,35]) in the extraction of the current activation waveforms. Moreover, relying on aggregate datasets also presents the opportunity of exploring the applicability of the proposed WRG feature for multilabel appliance classification.

Author Contributions: Conceptualization, A.F.; Data curation, A.F.; Formal analysis, A.F. and L.P.; Methodology, A.F. and L.P.; Resources, A.F.; Software, A.F.; Supervision, L.P.; Validation, L.P.; Writing—original draft, A.F.; Writing—review & editing, A.F. and L.P. All authors have read and agreed to the published version of the manuscript.

Funding: Lucas Pereira has received funding from the Portuguese Foundation for Science and Technology (FCT) under grants CEECIND/01179/2017 and UIDB/50009/2020.

Conflicts of Interest: The authors declare no conflict of interest.

References

1. Cominola, A.; Giuliani, M.; Piga, D.; Castelletti, A.; Rizzoli, A. A Hybrid Signature-based Iterative Disaggregation algorithm for Non-Intrusive Load Monitoring. *Appl. Energy* **2017**, *185*, 331–344. [CrossRef]
2. Batra, N.; Singh, A.; Whitehouse, K. If You Measure It, Can You Improve It? Exploring The Value of Energy Disaggregation. In Proceedings of the 2nd ACM International Conference on Embedded Systems for Energy-Efficient Built Environments (BuildSys '15), Seoul, Korea, 4–5 November 2015; pp. 191–200. [CrossRef]
3. Huss, A. Hybrid Model Approach to Appliance Load Disaggregation. Ph.D. Thesis, KTH Royal Institute of Technology, Stockholm, Sweden, 2015.
4. Kelly, J.; Knottenbelt, W. The UK-DALE dataset, domestic appliance-level electricity demand and whole-house demand from five UK homes. *Sci. Data* **2015**, *2*, 150007. [CrossRef] [PubMed]
5. Makonin, S.; Popowich, F.; Bajić, I.V.; Gill, B.; Bartram, L. Exploiting HMM Sparsity to Perform Online Real-Time Nonintrusive Load Monitoring. *IEEE Trans. Smart Grid* **2016**, *7*, 2575–25857. [CrossRef]
6. Kelly, J.; Knottenbelt, W. Neural nilm: Deep neural networks applied to energy disaggregation. In Proceedings of the 2nd ACM International Conference on Embedded Systems for Energy-Efficient Built Environments, Seoul, Korea, 4–5 November 2015; pp. 55–64.
7. Zhang, C.; Zhong, M.; Wang, Z.; Goddard, N.; Sutton, C. Sequence-to-point learning with neural networks for non-intrusive load monitoring. In Proceedings of the Thirty-Second AAAI Conference on Artificial Intelligence, New Orleans, LA, USA, 2–7 February 2017.
8. Murray, D.; Stankovic, L.; Stankovic, V.; Lulic, S.; Sladojevic, S. Transferability of Neural Network Approaches for Low-rate Energy Disaggregation. In Proceedings of the 2019 IEEE International Conference on Acoustics, Speech and Signal Processing (ICASSP), Brighton, UK, 12–17 May 2019; pp. 8330–8334.
9. De Baets, L.; Dhaene, T.; Deschrijver, D.; Develder, C.; Berges, M. VI-Based Appliance Classification Using Aggregated Power Consumption Data. In Proceedings of the 2018 IEEE International Conference on Smart Computing (SMARTCOMP), Taormina, Italy, 18–20 June 2018; pp. 179–186. [CrossRef]
10. De Baets, L.; Ruyssinck, J.; Develder, C.; Dhaene, T.; Deschrijver, D. Appliance classification using VI trajectories and convolutional neural networks. *Energy Build.* **2018**, *158*, 32–36. [CrossRef]
11. Gomes, E.; Pereira, L. PB-NILM: Pinball Guided Deep Non-Intrusive Load Monitoring. *IEEE Access* **2020**, *8*, 48386–48398. [CrossRef]
12. Liu, Y.; Wang, X.; You, W. Non-Intrusive Load Monitoring by Voltage–Current Trajectory Enabled Transfer Learning. *IEEE Trans. Smart Grid* **2019**, *10*, 5609–5619. [CrossRef]
13. Pereira, L.; Nunes, N. Performance evaluation in non-intrusive load monitoring: Datasets, metrics, and tools—A review. *Wiley Interdiscip. Rev. Data Min. Knowl. Discov.* **2018**, *8*, e1265, doi:10/gfb8gr. [CrossRef]

14. Baptista, D.; Mostafa, S.; Pereira, L.; Sousa, L.; Morgado, D.F. Implementation Strategy of Convolution Neural Networks on Field Programmable Gate Arrays for Appliance Classification Using the Voltage and Current (V–I) Trajectory. *Energies* **2018**, *11*, 2460. [CrossRef]
15. Faustine, A.; Mvungi, N.H; Kaijage, S.; Kisangiri, M. A Survey on Non-Intrusive Load Monitoring Methodies and Techniques for Energy Disaggregation Problem. *arXiv* **2017**, arXiv:1703.00785.
16. Du, L.; He, D.; Harley, R.G.; Habetler, T.G. Electric Load Classification by Binary Voltage–Current Trajectory Mapping. *IEEE Trans. Smart Grid* **2016**, *7*, 358–365. [CrossRef]
17. Sadeghianpourhamami, N.; Ruyssinck, J.; Deschrijver, D.; Dhaene, T.; Develder, C. Comprehensive feature selection for appliance classification in NILM. *Energy Build.* **2017**, *151*, 98–106. [CrossRef]
18. Lam, H.Y.; Fung, G.S.K.; Lee, W.K. A Novel Method to Construct Taxonomy Electrical Appliances Based on Load Signaturesof. *IEEE Trans. Consum. Electron.* **2007**, *53*, 653–660. [CrossRef]
19. Li, L.; Zhao, Y.; Jiang, D.; Zhang, Y.; Wang, F.; Gonzalez, I.; Valentin, E.; Sahli, H. Hybrid Deep Neural Network–Hidden Markov Model (DNN-HMM) Based Speech Emotion Recognition. In Proceedings of the 2013 Humaine Association Conference on Affective Computing and Intelligent Interaction, Geneva, Switzerland, 2–5 September 2013; pp. 312–317. [CrossRef]
20. Wang, A.L.; Chen, B.X.; Wang, C.G.; Hua, D. Non-intrusive load monitoring algorithm based on features of V–I trajectory. *Electr. Power Syst. Res.* **2018**, *157*, 134–144. [CrossRef]
21. Gao, J.; Kara, E.C.; Giri, S.; Bergés, M. A feasibility study of automated plug-load identification from high-frequency measurements. In Proceedings of the 2015 IEEE Global Conference on Signal and Information Processing (GlobalSIP), Orlando, FL, USA, 14–16 December 2015; pp. 220–224. [CrossRef]
22. Hassan, T.; Javed, F.; Arshad, N. An Empirical Investigation of V–I Trajectory Based Load Signatures for Non-Intrusive Load Monitoring. *IEEE Trans. Smart Grid* **2014**, *5*, 870–878. [CrossRef]
23. Garcia-Ceja, E.; Uddin, M.Z.; Torresen, J. Classification of Recurrence Plots' Distance Matrices with a Convolutional Neural Network for Activity Recognition. *Procedia Comput. Sci.* **2018**, *130*, 157–163. [CrossRef]
24. Hatami, N.; Gavet, Y.; Debayle, J. Classification of Time-Series Images Using Deep Convolutional Neural Networks. *arXiv* **2017**, arXiv:1710.00886.
25. Tsai, Y.; Chen, J.H.; Wang, C. Encoding Candlesticks as Images for Patterns Classification Using Convolutional Neural Networks. *arXiv* **2019**, arXiv:1901.05237.
26. Popescu, F.; Enache, F.; Vizitiu, I.; Ciotîrnae, P. Recurrence Plot Analysis for characterization of appliance load signature. In Proceedings of the 2014 10th International Conference on Communications (COMM), Bucharest, Romania, 29–31 May 2014; pp. 1–4. [CrossRef]
27. Rajabi, R.; Estebsari, A. Deep Learning Based Forecasting of Individual Residential Loads Using Recurrence Plots. In Proceedings of the 2019 IEEE Milan PowerTech, Milan, Italy, 23–27 June 2019; pp. 1–5.
28. Dokmanic, I.; Parhizkar, R.; Ranieri, J.; Vetterli, M. Euclidean Distance Matrices: Essential theory, algorithms, and applications. *IEEE Signal Process. Mag.* **2015**, *32*, 12–30. [CrossRef]
29. Tamura, K.; Ichimura, T. MACD-histogram-based recurrence plot: A new representation for time series classification. In Proceedings of the 2017 IEEE 10th International Workshop on Computational Intelligence and Applications (IWCIA), Hiroshima, Japan, 11–12 November 2017; pp. 135–140. [CrossRef]
30. Gao, J.; Giri, S.; Kara, E.C.; Bergés, M. PLAID: A Public Dataset of High-resolution Electrical Appliance Measurements for Load Identification Research: Demo Abstract. In Proceedings of the 1st ACM Conference on Embedded Systems for Energy-Efficient Buildings (BuildSys '14), Memphis, TN, USA, 3–6 November 2014; ACM: New York, NY, USA, 2014; pp. 198–199. [CrossRef]
31. Kahl, M.; Haq, A.U.; Kriechbaumer, T.; Jacobsen, H.A. WHITED-A Worldwide Household and Industry Transient Energy Data Set. In Proceedings of the 3rd International Workshop on Non-Intrusive Load Monitoring (NILM), Vancouver, BC, Canada, 14–15 May 2016.
32. Picon, T.; Nait Meziane, M.; Ravier, P.; Lamarque, G.; Novello, C.; Le Bunetel, J.C.; Raingeaud, Y. COOLL: Controlled On/Off Loads Library, a Public Dataset of High-Sampled Electrical Signals for Appliance Identification. *arXiv* **2016**, arXiv:1611.05803 .
33. Pereira, L.; Nunes, N. A comparison of performance metrics for event classification in Non-Intrusive Load Monitoring. In Proceedings of the 2017 IEEE International Conference on Smart Grid Communications (SmartGridComm), Dresden, Germany, 23–27 October 2017; pp. 159–164, doi:10.1109/SmartGridComm.2017.8340682. [CrossRef]

34. Pereira, L. Developing and evaluating a probabilistic event detector for non-intrusive load monitoring. In Proceedings of the 2017 Sustainable Internet and ICT for Sustainability (SustainIT), Funchal, Portugal, 6–7 December 2017; IEEE: Funchal, Portugal, 2017; pp. 1–10. [CrossRef]
35. De Baets, L.; Ruyssinck, J.; Develder, C.; Dhaene, T.; Deschrijver, D. On the Bayesian optimization and robustness of event detection methods in NILM. *Energy Build.* **2017**, *145*, 57–66. [CrossRef]

© 2020 by the authors. Licensee MDPI, Basel, Switzerland. This article is an open access article distributed under the terms and conditions of the Creative Commons Attribution (CC BY) license (http://creativecommons.org/licenses/by/4.0/).

Article

Combine Clustering and Machine Learning for Enhancing the Efficiency of Energy Baseline of Chiller System

Chun-Wei Chen, Chun-Chang Li * and Chen-Yu Lin

Intelligent Machining Division, Taiwan Instrument Research Institute, NARL, Hsinchu City 300, Taiwan; rich@narlabs.org.tw (C.-W.C.); chenyulin@narlabs.org.tw (C.-Y.L.)
* Correspondence: 1709873@narlabs.org.tw; Tel.: +886-3-5779911 (ext. 171)

Received: 13 July 2020; Accepted: 20 August 2020; Published: 24 August 2020

Abstract: Energy baseline is an important method for measuring the energy-saving benefits of chiller system, and the benefits can be calculated by comparing prediction models and actual results. Currently, machine learning is often adopted as a prediction model for energy baselines. Common models include regression, ensemble learning, and deep learning models. In this study, we first reviewed several machine learning algorithms, which were used to establish prediction models. Then, the concept of clustering to preprocess chiller data was adopted. Data mining, K-means clustering, and gap statistic were used to successfully identify the critical variables to cluster chiller modes. Applying these key variables effectively enhanced the quality of the chiller data, and combining the clustering results and the machine learning model effectively improved the prediction accuracy of the model and the reliability of the energy baselines.

Keywords: energy baselines; machine learning; clustering

1. Introduction

With the popularity of sustainable development concepts, an increasing number of enterprises are adopting energy conservation and carbon reduction as a significant aspect of corporate development. In most current enterprises, air-conditioning systems are the most energy-intensive equipment. Subsequently, chiller system are the most energy-intensive subsystems in air-conditioning systems. Therefore, improving the energy efficiency of chiller system can significantly reduce the energy consumption of entire systems.

Once the energy efficiency of chiller system is improved, our next focus is the effectiveness and benefits of the improvement methods. In this stage, accurately assessing the energy efficiency of improvement methods becomes a critical topic. Currently, the most widely used method is the establishment of energy baselines. An energy baseline refers to the collection of data within a time period before equipment improvement. The collected data can then be used to establish the mathematical equations that can describe the operation modes of equipment. This process is known as baseline modeling. Then, data are collected within a time period after equipment improvement to determine the prediction values of the post-improvement data in the baseline model. Finally, energy efficiency can be calculated by comparing the prediction values and post-improvement data.

Because energy baselines are an essential approach for assessing the improvement performance of chiller system, many studies have focused on developing chiller prediction models. The models can be predominantly classified into semi-empirical models and empirical models. Semi-empirical models refer to the use of equations derived from relevant laws of physics to describe performance of chiller system. For example, Lee and Reddy developed regression models to predict the coefficient of performance (COP) of screw chillers and centrifugal chillers [1,2]. Empirical models are data-oriented models. Equations that describe chiller performance can be established without having to collected chiller-related system data. For example, Adnan et al. combined artificial neural network (ANN) models of different structures and used three variables, specifically refrigeration ton, inlet temperature, and outlet temperature, to create a chiller prediction model [3]. Kim et al. used different combinations of input variables to identify the ANN model with the highest prediction accuracy [4]. Yu et al. used random forest model to predict the operating parameters that maximize chiller COP under different working conditions [5,6].

The development of prediction models can effectively enhance the accuracy of energy baseline predictions. Nonetheless, chiller system are intricate pieces of equipment. Many operating parameters must be collected, and operating modes may vary depending on the setting. Appropriately preprocessing data can facilitate overall analysis efficiency. Clustering is an excellent data preprocessing approach. It functions by calculating the relationships between data points and identifying hidden data structures. Malinao et al. applied the X-means clustering method to cluster chiller system and identify different operating modes [7]. Habib et al. used a two-layer K-means algorithm to cluster chiller system and identify and remove outliers to enhance energy analysis efficiency [8]. Habib et al. combined K-means, BoWR, and hierarchical clustering to preprocess chiller data. The researchers proposed a model to automatically detect the energy systems of different constructs. The model can be used for fault detection and diagnosis [9].

The operating modes in different conditions can be identified by clustering chiller data. This process enhances data quality and usability, thereby improving analysis efficiency. However, existing studies mostly used clustering for fault detection and diagnosis and rarely used preprocessed data in the development of prediction models. Therefore, using the COP of chiller system as the target of research, we applied a clustering method to preprocess chiller data and identify the operating modes of chiller system in different settings. In addition, a machine learning method was used to create prediction models for various operating modes.

The contribution of this paper is the proposal of a methodology for improving the prediction accuracy of chiller system. The chiller system examined in this study was a 230RT air-conditioning chiller equipped with a variable-frequency, centrifugal compressor. The methodology first selected K-means as clustering method based on characteristics of data. Then, we used data mining and statistical techniques to identify the critical variables for clustering method. After successfully identifying the critical variables, we applied K-means clustering and gap statistic to cluster chiller modes. For finding the best prediction accuracy of chiller system, the optimal number of clusters was calibrated, if needed. Finally, we combined the clustering results and machine learning models to establish a prediction model of chiller system. The simulation showed that the error rate of prediction model was successfully reduced and the prediction accuracy of chiller energy baselines without excessively increasing computational cost was enhanced.

The structure of this paper is as follows. In Section 2, we introduce commonly used chiller-related prediction models, such as regression models, ANN models, and random forest models. Extreme gradient boosting model is compared, which has gained considerable popularity in recent data analysis competitions. In Section 3, data, modeling, and model assessment criteria are discussed. In Section 4, a prediction simulation on the data is performed and we discuss the results. In Section 5, a conclusion to this study is provided.

2. Review of Machine Learning Algorithm

In this section, we review several machine learning algorithms which were used to establish prediction models of chiller system or related work. Here, we briefly review the final mathematical form of each model, and a detailed formulation is described in Appendix A.

2.1. Regression Model

2.1.1. Lee Simplified Model

Lee combined law of thermodynamics and heat exchanger to develop a prediction model of screw chillers [1]. Equation (1) describes the prediction model of coefficient of performance (COP):

$$\frac{1}{\text{cop}} = -1 + \frac{T_{ci}}{T_{wi}} + \frac{1}{Q_e}\left[-A_0 + A_1 T_{ci} - A_2 \frac{T_{ci}}{T_{wi}}\right] \qquad (1)$$

where A_0, A_1, and A_2 are coefficients of model and can be derived by regression analysis (see Appendix A).

2.1.2. Multivariate Polynomial Regression Model

Reddy and Andersen used three variables, specifically cooling capacity, cooling water inlet temperature, chilled water outlet temperature, and their interaction, to create a multivariate regression model of centrifugal chillers [2]. Equation (2) describes the prediction model:

$$\text{COP} = \beta_0 + \beta_1 Q_e + \beta_2 T_{wi} + \beta_3 T_{ci} + \beta_4 Q_e^2 + \beta_5 T_{wi}^2 + \beta_6 T_{ci}^2 + \beta_7 Q_e T_{wi} + \beta_8 Q_e T_{ci} + \beta_9 T_{wi} T_{ci} \qquad (2)$$

2.2. Artificial Neural Networks

A basic ANN framework is illustrated in Figure 1. Blue circles mark the neurons. They are responsible for recording values. The arrows illustrate the neural connections and the direction of data transfer. The framework can be broadly categorized into an input layer, hidden layer, and output layer. The hidden layer is responsible for receiving and converting data from the input layer and transferring the converted data to the output layer to derive a solution. The structure of the hidden layer and the data conversion method influence the quality of the overall ANN.

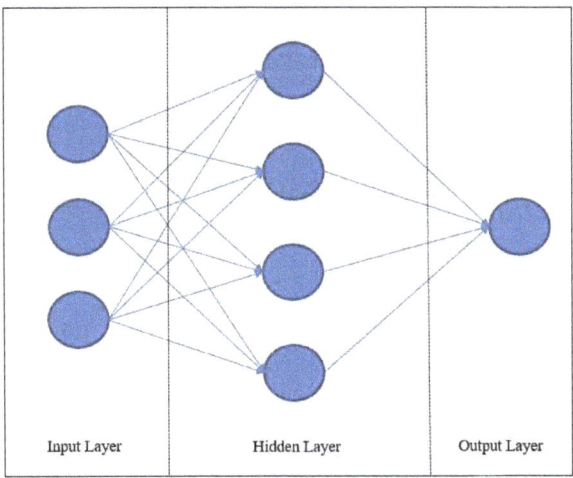

Figure 1. Structure of the artificial neural network (ANN).

Equation (3) describes the relationship of inputs x_i and the jth node in the hidden layer:

$$net_j = \sigma\left(\sum_{i=1}^{n} w_{ij} x_i + b_j\right) \qquad (3)$$

where w_{ij} is connection weight, b_j is bias; i is the number of input nodes, and j is the number of hidden nodes. σ is a activation function that transfer the inputs to the hidden layer by way of nonlinear transformation. The widely used activation function are sigmoid function, relu function, and softmax function.

Equation (4) describes the relationship of jth node in the hidden layer and output $\hat{y}_k$:

$$\hat{y}_k = \sigma\left(\sum_j w_{jk} net_j + b_k\right) \quad (4)$$

ANN models can derive the optimal solution for parameters (w, b) by differentiating the loss function, whereby the loss function is expressed as L = loss (y, $\hat{y}$). If the hidden layer comprises more than one sublayer, it may be challenging to derive the optimal solutions for the parameters of the various layers using common differentiation methods. In this instance, the chain rules in calculus can be applied to derive the solutions.

2.3. Ensemble Learning

2.3.1. Random Forest

Random forest is a classic ensemble learning algorithm. Predictions are carried out by combining the results of multiple classifications and regression tree (CART) models. When developing a CART in a random forest, the data and the variables are repeatedly sampled to increase the differences between models and prevent the overfitting problem common to CART models. The form of random forest can be written as:

$$\hat{y}_i = \sum_{m=1}^{M}\sum_{i=1}^{n}\sum_{k=1}^{K} C_k I(x_i \in R_k) \quad (5)$$

where R_k is the kth output space, C_k is average value of R_k, and m is the number of CART in the random forest model.

2.3.2. Extreme Gradient Boosting

Extreme gradient boosting (XGBoost) is a popular method used in data analysis competitions recently. It is a strong ensemble learning algorithm improved from gradient boosting decision tree algorithm (GBDT) [10]. In recent years, XGBoost have been actively applied to energy related issues [11–14].

XGBoost combines the results of CART models one by one to establish the prediction model, and uses residual as prediction target. For a given data set with n examples and d features $\mathcal{D} = \{(x_i, y_i) | x_i \in \mathbb{R}^d, y_i \in \mathbb{R}, i = 1, \ldots, n\}$, Equation (6) describes a tree ensemble model using K additive functions to predict the output:

$$\hat{y}_i = \sum_{k=1}^{K} w_{q(x_i)} \quad (6)$$

where $w_{q(x_i)}$ is the CART model. To learn the optimal parameters used in prediction model, Equation (7) describes the regularized objective function Obj:

$$Obj = \sum_{i=1}^{n} l(y_i, \hat{y}_i) + \sum_{k=1}^{K} \Omega(f_k) \quad (7)$$

where l is a differentiable convex loss function and Ω is the complexity of the model. For a fixed structure $q(x_i)$, the optimal parameter w_j^* and corresponding value Obj^* of output space j can be calculated by

$$w_j^* = -\frac{G_j}{H_j + \lambda} \tag{8}$$

$$Obj^* = -\frac{1}{2}\sum_{j=1}^{T}\frac{G_j^2}{H_j + \lambda} + \gamma T \tag{9}$$

where G_j and H_j represents the sum of first and second-order gradient statistics in output space j.

2.4. Clustering

Clustering is an unsupervised machine learning method. The purpose of clustering is to analyze the distal relationships of data points and identify underlying data structures, thereby facilitating users in carrying out advanced data analysis. Depending on the nature of the data, clustering approaches can be based on data prototype, class, density, or graphics. Table 1 summarized common clustering algorithm and their applicability from popular machine learning web, scikit-learn (https://scikit-learn.org/stable/modules/clustering.html). This subsection introduces the K-means clustering and gap statistic used in this research.

Table 1. Summary of clustering algorithm.

Method Name	Scalability	Use Case	Geometry
K-means	very large sample, medium clusters	1. general-purpose 2. even cluster size 3. flat geometry 4. not too many clusters	distances between points
Spectral clustering	medium sample, small clusters	1. few clusters 2. even cluster size 3. non-flat geometry	graph distance
Ward hierarchical clustering	large sample, large clusters	1. many clusters, 2. possibly connectivity constraints	distances between points
DBSCAN	very large sample, medium clusters	1. non-flat geometry 2. uneven cluster sizes	distances between nearest points
Birch	large sample large clusters	1. large dataset 2. outlier removal 3. data reduction.	Euclidean distance between points
Mean-shift	not scalable with samples	1. many clusters, 2. uneven cluster size 3. non-flat geometry	distances between points
OPTICS	not scalable	1. non-flat geometry 2. uneven cluster size 3. variable cluster density	distances between points
HDBSCAN	very large sample, medium clusters	1. non-flat geometry 2. uneven cluster sizes	distances between nearest points

2.4.1. K-Means

K-means is a clustering method with relatively simple computational procedures [15]. Although K-means fails to obtain good results in some cases, such as nonspherical, different variance, and different density, it is still popular for its simplicity to implement, known limitations, and excellent fine-tuning capabilities [16]. Several researchers have proposed different methods to solve different problems [17,18].

K-means can be performed in three steps. First, a k number of cluster centers are randomly established. Then, the Euclidean distance between each sample and the k cluster center is determined, and the sample point is classified into its nearest cluster. Finally, the centers of each cluster are updated using the detailed data until all sample groups reach the shortest distance to the core of their clusters. A detailed formulation is described in Appendix A.

2.4.2. Gap Statistic

The idea of the gap statistic is to compare the total within intracluster variation W_c with its expectation under an appropriate null reference distribution of the data [19]. The estimate of the optimal k is the value for which the total within intracluster variation falls the farthest below this reference curve. Hence, the optimal k is the smallest value k, satisfied in Expression (10):

$$\text{Gap}(k) \geq \text{Gap}(k+1) - s_{k+1} \tag{10}$$

$\text{Gap}(k)$ and s_{k+1} described in Equations (11) and (12).

$$\text{Gap}(k) = \frac{1}{B}\sum_{b=1}^{B} \log\left(W_{c,b}^*\right) - \log(W_c) \tag{11}$$

$$s_k = \sqrt{\frac{1+B}{B}} \sqrt{\frac{1}{B}\sum_{b=1}^{B} \left(\log\left(W_{c,b}^*\right) - \frac{1}{B}\sum_{b=1}^{B} \log\left(W_{c,b}^*\right)\right)^2} \tag{12}$$

where B is the number of sampling.

3. Methodology

3.1. Data Description and Statistic

The data examined in this study were from a chiller monitoring system in an undisclosed research center. The system was a 230RT air-conditioning chiller equipped with a variable-frequency, centrifugal compressor. The operating data between April 2018 and May 2019 were collected. Each data point represents one minute. After excluding the idle and maintenance times, a total of 316,749 data points and 28 variables were retained. Using a ratio of 8:2, 253,399 data points were used for training, and 63,350 data points were used for testing. The target of research was the COP of chiller system. The descriptive statistics of the training data and the key variables are illustrated in Figure 2 and tabulated in Table 2.

Table 2. Descriptive statistics of the key variables of chiller system.

Variables	Mean	Standard Deviation	Maximum	Minimum
COP	4.411	0.786	12.329	0.424
Power (kW)	38.139	6.045	127.224	30.001
Load rate (%)	20.76	4.853	62.358	1.825
Flow (GPM)	558.238	89.15	738.068	87.912

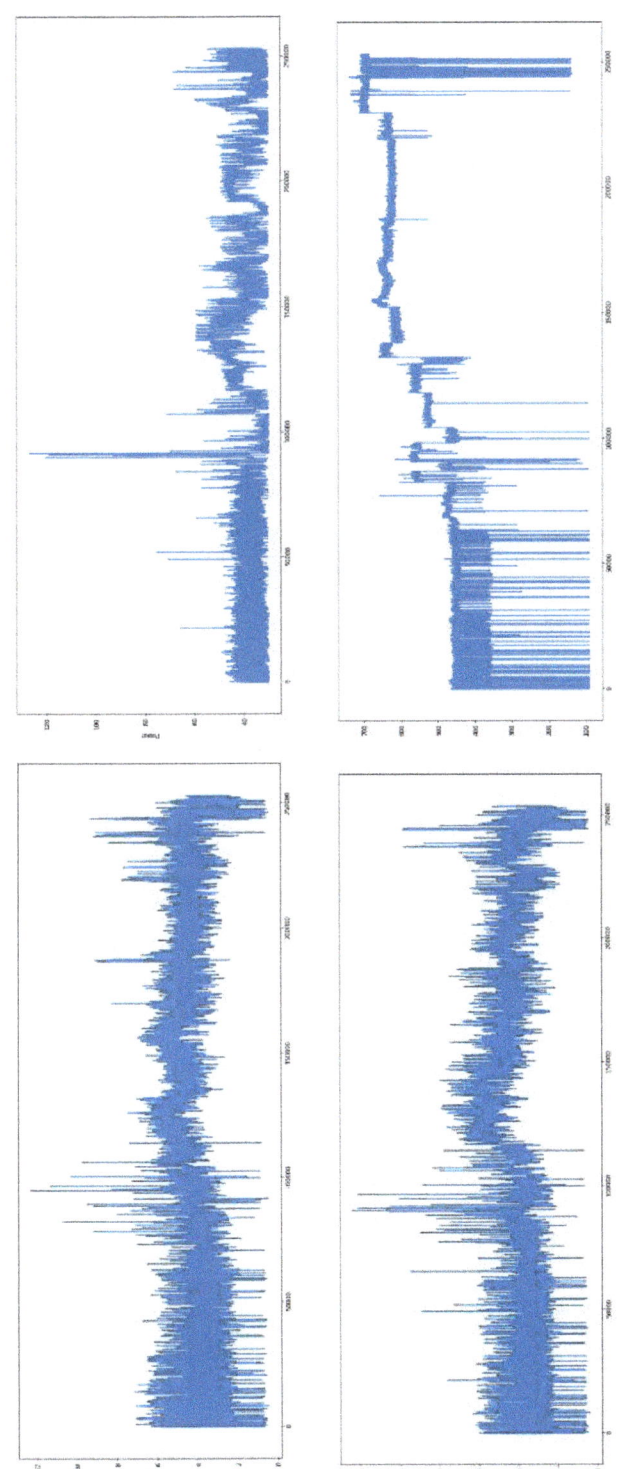

Figure 2. Trend chart of the key variables of chiller system.

The top left image in Figure 2 is a trend chart for COP. The chart shows that the COP values were predominantly distributed between 2 and 6. The top right figure is a trend chart for power consumption. The chart shows that power consumption was significantly higher in specific periods. The full distance of the data approximated 100. The lower left figure is a trend chart for load rate. The distribution was similar to COP. The lower right figure is a trend chart for chilled water flow.

Then, calculate the maximal information coefficient (MIC) for COP. MIC provides a measure of the strength of the linear or nonlinear association between two variables [20]. To ensure a fair comparison, MIC normalized the values and obtained modified values between zero and one. Table 3 tabulated some variables with higher correlation coefficient.

Table 3. Maximal information coefficient of performance (COP).

Variables	kW/RT	Exhaust Temperature (°C)	Load	Supply Cooling Water Temperature Different (°C)	Inhale Temperature (°C)	Chilled Water Flow (GPM)
Maximal information coefficient	0.9634	0.5342	0.4907	0.3255	0.3130	0.2714

Subsequently, a scatter diagram was plotted to observe the distribution relationships between each variable. Scatter relationships of interest are plotted in Figures 3–5. Figure 3 is a scatter diagram of COP and kW/RT. COP and kW/RT presented a reciprocal relationship. The anticipated results were a curve presenting a convex to origin. Instead, five curves and numerous sporadic scatter points were plotted in Figure 3. Therefore, we speculated that other variables influencing the scattering of COP and kW/RT were present.

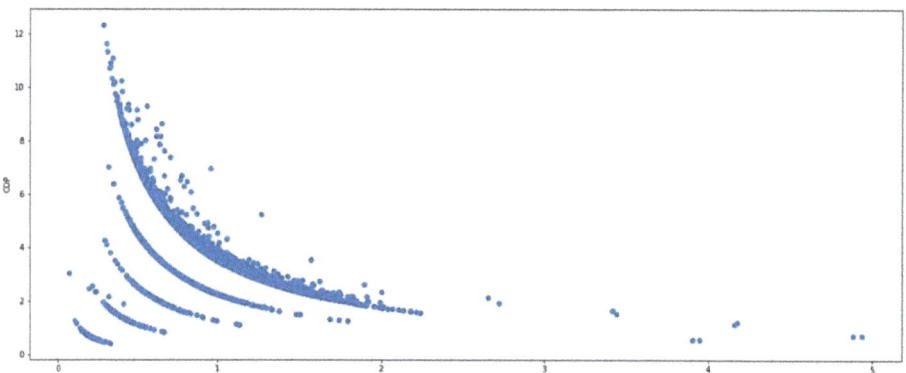

Figure 3. Scatter diagram of the kW/RT and COP.

Figure 4 is a scatter diagram of the condenser flow trend and COP. Figure 4 shows that the data were distributed into six distinct clusters in an apparent manner. Most of the condenser flow trend values ranged between 175 and 200, and the degree of COP dispersion increased concurrently with the condenser flow trend. Figure 5 is a scatter diagram of the chilled water flow and COP. The degree of COP dispersion increased concurrently with the chilled water flow. A block distribution of data points could be vaguely observed.

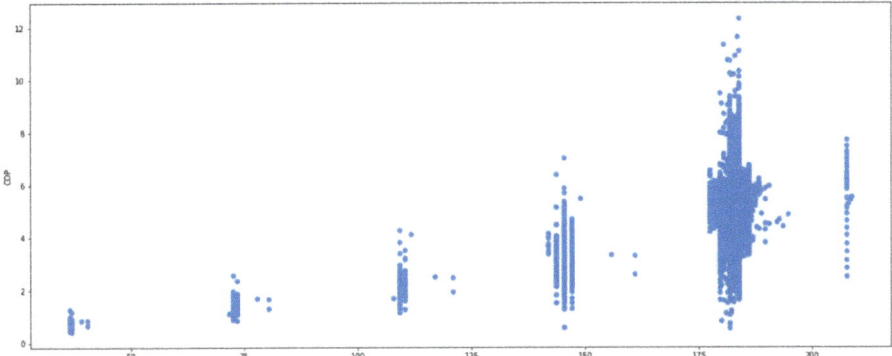

Figure 4. Scatter diagram of the condenser flow trend and COP.

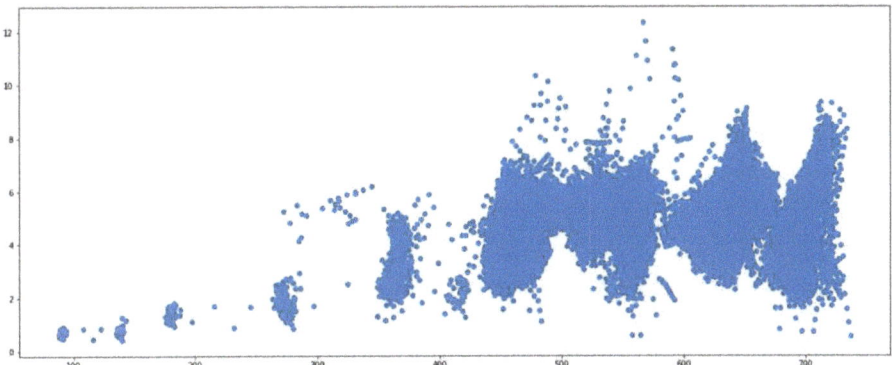

Figure 5. Scatter diagram of the chilled water flow and COP.

3.2. Model

This subsection describes the integration of clustering and machine learning. First, a suitable clustering approach was selected based on the data characteristics. In order to obtain a robust clustering effect, we also recommend using other clustering methods as validation. The necessity of estimating the optimal clustering value *k* was determined based on the approach. Estimation methods primarily included the elbow method, silhouette coefficient, and gap statistic. Third, the clustering method was employed to cluster the trained data, and the necessity of adjusting the clustering value *k* was determined by observing the clustering trends. Fourth, the clusters were then incorporated into a chiller prediction model to optimize the parameters and derive the final prediction model. Finally, the results of the different prediction models were compared based on the test data and the model assessment standards. Figure 6 summary the flow chart of establishing prediction model.

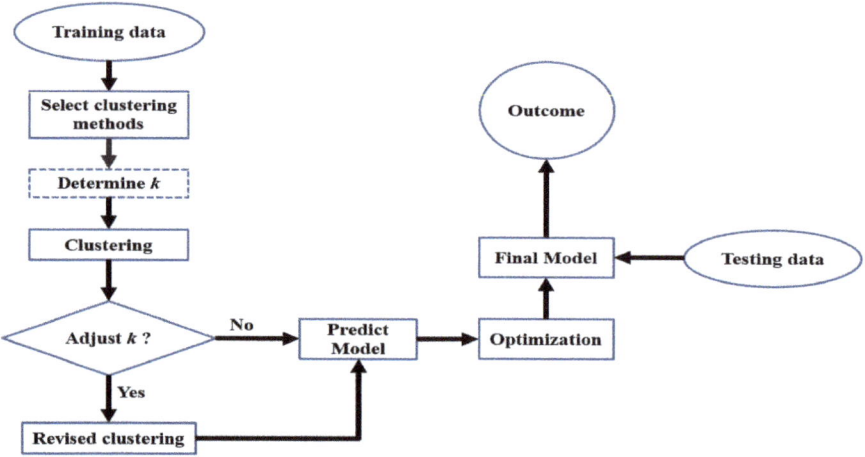

Figure 6. Flowchart of establishing prediction model. The procedure first selected a suitable clustering method according to the training data. Then, we determined the best number of cluster k, if the clustering method was needed. After obtaining the result of clustering, we drew and observed the scatterplot of clustering to determine whether to adjust k or not. Finally, we used the machine learning algorithm to train each cluster to obtain the prediction models, and optimized these models to obtain the final model.

3.3. Evaluation Metrics

To evaluate the performance of the prediction models, three different metrics were used: The MSE (mean square error; Equation (13)), the CVRMSE (coefficient of variation of root-mean squared error; Equation (14)) and the MAPE (mean absolute percentage error; Equation (15)).

$$\text{MSE} = \frac{\sum_{i=1}^{N}(y_i - \hat{y}_i)^2}{N} \tag{13}$$

$$\text{CVRMSE} = \frac{\sqrt{\frac{\sum_{i=1}^{N}(y_i - \hat{y}_i)^2}{N}}}{\frac{1}{N}\sum_{i=1}^{N} y_i} * 100 \tag{14}$$

$$\text{MAPE} = \frac{1}{N}\sum_{i=1}^{N} \frac{|y_i - \hat{y}_i|}{y_i} \tag{15}$$

where $\hat{y}_i$ is the predicted value, y_i is the actual value, and N is the total number of data.

MSE intuitively represent the error of predicted value and actual values. CVRMSE gives an indication of the model's ability to predict the overall load shape that is reflected in the data. MAPE provides an overall assessment of the general percent error [21]. In addition to these three metrics, we also took computation speed into account.

4. Discussion

In this chapter, we elucidate whether integrating clustering and machine learning improved the model's predictive accuracy of energy baselines. The aforementioned machine learning model and chiller data were used to train and validate the prediction model. The target of validation was chiller COP, and the variables used in this research were the variables with high MIC values. The simulation environment was Anaconda, the popular data science platform, and the machine learning models were package from scikit-learn (https://scikit-learn.org/stable/preface.html). The assessment results of the test data are tabulated in Table 4.

Table 4. Evaluation metrics of predict model for COP.

Model	MSE	CVRMSE	MAPE	Time (s)
Linear regression	0.0341	0.0456	0.0351	0.24
Lee simplified model	0.5057	0.1758	0.1608	0.44
Multivariate polynomial regression	0.4263	0.1615	0.1467	0.29
ANN	0.013	0.0282	0.0205	38.6
Random forest	0.003347	0.0143	0.0069	54.6
XGBoost	0.003326	0.0143	0.0075	19.2

In Table 4, the four evaluation metrics, MSE, CVRMSE, MAPE, and Time(s), are calculated. The results indicate that ensemble learning model, random forest, and XGBoost had the better prediction error. The three-error metric of the XGBoost model and random forest model were relatively similar, and the computation speed of XGBoost model was faster than random forest model. Although the evaluation metrics of the three regression models were acceptable, they were less favorable in terms of performance compared to the ensemble learning model, only outperforming the ensemble learning model in computation time. The performance of ANN model was between the regression models and ensemble learning. Then, we assessed whether integrating clustering and machine learning improved the accuracy of the prediction models.

According to the Figure 4, the data were distributed into six distinct clusters in an apparent manner. Although the data seemed a bit uneven, they were well separated from each other. So, we tried to use K-means as the clustering method. Gap statistic is the ideal method for calculating the clustering value k. To validate the choice, we also tried to run and compare different clustering methods. The outcome is presented in Appendix B. From the results, K-means was a great choice in this research.

K-means clustering and gap statistic were performed on the 28 variables of the chiller data. The clustering results were then consolidated onto a graph. Based on the calculation results, the condenser flow trend was the most suitable variable of the 28 variables for clustering. Figure 7 is a scatter diagram of the condenser flow trend and COP after clustering. The diagram shows that K-means distributed the data into ten clusters.

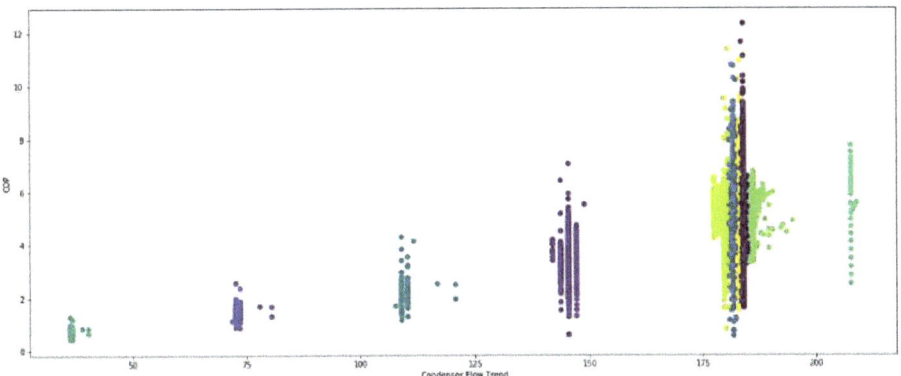

Figure 7. Scatter diagram of the condenser flow trend and COP after clustering.

Figure 8 is a scatter diagram of kW/RT and COP after clustering using the condenser flow trend. The diagram shows that besides a small number of scatter data, the data points of each cluster presented a convex to origin. The data distribution mode was more precise than that plotted chart in Figure 3.

Based on the aforementioned two points, we validated that the condenser flow trend was a suitable variable for clustering chiller COP data.

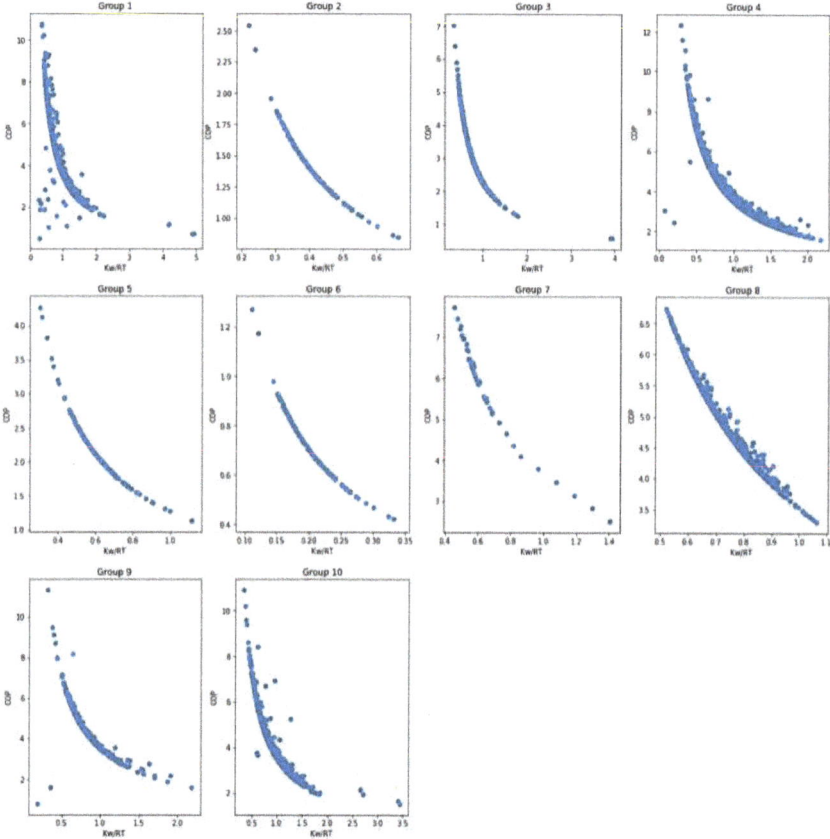

Figure 8. Scatter diagram of the kW/RT and COP after clustering.

Figure 9 shows the outcome of gap statistic. The x-coordinate is the number of cluster k, and the y-coordinate is the gap value $Gap(k)$. The optimal value for clustering is the smallest value k satisfied Expression (10). Here, the optimal value for clustering was $k = 10$. Subsequently, the clustered data was incorporated into the prediction models, and the individual test error and overall test error of 10 clusters were calculated. The results were presented as sum of squares (SSE) and MSE, where SSE was the value of MSE without average. The ideal results and post-integration performance of the different prediction models are tabulated in Tables 5 and 6.

Solely examining the overall error of the models, the performance of the models was similar for the clustered data and the unclustered data. A closer observation of the performance of individual clusters revealed that the models performed better in 7 of the 10 clusters compared to the unclustered data, suggesting that poor model performance was a direct result of a few individual clusters. We performed an in-depth review into the clustering results to explain this phenomenon and found that Clusters 1, 4, 8, 9, and 10 were the aforementioned larger data clusters with values ranging between 175 and 200. The cluster boundaries of these clusters were less prominent compared to the other clusters. We speculate that the clustering approach adopted in this study was less capable of processing the data volume, resulting in the clustering results not fully reflecting the data modes. In response, we attempted to calibrate the clusters to resolve this issue.

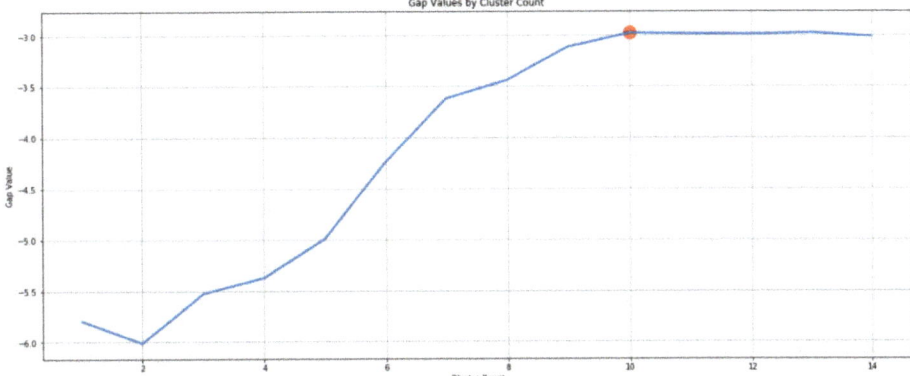

Figure 9. Output of gap statistic. The optical value for clustering was $k = 10$.

Table 5. Evaluation metrics of predict model for COP after clustering of each group.

Group	Group 1	Group 2	Group 3	Group 4	Group 5
SSE	19.0886	0.17391	0.0608	140.049	0.13358
MSE	0.00201	0.00295	0.00011	0.00305	0.0014
Group	Group 6	Group 7	Group 8	Group 9	Group 10
SSE	0.0521	1.609	293.0232	0.1844	14.4399
MSE	0.00084	0.04597	0.0673	0.00121	0.00536

Table 6. Evaluation metrics of predict model for COP after clustering.

Evaluation Metrics	Total MSE	Total CVRMSE	Total MAPE
Value	0.00707	0.01906	0.00904

Two calibration methods were adopted. The first method involved independently clustering the five sets of data to eliminate the effects of the other data. The second method was grouping the data in the five clusters without clear boundaries into one cluster for analysis. The assessment results of the two calibration methods are tabulated in Table 7.

Table 7. Evaluation metrics of predict model for COP calibrated.

	Method 1	Method 2
Total MSE	0.003386	0.002616
Total CVRMSE	0.014329	0.012591
Total MAPE	0.006657	0.006075

The table shows that the calibrated results produced using the first method were similar to the initial clustering results. In contrast, the calibrated results produced using the second method were better than the original clustering results, suggesting that integrating clustering and machine learning can improve model predictions after appropriate calibration.

The percentages of improvement between the results of this study and those of the original prediction models are tabulated in Table 8. The target of comparison was the XGB model, which had the best performance among the original prediction models. The results show that although computation time increased by 80% after clustering and calibration, the MSE, CVRMSE, and MAPE of the proposed method reduced by 21.35%, 11.96%, and 19%, respectively, suggesting a significant improvement in prediction accuracy.

Table 8. Lift percentage of proposed model.

Model	MSE	CVRMSE	MAPE	Time (s)
Proposed model	21.35%	11.96%	19%	−80%

The results confirm that clustering can effectively enhance the quality of chiller data and increase the efficiency of incorporating machine learning in the prediction of chiller data if the limitations were satisfied: (1) If the data could be clustered well or (2) if the clustering method failed to get good results, the revised approach must work.

5. Conclusions

In this study, we first simulated the common prediction models for chiller system. The best results were produced by the random forest and XGBoost models. Then, we employed statistical analysis methods, K-means clustering, and gap statistic to identify the ideal clustering variables and clustering value k. We successfully identified the key variables suitable for clustering and enhanced data quality and usability for prediction. We adopted MSE, CVRMSE, MAPE, and times as the assessment standards. After simulation and suitable calibration, MSE, CVRMSE, and MAPE improved by 21.35%, 11.96%, and 19%, respectively, without drastically increasing computation time. Therefore, we successfully improved the prediction accuracy of the model.

The findings of this study may serve as a reference for third parties responsible for assessing energy efficiency in the future. Applying the procedures outlined in this study for establishing a prediction model can effectively improve the accuracy of energy efficiency verification, reduce prediction error, and enhance the reliability of the improvement method.

In this research, the situations in which clustering methods may fail to get good results were not fully listed. In the future, the flowchart of establishing prediction model can be expanded for application in general contexts.

Author Contributions: Methodology, C.-C.L.; Project administration, C.-Y.L.; Writing—original draft, C.-C.L.; Writing—review & editing, C.-W.C.; Supervision, C.-W.C. All authors have read and agreed to the published version of the manuscript.

Funding: This research received no external funding.

Conflicts of Interest: The authors declare no conflict of interest.

Abbreviations

COP	Coefficient of performance
T_{ci}	Cooling water inlet temperature
T_{wi}	Chilled water outlet temperature
Q_e	Cooling capacity
XGBoost	Extreme gradient boosting
ANN	Artificial neural networks
MSE	Mean-square error
CVRMSE	Coefficient of variation of root-mean squared error
MAPE	Mean absolute percentage error
MIC	Maximal information coefficient

Appendix A. Review of Detailed Machine Learning Algorithm

Appendix A.1. Lee Simplified Model

Equation (A1) describe the prediction model of coefficient of performance (COP):

$$\frac{1}{cop} = -1 + \frac{T_{ci}}{T_{wi}} + \frac{1}{Q_e}\left[-A_0 + A_1 T_{ci} - A_2 \frac{T_{ci}}{T_{wi}}\right] \quad (A1)$$

where A_0, A_1 and A_2 are coefficients of model and can be derived by regression analysis. Let $\alpha = \left(\frac{1}{COP} + 1 - \frac{T_{ci}}{T_{wi}}\right) * Q_e$, Equation (A1) becomes:

$$\alpha = -A_0 + A_1 T_{ci} - A_2 \frac{T_{ci}}{T_{wi}} \quad (A2)$$

then set $\beta = \alpha + A_2 \frac{T_{ci}}{T_{wi}}$, Equation (A2) becomes:

$$\beta = A_1 T_{ci} - A_0 \quad (A3)$$

The coefficient A_2 can be calculated by regressing α on $\frac{T_{ci}}{T_{wi}}$, and the coefficients A_0 and A_1 can be calculated by regressing β on T_{ci}.

Appendix A.2. Random Forest

Let (x_n, y_n) represent a data set with n instances, the form of CART can be written as:

$$\sum_{i=1}^{n} \sum_{k=1}^{K} C_k I(x_i \in R_k) \quad (A4)$$

where R_k is the kth output space and C_k is average value of R_k. Output space are split by calculating feature j and node s satisfied Expression (A5):

$$\min_{j,s}[\min_{C_1} \sum_{x_i \in R_1(j,s)} (y_i - c_1)^2 + \min_{C_1} \sum_{x_i \in R_2(j,s)} (y_i - c_2)^2] \quad (A5)$$

Combine Expression (A4) and Expression (A5), the form of random forest can be written as:

$$\hat{y}_i = \sum_{m=1}^{M} \sum_{i=1}^{n} \sum_{k=1}^{K} C_k I(x_i \in R_k) \quad (A6)$$

where m is the number of CART in random forest model.

Appendix A.3. Extreme Gradient Boosting

For a given data set with n examples and d features $\mathcal{D} = \{(x_i, y_i) | x_i \in \mathbb{R}^d, y_i \in \mathbb{R}, i = 1, \ldots, n\}$, Equation (A7) describes a tree ensemble model using K additive functions to predict the output:

$$\hat{y}_i = \sum_{k=1}^{K} f_k(x_i) \quad (A7)$$

where f_k is the kth CART model. The CART model can be expressed as Equation (A8):

$$f_k(x_i) = w_{q(x_i)} \quad (A8)$$

where q is the structure of CART that maps the inputs x_i to the corresponding output space, w is the weights of output space. To learn the optimal parameters used in prediction model, Equation (A9) describes the regularized objective function Obj:

$$Obj = \sum_{i=1}^{n} l(y_i, \hat{y}_i) + \sum_{k=1}^{K} \Omega(f_k) \quad (A9)$$

where l is a differentiable convex loss function and Ω is the complexity of the model. Here, the loss function is least squares method $(y_i - \hat{y}_i)^2$, and Ω is defined as Equation (A10):

$$\Omega(f_k) = \gamma T + \frac{1}{2}\lambda \sum_{j=1}^{T} w_j^2 \tag{A10}$$

where T is the number of output space, γ and λ are hyper parameters.

Because tree ensemble model is an additive function, the objective function should satisfy $Obj^{(t)} < Obj^{(t-1)}$. Let $\hat{y}_i^{(t)}$ be the prediction of the ith instance at the tth iteration, Equation (A11) becomes:

$$\hat{y}_i^{(t)} = \sum_{k=1}^{t} f_k(x_i) = \hat{y}_i^{(t-1)} + f_t(x_i) \tag{A11}$$

and Equation (A9) becomes:

$$Obj^{(t)} = \sum_{i=1}^{n} l\left(y_i, \hat{y}_i^{(t-1)} + f_t(x_i)\right) + \Omega(f_t) + constant \tag{A12}$$

Here, the term $\sum_{k=1}^{t} \Omega(f_k)$ can be expanded to $\Omega(f_t) + \sum_{k=1}^{t-1} \Omega(f_k)$, and $\sum_{k=1}^{t-1} \Omega(f_k)$ can be regarded as a constant.

To minimize the objective function, Equation (A12) can be expanded and rewritten as following.

$$\begin{aligned} Obj^{(t)} &= \sum_{i=1}^{n}\left[y_i - \left(\hat{y}_i^{(t-1)} + f_t(x_i)\right)\right]^2 + \Omega(f_t) + constant \\ &= \sum_{i=1}^{n}\left[\left(y_i - \hat{y}_i^{(t-1)}\right) - f_t(x_i)\right]^2 + \Omega(f_t) + constant \\ &= \sum_{i=1}^{n}\left[l\left(y_i, \hat{y}_i^{(t-1)}\right)^2 - 2l\left(y_i, \hat{y}_i^{(t-1)}\right)f_t(x_i) + f_t^2(x_i)\right] + \Omega(f_t) + constant \\ &= \sum_{i=1}^{n}\left[l\left(y_i, \hat{y}_i^{(t-1)}\right)^2 + g_i f_t(x_i) + \frac{1}{2}h_i f_t^2(x_i)\right] + \Omega(f_t) + constant \end{aligned} \tag{A13}$$

where $g_i = \frac{\partial l(y_i, \hat{y}_i^{(t-1)})}{\partial \hat{y}_i^{(t-1)}}$ and $h_i = \frac{\partial^2 l(y_i, \hat{y}_i^{(t-1)})}{\partial \hat{y}_i^{(t-1)}}$ are first- and second-order gradient statistics on the loss function. Then, remove the constant term, and the objective function becomes Equation (A14):

$$Obj^{(t)} = \sum_{i=1}^{n}\left[g_i f_t(x_i) + \frac{1}{2}h_i f_t^2(x_i)\right] + \Omega(f_t) \tag{A14}$$

Finally, $f_t(x_i)$ and $\Omega(f_t)$ are substituted by Equation (A8) and (A10):

$$\begin{aligned} Obj^{(t)} &= \sum_{i=1}^{n}\left[g_i f_t(x_i) + \frac{1}{2}h_i f_t^2(x_i)\right] + \Omega(f_t) \\ &= \sum_{i=1}^{n}\left[g_i w_{q(x_i)} + \frac{1}{2}h_i w_q^2(x_i)\right] + \gamma T + \frac{1}{2}\lambda \sum_{j=1}^{T} w_j^2 \\ &= \sum_{j=1}^{T}\left[\left(\sum_{i \in I_j} g_i\right)w_j + \frac{1}{2}\left(\sum_{i \in I_j} h_i + \lambda\right)w_j^2\right] + \gamma T \\ &= \sum_{j=1}^{T}\left[G_j w_j + \frac{1}{2}(H_j + \lambda)w_j^2\right] + \gamma T \end{aligned} \tag{A15}$$

where $G_j = \left(\sum_{i \in I_j} g_i\right)$ and $H_j = \left(\sum_{i \in I_j} h_i\right)$ represents the sum of first- and second-order gradient statistics in output space j.

For a fixed structure $q(x_i)$, the optimal parameter w_j^* and corresponding value Obj^* of output space j can be calculated by

$$w_j^* = -\frac{G_j}{H_j + \lambda} \tag{A16}$$

$$Obj^* = -\frac{1}{2}\sum_{j=1}^{T}\frac{G_j^2}{H_j + \lambda} + \gamma T \tag{A17}$$

Appendix A.4. K-Means

Let $\{x_i | x_i \in \mathbb{R}^d, i = 1, \ldots, n\}$ be the set of d-dimensional points to be clustered into a set of k clusters, $\{\mu_c^{(t)} | \mu_c^{(t)} \in \mathbb{R}^d, c = i, \ldots, k\}$ be the cluster centers. Equation (A18) calculates the Euclidean distance of each sample and classified into its nearest cluster $S_c^{(t)}$ at the tth iteration:

$$S_c^{(t)} = \left\{x_i : \|x_i - u_c^{(t)}\|^2 < \|x_i - u_{c'}^{(t)}\|^2, \forall i = 1, \ldots, n\right\} \tag{A18}$$

Equation (A19) describes how to update $\mu_c^{(t)}$:

$$u_c^{(t+1)} = \frac{1}{n_c}\sum_{x_i \in S_c^{(t)}} x_i \tag{A19}$$

where n_c is the number of points in c^{th} cluster. K-means repeats formula (A18) and (A19) until $S_c^{(t+1)} = S_c^{(t)}$.

Appendix A.5. Gap Statistics

Using data set defined in Appendix A.4, let D_c be the sum of the pairwise distances for all points in cluster S_c and W_c be the pooled within-cluster sum of squares around the cluster means. Equation (A20) and (A21) describe the formula of D_c and W_c:

$$D_c = \sum_{x_i \in S_c}\sum_{x_j \in S_c} \|x_i - x_j\|^2 = 2n_c * \sum_{x_i \in S_c}\|x_i - u_c\|^2 \tag{A20}$$

$$W_c = \sum_{c=1}^{k}\frac{1}{2n_c}D_c = \sum_{c=1}^{k}\sum_{x_i \in S_c}\|x_i - u_c\|^2 \tag{A21}$$

The idea of gap statistic is to standardize the graph of $\log(W_c)$ by comparing it with its expectation under an appropriate null reference distribution of the data [19]. The estimate of the optimal k is the value for which $\log(W_c)$ falls the farthest below this reference curve. Hence, the optimal k is the smallest value k satisfied expression (A22):

$$Gap(k) \geq Gap(k+1) - s_{k+1} \tag{A22}$$

$Gap(k)$ and s_{k+1} are described in Equation (A23) and (A24).

$$Gap(k) = \frac{1}{B}\sum_{b=1}^{B}\log(W_{c,b}^*) - \log(W_c) \tag{A23}$$

$$s_k = \sqrt{\frac{1+B}{B}}\sqrt{\frac{1}{B}\sum_{b=1}^{B}\left(\log(W_{c,b}^*) - \frac{1}{B}\sum_{b=1}^{B}\log(W_{c,b}^*)\right)^2} \tag{A24}$$

where B is the number of sampling.

Appendix B. Compare of Different Clustering Methods

In this appendix, we ran and compared different clustering methods to validate whether K-means is a good choice or not. In total, we ran four clustering methods to compare with K-means. The four clustering methods are Mean-shift, OPTICS, Birch, and HDBSCAN. We summarized a detailed information of each clustering methods. Table A1 describes the detailed information.

Table A1. Detailed information of each clustering methods.

Methods	Parameters	Number of Clustering	Time (s)
Mean-shift	bandwidth	12	617
OPTICS	epsilon MinPts	40	2432
Birch	Not necessary	3	3
HDBSCAN	Not necessary	18	40
K-means	number of clustering	10	2

From Table A1, the computation speed of Birch, HDBSCAN and K-means are better than Mean-shift and OPTICS. Then, we plotted the scatter diagram of each clustering methods in Figure A1. From Figure 1, none of these five methods could perfectly separate the data, and a calibration method was necessary for the next research. Observing the scatter diagram, K-means seems to be a better method. It well separated data from each other without noises except data, which values ranging between 175 and 200. The calibration of K-means appeared easier than others. Hence, we selected K-means as the clustering method used in this research.

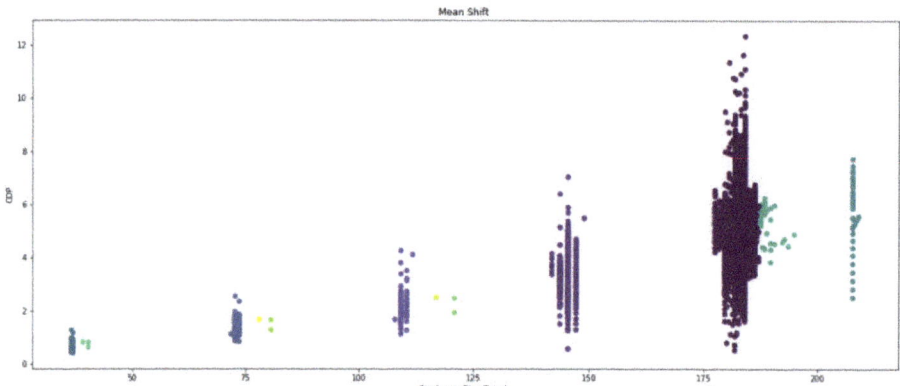

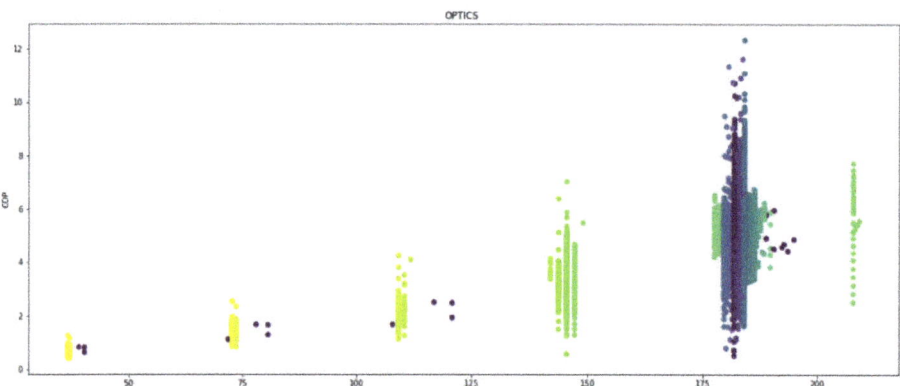

Figure A1. *Cont.*

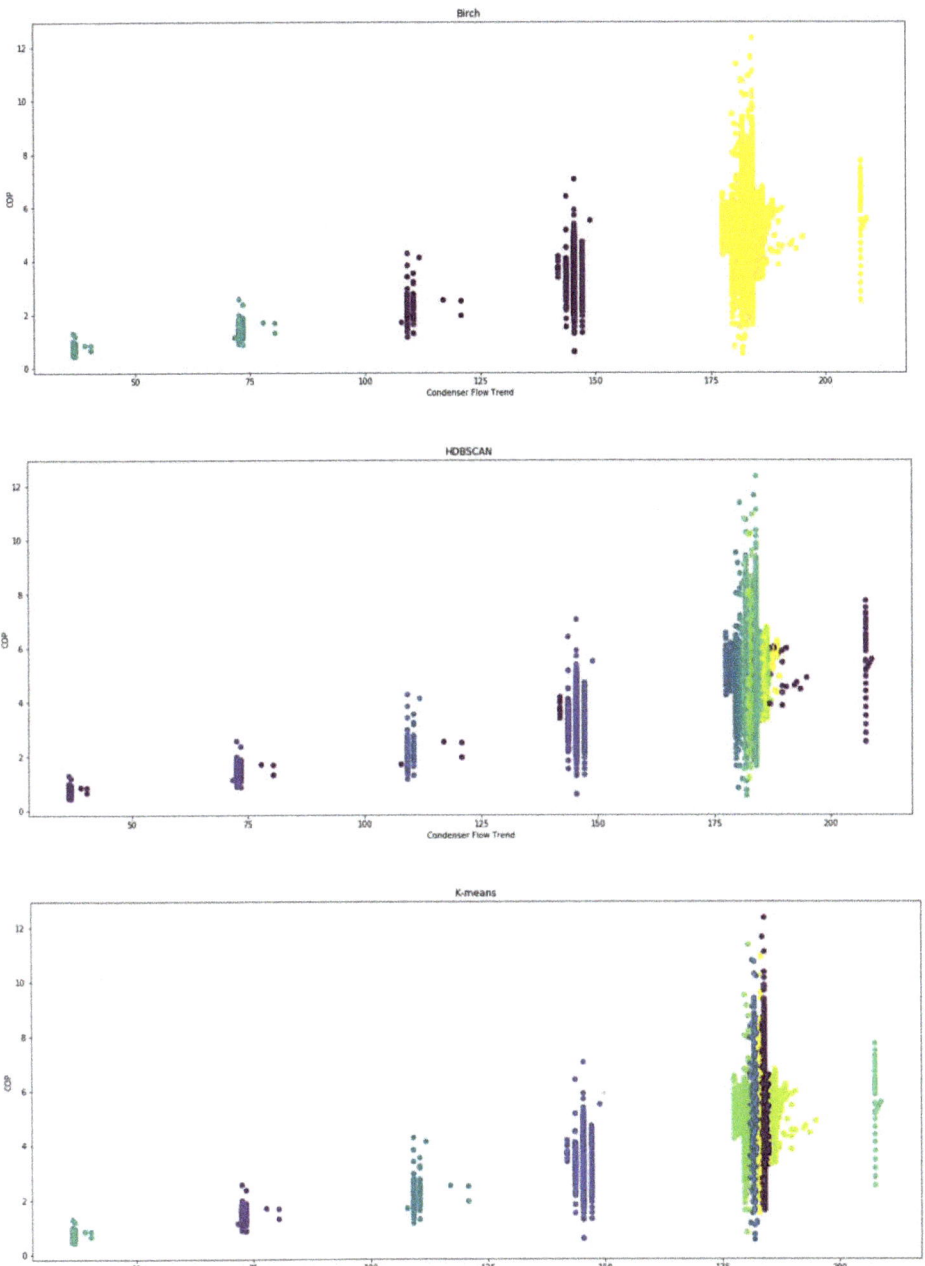

Figure A1. Scatter diagram of the condenser flow trend and COP in different clustering methods. There were five methods validated in this research. The scatter diagram are Mean-shift, OPTICS, Birch, HDBSCAN, and K-means from top to bottom.

References

1. Lee, T.S. Thermodynamic Modeling and Experimental Validation of Screw Liquid Chillers. *Ashrae Trans.* **2004**, *110*, 206–216.
2. Reddy, T.A.; Andersen, K.K. An Evaluation of Classical Steady-State Off-Line Linear Parameter Estimation Methods Applied to Chiller Performance Data. *HVAC&R Res.* **2002**, *8*, 101–124. [CrossRef]
3. Adnan, W.N.W.M.; Dahlan, N.Y.; Musirin, I. Modeling baseline electrical energy use of chiller system by artificial neural network. In Proceedings of the 2016 IEEE International Conference on Power and Energy (PECon), Melaka, Malaysia, 28–29 November 2016; pp. 500–505.
4. Kim, J.-H.; Seong, N.C.; Choi, W. Modeling and Optimizing a Chiller System Using a Machine Learning Algorithm. *Energies* **2019**, *12*, 2860. [CrossRef]
5. Yu, F.; Ho, W.; Chan, K.; Sit, R. Probabilistic and electricity saving analyses of Mist Coolers for Chiller System in a Hotel. *Energy Procedia* **2017**, *143*, 154–160. [CrossRef]
6. Yu, F.W.; Ho, W.; Chan, K.; Sit, R. Critique of operating variables importance on chiller energy performance using random forest. *Energy Build.* **2017**, *139*, 653–664. [CrossRef]
7. Malinao, J.; Judex, F.; Selke, T.; Zucker, G.; Caro, J.; Kropatsch, W. Pattern mining and fault detection via COP_therm-based profiling with correlation analysis of circuit variables in chiller systems. *Comput. Sci. Res. Dev.* **2016**, *31*, 79–87. [CrossRef]
8. Habib, U.; Zucker, G.; Blochle, M.; Judex, F.; Haase, J. Outliers detection method using clustering in buildings data. In Proceedings of the IECON 2015—41st Annual Conference of the IEEE Industrial Electronics Society, Yokohama, Japan, 9–12 November 2015; pp. 694–700.
9. Habib, U.; Hayat, K.; Zucker, G. Complex building's energy system operation patterns analysis using bag of words representation with hierarchical clustering. *Complex Adapt. Syst. Model.* **2016**, *4*, 1762. [CrossRef]
10. Chen, T.; Guestrin, C. Xgboost: A scalable tree boosting system. In Proceedings of the 22nd ACM SIGKDD International Conference on Knowledge Discovery and Data Mining, San Francisco, CA, USA, 13–17 August 2016; pp. 785–794.
11. Chakraborty, D.; Elzarka, H. Advanced machine learning techniques for building performance simulation: A comparative analysis. *J. Build. Perform. Simul.* **2019**, *12*, 193–207. [CrossRef]
12. Park, S.; Moon, J.; Jung, S.; Rho, S.; Baik, S.W.; Hwang, E. A Two-Stage Industrial Load Forecasting Scheme for Day-Ahead Combined Cooling, Heating and Power Scheduling. *Energies* **2020**, *13*, 443. [CrossRef]
13. Wang, Z.; Hong, T.; Piette, M.A. Building thermal load prediction through shallow machine learning and deep learning. *Appl. Energy* **2020**, *263*, 114683. [CrossRef]
14. Zheng, H.; Yuan, J.; Chen, L. Short-Term Load Forecasting Using EMD-LSTM Neural Networks with a Xgboost Algorithm for Feature Importance Evaluation. *Energies* **2017**, *10*, 1168. [CrossRef]
15. Jain, A.K. Data clustering: 50 years beyond K-means. *Pattern Recognit. Lett.* **2010**, *31*, 651–666. [CrossRef]
16. Fränti, P.; Sieranoja, S. How much can k-means be improved by using better initialization and repeats? *Pattern Recognit.* **2019**, *93*, 95–112. [CrossRef]
17. Liang, J.; Bai, L.; Dang, C.; Cao, F. The K-Means-Type Algorithms Versus Imbalanced Data Distributions. *IEEE Trans. Fuzzy Syst.* **2012**, *20*, 728–745. [CrossRef]
18. Melnykov, I.; Melnykov, V. On K-means algorithm with the use of Mahalanobis distances. *Stat. Probab. Lett.* **2014**, *84*, 88–95. [CrossRef]
19. Tibshirani, R.; Walther, G.; Hastie, T. Estimating the number of clusters in a data set via the gap statistic. *J. R. Stat. Soc. Ser. B Stat. Methodol.* **2001**, *63*, 411–423. [CrossRef]
20. Reshef, D.N.; Reshef, Y.A.; Finucane, H.K.; Grossman, S.R.; McVean, G.; Turnbaugh, P.J.; Lander, E.S.; Mitzenmacher, M.; Sabeti, P.C. Detecting Novel Associations in Large Data Sets. *Science* **2011**, *334*, 1518–1524. [CrossRef] [PubMed]
21. Granderson, J.; Touzani, S.; Custodio, C.; Sohn, M.; Fernandes, S.; Jump, D. *Assessment of Automated Measurement and Verification (M&V) Methods*; Lawrence Berkeley National Laboratory: Berkeley, CA, USA, 2015.

© 2020 by the authors. Licensee MDPI, Basel, Switzerland. This article is an open access article distributed under the terms and conditions of the Creative Commons Attribution (CC BY) license (http://creativecommons.org/licenses/by/4.0/).

Article

Neural Methods Comparison for Prediction of Heating Energy Based on Few Hundreds Enhanced Buildings in Four Season's Climate

Tomasz Szul [1,*], Krzysztof Nęcka [1] and Thomas G. Mathia [2]

1 Faculty of Production and Power Engineering, University of Agriculture, 30-149 Kraków, Poland; k.necka@urk.edu.pl
2 Laboratoire de Tribologie et Dynamique des Systèmes, École Centrale de Lyon, 69130 Écully, France; Thomas.Mathia@ec-lyon.fr
* Correspondence: t.szul@urk.edu.pl; Tel.: +48-12-662-46-47

Received: 16 September 2020; Accepted: 15 October 2020; Published: 19 October 2020

Abstract: Sustainable development and the increasing demand for equitable energy use as well as the reduction of waste of energy are the author's social and scientific motivations. This new paradigm is the selection of a pertinent methodology to evaluate the efficiency of habitat thermomodernization, which is one of the scientific tasks of the presented study. In order to meet the social and scientific requirements, 380 buildings from the end of the last century (made of large plate technology), which were thermally improved at the beginning of the XXI century, were designed for a comparative analysis of the predictive modelling of heating energy consumption. A specific set of important variables characterizing the examined buildings has been identified. Groups of variables were used to estimate the energy consumption in such a way as to achieve a compromise between the difficulty of obtaining them and the quality of forecast. To predict energy consumption, the six most appropriate neural methods were used: artificial neural networks (ANN), general regression trees (CART), exhaustive regression trees (CHAID), support regression trees (SRT), support vectors (SV), and method multivariant adaptive regression splines (MARS). The quality assessment of the developed models used the mean absolute percentage error (MAPE) also known as mean absolute percentage deviation (MAPD), as well as mean bias error (MBE), coefficient of variance of the root mean square error (CV RMSE) and coefficient of determination (R^2), which are accepted as statistical calibration standards by (American Society of Heating, Refrigerating and Air-Conditioning Engineers) ASHRAE. On this basis, the most effective method has been chosen, which gives the best results and therefore allows to forecast with great precision the energy consumption (after thermal improvement) for this type of residential building.

Keywords: neural methods; machine learning; smart intelligent systems; building energy consumption; building load forecasting; energy efficiency; thermal improved of buildings

1. Introduction

1.1. Scientific Context and Recent Trends in through Data-Driven Modeling

Tomorrow, and in some cases today, our everyday life will operate within more and more structured smart cyber-physical systems monitoring the physical processes of (personal interests and mobility, commercial and financial activity, electrical energy and water consumption, transport traffic, telecommunication, connected objects, etc.) in our environment, highly contributing to centralized decisions [1]. Deliberately, this study is devoted to only one aspect of energy consumption, limited to the selection of the most efficient methodology to predict the energy consumption of a human habitat in a four-season climate according to Köppen–Geiger climate classification. Dfb is designing warm-summer humid continental climate covering the largest part of Europe and part of the USA and Canada. In contrast to the modern perception of energy, "ἐνέργεια—energeia" was in ancient Greece a qualitative philosophical concept, broad enough to include ideas such as happiness, comfort, and pleasure. Today, energy has become a central problem for each of us, particularly in terms of personal serenity, mainly if financial and/or authorities restrictions play a main role. From one side, quasi monopolistic positioning of energy generation and/or distribution becomes problematic from a social point of view for humans, and on another side, its equitable selection and distribution, as well as general saving become vital [1].

Therefore, the influence and manipulation of decision-makers offer new fields for artificial intelligence (AI) expansion. The development, proliferation, and use of different algorithms for predictive model selection and their validation is one of its important aspects. Big data collection and their treatment are consequently fundamental terms of in system influences [2].

There is no place here to polemicize on the data rich and information poor (DRIP) dilemma. That concept (DRIP) was first used in the 1983 to describe organizations rich in data, but lacking the processes to produce meaningful information and create a competitive advantage. DRIP was since defeated in the private sector with the wise implementation of information technology. That is a part of the Industry 4.0 (shortened to simply I4.) scheme referred to as the fourth industrial revolution. That name is given to the current trend of cognitive computation comprising AI. Many tools are used in AI, including different versions of mathematical optimization based on statistics, rough set methods, artificial neural networks, and economics [3,4]. The AI cognitive aspects draw upon information engineering, including monitoring and computer sciences, as well as philosophy, linguistics, and psychology and many other fields of cognition sciences. Growing digitization contributes to a rising social gap of knowledge also in developed countries due to the positioning of "decision-makers" in "complex situations". Increasing demands for equitable energy use and the reduction of waste of energy is one of author's scientific motivations.

1.2. Habitat Thermal Comfort Versus Cognitive and Emotional Dissonance

Human comfort is a feeling of well-being that has a triple origin (physical, functional, and psychic). One of the fundamental characteristics of the human habitat besides location and architecture, is the comfort and particularly in four-season countries, particularly thermal aspects of it.

The most commonly used definition for thermal comfort according to the American Society of Heating, Refrigerating, and Air-Conditioning Engineers (ASHRAE) [5] is "that condition of mind which expresses satisfaction with the thermal environment and is assessed by subjective evaluation". Immediately the cost of it comes to our mind event if that aspect is omitted. Although thermal sensitivity varies from one person to another, according style of life, to age (the very young and very old being particularly sensitive), gender, dress, education, activity, cultural habits, etc., the basic principles behind thermal comfort are largely universal.

The recent trends in prediction due to credulous and naïve thermomodernization audit should be very carefully analyzed. Such forecasts often do not take into account information about the use of buildings, which leads to discrepancies between theoretical and actual energy consumption.

Moreover, material scientists, architects, and civil engineers are very preoccupied by the methodology of energy consumption evaluation of buildings to be fashioned as well as the improvement of heritage constructions.

Thermal comfort is linked on the one hand to the quality of the thermal insulation and the thermal inertia of the housing, and on the other hand, to the ambient humidity level (hygro-thermal comfort) depending on climate conditions. There is no direct link between thermal comfort and energy bill that varies according to the climatic context and according to the quality of the building.

From the 1960s to the 1980s, the technology of large panels (prefabricated) was very popular in Polish housing construction. The period of the greatest development of housing construction, based on large plate technology, falls in the 1970s. It was a period of planning and the construction of new, large housing estates. It was on them that prefabricated blocks of flats were erected. The assembly of prefabricated buildings on construction sites took place at a fairly fast pace. A characteristic problem for the construction of this period, which was particularly noticeable in the production of prefabricated elements, was the low quality of workmanship. A large percentage of sub-standard, defective elements often hindered and disorganized work on building assembly. Despite many improvements made at the place where the panels were joined, their joints were still difficult to seal. After a short period of use of residential buildings, physical defects could be observed, such as freezing and ventilation of vertical and horizontal joints of prefabricated large panels. This resulted in the formation of moisture and fungus. Sealing with impregnated hemp ropes did not meet the thermal requirements. In addition, the wall thermal insulation standards in force at that time were more than three times lower than those required today. These buildings were characterized by very high energy consumption.

The authors' interest in this type of building results from the fact that there are about 3.5 million of them in Poland accomodating about 12 million people.

Poland is currently experiencing a big turnaround in regard to national housing policy, with the introduction of specific programs (e.g., Home Plus & Habitat for Humanity) as well as the revision of the thermomodernization policy being an important part of the process. The framework of thermo-modernization in Poland covers the thermal refurbishment of all types of residential and municipal buildings (including schools and hospitals); the local district heating network and local sources of heating; and the installation of renewable energy sources or high efficiency energy equipment. That is the fundament reason for fantastic space selection for scientific studies of different methods.

The new paradigm is the selection of pertinent methodology to evaluate the efficiency of habitat thermomodernization what is one of the tasks of presented study (Figure 1). To satisfy social as well as scientific requirements, the 380 buildings (buildings made of prefabricates) from the end of the last century thermally improved at the beginning of 21st century were selected.

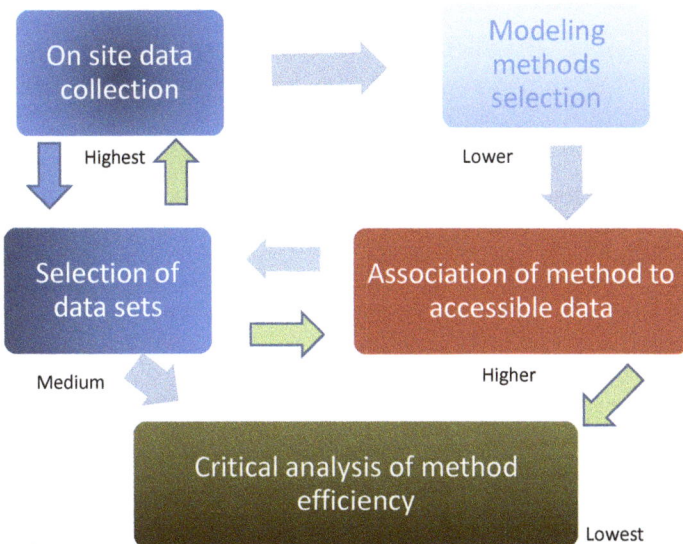

Figure 1. Methodological Flow Chart of different tasks and relative intellectual investment and time-consuming visualization.

2. Critical Bibliographical Analysis of Estimation Methods for Building's Energy Demand

The aim here is comparing the estimation methods of energy demand, their capabilities, strengths, and weakness in analyzed examples.

There are numerous methods for forecasting current and future energy needs of buildings which may be divided into engineering, statistical methods, and those based on the artificial intelligence (and also hybrid methods which combine the specified models) [3,4,6,7]. Engineering methods allow to make accurate forecasts of energy demand in a building, but they require a lot of work to carry out the thermal balance of the building. This analysis takes into account the actual operating parameters of individual systems: heating, cooling, and hot water preparation. Such a set of data characterizing the energy needs of buildings allows to determine the energy characteristics of individual buildings and to develop energy demand forecasts for them to ensure thermal comfort (user comfort). Due to the period of time that the balance sheet concerns, these methods can be divided into dynamic and static. Dynamic methods are mainly based on the measurement methodology presented in EN 16798 [8]. This refers to the values characterizing the thermal comfort of a building in particular seasons of the year. The methods from this group are mainly used for thermal calculations in new energy-saving and passive buildings [9–11]. They allow to perform a thermal balance of the building in short intervals of time, e.g., hours. They also provide the possibility of very accurate analyses of the building's thermal balance, taking into account thermal phenomena connected with energy accumulation of building's structural elements.

The second group of methods, i.e., static models, are based on the EN 13790 [12] standard supplemented by the EN 12831 [13] standard. Contrary to dynamic methods, analyzes of the heat balance are performed over long computational periods, most often covering the entire heating season. Examples of such analyzes are presented, among others in studies [14–16].

Statistical methods are usually regression models that are built on the basis of historical results. Regression models are used to forecast energy consumption based on such data as, for example: geometric dimensions, shape coefficient, area of partitions through which heat losses occur, thermal resistance of partitions, air temperature inside and outside the building and the period in which the building was built. Model calculations are performed both at the level of a single building as well as for entire building systems—groups of buildings and even entire cities. In some simplified models, regression is used to find the relationship between the final energy demand and climatic data, e.g., degrees-day of heating season in order to obtain the energy performance index [3,17–28]. Artificial neural networks are most often used in artificial intelligence-based forecasting models. These types of model are based on solving non-linear problems, where they are reliably suitable for estimating energy efficiency in various types of buildings. With the use of artificial neural networks, energy consumption was estimated for such processes as, for example: heating and cooling, thermal resistance of partitions, optimization of energy consumption and evaluation of operational parameters, as well as electricity consumption. The use of artificial neural networks for forecasting energy consumption can be found in the works of many authors [3,29–34]. These models are built for various types of buildings, where they estimate energy consumption with high precision [3,34].

Most of the presented calculation methods are effective in determining the energy efficiency of buildings. However, there is a need for further research to check the suitability of forecasting methods that could be applied to real buildings with different availability and accuracy of data describing the object from the thermal and operational point of view. Forecasting models focus mainly on estimating energy consumption in existing or simulated facilities, those newly built, and energy-saving (passive) buildings [9,28], where it is possible to obtain reliable data on the insulation of building partitions, ventilation air streams, and the number of their inhabitants [7,9].

However, few works concern residential buildings, in particular, there are no studies on actual residential buildings made of large plate technology (prefabricated), for which it is difficult to obtain detailed and reliable data. In buildings of this type, a frequent problem in thermal calculations is the lack of complete architectural and construction documentation. Moreover, there are other factors that affect the accuracy of calculations, which are caused by, e.g., moisture, aging of the material, the size of ventilation air flow, etc. Therefore, the aim of the research was to determine the usefulness of models based on artificial neural networks for estimating thermal energy consumption in multi-family residential buildings made of prefabricated (made of large panels), which have been thermally improved. Due to different availability and accuracy of data describing the building, different configurations of input variables will be applied and tested during model construction in order to achieve a compromise between the auditor's efforts to obtain them and the quality of the forecast.

3. Proposed Methodology of Investigations—Experimental Sites and Structure Model

Modelling of the impact of thermal efficiency improvement that works on the heat demand in residential buildings is a very difficult problem mainly due to the fact that it is influenced by a great number of factors. Very generally, they can be divided into factors non 'epistemologically "named" and related to:

- the "construction technology",
- the "geometry" of the building",
- the "meteorological" environmental conditions, and
- the "preferences" of their inhabitants.

At each stage of conducting audit calculations, there is a probability of inaccurate estimation of some of the volumes, most often it concerns the physical parameters of buildings and the method of use of the object, which results from the difficulty of collecting all numerical values of the object and its surroundings at a sufficiently high level of precision. This applies in particular to the value of the heat transfer coefficient U of the building shell. The heat transfer coefficient is seemingly an example of a well-defined parameter. The measurement and computational methods for estimating these values are known and quite accurately described. Unfortunately, however, in addition to a few simple cases, proper determination of this value requires a considerable amount of time, in the case of measurement methods, or the use of computer programs, if you want to use computational methods. A frequent problem in auditing activities is the lack of complete architectural and construction documentation of the analyzed objects. In this case, the auditor carries out partitions tests and then calculates the U heat transfer coefficient. Even a correct calculation of the U coefficient may be burdened with an error, because it is necessary to accurately determine the thermal conductivity and thickness of individual layers, which is not always possible, especially in real buildings. Therefore, auditors often use information contained in industry regulations. This approach is the most correct, but in the case of existing buildings it can sometimes lead to a significant error, with the poor condition of the partition, e.g., due to its moisture, aging of the material, etc., results in a higher than normative penetration rate. In many cases, the partition structure is incompatible with the standard requirements, which usually reveals a higher than estimated value of the U-factor. On account of the complexity of this problem, attempts were made to verify the usefulness of the alternative regression method for modelling of the percentage reduction of the annual energy demand in apartment buildings subjected to the improvement of thermal efficiency. From among many available methods of work, this paper investigates effectiveness of the following models: artificial neural networks (ANN), general regression trees (CART), exhaustive regression trees (CHAID), support regression trees (SRT), support vectors (SV), and method multivariant adaptive regression splines (MARS).

The first of the investigated methods were artificial neural network models which originate in the research carried out in the field of artificial intelligence. Research studies on the structure of the models of basic structures occurring in a brain had significant meaning for their development. These papers aimed mainly at the following characteristic features for biological nervous systems which will enable their practical use in technical issues.

The ANN module available in Statistica 13 program was used for construction of the model. When searching for an optimal structure of the network, the number of neurons in the hidden layer was changed from 3 to 15. In the structure of the network, linear, logistic, tangential, exponential, and sinusoidal functions were used as a function activating the transitional and output layer. Calculations were repeated for three teaching network algorithms, i.e., the fastest decrease method, the Broydena–Fletchera–Goldfarba–Shanno (BFGS) algorithm, and the conjugate gradient algorithm.

The second group covered the regression trees models (CART, CHAID), boosted regression trees (SRT) and support vectors (SV). They generate tress where each node (except for leaves) includes the condition for a division and their aim is optimal prediction of the quantity dependent variable. A classic algorithm of CART method was popularized by Breiman [30,35]. On the other hand, (CHAID) algorithm is one of the oldest methods of trees suggested by Kassa [36]. Multivariant adaptive regression splines (MARS) is an implementation of generalization of the technique introduced to common use by Friedman [37,38].

4. Description of Research Methodology and Application

Before the implementation of the main goal of the work, analyzes were carried out to establish a potential list of explanatory variables. During the research, a very extensive database was created, covering 380 buildings made of prefabricated panels for which energy audits were carried out. In particular, the energy consumption in the existing state before thermal modernization was calculated (Figure 2).

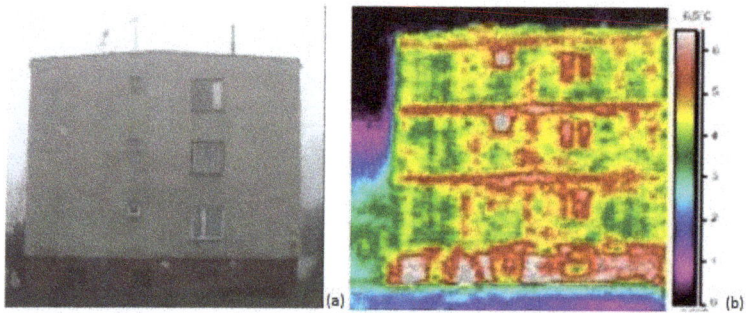

Figure 2. Representative image of one of few hundreds explored buildings (**a**) before thermomodernization and (**b**) its thermogram indicating heat flows.

For individual buildings the optimum thickness of the insulation layer of individual partitions has been assumed due to the shortest time of return on investment (Figure 3).

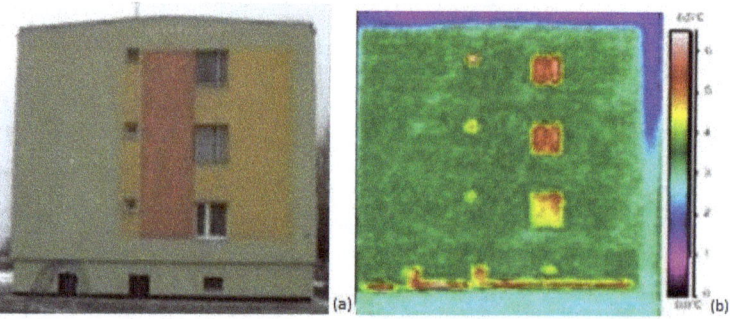

Figure 3. Representative image of (**a**) one of few hundreds explored buildings and (**b**) its thermogram indicating residual heat flows after thermomodernization.

The analyzed buildings are heated from the municipal heating network. Therefore, information was collected (based on thermal energy bills) on the actual consumption of heat for heating during the heating season (before and after thermal improvement). To exclude seasonal fluctuations, the actual energy consumption values have been converted (adjusted) to standard season conditions.

The analyzed buildings were described with many parameters. For experimental reasons, most relevant characteristics have been selected. In the first step these sizes were eliminated which were not statistically significantly correlated with the explained size or had a variability coefficient with the value below 10% or were very strongly correlated with each other. The strength of the correlation between the variables was assessed in the Statistica programme. The r-Pearson correlation coefficient would be statistically significant for the significance level $p = 0.05$. These requirements were met by 31 variables. These variables will be further divided into sets, which were used to check the usefulness of selected models for forecasting.

For the purpose of the work, analyzes were carried out to select the variables that affect the heat demand in the buildings. These buildings had energy audits prepared, on the basis of which the optimum variants of thermal modernization were selected, the partitions that should be modernized were indicated, and the appropriate thicknesses of layers of thermal insulation materials were selected. Some of them are measured and others calculated, as pointed out in Table 1. The table does not show the characteristics of 7 independent variables informing which of the partitions was thermally upgraded. The information concerning heat transfer coefficients contained below refers to the condition before thermo modernization.

Table 1. Characteristics of potential variables influencing the energy needs of buildings undergoing thermal efficiency improvement.

No.	Parameter	Abbreviation	Average	Median
1	construction year of a building, [year]	C_A	1970	1971
2	calculated from exterior measurements the heated volume of building, [m^3]	V_e	6393.1	5409.4
3	calculated from interior measurements total (net internal area), [m^2]	A_{in}	1764.0	1565.8
4	calculated surface of heated floors from interior measurements, [m^2]	A_f	1568.5	1523.8
5	calculated from exterior measurements surface of roof projection area (net), [m^2]	A_r	467.0	382.2
6	calculated from exterior measurements total walls' surface (net) area, [m^2]	A_w	1096.8	979.4
7	calculated surface of floor from interior measurements (floor over basement or floor on the ground), [m^2]	A_{fl}	395.4	360
8	calculated from exterior measurements total windows area, [m^2]	A_{tw}	290.7	254.9
9	number of stores, [pc.]	N_{Os}	4.3	4
10	number of residential flats, premises [pc.]	N_{Op}	32.4	29
11	number of living persons per building [N$_b$]	N_{Opb}	73.9	64
12	shape coefficient of buildings (the ratio surface to volume), [m$^2 \cdot$m^{-3}], [m^{-1}]	S/V_e	0.46	0.42

Table 1. *Cont.*

No.	Parameter	Abbreviation	Average	Median
13	calculated thermal transmittance of walls components, [W·m^{-2}·K^{-1}]	U_w	1.1	1.16
14	calculated thermal transmittance of peak walls components, [W·m^{-2}·K^{-1}]	U_{pw}	1.0	0.94
15	calculated thermal transmittance of roof projections components, [W·m^{-2}·K^{-1}]	U_r	1.25	0.72
16	calculated thermal transmittance of floor components on the ground, [W·m^{-2}·K^{-1}]	U_g	1.61	1.41
17	calculated thermal transmittance of floors components (floor over basement), [W·m^{-2}·K^{-1}]	U_f	1.17	1.1
18	thermal transmittance of windows (commercial data), [W·m^{-2}·K^{-1}]	U_{win}	1.88	1.6
19	calculated heating consumed power, [kW]	Φ_h	189.9	168.8
20	measured, annual energy consumption for heating, [GJ·year^{-1}]	Q_h	1524.4	1316.9
21	measured, annual energy consumption for hot water provision, [GJ·year^{-1}]	$Q_{w,w}$	364.1	276.47
22	measured, the annual heat consumption for building heating converted to the conditions of the standard heating season + energy for hot water provision, [GJ·year^{-1}]	$Q_{r,h+w,w}$	1824.1	1710.5
23	index of final energy demand for heating and domestic hot water preparation before modernization, [kWh·m^{-2}·year^{-1}]	FE_0	253.54	222.41
24	index of final energy demand for heating and domestic hot water preparation after modernization, [kWh·m^{-2}·year^{-1}]	FE_1	143.6	121.6

The variables designated after the initial selection were used to create sets of input variables based on the suitability of alternative regression methods to estimate the energy consumption of the building after performing the thermomodernization procedures. These variables were used to develop 5 sets of input data characterized by varying degrees of impact on energy consumption and the difficulty of acquiring them. Individual sets of variables were created by the authors on the basis of statistical analyses performed so far. Independent variables were required to be statistically significantly correlated with the independent variable. Independent variables could not be correlated with each other more than 0.3. The authors separated 5 sets of variables meeting these requirements. During the creation of the author's sets of variables, they also took into account the required effort to collect all necessary information. Some of the buildings in use have complete documentation describing their technical condition and equipment enabling monitoring of energy needs. Unfortunately, but especially in older buildings, we have a problem with obtaining reliable and up-to-date data about their energy needs. In the study, therefore, an attempt was made to assess changes in the energy needs of buildings undergoing thermomodernisation on the basis of different sets of diagnostic variables. These sets differ not only in the number of variables but also in the type of information provided. Some of the variables have a typical energy character (Q_h, Q_{ww}, Φ_h, $Q_{r,h+ww}$) and others describe, e.g., structural (A_f, A_{tw}) or utility parameters of the building (N_{opb}). Detailed characteristics of individual sets of variables are presented below and in Table 2.

Table 2. Selected sets of input variables for modelling heating energy needs for improved buildings in a four-season climate.

Set:	Parameter:	Standard [13,39,40]
I	Q_h—measured, consumed annual energy for heating [GJ·year^{-1}], Q_{ww}—measured, consumed annual energy for hot water provision [GJ·year^{-1}]	
II	Φ_h—calculated heating consumed power [kW], Q_{rh+ww}—measured, the annual heat consumption for building heating converted to the conditions of the standard heating season + energy for hot water provision [GJ·year^{-1}]	ISO 12831-1:2017-08
III	V_e—calculated from exterior measurements the heated volume of building [m^3], A_f—calculated surface of heated floors from interior measurements [m^2] A_w—calculated from exterior measurements total walls' surface (net) area [m^2] A_r—calculated from exterior measurements surface of roof projection area (net) [m^2] A_{tw}—calculated from exterior measurements total windows area [m^2] A_{in}—calculated from interior measurements total (net internal area) [m^2] No_{pb}—number of living persons per building [Nb] No_p—number of residential flats, premises [pcs.] S/V_e—shape coefficient of buildings (the ratio surface to volume) [m^2·m^{-3}], [m^{-1}]	ISO 12831-1:2017-08 ISO 12831-1:2017-08 ISO 9836:1997 ISO 12831-1:2017-08 ISO 12831-1:2017-08 ISO 12831-1:2017-08 ISO 9836:1997
IV	U_w—calculated thermal transmittance of walls components [W·m^{-2}·K^{-1}] U_{pw}—calculated thermal transmittance of peak walls components [W·m^{-2}·K^{-1}] U_r—calculated thermal transmittance of roof projections components [W·m^{-2}·K^{-1}] U_f—calculated thermal transmittance of floors components (floor over basement) [W·m^{-2}·K^{-1}] U_{win}—thermal transmittance of windows (commercial data) [W·m^{-2}·K^{-1}] U_g—calculated thermal transmittance of floor components on the ground [W·m^{-2}·K^{-1}] V_e—calculated from exterior measurements the heated volume of building [m^3] S/V_e—shape coefficient of buildings (the ratio surface to volume) [m^2·m^{-3}], [m^{-1}] A_f—calculated surface of heated floors from interior measurements [m^2] A_w—calculated from exterior measurements total walls' surface (net) area [m^2] A_r—calculated from exterior measurements surface of roof projection area (net) [m^2] A_{tw}—calculated from exterior measurements total windows area [m^2] A_{in}—calculated from interior measurements total (net internal area) [m^2] No_{pb}—number of living persons per building [Nb] No_p—number of residential flats, premises [pc.]	ISO 6946:2017-10 ISO 6946:2017-10 ISO 6946:2017-10 ISO 6946:2017-10 ISO 6946:2017-10 ISO 6946:2017-10 ISO 9836:1997 ISO 9836:1997 ISO 12831-1:2017-08 ISO 9836:1997 ISO 12831-1:2017-08 ISO 12831-1:2017-08 ISO 12831-1:2017-08
V	U_w—calculated thermal transmittance of walls components [W·m^{-2}·K^{-1}] U_{pw}—calculated thermal transmittance of peak walls components [W·m^{-2}·K^{-1}] U_r—calculated thermal transmittance of roof projections components [W·m^{-2}·K^{-1}] U_f—calculated thermal transmittance of floors components (floor over basement) [W·m^{-2}·K^{-1}] U_{win}—thermal transmittance of windows (commercial data) [W·m^{-2}·K^{-1}] U_g—calculated thermal transmittance of floor components on the ground [W·m^{-2}·K^{-1}] A_f—calculated surface of heated floors from interior measurements [m^2] A_w—calculated from exterior measurements total walls' surface (net) area [m^2] A_r—calculated from exterior measurements surface of roof projection area (net) [m^2] A_{tw}—calculated from exterior measurements total windows area [m^2]	ISO 6946:2017-10 ISO 6946:2017-10 ISO 6946:2017-10 ISO 6946:2017-10 ISO 6946:2017-10 ISO 6946:2017-10 ISO 12831-1:2017-08 ISO 9836:1997 ISO 12831-1:2017-08 ISO 12831-1:2017-08

Sets of variables (before thermomodernization) (Recorded in the form of 0–1 information whether the peak wall, external wall, floors, ground floors, windows and flat roof to be thermomodernized).

A very limited set of indicators was selected for the first set (set I) of variables explaining the changes in energy consumption to the heating of the building after its thermal renovation. It contained only information on the measures taken (i.e., which will be isolated from the bulkheads) and the results of calculations for the measured (standard) energy consumption of the building.

In the second set of variables (set II), the results of the calculation of the heat output of the heating system prior to the modernization and information on the scope of the activities are supplemented by measurements of energy consumption for heating. The practical use of this kit will therefore only be possible in the facilities where the energy consumption of heating is carried out (measured) and archived. The first two sets use the variables most closely correlated with energy consumption. They could not be used together because they are strongly correlated with each other.

The next set of variables (set III) therefore eliminates the energy consumption of the building for heating and replaces it with information on the characteristic dimensions of the building components, i.e., the area of the individual compartments, the area and the volume of the building and the indicators characterizing the building (number of persons using the building, number of habitations).

The previous set of variables contained information that could be reasonably easily obtained for any residential building, but it did not contain a very important parameter that would characterize the thermal insulation of the individual compartments in the existing state. The next set of variables (set IV) is therefore supplemented by heat transfer coefficients for individual compartments. Gathering such an extensive range of information allows for the exact characteristics of the object, but requires a lot of effort to prepare it reliably.

Since the above set of variables has been very extensive and the gathering of such a large range of data is time consuming, from the last set (set V) of inputs, we removed variables based on the analysis of the correlations, variability, and materiality of their effect on the final result of the calculation.

A similar group of input variables (4 sets) was used to check the suitability of a method using rough set theory (RST) to forecast energy consumption on a group of 109 buildings undergoing thermomodernization [7].

After a possible list of independent variables was selected the developed data base was divided into the teaching set to which 75% of the investigated buildings and the test set formed from the remaining objects were randomly selected. For the construction of models which enable determination of the annual heat demand and modernization costs for residential apartment buildings, a working space Data Miner available in Statistica (StatSoft®) program was applied. A schematic view of the working space with particular blocks were presented in Figure 4.

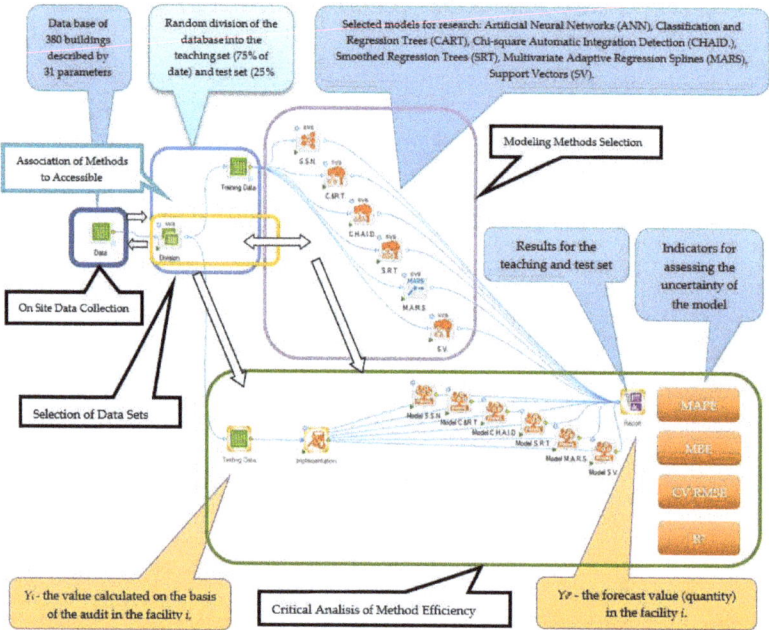

Figure 4. View of working space Data Miner visualizing global strategy of adopted methodology.

Four areas may be distinguished in the working space presented in Figure 4. In the first one there is a data source used for construction of prognostic models. It includes 380 observations described by the selected 31 parameters.

In present paper the artificial neural networks (ANN), general regression trees (CART), exhaustive regression trees (CHAID), support regression trees (SRT), support vectors (SV), and method MARS were selected. Following investigations on the effectiveness of artificial neural networks, it was decided to select an automatic network designer, which during the network construction according to its own algorithm selected the number of neurons in the hidden layer from the range 3 to 15. Except for the number of neurons, the impact of the functional type of neurons activation in the hidden layer and the output one on the quality of the model were also examined.

For assessment of past due forecasts use the mean absolute percentage error (*MAPE*) also known as mean absolute percentage deviation (*MAPD*), as well as mean bias error (*MBE*), coefficient of variance of the root mean square error (*CV RMSE*) and coefficient of determination (R^2) which are accepted as statistical calibration standards by ASHRAE Guideline 14-2014 [41,42]:

$$MAPE = \frac{1}{n_g} \sum_{m=1}^{n_g} \left| \frac{y_i - y_i^P}{y_i} \right| \cdot 100\% \quad m = 1, 2, 3 \ldots, n_g \qquad (1)$$

$$MBE = \frac{\sum_{m=1}^{n_g} (y_i - y_i^P)}{\sum_{m=1}^{n_g} y_i} \cdot 100\% \quad m = 1, 2, 3 \ldots, n_g \qquad (2)$$

$$CV\ RMSE = \frac{\sqrt{\sum_{m=1}^{n_g} \frac{(y_i - y_j^P)^2}{y_i}}}{\frac{1}{n_g} \sum_{m=1}^{n_g} y_i} \cdot 100\% \quad m = 1, 2, 3 \ldots, n_g \qquad (3)$$

$$R^2 = \left(\frac{n_g \cdot \sum_{m=1}^{n_g} y_i \cdot y_i^P - \sum_{m=1}^{n_g} y_i \cdot \sum_{m=1}^{n_g} y_i^P}{\sqrt{\left(n_g \cdot \sum_{m=1}^{n_g} y_i^2 - \left(\sum_{m=1}^{n_g} y_i\right)^2\right) \cdot \left(n_g \cdot \sum_{m=1}^{n_g} y_i^{P\ 2} - \left(\sum_{m=1}^{n_g} y_i^P\right)^2\right)}} \right)^2 \qquad (4)$$

where y_i is the actual value (quantity) in the facility *i*, and $y^p{}_i$ is the forecast value (quantity) in the facility *i*. The difference between y_i and $y^p{}_i$ is divided by the actual value y_i and *m* the number of the test object ($m = 1, 2, 3, \ldots, n_g$).

5. Results and Discussion

The results obtained for particular models (for the learning and test set) depending on the selected set of input variables are presented in Figures 5 and 6.

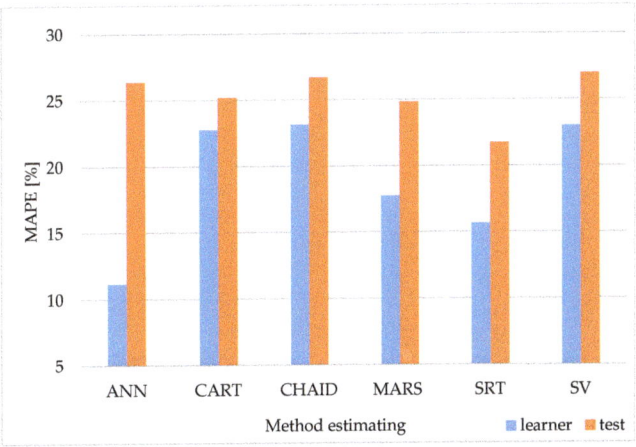

Figure 5. Comparison of the average quality indicators (*MAPE*), of selected methods estimating the reduction energy requirements for all accessible taking into account all accessible input variables (sets I–V).

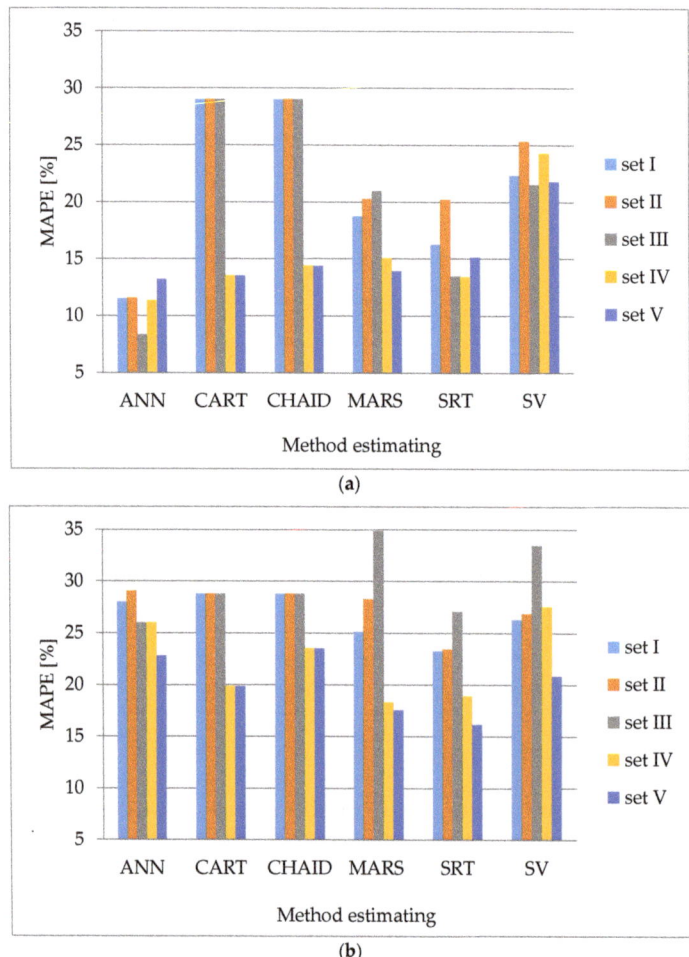

Figure 6. Comparison of the average quality indicators (*MAPE*), of selected methods estimating the reduction energy requirement taking into account all accessible input variables versus different set's selection for: (**a**) learner, (**b**) test.

The analysis carried out for artificial neural network methods shows that the lowest error MAPE when estimating the reduction of the energy requirement in a building after the completion of the thermomodernization designated for the learners irrespective of the selected set of input variables is expected. However, this method characterized a relatively high error of forecast (26%) set on test data not participating in network learning. A very promising result was obtained for the support regression trees (SRT) method. For the collection of learners, the error for this method was more than 5% higher than the ANN, but on the data that is a test collection allowed to most relevant predictions risky a map error of less than 22%. Based on the analysis of the quality assessment indicators, further analysis will also include the MARS method but only for selected sets of independent variables. The worst methods in the comparative analysis were: general regression trees (CART), exhaustive regression trees (CHAID) and support vectors (SV), and the error values of the MAPE oscillated between 23% and 27% (Figure 5).

In the next part of the work, studies were performed to see how the selection of the input variable set affects the quality of the forecasts analyzed by methods. Figure 6 shows error values for all methods depending on the set of input variables.

The analysis performed shows that the best quality forecasts regardless of the method selection can be obtained for the fourth and fifth sets of variables. The only exception for the ANN, SRT and SV method was the third set that the data in the learner collection generated the best quality forecasts, but the error was higher than for the other sets of variables on the test collection (Figure 6). For this reason, in the remainder of the work, this kit was not analyzed.

In order to get the lowest possible errors, the energy consumption forecasts in multi-family buildings after thermomodernization can be obtained using the support regression trees (SRT) method and the MARS method, for which as variables input uses variables selected for the IV and V set of independent variables.

The quality assessment of the developed models was not only based on the MAPE error analysis, but was extended by the price of MBE, CV RMSE, and R^2. The indicators were selected based on ASHRAE Guideline 14 [41,42] and the Federal Energy Management Program FEMP criteria [43]. Table 3 presents the MBE, CV RMSE and R^2 evaluation indicators for selected methods of estimating energy demand reduction taking into account all available input variables.

Table 3. Comparison of the Mean Bias Error (MBE), Coefficient of Variation of the Root Mean Square Error) (CV RMSE), coefficient of determination (R^2), of selected methods estimating the reduction energy requirement taking into account all accessibles input variables for test.

Index	Set	Method Estimating					
		ANN	CART	CHAID	MARS	SRT	SV
MBE [%]	I	12.9	8.7	8.7	14.3	9.9	8.6
	II	9.5	8.7	8.7	8.7	5.6	7.9
	III	8.8	8.7	8.7	18.4	12.2	14.0
	IV	4.0	9.5	4.0	4.0	4.7	2.8
	V	4.0	9.5	4.0	6.0	6.0	1.7
CV RMSE [%]	I	23.8	28.1	28.1	29.7	27.5	26.1
	II	23.8	28.1	28.1	33.9	25.7	26.8
	III	20.5	28.1	28.1	37.4	27.0	39.4
	IV	13.7	20.7	24.6	14.8	13.9	28.4
	V	13.7	20.7	24.6	17.8	16.4	20.7
R^2	I	0.6	0.3	0.3	0.4	0.4	0.4
	II	0.6	0.3	0.3	0.3	0.4	0.3
	III	0.7	0.3	0.3	0.3	0.4	0.1
	IV	0.8	0.7	0.4	0.8	0.8	0.3
	V	0.8	0.7	0.4	0.7	0.8	0.6

The MBE value assesses the absolute differences between the value obtained from the developed model and the actual value. It can take both positive and negative values. According to the evaluation criteria [41–43], the value of this indicator should amount to ±5. The results of the study (Table 3) show that on the test set the MBE value for all evaluated models and analyzed sets of variables was positive. Thus, the models developed underestimate the estimated reduction of energy demand in buildings undergoing thermal upgrading. For most models, for which the input variables constituted the fourth and fifth set of variables, the index values were very low and oscillated around 2–4%. This indicator is commonly used to assess the quality of the model, but it has a certain disadvantage, because in case of positive and negative values, the total value decreases significantly.

To assess the quality of the models built, CV RMSE index was therefore used, where there is no error cancellation problem caused by changing the index sign (positive with negative). According to the criteria the Federal Energy Management Program (FEMP) and ASHRAE Guideline 14 the index value should not exceed 20–30% for hourly data and 15% for monthly data [41–43]. The paper assumes that correctly calibrated models are to have a coefficient of variation of the square root mean error at a level not higher than 15%. The analysis shows that this assumption is fulfilled by the ANN model for the IV and IV set of variables and the MARS and SRT models for the IV set of variables.

ASHRAE Guideline 14 also recommends assessing the quality of the model based on the analysis of the coefficient of determination R^2 and to take 0.75 as a minimum value for well calibrated models. This requirement has been met by ANN, MARS and SRT models for 4 and 5 sets of variables, just as for the previously analysed indicators (Table 3).

6. Conclusions and Perspectives

Based on analyses carried out on a group of several hundred residential buildings in a four-season climate, for which the authors of the study developed energy audits, specific sets of deliberately selected variables characterizing the buildings were distinguished. The variables are grouped into five sets depending on the strength of impact on energy consumption after thermal renovation and difficulties in obtaining them. The first two collections use the indicators most closely correlated with the energy consumption of the building. These variables were divided into two sets because the independent variables were strongly correlated with each other. In the next sets it was analyzed how extending the variables with information related to the structural and thermal parameters of the building will affect the quality of the models. The models developed in the future will allow for a quick determination of the energy saving potential after the completion of the thermal modernization for buildings made using large plate technology (prefabricated).

- When assessing the quality of individual methods solely on the basis of the MAPE index (the index most frequently used for assessment) determined for the test set, it can be said that the best quality energy consumption forecasts after thermal rehabilitation were obtained by SRT and ANN methods, for which it was necessary to use the data from the V set as input variables. The error value was 12.1% and 12.5% respectively. Slightly worse quality forecasts, because they were burdened with a MAPE error of 14%, were obtained for the IV set of input variables and methods ANN, MARS, and SRT.
- When evaluating the methods according to the indicators proposed by ASHARE, the SV model together with IV and V sets of input variables should be considered the best in terms of MBE error. Slightly worse results, at the error level of about 4%, were obtained for the two best methods in terms of MAPE error, i.e., ANN and SRT and CHID and MARS methods. Unfortunately, CHID and SV methods were characterized by twice as high RMSE CV error as the other indicated methods. Also, the correlation coefficient for them did not meet the assumed assumptions, as it was only 0.3–0.6.
- Taking into account all quality assessment indicators, the ANN models should be indicated as preferred, together with an IV or V set of independent variables. For these sets of variables, the use of SRT models, followed by MARS, can also be considered. These models were in most cases burdened with only slightly larger errors.

In the future, the studied group of objects will be used to test other forecasting methods, e.g., hybrid methods (combining artificial neural networks and fuzzy logic), so that research results can be compared with each other. In further research, the authors also plan to test the usefulness of these methods for forecasting energy consumption in other types of buildings, such as schools, kindergartens, and others.

Author Contributions: Conceptualization, T.S.; software, T.S. and K.N.; data curation, T.S.; investigation, T.S. and K.N.; methodology, T.S.; project administration, T.S.; supervision, T.G.M.; writing—original draft, T.S. and K.N.; writing—reviewing and editing, T.G.M. and T.S. All authors have read and agreed to the published version of the manuscript.

Funding: This research was financed by the Ministry of Science and Higher Education of the Republic of Poland.

Acknowledgments: We are grateful to Sylwester Tabor and Sławomir Kurpaska from the University of Agriculture in Krakow, Poland, Faculty of Production and Power Engineering for very fruitful discussions, scientific orientations and stimulations in Analysis of Heat and Mass Transfer.

Conflicts of Interest: The authors declare no conflict of interest.

Nomenclature

ANN	Artificial Neural Network
CART	Classification and Regression Tree
CHAID	Chi-square Automatic Interaction Detector
CV RSME	Coefficient of Variance of the Root Mean Square Error, [%]
MAPE	Mean Absolute Percentage Error, [%]
MARS	Multivariate Adaptive Regression Splines
MBE	Mean Bias Error, [%]
R^2	Coefficient of determination
SRT	Support Regression Trees
SV	Support Vectors
A_f	calculated surface of heated floors from interior measurements, [m^2]
A_{f1}	calculated surface of floor from interior measurements (floor over basement or floor on the ground), [m^2]
A_{in}	calculated from interior measurements total (net internal area), [m^2]
A_r	calculated from exterior measurements surface of roof projection area (net), [m^2]
A_{tw}	calculated from exterior measurements total windows area, [m^2]
A_w	calculated from exterior measurements total walls' surface (net) area, [m^2]
C_A	construction year of a building, [year]
FE_0	final energy demand for heating and domestic hot water before modernization, [kWh·m^{-2}·year^{-1}]
FE_1	final energy demand for heating and domestic hot water after modernization, [kWh·m^{-2}·year^{-1}]
m	number of objects
No_p	number of residential flats, premises, [pc.]
No_{pb}	number of living persons per building, [Nb]
No_s	number of stores, [pc.]
Q_h	measured, consumed annual energy for heating, [GJ·year^{-1}]
$Q_{r,h+ww}$	measured, annual heat consumption for building heating converted to the conditions of the standard heating season + energy for hot water provision, [GJ·year^{-1}]
Q_{ww}	measured, consumed annual energy for hot water provision, [GJ·year^{-1}]
S/V_e	shape coefficient of buildings (the ratio surface to volume), [m^2·m^{-3}], [m^{-1}]
U_f	calculated thermal transmittance of floors components (floor over basement), [W·m^2·K^{-1}]
U_g	calculated thermal transmittance of floor components on the ground, [W·m^{-2}·K^{-1}]
U_{pw}	calculated thermal transmittance of peak walls components, [W·m^{-2}·K^{-1}]
U_r	calculated thermal transmittance of roof projections components, [W·m^{-2}·K^{-1}]
U_w	calculated thermal transmittance of walls components, [W·m^{-2}·K^{-1}]
U_{win}	ansmittance of windows (commercial data), [W·m^{-2}·K^{-1}]
V_e	calculated from exterior measurements the heated volume of building, [m^3]
y_i	the actual quantity in the facility i
y_{pi}	the forecast quantity in the facility i
Φ_h	calculated heating consumed power, [kW]

References

1. Reckel, P. *Effet de Serres Sur le €O2. 2040 Quel Climat en France Métropolitaine*; Amazon: Paris, France, 2019.
2. Frezal, B.; Leininger-Frezal, C.; Mathia, T.G.; Mory, B. *Influence et Systèmes–Introduction Provisoire à la Théorie de L'Influence et de la Manipulation*; L'Interdisciplinaire: Québec, QC, Canada, 2011.
3. Bourdeau, M.; Zhai, X.-Q.; Nefzaoui, E.; Guo, X.; Chatellier, P. Modelling and forecasting building energy consumption: A review of data-driven techniques. *Sustain. Cities Soc.* **2019**, *48*, 101533. [CrossRef]

4. Dong, B.; Li, Z.; Rahman, S.M.M.; Vega, R. A hybrid model approach for forecasting future residential electricity consumption. *Energy Build.* **2016**, *117*, 341–351. [CrossRef]
5. ASHRAE. *ASHRAE Handbook–Fundamentals—Energy Estimation and Modeling Methods*, 6th ed.; American Society of Heating, Refrigerating and Air-Conditioning Engineers, Inc. (ASHRAE): Atlanta, GA, USA, 2009; ISBN 978-1-61583-170-8. Available online: https://app.knovel.com/web/toc.v/cid:kpASHRAE37/viewerType:toc/ (accessed on 5 November 2019).
6. Zhao, H.; Magoulès, F. A review on the prediction of building energy consumption. *Renew. Sustain. Energy Rev.* **2012**, *16*, 3586–3592. [CrossRef]
7. Szul, T.; Kokoszka, S. Application of Rough Set Theory (RST) to forecast energy consumption in buildings undergoing thermal modernization. *Energies* **2020**, *13*, 1309. [CrossRef]
8. CEN. Energy Performance of Buildings. Ventilation for Buildings. Indoor Environmental Input Parameters for Design and Assessment of Energy Performance of Buildings Addressing Indoor Air Quality, Thermal Environment, Lighting and Acoustics. Module M1-6; ISO 16798-1:2019-06. Available online: https://standards.globalspec.com/std/14317955/bs-en-16798-1-tc (accessed on 23 September 2020).
9. Costanzoa, V.; Fabbrib, K.; Piraccini, S. Stressing the passive behavior of a Passivhaus: An evidence-based scenario analysis for a Mediterranean case study. *Build. Environ.* **2018**, *142*, 265–277. [CrossRef]
10. Djamila, H. Indoor thermal comfort predictions: Selected issues and trends. *Renew. Sustain. Energy Rev.* **2017**, *74*, 569–580. [CrossRef]
11. Wang, Y.; Kuckelkorn, J.; Zhao, F.-Y.; Spliethoff, H.; Lang, W. A state of art of review on interactions between energy performance and indoor environment quality in Passive House buildings. *Renew. Sustain. Energy Rev.* **2017**, *72*, 1303–1319. [CrossRef]
12. CEN. European Standard: Energy Performance of Buildings-Calculation of Energy Use for Space Heating and Cooling; ISO 13790:2008. 2008. Available online: https://www.iso.org/standard/41974.html (accessed on 5 November 2019).
13. CEN. European Standard: Heating Systems in Buildings; ISO 12831-1:2017-08. 2017. Available online: https://sklep.pkn.pl/pn-en-12831-3-2017-08e.html (accessed on 17 November 2019).
14. Ballarini, I.; Corrado, V. Application of energy rating methods to the existing building stock. Analysis of some residential buildings in Turin. *Energy Build.* **2009**, *4*, 790–800. [CrossRef]
15. Crawley, D.B.; Lawrie, L.K.; Winkelmann, F.C.; Buhl, W.F.; Huang, Y.J.; Pedersen, C.O.; Strand, R.K.; Liesen, R.J.; Fisher, D.E.; Witte, M.J.; et al. Energyplus: Creating a new-generation building energy simulation program. *Energy Build.* **2001**, *33*, 319–331. [CrossRef]
16. Rivers, N.; Jaccard, M. Combining top-down and bottom-up approaches to energy–economy modeling using discrete choice methods. *Energy J.* **2005**, *26*, 83–106. [CrossRef]
17. Allard, I.; Olofsson, T.; Hassan, O.A.B. Methods for energy analysis of residential buildings in Nordic countries. *Renew. Sustain. Energy Rev.* **2013**, *22*, 306–318. [CrossRef]
18. Asadi, S.; Amiri, S.S.; Mottahedi, M. On the development of multi-linear regression analysis to assess energy consumption in the early stages of building design. *Energy Build.* **2014**, *85*, 246–255. [CrossRef]
19. Asadi, S.; Marwa, H.; Beheshti, A. Development and validation of a simple estimating tool to predict heating and cooling energy demand for attics of residential buildings. *Energy Build.* **2012**, *54*, 12–21. [CrossRef]
20. Caldera, M.; Corgnati, S.P.; Filippi, M. Energy demand for space heating through a statistical approach: Application to residential buildings. *Energy Build.* **2008**, *40*, 1972–1983. [CrossRef]
21. Chou, J.S.; Bui, D.K. Modeling heating and cooling loads by artificial intelligence for energy-efficient building design. *Energy Build.* **2014**, *82*, 437–446. [CrossRef]
22. Fumo, N.; Biswas, R. Regression analysis for prediction of residential energy consumption. *Renew. Sustain. Energy Rev.* **2015**, *47*, 332–343. [CrossRef]
23. Lü, X.; Lu, T.; Kibert, C.J.; Viljanen, M. Modeling and forecasting energy consumption for heterogeneous buildings using a physical–statistical approach. *Appl. Energy* **2015**, *144*, 261–275. [CrossRef]
24. Ma, Z.; Li, H.; Sun, Q.; Wang, C.; Yan, A.; Starfelt, F. Statistical analysis of energy consumption patterns on the heat demand of buildings in district heating systems. *Energy Build.* **2014**, *85*, 464–472. [CrossRef]
25. Praznik, M.; Butala, V.; Zbašnik-Senegačnik, M. Simplified evaluation method for energy efficiency in single-family houses using key quality parameters. *Energy Build.* **2013**, *67*, 489–499. [CrossRef]

26. Sekhar-Roy, S.; Roy, R.; Balas, V.E. Estimating heating load in buildings using multivariate adaptive regression splines, extreme learning machine, a hybrid model of mars and elm. *Renew. Sustain. Energy Rev.* **2018**, *82*, 4256–4268. [CrossRef]
27. Tiberiu, C.; Virgone, J.; Blanco, E. Development and validation of regression models to predict monthly heating demand for residential buildings. *Energy Build.* **2008**, *40*, 1825–1832. [CrossRef]
28. Tsanas, A.; Xifara, A. Accurate quantitative estimation of energy performance of residential buildings using statistical machine learning to OLS. *Energy Build.* **2012**, *49*, 560–567. [CrossRef]
29. Biswas, M.; Robinson, M.D.; Fumo, N. Prediction of residential building energy consumption: A neural network approach. *Energy* **2016**, *117*, 84–92. [CrossRef]
30. Breiman, L.; Friedman, J.H.; Olshen, R.A.; Stone, C.J. *Classification and Regression Trees*; Wadsworth & Brooks/Cole Advanced Books & Software: Monterey, CA, USA, 1984.
31. Ekici, B.B.; Aksoy, U.T. Prediction of building energy consumption by using artificial neural networks. *Adv. Eng. Softw.* **2009**, *40*, 356–362. [CrossRef]
32. Li, K.; Sua, H.; Chua, J. Forecasting building energy consumption using neural networks and hybrid neuro-fuzzy system: A comparative study. *Energy Build.* **2011**, *43*, 2893–2899. [CrossRef]
33. Kumar, R.; Aggarwal, R.K.; Sharma, J.D. Energy analysis of a building using artificial neural network: A review. *Energy Build.* **2013**, *65*, 352–358. [CrossRef]
34. Seyedzadeh, S.; Rahimian, F.; Glesk, I.; Roper, M. Machine learning for estimation of building energy consumption and performance: A review. *Vis. Eng.* **2018**, *6*, 5. [CrossRef]
35. Ripley, B.D. *Pattern Recognition and Neural Networks*; Cambridge University Press: Cambridge, UK, 1996; ISBN 0-521-46086-7.
36. Kass, G.V. An exploratory technique for investigating large quantities of categorical data. *Appl. Stat.* **1980**, *29*, 119–127. [CrossRef]
37. Friedman, J. Multivariate adaptive regression splines (with discussion). *Ann. Stat.* **1991**, *19*, 1–141. [CrossRef]
38. Hastie, T.; Tibshirani, R.; Friedman, J.H. *The Elements of Statistical Learning: Data Mining, Inference, and Prediction*; Springer: New York, NY, USA, 2001.
39. CEN. Performance in Construction-Determination and Calculation of Surface and Volume Indicators. ISO 9836:1997. Available online: https://www.iso.org/standard/73149.html (accessed on 7 November 2019).
40. CEN. Building Components and Building Elements—Thermal Resistance and Thermal Transmittance—Calculation Methods. ISO 6946:2017-10. Available online: https://www.iso.org/standard/65708.html (accessed on 9 November 2019).
41. American Society of Heating, Ventilating, and Air Conditioning Engineers (ASHRAE). *Guideline 14-2014, Measurement of Energy and Demand Savings*; Technical Report; American Society of Heating, Ventilating, and Air Conditioning Engineers: Atlanta, GA, USA, 2014.
42. Ruiz, G.R.; Bandera, C.R. Validation of Calibrated Energy Models: Common Errors. *Energies* **2017**, *10*, 1587. [CrossRef]
43. Webster, L.; Bradford, J.; Sartor, D.; Shonder, J.; Atkin, E.; Dunnivant, S.; Frank, D.; Franconi, E.; Jump, D.; Schiller, S.; et al. *M&V Guidelines: Measurement and Verification for Performance-Based Contracts*; Version 4.0, Technical Report; U.S. Department of Energy Federal Energy Management Program: Washington, DC, USA, 2015.

Publisher's Note: MDPI stays neutral with regard to jurisdictional claims in published maps and institutional affiliations.

© 2020 by the authors. Licensee MDPI, Basel, Switzerland. This article is an open access article distributed under the terms and conditions of the Creative Commons Attribution (CC BY) license (http://creativecommons.org/licenses/by/4.0/).

Article

Investigation on the Mechanism of Heat Load Reduction for the Thermal Anti-Icing System

Rongjia Li [1], Guangya Zhu [2] and Dalin Zhang [2,*]

[1] College of Aerospace Engineering, Nanjing University of Aeronautics and Astronautics, Nanjing 210016, China; Rongjia_Li_NUAA@outlook.com
[2] Interdisciplinary Research Institute of Aeronautics and Astronautics, Nanjing University of Aeronautics and Astronautics, Nanjing 210016, China; zgyhappy@nuaa.edu.cn
* Correspondence: zhangdalin@nuaa.edu.cn

Received: 10 October 2020; Accepted: 6 November 2020; Published: 12 November 2020

Abstract: The aircraft ice protection system that can guarantee flight safety consumes a part of the energy of the aircraft, which is necessary to be optimized. A study for the mechanism of the heat load reduction in the thermal anti-icing system under the evaporative mode was presented. Based on the relationship between the anti-icing heat load and the heating power distribution, an optimization method involved in the genetic algorithm was adopted to optimize the anti-icing heat load and obtain the optimal heating power distribution. An experiment carried out in an icing wind tunnel was conducted to validate the optimized results. The mechanism of the anti-icing heat load reduction was revealed by analyzing the influences of the key factors, such as the heating range, the surface temperature and the convective heat transfer coefficient. The results show that the reduction in the anti-icing heat load is actually the decrease in the convective heat load. In the evaporative mode, decreasing the heating range outside the water droplet impinging limit can reduce the convective heat load. Evaporating the runback water in the high-temperature region can lead to the less convective heat load. For the airfoil, the heating power distribution that has an opposite trend with the convective heat transfer coefficient can reduce the convective heat load. Thus, the optimal heating power distribution has such a trend that is low at the leading edge, high at the water droplet impinging limit and zero at the end of the protected area.

Keywords: anti-icing; heat and mass transfer; heating power distribution; heat load reduction; optimization method; experimental validation

1. Introduction

Ice accretion always occurs on aircraft wings and stabilizers when the aircraft is flying through super-cooled water droplet clouds. This phenomenon may have adverse impacts on flight safety where aerodynamic and maneuvering performances are threatened if no adequate protection is supplied [1]. To prevent the aircraft wings and stabilizers from ice accretion, all commercial aircrafts are equipped with ice protection systems [2]. Generally, the thermal anti-icing system is the most widely used for large commercial aircraft and it also accounts for about 20% energy consumption of the aircraft engines [3–5]. Therefore, it is critical to optimize the thermal anti-icing system to achieve energy conservation, which can lighten the take-off weight and extend the flying range [6,7].

To prevent ice accretion, the aircraft is equipped with many kinds of anti-icing systems, which can be classified as passive and active anti-icing systems. The passive systems utilize hydrophobic or icephobic materials [8,9] to coat the surfaces of the protected components. The hydrophobic or icephobic properties can keep the surfaces as clean as possible so that ice cannot easily accumulate [10–12]. However, in many cases, the passive systems alone are difficult to keep the surfaces free from ice completely and need the active systems to operate together [13]. At present, most active systems are mainly thermal anti-icing systems. The thermal anti-icing system raises the surface temperature of the protected area above the freezing point. The surface temperature can be varied depending on the external environment and the supplied energy, which can lead to different anti-icing modes, i.e., dry surface mode, evaporative mode and runback water mode [14]. The dry surface mode ensures that no water exists within the protected area, which keeps the aircraft quite safe, but wastes massive energy. The runback water mode barely evaporates water and just maintains the surface temperature slightly above the freezing point. Despite its low energy consumption, it risks the runback ice [15], which is not permitted on the lifting and handling surfaces, or the air intakes of aircraft engines [16,17]. The evaporative mode means that the runback water is allowed but will be completely evaporated within the protected area. The energy consumption in this mode is between that in the dry surface mode and the runback water mode. For the sake of flight safety and energy conservation, the thermal anti-icing system usually works in the evaporative mode.

The energy required in the evaporative mode is determined by the heat load of the anti-icing process. There have been many advanced computational codes that can be used for predicting the anti-icing heat load under the evaporative mode, such as LEWICE [18,19], CANICE [20,21], and FENSAP-ICE [22,23]. Al-khalil [24] carried out the validation test of ANTICE code with an NACA0012 airfoil at the NASA Lewis Icing Research Tunnel. The test investigated the performances of the electro-thermal anti-icing system in the evaporative mode and presented the airfoil surface temperature distributions corresponding to different heat flux distributions and icing conditions. The test manifested that the predictions of ANTICE code were in good agreement with the experimental results. Further analysis indicated that there were a series of heat flux distributions enabled the anti-icing system to operate in the evaporative mode, which led to different anti-icing heat loads. Among all the heat flux distributions that keep the system in the evaporative mode, there will be an optimal heat flux distribution that can cause a lesser anti-icing heat load and reduce the energy consumption.

To achieve energy conservation under the evaporation model, many works have been done. Saeed and Paraschivoiu [25] presented a genetic algorithm-based optimization method to determine the optimum characteristics of a hot-air jet. The results enhanced the heat transfer process and improved the efficiency of a hot-air-based anti-icing system. Pellissier and Habashi [26] combined the reduced-order models and genetic algorithms with 3D computational fluid dynamics (CFD) to determine the optimal configuration of the piccolo tube, including jet angles, spacing of holes, and position from the leading edge. The results reduced the runback water mass flow rate and made good use of hot-air energy. Long Chen et al. [27] optimized the heat transfer in the anti-icing component for helicopter rotor, which considered the wiring pattern and heat transfer parameters of the anti-icing component. Mahdi Pourbagian and Habashi [28,29] conducted the optimization for the electro-thermal wing anti-icing systems through the surrogate-based model in conjunction with the Kriging algorithm. The set of design variables included the power density and the length of every heater. The optimization results obtained the minimum anti-icing heat load under different constrained conditions and figured out the corresponding distributions of the power density as well as the surface temperature. The results showed that, in the evaporative mode, the optimal heat flux distribution tended to keep a low value at the leading edge and increase immensely at the end of the protected area. Then, based on the previous works, Mahdi Pourbagian et al. [30] proposed more different constrained problem formulations from the physical and mathematical viewpoints and investigated the models on the convergence speed and the quality of the obtained design solutions. Chang et al. [31] proposed an approach to predict the minimum anti-icing heat load based on the icing limit state in the runback water mode. The numerical simulation was conducted with a DFVLR R-4 airfoil under different conditions. The results revealed that the optimal heating power distribution had a minimum value in the stagnation point and increased along the lower surface.

The previous work mentioned above could achieve energy conservation for the thermal anti-icing system. However, the general underlying mechanism of the anti-icing heat load reduction has not been revealed. Moreover, there is a lack of experimental investigations on the mechanism of the anti-icing heat load reduction. The influence of key parameters on the optimal heat flux distribution has not been fully studied. Therefore, in this paper, the mechanism of anti-icing heat load reduction was uncovered through both numerical simulation and experimental validations. The influences of the heating range, the surface temperature and the convective heat transfer coefficient on the anti-icing heat load reduction were also investigated. The outline of this paper is as follows. First of all, Section 2 presents the modeling and optimization methods of the thermal anti-icing system. Then, to demonstrate the applicability of the numerical models and the optimization methods, an experimental test is conducted and introduced in Section 3. Section 4 gives the numerical and experimental results and discusses the underlying mechanism of the anti-icing heat load reduction. The conclusion is presented in Section 5.

2. Numerical Simulation and Optimization Method

2.1. Modeling of the Anti-Icing Process

According to the Messinger model [32], the mass and energy conservation equations of a control volume for the runback water on the anti-icing surface can be formulated from Figure 1:

$$\dot{m}_{in} + \dot{m}'_{imp} dx = \dot{m}_{out} + \dot{m}'_{evap} dx \tag{1}$$

$$Q_{w,in} + (q_w + q_a + q_n) dx = (q_{evap} + q_{conv}) dx + Q_{w,out} \tag{2}$$

where $\dot{m}_{in}$ is the mass coming in from the previous control volume, $\dot{m}_{out}$ is the mass flowing into the next control volume, $\dot{m}'_{imp}$ is the mass of water droplets impingement per unit length, $\dot{m}'_{evap}$ is the mass of evaporation per unit length, q_w is the heat flux converted from the kinetic energy of the water droplets impingement, q_a is the aerodynamic heating flux, q_n is the heat flux supplied by the thermal anti-icing system, q_{evap} is the evaporative heat flux, q_{conv} is the convective heat flux, $Q_{w,in}$ is the energy coming in from the previous control volume, and $Q_{w,out}$ is the energy flowing into the next control volume. The above mass terms are detailed as follows:

$$\dot{m}'_{imp} = \beta \cdot u_\infty \cdot LWC \tag{3}$$

$$\dot{m}'_{evap} = \frac{\alpha}{c_{p,air}} \cdot \left(\frac{Pr}{Sc}\right)^{2/3}_{air} \cdot \frac{M_{water}}{M_{air}} \cdot \left(\frac{p_{v,s} - p_{v,e}}{p_e - p_{v,s}}\right) \tag{4}$$

$$p_v = 602.4 \times 10^{\frac{7.45 \cdot (T-273.15)}{T-38.15}} \tag{5}$$

where β is the local water droplet collection efficiency, u_∞ is the freestream air velocity, LWC is the liquid water content, α is the local convective heat transfer coefficient, $c_{p,air}$ is the specific heat of air, Pr is the Prandtl number, Sc is the Schmidt number, M_{water} is the relative molecular mass of water, M_{air} is the relative molecular mass of air and p_e is the static pressure at the edge of the boundary layer. $p_{v,s}$ and $p_{v,e}$ are the saturation vapor pressure of water on the airfoil surface and at the edge of the boundary layer, respectively. The above energy terms are detailed as follows:

$$Q_{w,in} = c_{p,w} \cdot \dot{m}_{in} \cdot (T_{s,in} - T_r) \tag{6}$$

$$Q_{w,out} = c_{p,w} \cdot \dot{m}_{out} \cdot (T_s - T_r) \tag{7}$$

$$q_w = \dot{m}'_{imp} \cdot \left[\frac{u_\infty^2}{2} + c_{p,w} \cdot (T_\infty - T_r)\right] \tag{8}$$

$$q_a = \frac{\alpha \cdot \gamma \cdot u_e^2}{2 c_{p,air}} \tag{9}$$

$$q_{evap} = \dot{m}'_{evap} \cdot r + \dot{m}'_{evap} \cdot c_{p,w} \cdot (T_s - T_e) \tag{10}$$

$$q_{\text{conv}} = \alpha \cdot (T_s - T_e) \tag{11}$$

$$T_e = T_\infty + \frac{u_\infty^2 - u_e^2}{2c_{p,\text{air}}} \tag{12}$$

where $c_{p,w}$ is the specific heat of water, $T_{s,\text{in}}$ is the temperature of the previous control volume, T_s is the temperature of the current control volume, T_r is the reference temperature (273.15K), T_e is the temperature at the edge of the boundary layer, T_∞ is the freestream air temperature, γ is the recovery factor, u_e is the velocity at the edge of the boundary layer and r is the latent heat of water evaporation.

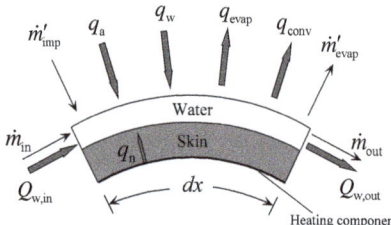

Figure 1. Control volume for the runback water on the airfoil surface.

Some parameters involved in the calculation of the anti-icing heat load, such as α, β and p_e, are determined by the solution of flow field, which can be divided into two steps. The first step is to solve the air flow field by using ANSYS FLUENT CFD code. The Spalart–Allmaras model was selected as the turbulence model. The second step is to calculate the water droplet impingement characteristics by means of the Eulerian approach [33]. A UDF (User Defined Function) [34] was built to solely calculate the water droplets' movement based on the simulation results of the air flow field. To calculate the anti-icing heat load precisely, the heat conduction calculation was also taken into consideration [35,36].

2.2. Optimization Method of the Anti-Icing Heat Load

Based on the numerical simulation of the anti-icing process, an optimization method was proposed to optimize the heat flux distribution. For the convenience of practical application, the entire protected area was divided into multiple heating zones, as illustrated in Figure 2 whose heating power can be adjusted independently. The heating power of each zone can be treated as an individual variable and all these independent variables ultimately constituted the heating power distributions. By organizing a set of equations described in Section 2.1, the function for calculating the anti-icing heat load was established. The input of this function was the heating power distribution, and the output was the anti-icing heat load. The optimization goal is to find an optimal heating power distribution that can reduce the anti-icing heat load in the evaporative mode and the constraint condition can be expressed as follows:

$$Q_t = \min \sum_{i=1}^{n} (q_{n,i} \cdot \Delta s_i) \tag{13}$$

subject to

$$\dot{m}_{\text{out,end}} = 0 \tag{14}$$

$$275K \leq T_i \leq T_{\max} \tag{15}$$

where the subscript end denotes the end of the protected area. Equation (14) means that the runback water does not flow out of the protected area, ensuring the system operates in the evaporation mode. Equation (15) makes the protected area free of any ice. Moreover, the mechanical properties of the aircraft structure are greatly affected by temperature. The ultimate strength, the yield strength and the fatigue life of many composite materials decrease as temperature increases [37]. Furthermore, large temperature differences may cause non-uniform expansions in different parts of the structure, resulting in thermal stresses, added to the other imposed stresses [38]. As a consequence, it is recommended that the maximum temperature should be limited to the temperature at which the material is allowed to stand.

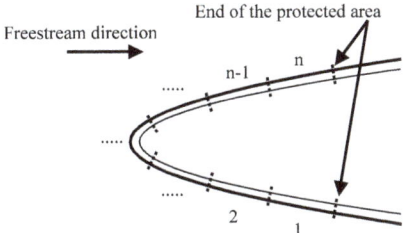

Figure 2. Division of heating zones within the protected area.

For the optimization problem, it is quite suitable to select the Genetic Algorithm (GA) [39]. The Genetic algorithm can deal with multiple individuals simultaneously in a population, which means that it evaluates multiple solutions in the searching space, reducing the risk of falling into the local optimal solution. Moreover, the fitness function is not constrained by continuous differentiability and its domain can be set arbitrarily. In the present study, a heating power distribution under the evaporative mode was encoded into the initial population. By following the selection, mutation and intersection, the initial population was evolved into the high fitness population through generations. Subsequently, the optimal heating power distribution that can reduce the anti-icing heat load was obtained. The flow chart of the optimization method is illustrated in Figure 3.

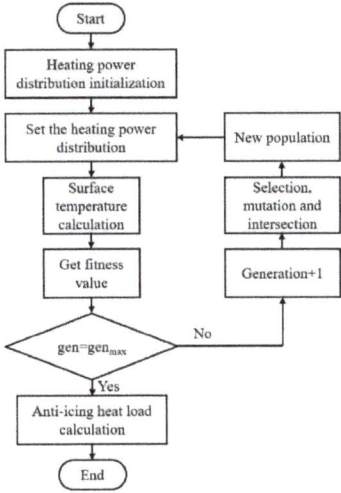

Figure 3. Flow chart of the optimization method by the genetic algorithm.

3. Experimental Setup and Test Model

In the present study, a comprehensive experimental campaign was performed to validate the numerical optimized results. The experimental campaign was conducted in an ejector-driven and straight-flow icing wind tunnel, as shown schematically in Figure 4. The icing wind tunnel consisted of three parts, namely the ejector-driven wind tunnel system, the temperature adjustment system and the spraying system. The ejector-driven wind tunnel system was controlled by a pressure-regulating valve in front of the ejector, and the wind speed in the test section can be regulated from 0 to 90 m/s. The temperature adjustment system was manipulated by another pressure-regulating valve ahead of the cooling turbine, and the ambient temperature inside the insulated chamber can be adjusted from −25 to 0 °C. The spraying system can simulate the icing weather condition of which the liquid water content (LWC) varies from 0.5 to 2 g/m^3 and the median volumetric diameter (MVD) varies from 15 to 40 µm. Additional details of the icing wind tunnel are provided in [40].

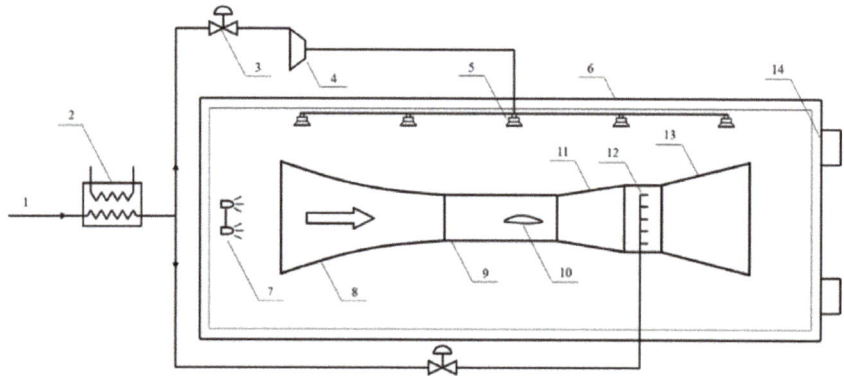

1. Compressed Air 2. Refrigerator Sets 3. Pressure Regulating Valve 4. Cooling Turbine 5. Air Diffuser 6. Insulated Chamber 7. Spray Nozzles
8. Entrance Section 9. Test Section 10. Test Model 11. Transition Section 12. Injector Section 13. Diffuser Section 14. Exhaust Vent

Figure 4. Schematic diagram of ejector-driven and straight-flow icing wind tunnel.

An NACA0012 airfoil with a chord length of 0.3 m and a span length of 0.2 m was designed as a scaled test model. As shown in Figure 5, the test model comprised one main body and two spliced parts. The main body was 20 mm wide and made of polymethyl methacrylate (PMMA). The spliced parts on both sides were 40 mm wide and made of polyurethane foam. Near the front, the insides of the main body and the spliced parts were hollowed out for wiring and temperature sensor installation. Three parts were bolted together and mounted vertically in the test section of the icing wind tunnel.

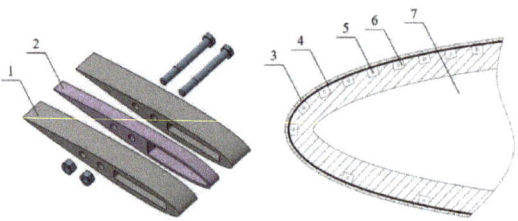

1. Spliced part (Polyurethane Foam) 2. Main Body (PMMA) 3. Erosion Shield (Stainless steel)
4. Heating Film 5. T-type Thermocouple 6. Copper Block 7. Interior (Elastic sealing foam)

Figure 5. Structure of the test model.

The internal structure, as well as the material composition inside the main body, is illustrated in Figure 5. The outermost layer was the erosion shield, made of stainless steel. To observe and record the location and the distribution of the water film during the experiment, marks were curved on the erosion shields of each spliced part. Next to the erosion shield was the electric heating film layer. The heating film was made of nickel-chromium alloys with the polyimide tape covering its both sides. The size of the heating part was 20 mm × 5 mm. The resistance of each heating film was calibrated before the experiment, and 24 V DC power supplies with the precision of ±0.01V were applied to control the heating power of each heating film, of which the maximum value can be reached to 60 kW/m². Since the NACA0012 airfoil was symmetrical, only one side needed to be investigated at the angle of attack (AOA) = 0°. Due to the size limitation of experimental conditions, the protected area on one side of the main body was divided into 8 heating zones to simulate various heating power distributions. Each heating zone was covered by an electric heating film which is displayed in Figure 6. The heating zone lengths streamwise are presented in Table 1. On the other side of the main body, the protected area was covered by a larger electric heating film of which the size was 80 mm × 20 mm. Similarly, the leading edges of the spliced parts were also wrapped by the electric heating films, as shown in Figure 6. These heating films were used to keep as much of the test model clean of ice to prevent ice accretion from interference in the measurement on the main body. Material properties of each layer are presented in Table 2.

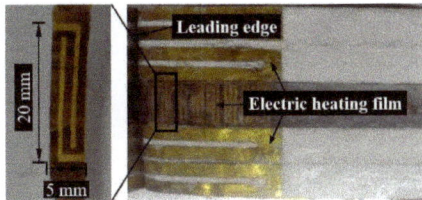

Figure 6. Configuration of the heating films on the test model.

Table 1. Heating zones length streamwise.

Heating Zones	Start (mm)	End (mm)	Heating Area (mm²)
1	0	2.5	50
2	2.5	7.5	100
3	7.5	12.5	100
4	12.5	17.5	100
5	17.5	22.5	100
6	22.5	27.5	100
7	27.5	32.5	100
8	32.5	37.5	100

Table 2. Material properties.

Material	Density, kg/m³	Specific Heat, kJ/(kg·K)	Conductivity, W/(m·K)	Thickness, mm
Stainless Steel	7930	0.5	16.3	0.10
Polyimide	1400	1.1	0.2	0.06
Nickel-Chromium Alloys	8400	0.46	12.2	0.03
PMMA(Poly Methyl Methacrylatemethacrylic Acid)	1190	1.47	0.19	4.00
Polyurethane Foam	3500	2.48	0.024	-

To obtain the surface temperature distribution without disturbing the heat transfer on the airfoil surface, several T-type thermocouples with the measurement range from −50 to 200 °C and the precision of ±0.5 °C, were installed beneath the heating film inside the main body. Each thermocouple was attached to a small piece of copper block which featured excellent thermal conductivity. Furthermore, the main body interior was filled with polyurethane elastic sealing foam which had a good adiabatic performance. As a consequence, the thermocouples were able to directly and precisely measure the surface temperature, which can be used to validate the numerical simulation and the optimization method.

4. Results and Discussions

According to the configuration of the icing wing tunnel and the test model, the computational domain of the numerical simulation was established and the boundary conditions were defined, which are displayed in Figure 7. After various tests, a structured grid with 3 million cells was used to calculate the flow field around the test model. The cells in the first boundary layer were refined to $y^+ \approx 1$. The experimental conditions are listed in Table 3. To validate the numerical simulation and the optimization methods, the numerical results were compared with the experimental results.

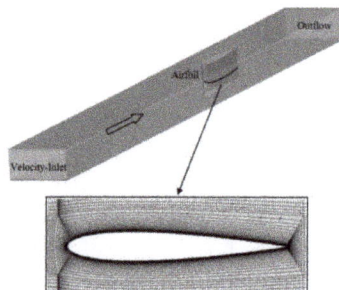

Figure 7. Computational domain size and boundary conditions.

Table 3. Experimental conditions.

Case	u_∞, m/s	T_∞, K	LWC, g/m³	MVD, μm
1	30	263.15	0.27	20
2	40	263.15	0.27	20
3	50	263.15	0.27	20

4.1. Validation of the Numerical Simulation

4.1.1. Convective Heat Transfer Coefficient

The convective heat transfer coefficient plays an important role in the calculation of the anti-icing heat load. In the icing wind tunnel test, the experimental cases were conducted without the spraying system turned on. When the steady state conditions were achieved, the heating films were adjusted to a uniform temperature, typically in the range of 32 to 38 °C [41]. Roughly three minutes were required to record the temperature and heat flux distribution. The convective heat transfer coefficient can be derived by

$$\alpha_i = \frac{q_i}{T_{s,i} - T_\infty} \qquad (16)$$

where q_i is the power density of the ith heating film. The measurements of the convective heat transfer coefficient were carried out from Case 1 to Case 3. The comparisons of the results of the numerical simulation and the experiment are displayed in Figure 8. As can be seen, the distributions of the convective heat transfer coefficient in all cases show a decreasing tendency, which drops more at the leading edge and less backwards. This kind of distribution means that the leading edge has intensive heat transfer. The maximum error between the numerical and experimental results is less than 15%. In general, there is an acceptable agreement between the numerical and the experimental results.

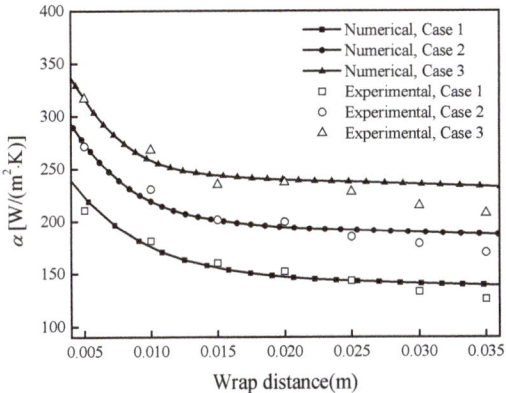

Figure 8. Comparisons of the convective heat transfer coefficients.

4.1.2. Water Droplet Impinging Limit

The water droplet impinging limit in each case was measured by the rime ice method, which can form the thin rime ice on the surface of the test model. The pictures of the experimental results are shown in Figure 9, which are 17.5 mm in Case 1, 20 mm in Case 2 and 22.5 mm in Case 3. As can be seen, the water droplet impinging limits increase with the increase in the wind speed. There is more ice accretion at the leading edge and less at the impinging limit, which means the water droplet collection efficiency has a decreasing tendency along with the chord. The comparison between experimental results and numerical simulation of the water droplet collection efficiencies are shown in Figure 10. The results indicate that the numerical water droplet impinging limits are generally consistent with the experimental ones, which means the numerical simulation and the experiments are reliable.

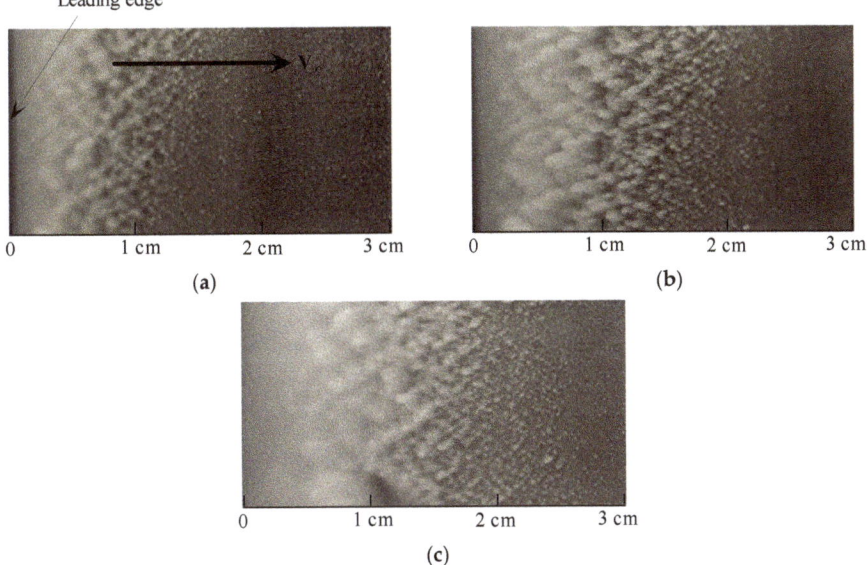

Figure 9. Experimental results of the water droplet impinging limits: (**a**) Case 1; (**b**) Case 2; (**c**) Case 3.

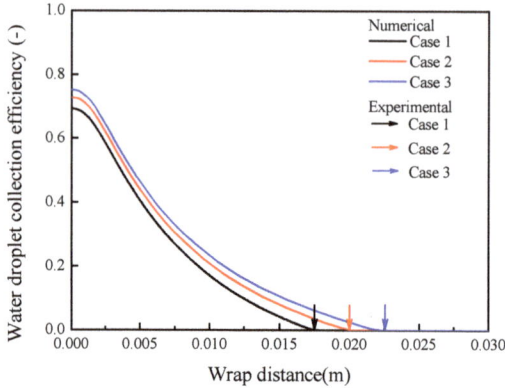

Figure 10. Numerical and experimental results of the water droplet impinging limits.

4.1.3. Surface Temperature

The heating power distributions used for the surface temperature validation are listed in Table 4. Figure 11 displays the numerical and experimental results of surface temperature distributions. As can be seen, the surface temperature distributions had humps in the middle of the protected area, which was caused by completely evaporating the runback water. There were small discrepancies between the experimental and numerical results in the low-temperature regions, while the differences became larger in the high-temperature regions. This was because the thermal conduction from the main body to the spliced parts of the test model was not considered in the numerical simulation. The maximum error between the numerical and experimental results was about 8.8%, and the average error was about 4.1%, which was acceptable.

Table 4. Heating power distributions for the surface temperature validation.

Case	Heating Film Power Density (kW/m^2)							
	1	2	3	4	5	6	7	8
1	19.9	17.2	15.4	14.9	13.1	7.2	7.3	7.2
2	24.8	21.0	18.4	15.1	9.0	8.8	9.0	8.9
3	30.3	27.1	19.6	18.6	17.9	10.7	10.9	10.8

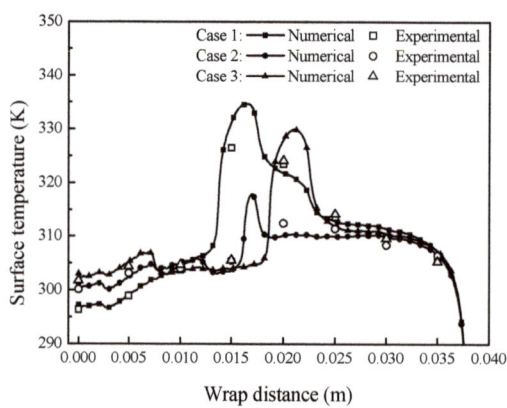

Figure 11. Numerical and experimental results of the surface temperature.

4.2. The Optimal Heating Power Distribution

To optimize the heating power distribution, the experiments started with the critical dry surface state which is the boundary between the dry surface mode and the evaporative mode. The dry surface mode was easily accessible in the experiment. Firstly, the heat power distribution was set up at a high level to ensure no runback water within the protected area. Then, from 8# to 1#, the power density of each heating film was reduced as low as possible until the critical dry surface state emerged. Then, the power density of 1# heating film was turned down and the power density of 2# heating film was turned up till the runback water covered 1# heating zone. After that, the power density of 1# and 2# heating films were turned down and the power density of 3# heating film was turned up till the runback water covered 2# heating zone, and so on till the runback water covered the entire protected area. Figure 12 shows the experimental heating power distributions with the runback water covering the different heating zones in each case. The corresponding anti-icing heat loads of the heating power distributions are also displayed in Figure 12. The results show that the anti-icing heat loads had a decreasing tendency as the runback water covered more protected areas. In Case 1, the anti-icing heat load had a minimum value when the runback water covered 4# heating zone and was reduced by 23.8% compared to the initial heating power distribution. In Cases 2 and 3, the anti-icing heat loads had minimum values when the runback water covered 5# heating zones and were reduced by 19.6% and 18.6%, respectively, compared to the initial heating power distributions. It can be seen from Table 2 and Figure 10 that the water droplet impinging limit of Case 1 was located in 4# heating zone while the water droplet impinging limits of Cases 2 and 3 were located in 5# heating zones. This indicates that the anti-icing heat load can be reduced to a minimum value as the runback water reaches the water droplet impinging limit.

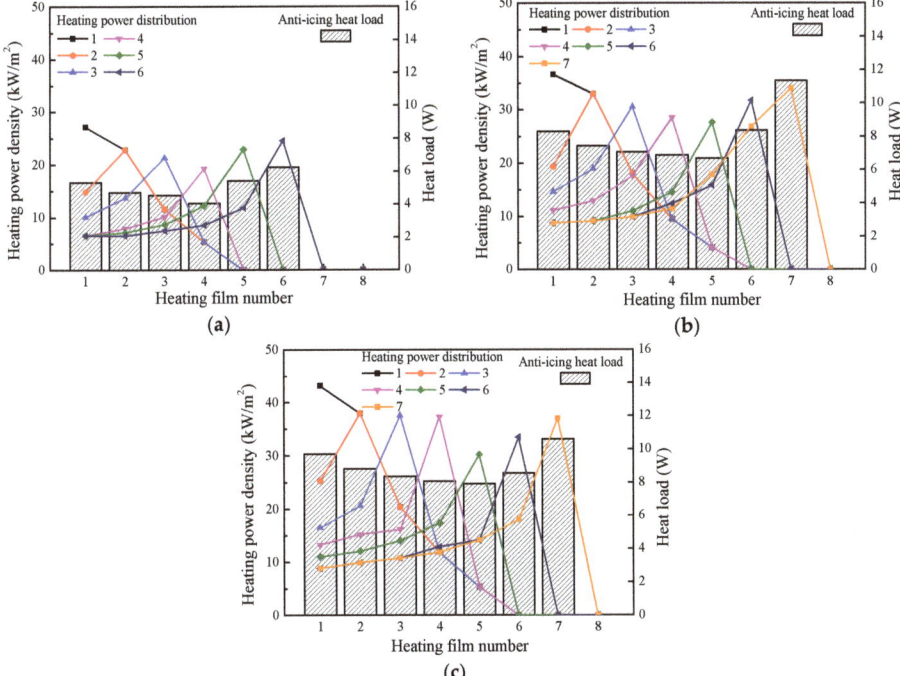

Figure 12. Heating power distributions and the anti-icing heat loads with different runback water locations: (**a**) Case 1; (**b**) Case 2; (**c**) Case 3.

Considering that the PMMA has a poor temperature tolerance among the materials of the test model, the maximum temperature in Equation (15) is set to be 353 K [42]. The comparison of the optimized and the experimental results are displayed in Figure 13. The optimal heating power distributions of the optimization and the experiment were generally consistent in the trends, which were both low at the leading edge, high at the water droplet impinging limit and zero at the end of the protected area. The anti-icing heat loads in the experiment were a little larger than those in the optimization because of the differences of the heating power distributions at the leading edge and the impinging limit. The difference between the optimizations and the experiments in the heating power distribution is that the experimental results are higher at the leading edge and lower at the water droplet impinging limit. As a matter of fact, during the experiment, when the heating power density at the leading edge was reduced excessively, the runback water film became unstable and easily turned into the rivulets, which failed the ice protection. However, the numerical simulation did not consider this process, which made the differences in the anti-icing heat load as well as the surface temperature.

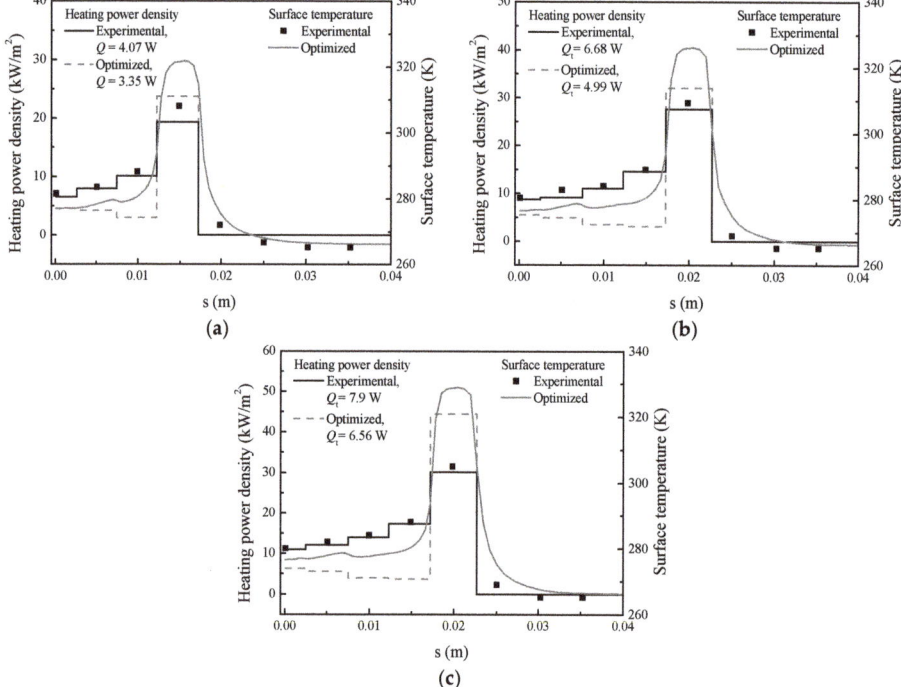

Figure 13. Comparison of the optimized and experimental results: (**a**) Case 1; (**b**) Case 2; (**c**) Case 3.

4.3. Mechanism of the Anti-Icing Heat Load Reduction

According to the results of the optimization and the experiments, the optimal heating power distribution has such a characteristic that is low at the leading edge, high at the water droplet impinging limit and zero at the end of the protected area. This tendency can lead to a less anti-icing heat load. To find out the mechanism behind this consequence, it is necessary to figure out the composition of the anti-icing heat load. Integrating the control volume within the protected area, Equation (2) can be written as:

$$\int_A q_n dx = \int_A \left(q_{evap} + q_{conv} - q_w - q_a \right) dx + \int_A \left(Q_{w,in} - Q_{w,out} \right) \tag{17}$$

where A refers to the protected area. The third term in Equation (16) should be zero because neither the inflow enthalpy nor the outflow enthalpy exists in the evaporative mode, except the enthalpy of water droplet impingement. According to References [24] and [31], q_w and q_a are usually much smaller than the others, which can also be neglected. Therefore, Equation (16) can be simplified as:

$$\int_A q_n dx = \int_A q_{evap} dx + \int_A q_{conv} dx \tag{18}$$

or

$$Q_t = Q_{evap} + Q_{conv} \tag{19}$$

where Q_t is the total anti-icing heat load, Q_{evap} is the evaporative heat load and Q_{conv} is the convective heat load.

It follows that the anti-icing heat load is mainly composed of the evaporative and convective heat loads. As can be seen from Equation (10), Q_{evap} includes both the latent part and the sensible part. In the evaporative mode, supposing the thermal anti-icing system operates in a stable environment, the total amount of the collected water droplets remains constant. Consequently, Q_{evap} does not change much even under different heating power distributions. As a result, the reduction in the anti-icing heat load can only be the decrease in Q_{conv}. It is well known that Q_{conv} is influenced by the heating range, the surface temperature as well as the convective heat transfer coefficient. Analyzing the influences of these factors is conducive to reveal the mechanism of the anti-icing heat load reduction.

4.3.1. Heating Range

The anti-icing heat loads reached the minimum value as the runback water exactly covered the water droplet impinging limit as shown in Figure 12. It indicates that the heating range is important to the anti-icing heat load reduction. To better investigate its influence, a uniform heating power distribution was experimentally tested. In this experiment, only the wet area covered by the runback water was heated, and the dry area was not heated. Hence, the heating range can be represented by the runback water length. Additionally, when the runback water length was less than the water droplet impinging limit, the heating range was fixed at the limit.

The experimental and the numerical results are displayed in Figure 14, which presents the relationship between the anti-icing heat load and the range of the runback water length. As can be seen, both the experimental and the numerical anti-icing heat loads had minimum values as the runback water lengths were at the water droplet impinging limits. The evaporative heat loads barely change with the heating power density. The trend of the convective heat load is similar to the anti-icing heat load, which has an inflection point corresponding to the impinging limit. This can be explained in two aspects. On one hand, when the heating power density was higher than the value at the impinging limit, the runback water length decrease. However, the heating range was fixed at the impinging limit, so the anti-icing heat load increased. On the other hand, when the heating power density was lower than the value at the impinging limit, both the runback water length and the heating range increased, as did the anti-icing heat load. Therefore, decreasing the heating range outside the water droplet impinging limit can effectively reduce the anti-icing heat load. As the heating range is equal to the impinging limit, the anti-icing heat load is the minimum.

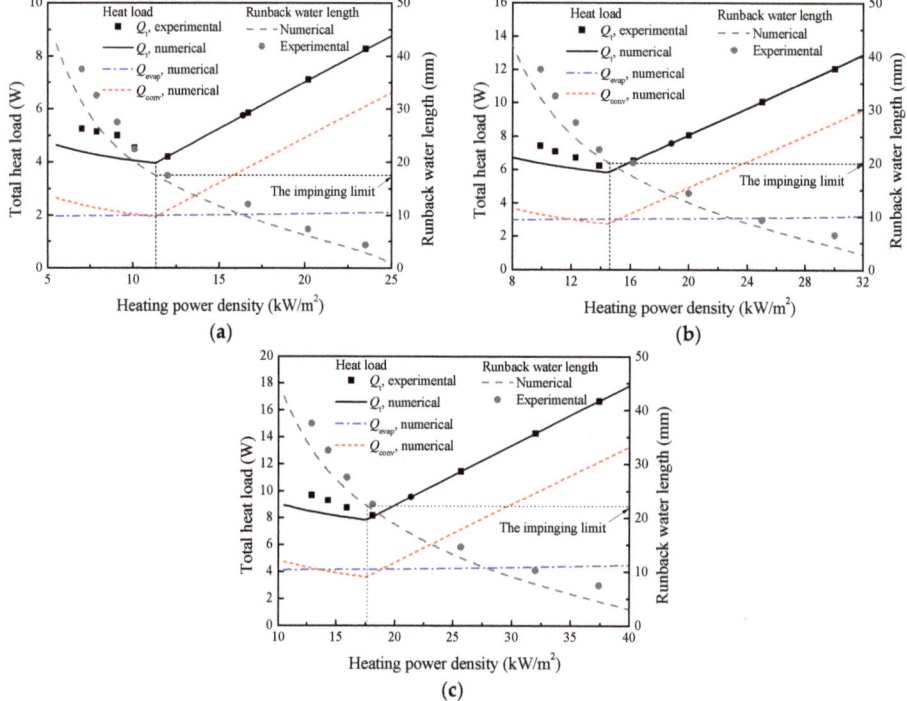

Figure 14. Relationship between the anti-icing heat load and the heating range: (**a**) Case 1; (**b**) Case 2; (**c**) Case 3.

4.3.2. Surface Temperature

Figure 15 displays the surface temperature distributions and the proportions of the convection and evaporation under the optimal heating power distributions. As can be seen, the evaporation has a higher proportion in the high-temperature regions, while the convection has a higher proportion in the low-temperature regions. This suggests that the temperature has different impacts on convection and evaporation. To better illustrate the influences of the surface temperature, the following parameters are selected as representative values: $\alpha = 200$ W/(m²·K), $T_e = 263.15$ K, $p_e = 101.325$ kPa. The changes in the evaporative and convective heat fluxes with the surface temperature are displayed in Figure 16. Noted that the evaporative heat flux can directly denote the evaporative mass transfer of the runback water according to Equation (10). According to Equations (4), (5), (10) and (11), the convective heat flux has a linear relationship while the evaporative heat flux has an exponential relationship with the surface temperature. As can be seen, when the same amount of water is evaporated simultaneously at both high and low temperatures, the temperature rise required in the high-temperature region is less than that in the low-temperature region. Moreover, the additional convective heat flux rise in the high-temperature region is less than that in the low-temperature region. For instance, as the evaporative heat flux increases from 0 to 30 kW/m², the temperature will have an increment of about 49 K. However, as the evaporative heat flux increases from 60 to 90 kW/m², the temperature rise is less than 10 K, which leads to a significant reduction in the convective heat load. Therefore, evaporating most runback water in the high-temperature region can surely reduce the convective heat load.

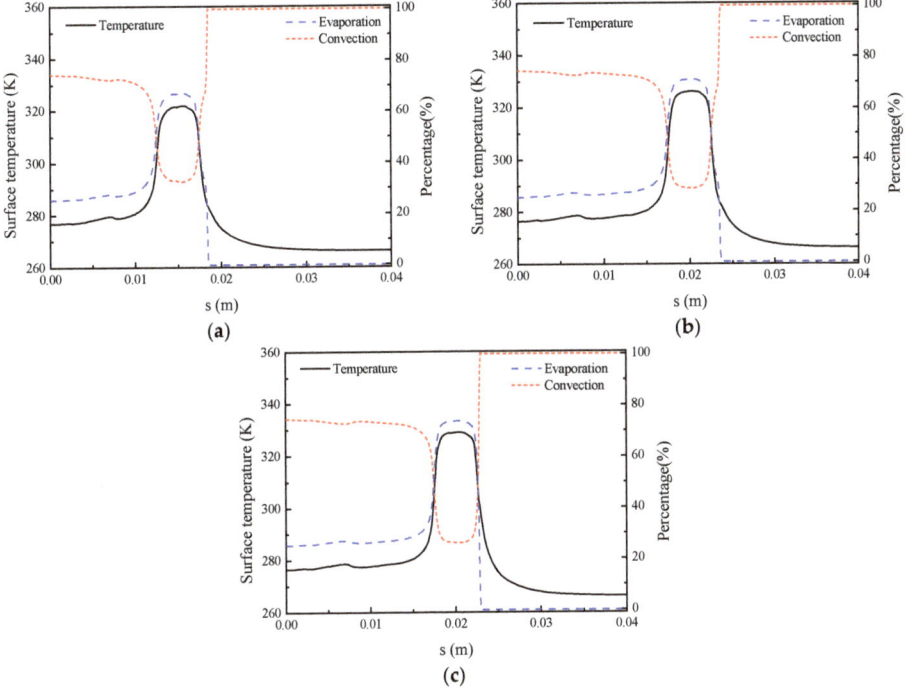

Figure 15. Surface temperature and the proportions of Q_{evap} and Q_{conv}: (**a**) Case 1; (**b**) Case 2; (**c**) Case 3.

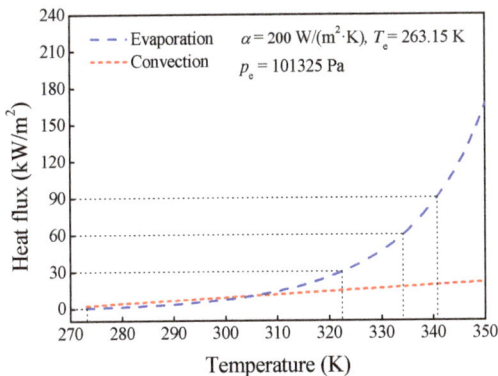

Figure 16. Changes of q_{evap} and q_{conv} with the surface temperature.

4.3.3. Convective Heat Transfer Coefficient

The surface temperature distribution is not only influenced by the heating power distribution, but also by the characteristics of the convective heat transfer. Supposed that a constant heating power density of 30 kW/m² is provided within the protected area, T_e and pe are selected as representative values: T_e = 263.15 K, p_e = 101.325 kPa. According to Equations (10), (11) and (18), the changes of q_{evap} and q_{conv} as well as the surface temperature with the convective heat transfer coefficient are displayed in Figure 17a. As can be seen with the increase in the convective heat transfer coefficient, q_{conv} tends to increase, while the surface temperature tends to decrease, so does q_{evap}. The results show that q_{evap}

has a higher proportion in the region with the small convective heat transfer coefficient, while q_{conv} has a higher proportion in the region with the large convective heat transfer coefficient.

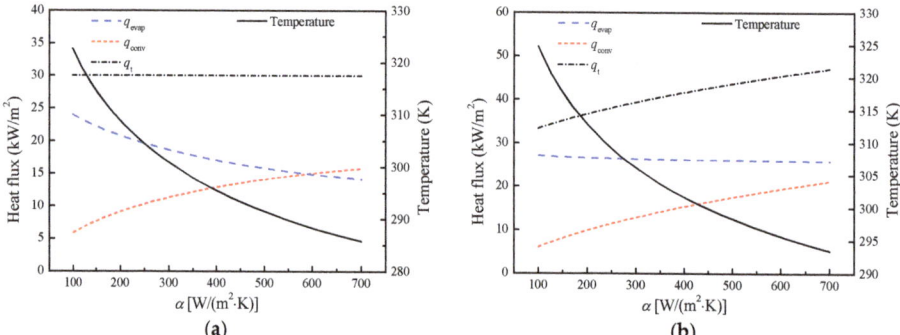

Figure 17. Changes of q_{evap}, q_{conv} and the surface temperature with α: (**a**) Constant q_t; (**b**) Constant $\dot{m}'_{evap}$.

Given the constant mass flow rate of the evaporation, of which $\dot{m}'_{evap}$ is equal to 0.01 kg/(m²·s), the changes of q_{evap} and q_{conv}, as well as the surface temperature with the convective heat transfer coefficient, are displayed in Figure 17b. As can be seen with the increase in the convective heat transfer coefficient, q_{conv} tends to increase, while the surface temperature tends to decrease. However, due to constant $\dot{m}'_{evap}$, the heating power density tends to increase. The results show that, when evaporating the same amount of water, the anti-icing heat load in the region with the small convective heat transfer coefficient is smaller than that in the region with the large convective heat transfer coefficient.

According to the influence of the surface temperature, evaporating the runback water in the high-temperature region can reduce the anti-icing heat load. The surface temperature can easily be raised in the region with the small convective heat transfer coefficient. For the flow field around the airfoil surface, the convective heat transfer coefficient is always large in the vicinity of the leading edge and small at the end of the protected area, due to the increase in the boundary layer thickness and the turbulence. The trend of the optimal heating power distribution is opposite to that of the convective heat transfer coefficient. Thus, the anti-icing heat load can be reduced.

5. Conclusions

In this paper, the optimal heating power distribution that leads to the less anti-icing heat load in the evaporative mode was investigated both in the numerical optimization and the experiment. By analyzing the influences of the key factors on the convective heat load, the mechanism of the anti-icing heat load reduction was revealed.

(1) The reduction in the anti-icing heat load is the decrease in the convective heat load. As the thermal anti-icing system operating in the evaporative mode, the evaporative heat load keeps nearly constant. The convective heat load can be varied with the surface temperature distribution which is influenced by the heating power distribution. Thus, there must be an optimal heating power distribution that can reduce the convective heat load as well as the anti-icing heat load.

(2) The optimal heating power density obtained by the numerical optimization and the experiment has such characteristics that are low at the leading edge, high at the water droplet impinging limit and zero at the end of the protected area. These characteristics are mainly influenced by the heating range, the surface temperature and the convective heat transfer coefficient. In the evaporative mode, decreasing the heating range outside the protected area can reduce the anti-icing heat load effectively. As the heating range is decreased to the impinging limit, the anti-icing heat load has the minimum value. Due to the different impacts of the surface temperature on the evaporative

and convective heat fluxes, it is better to evaporate the runback water in the high-temperature region, which can lead to a lesser additional convective heat load. The surface temperature distribution is affected by the convective heat transfer coefficient distribution of which the trend is high at the leading edge and decreases chordwise around the airfoil surface. As a consequence, the optimal heating power distribution has the opposite trend with the convective heat transfer coefficient distribution.

The present investigations on the mechanism of the anti-icing heat load reduction can provide valuable guidance for the design of the thermal anti-icing system, which can be used for wings, stabilizers and engine inlets of the aircraft as well as wind blades and cowlings of the wind turbines, or any component that has an aerodynamic profile. The configuration of the thermal anti-icing system can be improved according to the presented results, which can achieve the purpose of saving energy and reducing weight. However, the results obtained in this paper have certain limitations. Considering the anti-icing requirement in practical applications, the margins of both the anti-icing heat load and the protected area ought to be increased appropriately, and extra constraints such as maximum heating power density should also be taken into consideration.

Author Contributions: Conceptualization, R.L. and D.Z.; Methodology, R.L.; Software, R.L.; Validation, R.L. and G.Z.; Formal Analysis, R.L.; Investigation, R.L.; Resources, D.Z.; Data Curation, R.L.; Writing—Original Draft Preparation, R.L.; Writing—Review and Editing, G.Z. and D.Z.; Visualization, R.L.; Supervision, D.Z.; Project Administration, D.Z.; Funding Acquisition, D.Z. All authors have read and agreed to the published version of the manuscript

Funding: This research received no external funding.

Acknowledgments: The authors are grateful to Guangya Zhu and Qihang Lu for proofreading this manuscript.

Conflicts of Interest: The authors declare no conflict of interest.

References

1. Green, S. A Study of U.S. Inflight Icing Accidents and Incidents, 1978 to 2002. In Proceedings of the 44th AIAA Aerospace Sciences Meeting and Exhibit, Reno, NV, USA,, 9–12 January 2006. AIAA-2006-82.
2. Thomas, S.K.; Cassoni, R.P.; MacArthur, C.D. Aircraft anti-icing and de-icing techniques and modeling. *J. Aircr.* **1996**, *33*, 841–854. [CrossRef]
3. Cronin, M. The prospects and potential of all electric aircraft. Aircraft Design. In Proceedings of the Systems and Technology Meeting, Fort Worth, TX, USA, 17–19 October 1983. AIAA-83-2478.
4. Ingram, C.; Dendinger, T.; Inclan, E.; Charront, Y.; Handschuh, K.; Chakraborty, I.; García, E.; Mavris, D.N. Integrating Subsystem Sizing into the More Electric Aircraft Conceptual Design Phase. In Proceedings of the 53rd AIAA Aerospace Sciences Meeting, Kissimmee, FL, USA, 5–9 January 2015. AIAA-2015-1682.
5. Chakraborty, I.; Ozcan, M.F.; Mavris, D.N. Effect of Major Subsystem Power Off-takes on Aircraft Performance in More Electric Aircraft Architectures. In Proceedings of the 15th AIAA Aviation Technology, Integration, and Operations Conference, Dallas, TX, USA, 22–26 January 2015. AIAA-2015-3287.
6. Gandolfi, R.; Pellegrini, L.; De Oliveira, S. More Electric Aircraft Analysis Using Exergy as a Design Comparison Tool. In Proceedings of the 48th AIAA Aerospace Sciences Meeting Including the New Horizons Forum and Aerospace Exposition, Orlando, FL, USA, 4–7 January 2010. AIAA 2010-809.
7. Ensign, T.; Gallman, J. Energy Optimized Equipment Systems for General Aviation Jets. In Proceedings of the 44th Aerospace Sciences Meeting and Exhibit, Reno, NV, USA, 9–12 January 2006. AIAA 2006-228.
8. Wang, P.; Wei, W.; Li, Z.; Duan, W.; Han, H.; Xie, Q. A superhydrophobic fluorinated PDMS composite as a wearable strain sensor with excellent mechanical robustness and liquid impalement resistance. *J. Mater. Chem. A* **2020**, *8*, 3509–3516. [CrossRef]
9. He, Z.; Zhuo, Y.; Wang, F.; He, J.; Zhang, Z. Design and preparation of icephobic PDMS-based coatings by introducing an aqueous lubricating layer and macro-crack initiators at the ice-substrate interface. *Prog. Org. Coat.* **2020**, *147*, 105737. [CrossRef]

10. Brassard, J.-D.; Laforte, J.-L.; Blackburn, C.; Perron, J.; Sarkar, D.K. Silicone based superhydrophobic coating efficient to reduce ice adhesion and accumulation on aluminum under offshore arctic conditions. *Ocean. Eng.* **2017**, *144*, 135–141. [CrossRef]
11. Ma, L.; Wang, J.; Zhao, F.; Wu, D.; Huang, Y.; Zhang, D.; Zhang, Z.; Fu, W.; Li, X.; Fan, Y. Plasmon-mediated photothermal and superhydrophobic TiN-PTFE film for anti-icing/de-icing applications. *Compos. Sci. Technol.* **2019**, *181*, 107696. [CrossRef]
12. Lv, J.; Zhu, C.; Qiu, H.; Zhang, J.; Gu, C.; Feng, J. Robust icephobic epoxy coating using maleic anhydride as a crosslinking agent. *Prog. Org. Coat.* **2020**, *142*, 105561. [CrossRef]
13. Wang, P.; Yao, T.; Li, Z.; Wei, W.; Xie, Q.; Duan, W.; Han, H. A superhydrophobic/electrothermal synergistically anti-icing strategy based on graphene composite. *Compos. Sci. Technol.* **2020**, *198*, 108307. [CrossRef]
14. Silva, G.; Silvares, O.; Zerbini, E.; Hefazi, H.; Chen, H.-H.; Kaups, K. Differential Boundary-Layer Analysis and Runback Water Flow Model Applied to Flow Around Airfoils with Thermal Anti-ice. In Proceedings of the 1st AIAA Atmospheric and Space Environments Conference, San Antonio, TX, USA, 22–25 June 2009. AIAA 2009-3967.
15. Broeren, A.P.; Whalen, E.A.; Busch, G.T.; Bragg, M.B. Aerodynamic Simulation of Runback Ice Accretion. *J. Aircr.* **2010**, *47*, 924–939. [CrossRef]
16. Whalen, E.; Broeren, A.; Bragg, M.; Lee, S. Characteristics of Runback Ice Accretions on Airfoils and their Aerodynamics Effects. In Proceedings of the 43rd Aerospace Sciences Meeting and Exhibit, Reno, NV, USA, 10–13 January 2005. AIAA-2005-1065.
17. Alègre, N.; Hammond, D. Experimental Setup for the Study of Runback Ice at Full Scale. *J. Aircr.* **2011**, *48*, 1978–1983. [CrossRef]
18. Wright, W.B. *User's Manual for the Improved NASA Lewis Ice Accretion Code LEWICE 1.6*; CR-198355; NASA: Washington, DC, USA, 1995.
19. Wright, W.B. *User's Manual for the NASA Glenn Ice Accretion Code LEWICE Version 2.0*; CR-209409; NASA: Washington, DC, USA, 1999.
20. Morency, F.; Brahimi, T.; Tezok, F.; Paraschivoiu, I. Hot air anti-icing system modelization in the ice prediction code CANICE. In Proceedings of the 36th AIAA Aerospace Sciences Meeting and Exhibit, Reno, NV, USA, 12–15 January 1998. AIAA Paper 1998-0192.
21. Morency, F.; Tezok, F.; Paraschivoiu, I.; Para, F.; Morency, O. Anti-Icing System Simulation Using CANICE. *J. Aircr.* **1999**, *36*, 999–1006. [CrossRef]
22. Baruzzi, G.; Tran, P.; Habashi, W.; Narramore, J. Actuator Disk Implementation in FENSAP-ICE, a 3D Navier-Stokes In-Flight Simulation System. In Proceedings of the 41st Aerospace Sciences Meeting and Exhibit, Reno, NV, USA, 6–9 January 2003. AIAA-2003-0619.
23. Morency, F.; Beaugendre, H.; Habashi, W.G. FENSAP-ICE: A study of the effect of ice shapes on droplet impingement. In Proceedings of the 41st Aerospace Sciences Meeting and Exhibit, Reno, NV, USA, 6–9 January 2003. AIAA-2003-1223.
24. Al-Khalil, K.M.; Horvath, C.; Miller, D.R.; Wright, W. Validation of NASA Thermal Ice Protection Computer Codes. III –Validation of ANTICE. In Proceedings of the 35th Aerospace Sciences Meeting and Exhibit, Reno, NV, USA, 6–9 January 1997. AIAA 1997-51.
25. Saeed, F.; Paraschivoiu, I. Optimization of a Hot-Air Anti-Icing System. In Proceedings of the 41st Aerospace Sciences Meeting and Exhibit, Reno, NV, USA, 6–9 January 2003. AIAA-2003-0733.
26. Pellissier, M.P.C.; Habashi, W.G.; Pueyo, A. Optimization via FENSAP-ICE of Aircraft Hot-Air Anti-Icing Systems. *J. Aircr.* **2011**, *48*, 265–276. [CrossRef]
27. Chen, L.; Zhang, Y.; Wu, Q. Heat transfer optimization and experimental validation of anti-icing component for helicopter rotor. *Appl. Eng.* **2017**, *127*, 662–670. [CrossRef]
28. Pourbagian, M.; Habashi, W.G. Surrogate-Based Optimization of Electrothermal Wing Anti-Icing Systems. *J. Aircr.* **2013**, *50*, 1555–1563. [CrossRef]
29. Pourbagian, M.; Habashi, W. On Optimal Design of Electro-Thermal In-Flight Ice Protection Systems. In Proceedings of the 5th AIAA Atmospheric and Space Environments Conference, San Diego, CA, USA, 24–27 June 2013. AIAA 2013-2937.
30. Pourbagian, M.; Talgorn, B.; Habashi, W.G.; Kokkolaras, M.; Le Digabel, S. Constrained problem formulations for power optimization of aircraft electro-thermal anti-icing systems. *Optim. Eng.* **2015**, *16*, 663–693. [CrossRef]

31. Chang, S.; Zhao, Y.; Yang, B.; Leng, M.; Wang, C. Study on the Minimum Anti-Icing Energy Based on the Icing Limit State. *J. Aircr.* **2016**, *53*, 1690–1696. [CrossRef]
32. Messinger, B.L. Equilibrium Temperature of an Unheated Icing Surface as a Function of Air Speed. *J. Aeronaut. Sci.* **1953**, *20*, 29–42. [CrossRef]
33. Chen, W. Numerical Simulation of Ice Accretion on Airfoil. Ph.D. Thesis, Nanjing University of Aeronautics and Astronautics, Nanjing, China, 2007.
34. Villalpando, F.; Reggio, M.; Ilinca, A. Prediction of ice accretion and anti-icing heating power on wind turbine blades using standard commercial software. *Energy* **2016**, *114*, 1041–1052. [CrossRef]
35. Al-Khalil, K.M. Numerical Simulation of an Aircraft Anti-icing System Incorporating a Rivulet Model for the Runback Water. Ph.D. Thesis, The University of Toledo, Toledo, OH, USA, 1991.
36. Elangovan, R.; Olsen, R. Analysis of Layered Composite Skin Electro-Thermal Anti-Icing System. In Proceedings of the 46th AIAA Aerospace Sciences Meeting and Exhibit, Reno, NV, USA, 7–10 January 2008. AIAA 2008-446.
37. Mivehchi, H.; Varvani-Farahani, A. The effect of temperature on fatigue strength and cumulative fatigue damage of FRP composites. *Procedia Eng.* **2010**, *2*, 2011–2020. [CrossRef]
38. National Research Council. *Accelerated Aging of Materials and Structures*; The National Academies Press: Washington, DC, USA, 1996; pp. 24–25.
39. Goldberg, D.E. *Genetic Algorithms in Search, Optimization, and Machine Learning*; Addison-Wesley Professional: Longman, MA, USA, 1989; pp. 55–60.
40. Meng, F. Study on Key Problems in Airfoil Icing Simulation. Ph.D. Thesis, Nanjing University of Aeronautics and Astronautics, Nanjing, China, 2013.
41. Poinsatte, P.E.; Newton, J.E.; De Witt, K.J.; Van Fossen, G.J. Heat transfer measurements from a smooth NACA 0012 airfoil. *J. Aircr.* **1991**, *28*, 892–898. [CrossRef]
42. Abdel-Wahab, A.; Ataya, S.; Silberschmidt, V.V. Temperature-dependent mechanical behaviour of PMMA: Experimental analysis and modelling. *Polym. Test.* **2017**, *58*, 86–95. [CrossRef]

Publisher's Note: MDPI stays neutral with regard to jurisdictional claims in published maps and institutional affiliations.

© 2020 by the authors. Licensee MDPI, Basel, Switzerland. This article is an open access article distributed under the terms and conditions of the Creative Commons Attribution (CC BY) license (http://creativecommons.org/licenses/by/4.0/).

Article

A Framework for Big Data Analytical Process and Mapping—BAProM: Description of an Application in an Industrial Environment

Giovanni Gravito de Carvalho Chrysostomo [1], Marco Vinicius Bhering de Aguiar Vallim [1], Leilton Santos da Silva [2], Leandro A. Silva [1,*] and Arnaldo Rabello de Aguiar Vallim Filho [3,*]

1. Postgraduate Program in Electrical Engineering and Computing, Mackenzie Presbyterian University, Rua da Consolação, 896, Prédio 30—Consolação, São Paulo 01302-907, Brazil; giovannigravito@gmail.com (G.G.d.C.C.); vallim.marco@gmail.com (M.V.B.d.A.V.)
2. EMAE—Metropolitan Company of Water & Energy, Avenida Nossa Senhora do Sabará, 5312—Vila Emir, São Paulo 04447-902, Brazil; leilton@emae.com.br
3. Computer Science Department, Mackenzie Presbyterian University, Rua da Consolação, 896, Prédio 31—Consolação, São Paulo 01302-907, Brazil
* Correspondence: leandroaugusto.silva@mackenzie.br (L.A.S.); aavallim@mackenzie.br (A.R.d.A.V.F.)

Received: 30 July 2020; Accepted: 9 November 2020; Published: 18 November 2020

Abstract: This paper presents an application of a framework for Big Data Analytical Process and Mapping—BAProM—consisting of four modules: Process Mapping, Data Management, Data Analysis, and Predictive Modeling. The framework was conceived as a decision support tool for industrial business, encompassing the whole big data analytical process. The first module incorporates in big data analytical a mapping of processes and variables, which is not common in such processes. This is a proposal that proved to be adequate in the practical application that was developed. Next, an analytical "workbench" was implemented for data management and exploratory analysis (Modules 2 and 3) and, finally, in Module 4, the implementation of artificial intelligence algorithm support predictive processes. The modules are adaptable to different types of industry and problems and can be applied independently. The paper presents a real-world application seeking as final objective the implementation of a predictive maintenance decision support tool in a hydroelectric power plant. The process mapping in the plant identified four subsystems and 100 variables. With the support of the analytical workbench, all variables have been properly analyzed. All underwent a cleaning process and many had to be transformed, before being subjected to exploratory analysis. A predictive model, based on a decision tree (DT), was implemented for predictive maintenance of equipment, identifying critical variables that define the imminence of an equipment failure. This DT model was combined with a time series forecasting model, based on artificial neural networks, to project those critical variables for a future time. The real-world application showed the practical feasibility of the framework, particularly the effectiveness of the analytical workbench, for pre-processing and exploratory analysis, as well as the combined predictive model, proving effectiveness by providing information on future events leading to equipment failures.

Keywords: big data process; predictive maintenance; machine learning

---

1. Introduction

Interest in data-based knowledge applied to decision-making processes has been growing in different industrial segments [1]. The importance of this movement of data-driven decisions is understood, since organizations with better performance have used data analysis five times more than those with low performance [2].

This movement of implementing a so-called KDD—knowledge discovery in databases—environment is relatively new in industrial business, and it is due, on the one hand, to the huge volume of data generated (big data), which is largely the result of the Internet of Things (IoT), where sensors connected to a variety of objects, spread across the planet, have accelerated the big data phenomenon. On the other hand, data availability has sparked interest in using these historical data to support decisions, based on mathematical models and algorithms, mainly those of artificial intelligence (AI), which allow predictions of different types of events, such as the imminence of equipment failure, triggering a preventive maintenance schedule [3].

The combination of concepts, such as big data, IoT and AI, has had a considerable impact on industrial business, defining the main dimension of Industry 4.0, which can be defined as a concept that encompasses automation and information technology, transforming raw materials into value-added products from data-driven sources [3,4].

One of the main areas is AI-based predictive maintenance. In this type of maintenance rather than scheduling operation suspension for maintenance, based on fixed time intervals, the best stopping moment is defined based on AI inference, as a result of an analytical model, calibrated (trained) on the basis of historical data [4–6].

A continuous monitoring of equipment, by AI algorithms, can have an important impact by allowing the reduction of corrective maintenance, which occurs unexpectedly and is strongly undesirable, compromising budgets and industrial production. Advance information that an equipment failure is close allows for proactive and planned actions to mitigate these financial impacts. This is clearly a trade-off between investment in research and development and equipment productivity [7,8].

New companies are already starting operations considering the modern concepts of Industry 4.0, but traditional industries are also entering this new world, seeking to improve their processes by including Industry 4.0 elements.

1.1. Motivation

In this paper, we will deal with one of these cases. It is a real-world case of a hydroelectric power plant, operating since 1926, which despite being an operation within traditional standards, has, over time, been updated to receive monitoring systems based on data collection sensors. The objective now was to go one step further, developing an analytical "workbench" for data exploration and, furthermore, implementing applications of AI algorithms to support a predictive process.

So far, the plant updating process has been developed incrementally, but with little documentation. The mapping of processes and sensors, for example, were not fully updated. Therefore, if new improvements were desired, these mappings should be a must before any new action. Such mappings could provide a clear understanding of the power plant system and subsystems, as well as the types of sensors installed and variable observations collected. With an understanding of this entire universe, the road was open for new developments. As a result of these process mappings, as well as an exploratory data analysis, a favorable environment would be created for the application of AI algorithms to support the implementation of predictive models, and thus achieving a consistent KDD environment.

Therefore, the main motivation that led to the development of this paper was to report in the literature the experience obtained in this research project in which all phases of a big data process were covered and which led to the construction of a framework (BAProM) that can be used in industrial systems of different types.

The description of this framework, accompanied by an implementation in a real-world case, may lead other researchers to develop similar works, and professionals in the field to make better-informed decisions, and therefore, become more secure.

1.2. Research Question

This subsection presents the research question (RQ) that drove all the development of the study described in this paper.

RQ:
What are the phases and their respective internal structures to constitute a consistent framework focused on the big data process, which could be applied in real-world cases of predictive maintenance?

As the question states, its purpose is to define the phases, tasks and techniques that must be employed in each step of a big data process, considering from the identification of relevant processes and variables to be studied to the implementation of prediction models. Such a framework should be suitable for application in predictive maintenance use cases.

1.3. Objectives

Based on the RQ, the objective of this study, therefore, is to address these issues, and it must do so through a framework proposal that has been called BAProM—Big Data Analytical Process and Mapping.

As specific objectives of the study, we must:

(a) Define and test the BAProM framework as a pipeline of four modules: Process Mapping, Data Management, Data Analysis, and Predictive Modeling.
(b) Ensure the modules are adaptable to different types of industry and problems and can be applied independently.
(c) Develop an application of BAProM in the hydroelectric plant (UHB) as a decision support tool for predictive maintenance.
(d) Identify all relevant operational processes in UHB
(e) Identify all variables significantly associated with equipment failures.
(f) Conclude the application with the development of a prediction model of equipment failures
(g) The prediction model must have the ability to identify, by the values of the significant variables, whether an equipment would be close to a failure point or not.
(h) The prediction model must predict the probability of an equipment failure in a future period.

1.4. Implications and Contributions

The importance of studying the big data process is the relevance that the subject has acquired in Industry 4.0, since more and more stakeholders are adopting data-driven decision-making practices.

The implications of data analysis and prediction models, expected products of a big data process, are far beyond Industry 4.0. In fact, its benefits spread across all areas of activity.

In Industry 4.0, in particular, the implications of a framework that could be implemented as systematic procedures in the operation can be huge. Such models would lead to a minimization of corrective maintenance occurrences, in addition to optimizing the periodic maintenance schedule. Productivity can increase, as can profit. As the amounts involved in industry can be significantly high, so would be the benefits of costs savings.

This paper, therefore, can bring an important practical contribution to an important economic sector.

On the other hand, the conceptual and technical implications of the paper can also be significant, since novelties are proposed and validated by a complete implementation in a real-world case.

The mapping of processes and variables is often not present in the big data processes described in the literature, and this paper seeks to draw attention to this fact and show its relevance in the direction the project took.

The development of an analysis and data exploration tool, with the demonstration in the article of its use in different stages of the process, is another contribution of the study that should have implications in the way the projects are developed.

In addition, a combined prediction model, employing a decision tree complemented by an artificial neural network to forecast critical variables for a future period, as will be presented in this paper, is not often seen in the literature.

The article thus acquires some relevance with these contributions and may have positive implications both from a conceptual and practical point of view.

The description of the BAProM framework, as well as the real-world application case, is presented in the paper over five more sections. In Section 2, we give a literature overview of the works related to this research. Section 3 presents the methodology employed in the conception of the framework and shows how it could be implemented. In Section 4 we describe the Case Study developed in the hydroelectric power plant, and Section 5 shows and discusses the results of these practical applications. Finally, Section 6 presents the conclusions and gives directions for future works.

2. Related Works

Every industry, including power generation, wants its equipment to be as efficient as possible, which means operating at full load (or close to it), producing as much as possible and having the equipment for the maximum available time [9]. Therefore, maintenance aims to inspect any equipment to ensure its effectiveness, avoiding unexpected failures [10].

The most common type of maintenance is a periodic one, called preventive maintenance, which consists of stopping the equipment according to a predefined schedule, and performing scheduled services and inspections to check for additional repair needs. Most preventive maintenance stops can prove to be unnecessary, resulting in maintenance expenses and loss due to production stoppage. However, even so, this type of maintenance is sustained by the industry, as it is still the best resource to avoid corrective maintenance [11].

Corrective maintenance comes from a failure in an equipment throughout the industrial process, generating a high financial impact on budgets due, above all, to the immediate need for repair and spare parts, in addition to interrupting the production chain in an unplanned way [12,13].

The best scenario would be one in which the ideal time for maintenance is known in advance. But, this type of discovery is not trivial, as it involves a complex system of variables related to operation, maintenance, production and even the human order of those who are handling the equipment [14].

These questions increase the interest in installing sensors in a variety of equipment, collecting data almost in real time (in the order of seconds) about their mechanical, electrical or operational conditions. Having the data and developing analyses makes it possible to get to models supporting decisions regarding when maintenance should occur and what procedures should be adopted for eventual failures. Decisions, in this case, are supported and based on information extracted from data (Data-Driven approach) [7,8,15].

When a maintenance decision is based on information extracted from data collection, it generates a proactive action. In addition, this paradigm shift between reactive (corrective) to proactive maintenance actions is also seen in the literature by transforming time-based maintenance (TBM) into condition-based maintenance (CBM) [7,8].

Proactive maintenance uses concepts of Internet of Things (IoT), big data (BD) and artificial intelligence (AI). Simply put, for conceptualization purposes, the sensor used in monitoring is associated with the IoT component, the process of collecting and exploratory processing of data to the database is associated with BD, and the training of algorithms for the generation of models to be used for decision-making is addressed to AI.

Literature points towards a new industry revolution. After the mechanical, electrical and automation revolutions that brought mass production, assembly lines and information technology, raising workers' income and making technological competition the core of economic development, the fourth industrial revolution is characterized by a set of technologies, where the operation is modernized with sensors for monitoring, collecting, and storing data and using data-mining techniques, with intelligent algorithms to support decision-making [3,16,17].

The approaches of Industry 4.0 used together are optimistic because they can monitor, diagnose and predict possible failures in addition to indicating the best time for maintenance to occur. The papers focusing on anticipating the best time for maintenance define this approach as predictive maintenance [18–20].

Related work emphasizes the choice of specific algorithms or composite algorithms, in order to seek the best performance in predicting the best time for a maintenance service. Composite algorithms imply, on the one hand, the use of techniques for dimensionality reduction which may occur due to the high number of sensors. These are techniques such as the Principal Components Analysis (PCA) [15–17] or data clustering algorithms, as K- Means [21] or yet, probabilistic models such as the Bayesian Belief Network (BBN) [3]. On the other hand, there is the use of AI algorithms, where the most used in predictive maintenance are Support Vector Machines (SVM) [16,17,22], Artificial Neural Networks (ANN) [18,22], Bayesian Belief Network [3], Random Forest (RF) [22], Partial least squares (PLS) [15], Markov Chain and deterministic methods [23,24]. These mentioned works are discussed in more detail below.

Yin et al. present a survey of studies employing statistical methods for monitoring and detecting failures in large-scale industrial systems. As their main results, database problems stand out, and among them can be highlighted the high number of variables, wrong measurements and missing values. For variable treatment, especially dimensionality reduction, and monitoring to detect flaws, the authors conclude that the best approaches are PCA and regression by PLS. The combination also allows identification of the most significant variables in an equipment failure [15].

Another paper, developed by Jing and Hou used the Tennessee-Eastman Process (TEP) to simulate an industrial chemical environment in order to assess process control, process monitoring and diagnostic methods. As far as diagnosis is concerned, the authors used PCA to reduce the dimensionality of the data and SVM for the diagnostic classification [16].

A survey of articles from 2007 to 2015 using SVM to detect failures in industrial environments is presented in a paper of Yin and Hou. The main conclusion of this research was that the best results were obtained when the SVM was combined with some other dimensionality reduction technique [17].

Lee et al. proposed an analytical framework with Prediction-Health Management (PHM) algorithms aiming to learn how to operate normal equipment and to predict its lifespan. Self-analysis of the equipment is performed using unsupervised algorithms such as the ANN Self-Organizing Maps (SOM), defining normal operating standards. Therefore, when the operation comes to the point of having a certain level of dispersion in relation to its standard behavior, learned by SOM, the algorithm infers that it just started a degradation process [3].

The development of an ANN based on operation data of machining equipment is the content of a paper of Yan et al. The objective of the research was to estimate the remaining life of the most relevant component of that equipment. The work also proposes the need for a standardization of semi-structured and unstructured data from industrial processes, to improve the accuracy of the prediction algorithms. An improvement occurs because heterogeneous data, such as vibration signals from the machine and images of the machine's working environment, can provide important information for the prediction model after being structured and standardized [18].

Gatica et al. propose two approaches to predictive maintenance, named online and offline. The approaches have top-down and bottom-up strategies. In the "top-down" approach, the process begins with understanding the use case, as well as the machines employed. Following from this, a mental model of the process is made, where a hypothesis of how the process impacts data collection, is elaborated. Finally, the hypothesis is tested by analyzing the sensor data. In the 'bottom-up' strategy, the process has the following flow: data collection, exploratory analysis, selection of variables, predictive modeling and results validation based on the experience of the industrial process team [20].

A model to evaluate equipment failure time by collecting data with a vibration sensor was proposed by Sampaio et al. Their objective was to develop a relationship between the vibration levels and the equipment failure time, thus raising a characteristic curve that was learned by three AI algorithms: ANN, RF and DT. The lowest RMSE (Root Mean Square Error) was achieved by ANN [22];

Wang et al. presented a framework named Policy Semi-Markov Decision Process (PSMDP) to find the best time for predictive maintenance, based on the system deteriorating state. The proposal aimed to understand the equipment operating status, so that maintenance would be planned considering the aspects of production efficiency and maintenance expenses. The work aims to discover when equipment is about to present a failure and consequently establish an action plan for the best maintenance moment [23].

A paper developed by Gao et al. presented a bibliographic review of works dealing with approaches involving fault detection based on signals and methods of deterministic models. The result is a taxonomy of fault diagnosis approaches for deterministic systems, stochastic fault diagnosis methods, discrete and hybrid event diagnostic approaches, and diagnostic techniques for networked and distributed systems [24].

The works presented in this section focus on different aspects of predictive maintenance. Among all the works mentioned here, only Gatica et al., as explained above, thought of the problem in the form of a process [20]. The others focused on the techniques involved and among these, the problem of the data set is noted. The data collected from sensors has problems of outlier, missing values, standardization and dimensionality that were pointed out in full by only [18]. Others were concerned only with dimensionality reduction, which was resolved with the use of PCA. Regarding prediction processes, the SVM algorithm is widely used, but without further discussion of parameterization and the kernel used. In part, the strong use of this algorithm is due to its performance in comparison with other methods. However, most of the applications are in contexts that are not necessarily industrial environments.

A systematic review of Machine-Learning methods applied to Predictive Maintenance on two scientific databases: IEEE Xplore and Science Direct [25], gave an overview of the maintenance types—corrective, preventive and predictive—and tried to show the machine-learning methods being explored and the performance of the techniques. An analysis of the papers between 2009 and 2018 showed that techniques of the most diverse types have been widely used, such as: Decision Tree, RF—Random Forest, k-NN—k-Nearest Neighbors, , SVM—Support Vector Machine, Hierarchical clustering, k-means, Fuzzy C-means, ANN—Artificial Neural Network, LSTM- Long Short-Term Memory Network, ARIMA—Autoregressive Integrated Moving Average, ANOVA—Analysis of Variance, Linear Regression, GLM—Generalized Linear Model, and others.

In another paper, the authors presented a machine-learning approach for detecting drifting behavior—so-called concept drifts—in continuous data streams, as potential indication for defective system behavior and depict initial tests on synthetic data sets. The machine-learning techniques used in the study were LR, RF and Symbolic Regression (SR). They also presented a real-world case study with industrial radial fans and discuss promising results from applying their approach [26].

The literature also presents a predictive maintenance framework based on sensor measurements [27] and a prognostic is developed, oriented towards the requirements of operation planners, which is based on a Long Short-Term Memory network. Its performance is compared with two benchmark maintenance policies: a classical periodic and an ideal case (perfect prognostics information) called the ideal predictive maintenance (IPM). The mean cost rate of the proposed framework was lower than the periodic maintenance policy and close to the ideal case IPM. It is possible to find works yet, with confirmations that big data and IoT play a fundamental role in data-driven applications for Industry 4.0, as is the case of predictive maintenance [28]. The authors in this paper reviewed the strengths and weaknesses of open-source technologies for big data and stream processing and tried to establish their usage in some cases. As a result, they proposed some combinations of such technologies for predictive maintenance in two cases: one in the transportation industry, a railway maintenance, and another in the energy industry, a wind turbine maintenance.

Another study proposed a Weibull proportional hazards model to jointly represent degradation and failure time data. The authors explained that degradation refers to the cumulative change of the performance characteristic of an object over time, as the capacity of batteries of hybrid-electric vehicles, the leveling defects of railway tracks and so on. The proposed strategy was applied to the predictive maintenance of lead-acid batteries and proved to be adequate [29].

This review sought to provide an overview of the main aspects associated with the theme of this research. Thus, works were presented showing the context of the Industry 4.0 environment, involving the maintenance of equipment, the acquisition of data for monitoring, based on sensors, the use of AI algorithms based on ANN for failure prediction, the use of statistical methods for monitoring and fault detection, and other proposed analytical structures. A rich field of opportunities has been presented.

From this picture of opportunities, verified in the literature review, emerged one of those opportunities with the proposal of the big data Analytics Process Mapping framework, BAProM, which is the development of an analytical framework covering the entire big data process and also including a first phase of a detailed mapping of processes and variables, which is not frequently seen in the literature. As stated before, synthetically, the framework consists of four modules: Process Mapping, Data Management, Data Analysis and Predictive Modeling.

Such a framework, including the mapping of processes and variables to a predictive analysis and showing results of an implementation in a real-world case, is a novelty in the literature.

The details of each of these modules are presented in the next section, as well as the reasons for each technique selected to became part of this first version of the framework, which was validated in a real-world case of the Henry Borden hydroelectric plant Section 4.

In addition to its conceptual relevance, the research gains practical importance by being applied to a relevant industrial system in the real world creating mechanisms for monitoring the operation and predicting equipment failures, which could be avoided once they were known in advance.

3. Framework

A classical development of a big data project starts by data collection regarding the important variables of the system under study [1]. However, in some cases, it is not so clear what these variables are, since a comprehensive documentation may not be available. In these cases, an earlier phase of mapping processes and relevant variables to characterize the state of the system is necessary.

The framework proposed in this paper introduces in the big data process phase of mapping processes and variables as an initial fundamental part of the process, which is followed by data management, in which part lies the collection of primary data. After that, there would be a phase of data analysis, with more exploratory characteristics, and in the end there is a predictive modeling.

The entire process was consolidated into four modules, whose details are shown as follows:

Module 1: Mapping Process

- Process mapping to identify critical operation points of the system under study;
- Variables mapping to identify critical operation indicators;
- Analysis of technical reports to define the standard behavior for variables monitored by sensors;
- Interviews with specialists responsible for the operation of the system.

Module 2: Data Management

- Data Acquisition from sensors at critical points of the system, properly mapped;
- Aggregation to dataset any relevant historical data registered in other systems;
- Pre-processing of data involving preparation, transformation of the data into a final format for analysis and selection;
- Consolidation of data on a single database.

Module 3: Data Analysis

- Implementation of computational tools for analysis and visualization of information stored in dataset;
- Development of analyses and new insights about interrelations, correlations and/or operational trends;

Module 4: Predictive Modeling

- Design and Construction of an Incident Predictive Model;
- Validation of the predictive model;
- Application of the predictive model to optimize processes;

Figure 1 illustrates the complete framework, including the techniques and the computational tools applied in each step. Please note that the framework proposed is an extension of the big data process proposed by [1]. Here, the flow of activities incorporates mapping, which therefore becomes an integral part of a big data process. This, in a way, is recommended in the CRISP-DM (Cross Reference Industrial Standard Process for Data Mining) model, which suggests as initial phases the understanding of processes and data [30]. However, this understanding phase is not directly related to a mapping of processes or variables, in CRISP-DM, as it is here in this proposal.

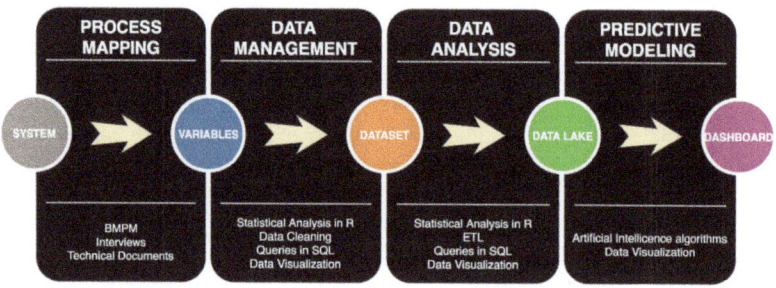

Figure 1. BAProM—Modules and techniques applied by module.

3.1. Process Mapping

The mapping of processes is a fundamental step, since it unveils the set of variables, which are those "keeping the knowledge" of the system under study, often obscured under a surface of a mass of data. This mapping of variables, which follows the mapping of process, opens the access doors to this knowledge. A process mapping can be defined as a modeling technique used to understand in a clear and simple way how a business unit is operating, representing each step of its operation in terms of inputs, outputs, and actions. As a result, a model of the system operation is built, with all its flows, relations, variables and complexities [31,32]. This is a fundamental step in research and development studies, as it provides a broader view of the object of study and makes it possible to improve the basis for decision-making, since at the modeling stage all processes are identified, mapped, understood and validated, which may lead to a process redesign. The characteristics of the processes (flows and/or activities) may be redesigned, aiming optimization and/or adaptation to recurrent needs.

All these concepts were initially applied to business processes, to improve and to automate a process. In fact, process automation by the means of applications is one of the major uses of process modeling [32]. However, by the characterization and validation of a process, it is possible to identify critical points in the system and, therefore, to identify and/or define critical variables, which form the basis for the data collection phase of a big data process. The start point for a consistent data collection is a set of representative variables of the system under study. Therefore, even though the aim here is the study of a big data process, the modeling process to identify this set of representative variables is similar to classical business process modeling. Thus, this paper tries to demonstrate how a tool originally designed for modeling business processes, the well-known software engineering tool BPMN—Business Process Model and Notation—can also be applied to a big data process.

BPMN is the notation of the methodology of business process management, widely used in software engineering for process modeling and validation of the process from the prototype generation of an application. The BPMN was developed by the Business Process Management Initiative (BPMI) and is currently maintained by the Object Management Group, maintaining the current version of BPMN in 2.0 [31,32].

A proposal [33] to use this process to align the business process with that of the analysis, corroborates the benefits pointed out in other articles [34]. The relevance of this type of application can also be demonstrated in a work which proposes, in an embryonic way, the improvement of a BPMN for better use in an analytical context [35].

The BPMN provides a standard notation, easily understood by all members of the business. Stakeholders include business analysts who create and refine the processes, the technical developers responsible for implementing the processes, and the business managers who monitor and manage the processes. Consequently, BPMN intends to serve as a common language to bridge the communication that often occurs between designing business processes and implementing a process automation. It is a process-modeling notation comprehensible to the process owner (definition); to the participant in the process (use); to system developers (automation); to the business manager (monitoring) and; to decrease the distance between definition and implementation of the defined solution [31,32]. Based on these characteristics, this proposed methodology considers the use of BPMN as an adequate tool for the development of the mapping of processes and variables, the initial stage of the big data process conceived here.

3.2. Data Management

When we talk about data, we are in fact referring to observations of a set of variables which is the fundamental pillar for an analytical description of a system. It represents a synthetic framework of the system knowledge map, and through the variables observations it is possible to penetrate often complex paths existing in the masses of data, obscured by a variety of noises, as random observations, missing value outliers and so on. Data management means collecting and dealing with these observed values of the variables, and assures quality to the data, since it is the base of the entire analytical process of the system. Data quality is essential for a descriptive analysis of the system and an understanding of its behavior, as well for predictive models.

As described at the beginning of this section, data management begins by the acquisition and recording steps, which are strongly dependent on the application domain. This collection step, based on the set of critical variables, is the basis for the next analytical phases. In the case of Industry 4.0, the theme of this work, sensors usually make the acquisition. However, it may also be done by data sources other than sensors, such as photos and/or sounds collected in the operating environment or even by very simple processes such as notes registering operating situations of equipment.

The second step of data management, referred to as extraction, cleaning and annotation, also known as pre-processing, is dedicated to improving data quality. The pre-processing has two fundamental segments: data preparation and dimensionality reduction.

Data preparation means, basically, cleaning, integration and representation or transformation of the data, preparing the data for the analytical phases.

The cleaning involves treatment of data noise, characterized mainly by outliers (points with behavior quite different from the others) and missing values (lack of observations). Due to the diversity of data sources from different databases, noise, inconsistencies or missing values are very common. Even data from a single database is not exempt from such problems, and neither is data collected automatically by sensors, as these are liable to fail [36–38]. The cleaning consists of eliminating noise, correcting inconsistencies and handling missing values. The treatment of noisy data consists of identifying attribute values outside an expected standard (outlier) or other unexpected behaviors. The causes are diverse, such as measurement variations of equipment, human interference or extraordinary events, among others. The solution can be by simply removing the value, if the observation is identified as an anomaly, or by treatment using binning, clustering or other procedures. The elimination of an outlier is the simplest solution, but, before eliminating such a value, it must be considered that an occurrence with a value other than the usual may be the result of a measurement never seen before and therefore it should be carefully studied rather than being eliminated. An outlier, in fact, may represent an opportunity of a discovery, which might conduct a research to new paths not considered before. Correcting data inconsistency is also a part of cleaning. Inconsistency is the presence of conflicting values in the same attribute, which in many cases may be caused by the integration of different databases. An example would be if each database uses a different scale to measure power. One could use kilowatt and the other megawatt. In integration, the values would be inconsistent. The correction can be done manually, automatically, in some cases, or even considering some kind of normalization (see Data Transformation, ahead in this section). Another cleaning task is to deal with the absence of data, which occurs when one or more attribute values do not exist. There can be several causes, such as failure to fill manually, no knowledge of the attribute, or low importance of the attribute, among others. The problem can be solved simply by removing the attribute or removing the entire sample, if this may cause a problem to other attributes of the same sample. There are other types of solutions with more elaborate techniques, such as to assign the mean, a moving average, or even the minimum or maximum values to those missing values [37]. Data cleaning is an essential step for the analytic stage. After cleaning there is the integration and representation or transformation, as a final data preparation for the analytic stage. These are pre-processing procedures applied to the data to gain efficiency and effectiveness. The integration activity occurs when one has many data sources, and seeks the construction of a single database. Otherwise, it loses importance. The representation in many cases means a data transformation, converting types and/or values of attributes. In some cases it is necessary, for example, transforming a continuous numerical value into a discrete value, or a discrete value for categorical ordinal, categorical nominal for discrete binary and categorical ordinal for discrete. It may be necessary, however, to normalize attributes that present values in broad ranges, in order to make them have the same level of importance in an analytical process. For normalization, the literature presents different methods, such as the z-score that transforms attribute values so that they remain with zero mean and standard deviation equal to one. Another method, considered as standard by many authors, is the min-max method [37]. The pre-processing so far included its first segment, the data preparation, involving cleaning, integration and representation or transformation.

Dimensionality reduction is a second segment of pre-processing. It is associated with data redundancy, which is another problem that must be treated. It occurs when two attributes have a dependency on each other. In this case, they may have the same values, or they may be very similar. It may happen for different reasons, such as lack of information of a database (metadata) that an attribute generates another one, or it may also exist between copies of a database. Typically, redundancy can be identified using correlation analysis, where the Pearson Correlation Coefficient is one of the most frequently used [37]. However, it may also be identified by using techniques such as factor analysis or Principal Components Analysis (PCA). The result of applying these techniques is a selection of records in the database and/or attributes, which will form the final database for the analysis phase. This selected data is a reduced database, without redundancy, but with equivalent analytical capacity.

It should be noted that each project has different needs and it is not always necessary to develop all pre-processing steps described here. Anyway, if all the steps are necessary, the natural sequence would be preparation, involving cleaning, integration and representation or transformation, and dimensionality reduction, in an iterative way and with interactions between the steps, in a feedback process, until the final data quality is effectively guaranteed [38]. A final step may still be necessary at this phase, which would be consolidating the data into a single database.

3.3. Data Analysis

This analytical module, as shown in Figure 1, is basically defined by exploratory analyses of the critical variables, which is essential for a descriptive analysis of the system, building a clear understanding of its behavior. Similar to the variables stored regarding the information about a system, once this data is properly explored and interpreted, the information obtained will represent an accumulated knowledge regarding the system.

The exploratory analysis is based on the observed values of the variables, and usually, it works with tools as the Structured Query Language (SQL) to create consolidated databases from multiple queries on different data sources. SQL allows data modeling, relating tables created by extracting, transforming and loading data, the so-called ETL process (extract, transform and load), and constructing analytical repositories appropriate for discoveries [39].

Typical examples of this analytical approach are multidimensional data models, supported by data warehouses (DW). A DW is a repository constructed with data extracted from transaction systems, the so-called OLTP (Online Transaction Processing) data, and is exclusively for analysis, and so, it is not constantly updated (non-volatile) [40].

Online analytical processing tools (OLAP) are useful instruments to explore a DW. This kind of tool provides the exploration of different perspectives of a database. Moreover, SQL and other statistical tools may provide aggregate functions to summarize data, generating descriptive statistics measures such as sum, mean, median, standard deviation, minimum and maximum values, counts, etc. As a result, the descriptive statistic provides a clear view of the behavior of the variables under study and furnishes indicators for consolidated reports.

The Interpretation of these indicators must be strongly supported by computational tools integrating statistical analysis with visualization resources, as different types of graphics, dashboards and other instruments. The implementation of such analytical tools is part of this proposal. With an analytical computational tool, the development of analyses and new insights about interrelations, correlations, and/or operational trends of the variables becomes a reality.

3.4. Predictive Modeling

Differently from the approach described in the previous section, the predictive module is based on Data-Mining (DM) techniques. DM is a process of analytically exploring databases for the purpose of making findings that are not obvious, whose outcomes are effective in decision-making processes. DM is a core component of a KDD process [38], and usually involves prediction, clustering, or data association techniques.

The prediction process can be developed based on AI algorithms, which are strongly based on the data, including an auto-adjustment of its internal free parameters, calibrating the model (the so-called "training" of the model) which is performed from data history. This parameter adjustment (the model training) makes the algorithm able to be applied in other datasets, distinct from the one where the training process took place. A training model can, for example, estimate future values of variables, as the probability of an equipment failure. In such an example, the prediction could support the estimation of an optimal period for equipment maintenance [1].

There are different types of algorithms for prediction. One of the classical ones is the Decision Tree (DT), which is a type of AI algorithm whose model, generated after the training process, can be interpreted by humans and machines [41].

In a DT algorithm, the training process is simple and intuitive. In DT, each variable (attributes) is analyzed in its capacity of estimating a class of an object in a dataset. The DT defines a sequence (in a hierarchical tree structure) of attributes to be used to estimate the category (the class) of the object under analysis and depending on this sequence, different results may be generated. Therefore, a metric must be employed to stablish the "best" attributes sequence. One of the most used indicators is the entropy, which is a measure of the uncertainty associated with an attribute. The entropy is computed in terms of separation between classes. The variables are combined, and a measure of the entropy is performed [37]. The final model is a hierarchical structure by variable importance leading to a process of classification of the objects.

In an industrial context, for example, a class may be an equipment failure or not. Based on the values of the attributes of an equipment, the DT algorithm decides if the values of its attributes in a certain point in time means an imminence of equipment failure or not. An important characteristic of a DT algorithm is its ability to allow interpretation by humans and not only by machines. It provides a reasonable understanding to experts of how the model is making its decisions, what leads stakeholders to trust the model. In this BAProM framework a DT algorithm has been developed to be used in the optimization of the maintenance programming of equipment.

Another important AI algorithm type is the ANN. ANN mimics or simulates the behavior of the human brain. In fact, it is a computational algorithm that implements a mathematical model inspired by the brain structure of intelligent organisms. As a result, it is possible to implement a simplified functioning of the human brain in computers [42]. The human brain receives information, processes and returns a response, and does so through neurons, connected in an immense network, and which communicate with each other, by electrical signals (synapses). An ANN seeks to imitate, in a simplified way, this process, to solve a problem. ANN, therefore, is an artificial network of neurons (nodes) connected. These artificial neurons are connected in layers: an input data layer, intermediate layers (varying from 0 to "n") and an output layer.

ANN is a powerful tool for solving complex problems, and can be used, for example, in classification, clustering, associations and in time series forecasts. In this BAProM framework an ANN was employed to forecast time series of critical variables defined in the DT model. The two models, therefore, worked together to forecast an equipment failure, allowing the operation team to act before the fail takes place.

4. Case Study

This section presents a more detailed description of the case study and the experimental methodology applied in real-world operation. The computational tools used in the experiment are also discussed.

Therefore, the core purpose that has been implemented in this study was mapping operation, facilities, and processes to identify variables that would be relevant for decision-making of maintenance. Then, with those variables identified, it would be possible to start an analytical repository, and, further, training machine-learning algorithms to the prediction.

4.1. Case Description

The case studied in this article is the Henry Borden Power Plant (UHB), located in Cubatão, about 60 km from São Paulo, capital of the state of São Paulo, in Brazil.

Its power generation complex is composed of two high drop-off power plants (720 m) called External and Underground, with 14 groups of generators powered by Pelton turbines, with an installed capacity of 889 MW. Pelton turbines are characterized by blade-shaped fins that are the main cause of maintenance [43].

The External Power Plant is the oldest. It has eight external forced ducts and a conventional powerhouse. The first unit started operations in 1926, the others were installed up to 1950, in a total of eight generator sets, with an installed capacity of 469 MW.

Each generator is powered by two Pelton turbines, which receive water flows from the Rio das Pedras reservoir. These flows arrive at the so-called "Valve House", where they pass through two butterfly valves in penstocks. Then, they descend a slope, reaching their respective turbines, covering a distance of approximately 1500 m.

The Underground Power Plant is composed of six generator sets, installed inside the rocky massif of Serra do Mar, in a 120 m long, 21 m wide and 39 m high cave with an installed capacity of 420 MW.

The first generator set went into operation in 1956. Each generator is triggered by a Pelton turbine driven by four jets of water. The operation of the UHB was developed according to an Integrated System of Generation of Electrical Energy composed of four large interdependent subsystems, interrelated in a continuous way, in the sense of generating electric energy delivered to the Brazilian Interconnected System, distributed cross country.

The general framework in UHB today is management practices combining modern instruments, such as computerized monitoring systems and dashboards for visualizations of different types of indicators with empirical practices based on its team experience. The system in the operation center runs uninterruptedly, allowing information from the entire system constantly. Therefore, appropriate decisions can be made at every moment. However, many of these operating parameters and metrics are established based on empirical practices. A typical example is the timeframe between inspections and preventive maintenance of turbines of the generating system. These parameters, which are determinant for the quantification of operational costs and level of the service of the electric system, should be periodically re-evaluated and, if possible, optimized, in order to find the optimal point of the tradeoff between costs and service levels.

Hydropower plants and generation facilities represent a high level of investments requiring management based on robust processes and standards, to guarantee the adequate return of the investments. Its operation and maintenance must be developed to guarantee the preservation and maximization of the use of this patrimony, within the operational conditions in which it operates.

The primary objective of such facilities is to maximize the availability of the energy generation and use of equipment. This is only achieved with high-level operating standards and procedures to guarantee the facilities productivity and the quality of the services offered.

The operational and maintenance standards of a power plant have their own costs, which may be considerable, given the complexity and size of the operations, inducing managers to search for practices leading to costs minimization.

Therefore, the use of BAProM framework (Section 3), seeking to establish optimized parameters to minimize operational costs and maintenance associated with equipment shutdowns could represent a relevant contribution to the operation of a hydroelectric plant. The BAProM framework was applied to this case, to develop a predictive model to establish the probable occurrence of an incident in Generating Units (GU) that could cause an interruption in the operation and, consequently, the need for corrective maintenance. Based on these predictions, it would be possible to establish optimal periods between maintenance.

In the following section, we present the approach and results involved in the predictive modeling.

4.2. Experimental Methodology

The methodology applied to the case study strictly followed the four modules of the proposed BAProM framework, but throughout the project, the technical team had to face some concrete questions, which only when an experimental methodology is effectively put into practice is it possible to have the real dimension of certain issues. Given the impact of such practical issues on the time dedicated by the team to resolve them, it is understood that they deserve a record and a discussion, as they can occur in many real projects. On the other hand, some steps that might have seemed difficult, in practice, demanded much less time and dedication from the team than one could imagine previously.

Thus, this section presents the four modules of the experimental methodology highlighting and discussing the main practical aspects related to the experience developed during the project. This type of record can be a useful contribution to the definition of the steps of a methodology, and also, to emphasize the attention that a team must dedicate to each step of the application of a methodology. In addition, it can also be an important contribution to scale, in a schedule, the time of each phase in a practical project.

Module 1: Mapping Process

The mapping of UHB operational processes involved the identification and characterization of the operation systems of the power plant, and the main physical variables (electrical, mechanical and electromagnetic) associated with the processes. The main procedure for gathering information to build the mapping focused on a search directly with the power plant staff, since the individuals working on the plant showed to have a consistent knowledge and deep domain of the business to be modeled. These professionals with relevant experience in management and operations showed to have knowledge not only of the general process, but also of the some important details, allowing a consistent and reliable description of the processes and their associated variables, identifying accurately some points to be mapped and highlighted. This module was one of the major challenges of the project, involving extensive discussion with the power plant operation team, to learn the operational process and the relevant variables and this is a lesson to be learned. Sometimes, it is not a trivial task for the technical data science team to learn the technicality of the business being modeled. In addition to the information extracted from the meetings with the operation personnel, other relevant information on equipment was obtained from documents provided by the company.

Module 2: Data Management

If the previous module represented one of the major challenges of the project, this data management module was the biggest one. First, it was decided that the data collection would be focused on two UHB Generating Units (UG), known as UG4 and UG6, both with the same mechanical, electrical and technical characteristics, and the data would be obtained from a supervisory system database fed by sensors coupled to the plant equipment, which were connected to this database. The problems started to appear when analyzing the collected data. The data has not been properly stored over the years. Most of the data collected was used just as input to dashboards and discarded after use. The fact is that although the hydroelectric plant had a good data collection infrastructure, the team did not have a culture of data analysis, but only used the information for an instant monitoring of the operation. In the team there was no qualification for data analysis, so what happened was that the data was used for monitoring and most of them was then discarded. In fact, there was little historical data to analyze. Therefore, what happened is that the effective data collection had to be started from the beginning of the study. This led to a considerable delay in the project's planned schedule. In addition, there was a great deal of heterogeneity among the collection time periods of the diverse variables. The intervals between two collections could be quite different from one variable to another. There was no standardization of these periods. Moreover, we found many variables without data (missing data) and many problems of noise, including inconsistency and outliers.

Beside these problems, during the project one of the Generating Units, UG4, had a technical problem and had to be deactivated for a long period. Therefore, the data collection had to be focused only on one of the Generating Units of the UHB, UG6, which became, therefore, the object of this study.

Anyway, all problems had to be solved, especially the interval between two consecutive collections, which was adjusted so that all variables were always collected at the same time stamp. New time series of observations of the variables started to be generated. Once these difficulties were overcome, the data was successfully collected and a succession of analyses could be conducted. The final collection period was from May 2017 to January 2018 and they kept being updated continuously.

Module 3: Data Analysis

This module did not present any significant practical problems. The challenge here was technical, related to the development of a computational tool to support the analytical phase, which should be effective, but also be friendly, so that it could also be used by the operation team, non-technical users. Therefore, as soon as the mapping phase ended, an analysis and visualization tool, an analytical workbench, was developed to be used not only in this phase 3, but also, in the previous one, data management, to assist in the characterization of the variables and in the identification of data quality problems. Each critical variable has been filtered by the dashboard tool, providing visualizations of their domains, through statistical diagrams and summaries, presenting time series graphs, boxplots and histograms to identify trends, seasonality, statistical distributions, presence of outliers and missing values, as well, metrics such as mean, median, standard deviation and quantiles. Once the analyses were completed, knowledge about the system increased significantly and the entire database was ready to be subjected to predictive modeling.

Module 4: Predictive Modeling

As the previous one, this fourth module did not present significant practical problems. Once more, the challenge here was technical, since the predictive modeling involves AI algorithms and data modeling, since the data should be properly prepared to input the models.

The modeling was subdivided in two predictive models: the first one was a Decision Tree, where relevant variables associated with equipment failure were identified, as well as, thresholds, indicating the imminence of a failure when a variable reaches that value; the second model was an ANN dedicated to forecast time series of the significant variables, and so, could be possible to foresee in a future period when one of these variables would reach a threshold. Therefore, this was a module in which the tasks went without unexpected occurrences, including the techniques and tools employed in the practical application, which proved to be well adapted to the tasks.

4.3. Computational Tools

This section discusses the computational instruments used in the case study, for the four modules of the proposed framework.

The mapping of operational processes and variables was the fundamental starting point of the methodology, first module of the BAProM framework. In this case, a tool originally designed for modeling business process, the software engineering tool, BPMN, could be applied even though this was a big data process. A graphical tool based on the last existing version of BPMN (v. 2.0) showed to be well suited for this development. The software provided appropriate resources for modeling processes allowing validation of operation rules, flows definition and identification of critical variables. Moreover, these features were essential for validation the mapping with the power plant team.

The next step, module 2 in the proposed methodology, was Data Management, where data collection played a relevant role. Data was provided from different sources, such as the supervisory system database, fed by a set of sensors, an application named Impediment Registry, a by-product of these project, and which records equipment occurrences, as well as some external data. The SQL Server Database Management System was the basis for data storage, in a unified repository.

Another step of this module 2, the pre-processing for data validation, as the data cleaning, had the support of the analysis and visualization tool mentioned earlier, an analytical workbench, developed specifically for this framework, in the R-Shiny, a language library and statistical environment in R. This computational tool was a fundamental support for the characterization of the variable's standards and identification of data quality problems, providing for example, the treatment of missing values and outliers.

In module 3, the complete exploratory analysis, was totally based on this analytical workbench. The Shiny package from R language made it possible to build interfaces for the application with a high level of usability, as well as the processing of basically, all kinds of statistical operations.

For analysis and visualization purposes the tool provided the flexibility of filters, allowing the selection of a generating unit, a specific subsystem and a variable, as for example, selects "UG6", subsystem "Generator" and variable "Stator Armature". The tool provided yet, diverse types of dashboard outputs, graphical and metrics, which represented the core of the data analysis in module 3. Its features included statistical summaries, graphical visualization of time series, boxplot and histograms.

Module 4 was developed basically, through algorithms coded in R. This language provides a variety of functionalities, as statistical and machine-learning functions, allowing the development of most of the data science algorithms, from the simplest ones to the most sophisticated, such as those of artificial intelligence algorithms. Both algorithms employed in module 4, DT and ANN, were developed in R, which proved to be well suited for the job.

5. Practical Application of BAProM: Results and Discussion

The practical application strictly followed the modules of the BAProM framework, which are presented in the following subsections.

5.1. Process Mapping Results and Discussion

The mapping of Processes and Variables, developed on the first module, was fundamental to identify and formalize all the relevant flows and processes of the UHB Integrated Energy Generation System, as well as all the relevant variables. An integrated macro model for the entire system was developed with the purpose of showing a more comprehensive view of all subsystems identified in the process. Therefore, it was possible to verify and analyze the major components of the four stages in their sequential order.

The modeling was developed, in most part through information gathering with the power plant team. Four subsystems were identified, making up the entire UHB energy generation process. These subsystems, which are: Adduction, Turbine, Generator and Transmission, are illustrated in Figure 2.

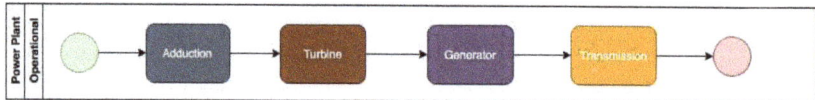

Figure 2. Macro view of the system with 4 subsystems.

These four subsystems make up, at UHB, an Integrated Electricity Generation System, which delivers energy to the Brazilian Interconnected Central System, composed of several power plants spread over the country, which in turn, distributes the energy throughout the country.

A synthetic description of the subsystems interaction, could be, as follows: the Adduction System carries a water flow from a reservoir descending a slope, to reach the turbines, covering a distance of approximately 1500 m (almost 1 mile). The pressure is enough to promote a high-speed rotation of the Turbine (Turbine System).

Each turbine, in turn, generates a rotation of the bearing axis on which it is supported, transmitting energy to the Generator to which it is connected.

The Generator by means of this kinetic energy, creates a magnetic field generating electrical current for the Transmission System. This system increases the voltage and prepares the energy ("packs") leading to transmission lines, integrating the Brazilian Interconnected System, for later distribution.

In this module, which represents the process mapping task of the BAProM approach, process modeling was applied to the entire system, which was a very extensive work, composed of vast documentation. Each of the four subsystems had its own modeled process, as well as the identification of its relevant variables.

For the purpose of illustrating this process, the mapping of one of the subsystems, the Generator, is presented here, with a special emphasis on one of its components, the "Stator Armature". The mapping of the other subsystems and their components was very similar to what is presented here.

The mapping of the Generator subsystem is shown in Figure 3, where the "Stator Armature" appears as its third component.

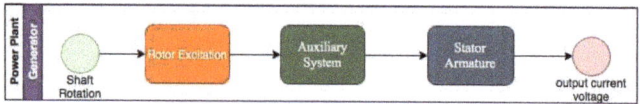

Figure 3. Generator Subsystem.

An integrated model for Stator Armature was developed showing a detailed view of this subsystem component (see Figure 4), and already including some aspects of data management, as well. This mapping provides a solid basis for applying the other framework modules, in their sequential order.

The mapping provides a broad overview of all critical variables. For the specific case of the Stator Armature, five critical variables were identified: Active Power, Active Energy, Armature Tension, Armature Current and Rotor Groove Temperature. These five variables, now, should be continually monitored by sensors, and their observed values subjected to an ETL process, for future analyses.

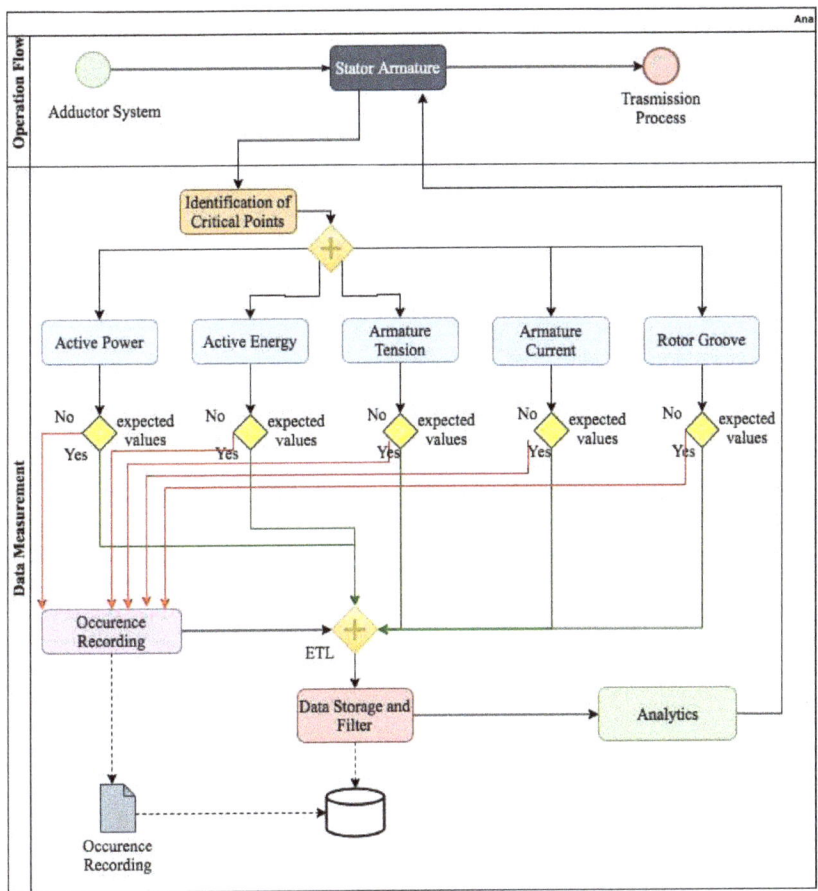

Figure 4. Mapping of the Component "Stator Armature".

The mapping of the complete operation of UHB was an effective practical contribution for the company, since it did not have this type of documentation, comprehensive and detailed, involving its entire operation.

Having completed the mapping, the next step was data management, which is the subject of the next section.

5.2. Data Management Results

The data management began with the data acquisition and recording, and it was favored by the previous phase, which provided an effective road map to the ETL procedure, by just following the flow throughout the mapping. In fact, as can be seen in Figure 4, whenever data is collected, a check is performed to verify that its value is within a specified range; if so, the values are extracted from the source, transformed into a compatible format and then loaded into the database. As the ETL procedure extracted and transformed the data for storage, simultaneously, was carried out an analysis of data quality, on all kinds of anomalies.

The data quality is essentially the pre-processing step, which was developed in Module 2. In this step, the data was submitted to a rigorous quality analysis process, based on data preparation, which involved cleaning, integration and transformation of the data into a final format for analysis.

The cleaning involved treatment of data noise, characterized mainly by outliers and missing values. This phase had the support of the analytical workbench, developed specifically for this framework, which provided statistical analysis and visualizations, having been a fundamental support for this cleaning task.

The number of variables resulting from the data quality checking for each subsystem (Figure 2) are summarized in Table 1. Please note that in percentage terms, the proportion of variables with outliers represented 57% of the total of variables, while variables with missing values were 43%.

Table 1. Distribution of variables among the operation subsystems and number of anomalies.

System	Number of Variables	Number of Variables with Outliers	Number of Variables with Missing Values
Adduction	12	3	9
Turbine	35	30	5
Generator	37	23	14
Transmission	16	1	15
Total	100	57	43

These are relatively high numbers and, therefore, were brought up for discussion with the UHB technical team, to understand the reasons for such values. Regarding outliers, while in some cases there was just a possibility of a value outside the expected standard, in other situations the observed values in fact corresponded to problems to be treated. As an example, some temperature sensors measured negative values. Since this scenario was impossible in the region of the power plant and the equipment should accompany the operating environment, it was clear that the observed negative temperatures were errors in the data collection, and consequently, those values were discarded. It was found that the errors were due to sensor failures. Another reason for outliers was data collections performed at system startup times. In these cases, peaks occur in certain variables, but they soon stabilize, entering in an equilibrium state. The missing values were also related to sensor problems. In this case, for a period, some sensors were disconnected from the system due to technical causes. The missing values were then treated. In most cases, they were filled with averages for near periods.

Another aspect identified during this phase was that some relevant data, collected in other systems operating at UHB, were not being integrated into the database of the supervisory system. As a combination of different sources can be useful to develop exploratory analyses, as well as robust predictive models, this integration has been implemented. One of the important data sets incorporated was a maintenance database, since the predictive models of this study are focused on maintenance. Thus, for exploratory and predictive analysis, the built repository integrated data from controls and records of equipment maintenance to the data of the critical variables of the system. Therefore, a single database started to store all the relevant variables for the analyses developed in Modules 3 and 4.

Once these problems had been solved, a last question arose, concerned with the time interval between successive data collections. This problem could be better perceived when analyzing the groups to which the variables belonged. The collected variables belong to four different types: electrical, pressure, temperature and speed regulation. This pattern was already part of a tacit knowledge of the UHB's operating team, which was formally defined in module 1 of process mapping.

Regarding these four groups, the periods between successive collections were too long, and there was still, a considerable heterogeneity among periods of collection of the different types of variables. There was no standardization of these periods.

The different collection periods can be seen in Table 2. These turned out to be a serious problem, since the analysis of variables for different timestamps creates basic problems under two aspects: analytical and systemically. Moreover, the value itself of each collection period, was a problem, since it varied from 5 min to 15 min. These were long periods for this type of data collection.

Table 2. Distribution of Variables in Categories and Collection Time Interval per Category.

Type of Variables	Number of Variables	Period of Collection (in Minutes)
Electrical	8	15
Pressure	14	5
Temperature	18	15
Speed Regulator	14	5

The question was analyzed with the UHB technical team and from these discussions came out a resulting standard period for all variables, defined in a fixed time interval of 30 s.

Once all quality problems were resolved, the data started to be regularly collected. By the end of this module, the result was a consistent dataset, without outliers and without missing values and with all variables on the same time scale (timestamp).

As a final comment, it could be highlighted that previously to this study, most of the data collected in UHB was just used as an input for computation and presentation of operation indicators on dashboards in the plant's supervisory system. The data, after use, was then discarded. There were no historical data and, consequently, no analytical treatment of the data. This was changed with this project.

Today, all variables have their historical data kept in the database of the supervisory system, for a period of 6 months. At the same time, there is now a data warehouse, built on a separate data server, where new data is continuously incorporated into the historical series of the variables, which can now be increased for an almost indefinite period. It is a very different scenario. In fact, it would be reasonable to consider that the results of this module 2, mainly the ETL procedure, the exclusive data server and the data warehouse were successful, being, thus, relevant contributions of this work and that could be followed in other applications.

5.3. Data Analysis Results

The data analysis was based on the analytical workbench, illustrated in Figure 5, developed specifically for this framework. This application was fundamental for this analytical module. Before describing the workbench, it must be remembered that it was designed for a Brazilian company and, therefore, for Brazilian users. Thus, all labels and titles in the application were defined in the Portuguese language. The figures presented here in this paper are maintaining the original screens of the tool; however, this aspect should not affect the understanding of the tool, in relation to its functionalities, since a detailed description of each one will be provided.

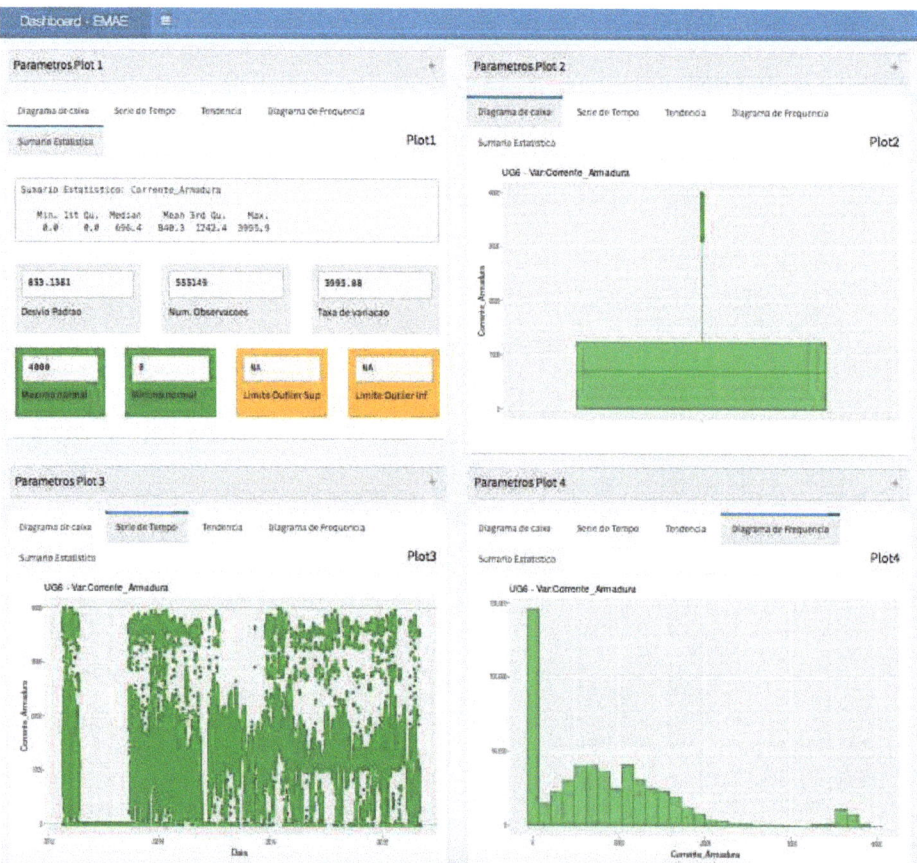

Figure 5. Variable "Armor Current"—Exploratory Analysis in the Analytical Workbench.

The analysis could be developed from many angles. The tool provided the filtering of a generating unit, a specific subsystem and a variable of that subsystem. To select the variables the tool follows the hierarchy, starting at the system, going through its subsystems, then, its components and finally, the variables. At any hierarchical level, an analysis can be defined.

Once the analysis parameters are defined, four types of outputs can be viewed: a statistical summary, a boxplot diagram, a time series plot and a histogram. The user can select all these features to analyze a single variable or one of them for a comparative analysis among variables.

The analysis results are presented by subdividing the screen into quadrants, and in each of the quadrants one of these four types of outputs is presented. Therefore, the output interface is, in fact, a dashboard, combining graphical visualizations and with statistical measures.

As in Section 5.1, component "Stator Armature" will be used here, once more, to demonstrate the tool. An analysis of one of its critical variables, the "Armor Current", will be shown. An exploratory analysis of this variable is represented in the four blocks of Figure 5, in which all possibilities of statistical metrics and graphic analyses can be visualized.

From that Figure 5 one analysis that can be done for the "Armor Current" variable (in Portuguese *VarCorrente_Armadura*), is based on the boxplot (see Plot 2, graphic at superior right in Figure 5), where it can be seen a group of values between 3000 and 4000, considering the scale of the vertical axes, distorting the visualization of a potential outlier. However, from the statistical summary (see Plot 1, graphic at superior left in Figure 5, the maximum expected value (in Portuguese: Máximo Normal) is 4000, indicating that there were no outliers in these data. A confirmation can be obtained by the maximum observed value of the variable which happens in the situation of high energy generation. The time series diagram and the histogram plot (Plot 3 and Plot 4, respectively from left to right in the bottom of Figure 5) also provide relevant information for analysis. In the case of plot 3, it is possible to identify the period in which the maximum value was reached and the histogram (plot 4) shows the distribution of observed values. In this case, value zero has the largest frequency, which stands the period when the GU was off for maintenance. Another type of analysis can be seen in the Figure 6, which shows the "Rotor Groove Temperature", another variable of the Stator Armature component. A comparison of the behavior of the variable in GU4 and GU6 is presented through the Boxplot and Time Series diagrams. The graphs show very similar behavior, as expected, even though the boxplot shows less dispersion for GU4, the green one. A complement to this comparison was developed based on the frequency histograms (Figure 7) and the same behavior was detected. With histograms, it can be seen more clearly the dispersion of the data.

This type of comparative analysis between the two generating units was developed for all variables, whenever data from both generating units were available.

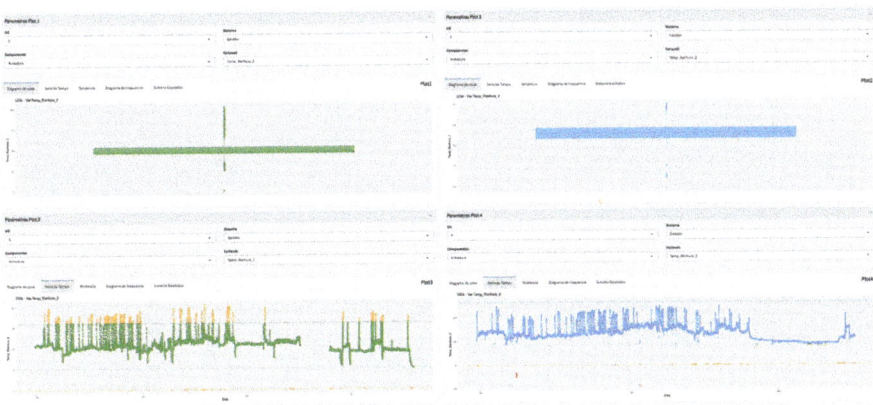

Figure 6. Rotor Groove—Comparison GU4 vs. GU6—Boxplot and Time Series.

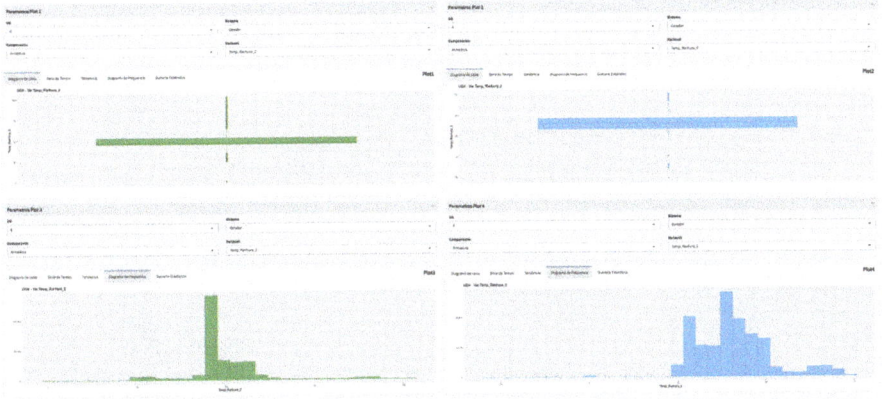

Figure 7. Rotor Groove—Comparison GU4 vs. GU6—Boxplot and Histogram.

A final analysis developed for all variables is illustrated in Figure 8, a time series decomposition, in this case for the Armature current. This is an important analysis, since when we look to the original data, many times we do not see certain behaviors as they are obscured by random effects. The time series decomposition shows three components of the series: the tendency, seasonality, and random effect (remainder). Through these decomposition tendencies, seasonality effects became much clearer, giving the stakeholders important information for the decision. These effects are clear in Figure 8. The figure shows in its upper part the original data. Then it presents the trend and seasonality curves in sequence. In addition, in its lower part it presents the random component (remainder). It is perfectly possible to see in the trend curve that in two moments in time the variable showed a growth trend, which was later reversed. Regarding seasonality, it can be seen that there are reasonably well-defined cycles, in which peaks occur. In addition, these peaks are reflected in the original data curve, as can be seen.

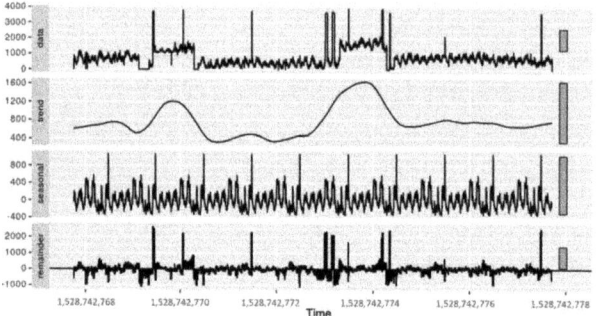

Figure 8. Armature Current—Time Series Decomposition.

Some important results were obtained in this module, and for this, the role of the analytical workbench in the developed analyses must be highlighted, not only in this Module 3 but also in Module 2, as already reported, having contributed significantly to the identification of anomalies associated with critical variables.

As stated earlier, the section showed some examples with focus on the Stator Armature component, but the figures and discussions presented in this section are just an illustration of the analysis developed. In fact, the entire set of variables was submitted to an exploratory analysis, which was a comprehensive and extensive work. Indeed, more than 750 diagrams have been generated, including dashboards of the types presented above, graphs of time series decomposition, and other types of diagrams involving comparisons and correlations among variables.

This extensive analysis provided a reasonably deep knowledge about the behaviors of the variables, individually and as a system. At the end of this module, the technical team was confident that the accumulated knowledge about the system at UHB was robust and that they could move on to the next module to develop predictive modeling, discussed in the next section.

5.4. Predictive Modeling Results

Before describing this last module of the framework is important to point out once more, the general objective of this application, which is to support the predictive maintenance decisions, by a minimization of corrective maintenance occurrence, and so, the objective of this application is to support predictive maintenance decisions, identifying when an equipment is in the imminence of a failure.

The predictive modeling was subdivided in two modules:

A first part of this application is a predictive model to identify the variables significantly associated with equipment failures, and, by the values of these significant variables, whether the equipment is close to a failure point or not.

The second part of the application is a time series forecasting model, developed to predict the values of the significant variables, and, thus, to predict the probability of an equipment failure in a future period.

The literature review presented in Section 2 shows an intense use of algorithms such as Artificial Neural Network, Support Vector Machine and others considered to be black box [41]. This term, black box, is used because the algorithm's decision criterion is not visible to humans. In this research, it was preferred for its first model, to use an AI algorithm more similar to a white box [41], where decision-making based on the algorithm, can be more easily interpreted by experts, and even by laypeople. In this sense, one of the algorithms employed in the predictive modeling, part 1, of BAProM was the Decision Tree (DT) and for the time series forecasting model was employed an ANN model.

The choice in both cases was technical, but in the first model it was also defined to better take advantage of the experience of the UHB team, who could better visualize the results and who, with their experience, with solid knowledge of the causes of maintenance, could better assess the outputs of the model. However, this model, as well as the whole framework, can be used for any industrial system.

Once again, the "Stator Armature", one of the components of the Generator subsystem (Figure 4), was used to illustrate the experiments carried out with DT, which are presented in this subsection. As mentioned before, the Stator Armature has five critical variables: Active Energy, Armature Tension, Armature Current, Active Power and Rotor Groove temperature. More than one DT were built to contemplate different possibilities of variables combinations. The DT presented here shows one of these DT, which included the three first variables:Active Energy, Armature Tension, Armature Current.

For this experiment, data from 2017 to 2018 were used, equivalent to 5000 samples. The data for training the model were classified with two types of labels: OP (operating normal) and CM (corrective maintenance), defined for data collected 15 days before and after the maintenance. The modeling of the DT algorithm follows the well-known cross-validation process, with 5-fold [37]. The resulting DT Model for this experiment is illustrated in Figure 9.

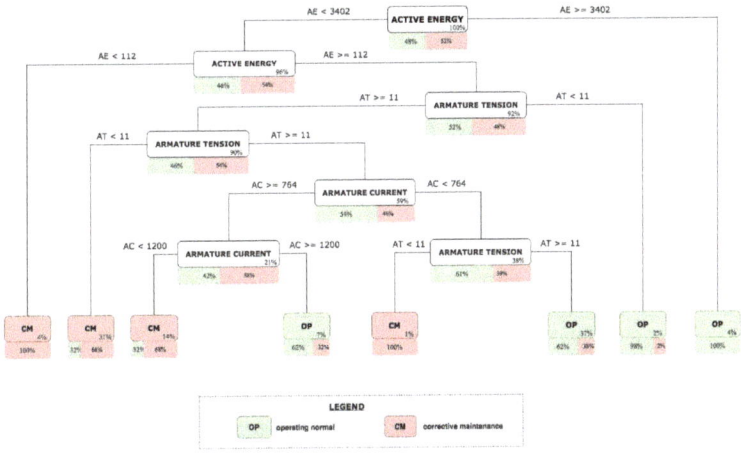

Figure 9. Predictive Decision Tree Model.

Once the decision tree has been generated, from the application of the technique to the data, it is possible to analyze the model output and identify the leaves whose classifications presented the best results in terms of accuracy and quantity, and retrace the path from these leaves to the root node to identify the rules that generated these leaves. With this knowledge of the rules, it will be possible to establish the degree of importance of each variable, defining those that deserve closer observation. Please note that the model provides the ranges of values and probabilities for each variable, which lead to the conditions of OP or CM. These allows the monitoring of these variables so that when reaching these thresholds, an alarm may be triggered to evaluate the possibility of having a maintenance stop before a failure occurs, generating corrective maintenance. The model furnishes, yet, for each node the percentage of observations of the dataset. In terms of performance, the accuracy of the different DT models developed, ranged from 70% to 96%. In addition, in this specific case, a qualitative analysis of the variables at the different levels of the decision tree was developed by UHB specialists, who agreed with the results, which showed the degrees of importance of the variables in the maintenance decision. The DT model, therefore, showed to be a consistent predictive maintenance tool, supporting the decision-making of scheduling equipment stops.

Complementing the DT model, a second type of predictive model based on ANN was developed to forecast the critical variables that would need to be monitored. Thus, in addition to monitoring the actual value of a variable, one can also identify in a future period, when one of these variables would reach a threshold that could lead to an equipment failure. An MLP—Multilayer Perceptron neural network was employed in this model and the forecasting results for the variable "Active Energy" are presented in Figure 10. In that figure, time is expressed in 30-s intervals, which were the time intervals used in data collection and there is a trend curve projected for the future, also showing the curves of the lower and upper limits, of confidence intervals for the forecasts. The intervals are presented for two confidence levels: 80% level, with a narrower range, and a 95% confidence level.

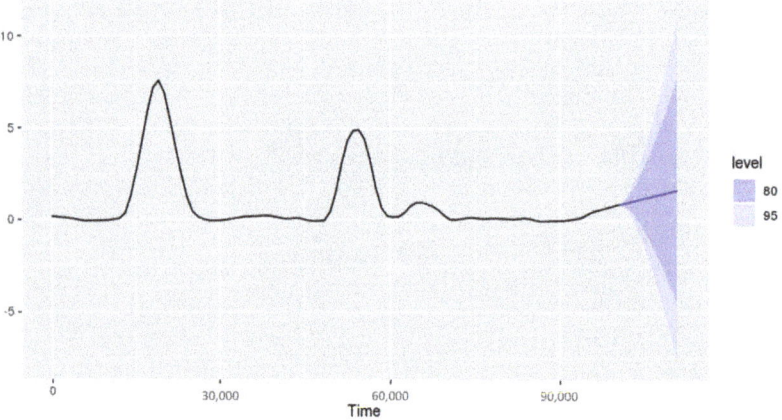

Figure 10. Active Energy Forecasting.

It should be noted that with the two predictive models working together, it can be said that there is a predictive modeling with reasonable robustness, once it can have reference parameters for monitoring the variables in real time, triggering preventive actions every time that a critical variable enters a level of equipment failure; and at the same time, there is an implementation of an effective instrument to project this type of situation for some time in the future, providing even more time, so that the operation teams can prepare and/or prevent such occurrences.

As said before, the research was conducted at UHB in a real-world environment. Therefore, the predictive model described here was tested with real data of UHB's operation. As previously stated, the data used in this study varied from May 2017 to January 2018. Therefore, to validate the model, what was done was to use data from the first months of this period to predict occurrences of failure for the final months of this period. In addition, since the actual data from these forecast months were known, it was possible to compare the predictions made by the model with the actual occurrences. The model was able to identify most of the failures that could have been avoided and to identify maintenance that could have been reprogrammed. These predictions would result in cost savings and productivity increasing.

6. Conclusions and Future Work

This paper presented an application of a methodological proposal, expressed by the framework BAProM—Big Data Analytical Process and Mapping—which sought to contemplate all the phases of a KDD process, from the mapping of processes and critical variables, going through data management, exploratory analysis and even implementing predictive models. The complete framework has been tested in a real-world application in an industrial environment, making it possible to validate and demonstrate its practical feasibility. This real-world application started with the mapping of the entire operational process of the plant and an ETL procedure. Next, a data analysis tool, an "analytical workbench", was developed and implemented. This workbench has been shown to be suitable for different types of analysis, such as pre-processing or exploratory analysis. The tool has multiple possibilities for graphical analysis and statistical metrics computation, in addition to allowing monitoring of system variables, indicating anomalous behavior. It was used in the pre-processing phase and in exploratory analyses with satisfactory results.

A predictive model was developed, based on decision trees, which allowed the identification of more relevant variable thresholds, indicating the imminence of an equipment failure which consequently allows the programming of a predictive maintenance, avoiding unplanned stops for corrective maintenance. The predictive model made it possible to implement a management process for critical variables. Operators can act before an interruption event occurs. The whole process proved to be effective and efficient, given the feasibility of its implementation in a real-world operation.

In addition, a time series forecasting model for these critical variables, based on ANN, was also designed and implemented, which made the process even more effective, since managers can have information on future times when these variables should reach their thresholds, leading to the need for corrective maintenance. The forecasts provide additional time for teams to act, avoiding unexpected equipment stops.

The main conclusions of the research can be expressed as follows:

(a) The phases and tools proposed in the framework proved to be well suited to an industrial process, allowing it to pass effectively through all stages of a big data process.
(b) The process and variable mapping, the first phase of the framework, is a novelty proposed in the research which proved to be a fundamental step. The knowledge obtained in this phase about the entire operation under study was an essential driver for the following phases, mainly to define the most relevant variables to be analyzed.
(c) The development of a computational tool focused on data exploration was essential to support the pre-processing of the data and also the analytical phase, where the behaviors of the variables and their interrelations are identified. The dashboard developed in the project was fundamental to identify non-standardized behaviors in some variables, as well as to identify reference parameters used to propose patterns for monitoring variables.
(d) A predictive model, based on a decision tree, proved to be well suited to identify, with reasonable accuracy, the critical variables that lead to equipment failures and to predict the limit values of those variables that can cause a failure. An additional advantage of this model is that as a decision tree is a "white box" model, the rules identified by the technique are totally clear and known, which favors an implementation to trigger alerts, whenever a threshold of a critical variable is reached.
(e) Another point to be highlighted is that in order to have a projection of the future, the decision tree model must be complemented by a model for forecasting the critical variables considered in the tree. Thus, it is possible to identify in a future period when one of these variables would reach a threshold, leading to equipment failure. An ANN prediction model for such variables proved to be an effective alternative.

Despite the positive points of this framework, it must be considered that there are some limitations that should be considered in future studies and projects. One of these improvements concerns ETL, which relies on operational personnel to transfer production data to a repository dedicated to analytic. This process could be automated. Another limitation refers to data pre-processing in which part of the work is done by inspecting the variables with the support of the dashboard. Some of these tasks could also be automated. Furthermore, the dashboard could be improved by automatically generating some standard graphics and metrics to all or to a group of variables.

Moreover, regarding future works, it would be important to implement on the dashboard the critical values identified in the predictive decision tree model, so that alarms would be automatically triggered without the need for human monitoring when one of those variables is close to those values.

Another opportunity for future work is the application of this methodology in other industrial systems, including other subsystems of the case studied. Finally, one can also develop a validation of the results obtained through decision trees with other types of predictive models, such as artificial neural networks and support vector machines.

Author Contributions: Conceptualization, L.A.S., A.R.d.A.V.F.; methodology, L.A.S., A.R.d.A.V.F. and G.G.d.C.C.; software, G.G.d.C.C. and M.V.B.d.A.V.; validation, L.A.S., A.R.d.A.V.F. and L.S.d.S.; formal analysis, M.V.B.d.A.V. and G.G.d.C.C.; investigation, M.V.B.d.A.V. and G.G.d.C.C.; resources, L.A.S. and L.S.d.S.; data curation, M.V.B.d.A.V. and G.G.d.C.C.; writing–original draft preparation, G.G.d.C.C., L.A.S. and A.R.d.A.V.F.; writing–review and editing, A.R.d.A.V.F., L.A.S., G.G.d.C.C. and M.V.B.d.A.V.; visualization, G.G.d.C.C. and M.V.B.d.A.V.; supervision, L.A.S.; project administration, A.R.d.A.V.F.; funding acquisition, L.S.d.S. All authors have read and agreed to the published version of the manuscript.

Funding: This research is a part of the R&D project "EMAE-ANEEL-P&D 00393-0008/2017", funded by EMAE—-Metropolitan Company of Water & Energy, of the state of São Paulo, Brazil.

Acknowledgments: We thank all the EMAE staff who participated in the R&D project "EMAE—ANEEL-P&D 00393-0008/2017", and all the faculty and student members of the BigMAAp research lab at Mackenzie Presbyterian University.

Conflicts of Interest: The authors declare no conflict of interest. The funders had no role in the design of the study; in the collection, analyses, or interpretation of data; in the writing of the manuscript, or in the decision to publish the results.

References

1. Gandomi, A.; Haider, M. Beyond the hype: Big data concepts, methods, and analytics. *Int. J. Inf. Manag.* **2015**, *35*, 137–144. [CrossRef]
2. Lavalle, S.; Lesser, E.; Shockley, R.; Hopkins, M.; Kruschwitz, N. Big Data, Analytics and the Path From Insights to Value. *MIT Sloan Manag. Rev.* **2011**, *52*, 21–32.
3. Lee, J.; Kao, H.A.; Yang, S. Service Innovation and Smart Analytics for Industry 4.0 and Big Data Environment. *Procedia CIRP* **2014**, *16*, 3–8. [CrossRef]
4. Li, Z.; Wang, Y.; Wang, K.S. Intelligent predictive maintenance for fault diagnosis and prognosis in machine centers: Industry 4.0 scenario. *Adv. Manuf.* **2017**, *5*, 377–387. [CrossRef]
5. Rigatos, G.; Siano, P. Power transformers' condition monitoring using neural modeling and the local statistical approach to fault diagnosis. *Int. J. Electr. Power Energy Syst.* **2016**, *80*, 150–159. [CrossRef]
6. Márquez, F.P.G.; Tobias, A.M.; Pérez, J.M.P.; Papaelias, M. Condition monitoring of wind turbines: Techniques and methods. *Renew. Energy* **2012**, *46*, 169–178. [CrossRef]
7. Bousdekis, A.; Papageorgiou, N.; Magoutas, B.; Apostolou, D.; Mentzas, G. A Proactive Event-driven Decision Model for Joint Equipment Predictive Maintenance and Spare Parts Inventory Optimization. *Procedia CIRP* **2017**, *59*, 184–189. [CrossRef]
8. Ahmad, R.; Kamaruddin, S. An overview of time-based and condition-based maintenance in industrial application. *Comput. Ind. Eng.* **2012**, *63*, 135–149. [CrossRef]
9. Froger, A.; Gendreau, M.; Mendoza, J.E.; Pinson, É.; Rousseau, L.M. Maintenance scheduling in the electricity industry: A literature review. *Eur. J. Oper. Res.* **2016**, *251*, 695–706. [CrossRef]
10. Stenström, C.; Norrbin, P.; Parida, A.; Kumar, U. Preventive and corrective maintenance – cost comparison and cost–benefit analysis. *Struct. Infrastruct. Eng.* **2015**, *12*, 603–617. [CrossRef]

11. Nasr, A.; Gasmi, S.; Sayadi, M. Estimation of the parameters for a complex repairable system with preventive and corrective maintenance. In Proceedings of the 2013 International Conference on Electrical Engineering and Software Applications, Hammamet, Tunisia, 21–23 March 2013.
12. Arno, R.; Dowling, N.; Schuerger, R. Equipment failure characteristics & RCM for optimizing maintenance cost. In Proceedings of the 2015 IEEE/IAS 51st Industrial & Commercial Power Systems Technical Conference (I&CPS), Calgary, AB, Canada, 5–8 May 2015.
13. Sheut, C.; Krajewski, L.J. A decision model for corrective maintenance management. *Int. J. Prod. Res.* **1994**, *32*, 1365–1382. [CrossRef]
14. Liu, B.; Xu, Z.; Xie, M.; Kuo, W. A value-based preventive maintenance policy for multi-component system with continuously degrading components. *Reliab. Eng. Syst. Saf.* **2014**, *132*, 83–89. [CrossRef]
15. Yin, S.; Ding, S.X.; Xie, X.; Luo, H. A Review on Basic Data-Driven Approaches for Industrial Process Monitoring. *IEEE Trans. Ind. Electron.* **2014**, *61*, 6418–6428. [CrossRef]
16. Jing, C.; Hou, J. SVM and PCA based fault classification approaches for complicated industrial process. *Neurocomputing* **2015**, *167*, 636–642. [CrossRef]
17. Yin, Z.; Hou, J. Recent advances on SVM based fault diagnosis and process monitoring in complicated industrial processes. *Neurocomputing* **2016**, *174*, 643–650. [CrossRef]
18. Yan, J.; Meng, Y.; Lu, L.; Li, L. Industrial Big Data in an Industry 4.0 Environment: Challenges, Schemes, and Applications for Predictive Maintenance. *IEEE Access* **2017**, *5*, 23484–23491. [CrossRef]
19. Civerchia, F.; Bocchino, S.; Salvadori, C.; Rossi, E.; Maggiani, L.; Petracca, M. Industrial Internet of Things monitoring solution for advanced predictive maintenance applications. *J. Ind. Inf. Integr.* **2017**, *7*, 4–12. [CrossRef]
20. Gatica, C.P.; Koester, M.; Gaukstern, T.; Berlin, E.; Meyer, M. An industrial analytics approach to predictive maintenance for machinery applications. In Proceedings of the 2016 IEEE 21st International Conference on Emerging Technologies and Factory Automation (ETFA), Berlin, Germany, 6–9 September 2016.
21. Vallim-Filho, A.R.A.; Okido, P.; Silva, L.A.; Vallim, M.V.B.A.; Silva, L.S. Data Dimensionality Reduction based on Variables Clustering. *XI Int. Stat. Congr.* **2019**, *1*, 1–10.
22. Sampaio, G.S.; de Aguiar Vallim Filho, A.R.; da Silva, L.S.; da Silva, L.A. Prediction of Motor Failure Time Using an Artificial Neural Network. *Sensors* **2019**, *19*, 4342. [CrossRef]
23. Wang, N.; Sun, S.; Si, S.; Li, J. Research of predictive maintenance for deteriorating system based on semi-markov process. In Proceedings of the 2009 16th International Conference on Industrial Engineering and Engineering Management, Beijing, China, 21–23 October 2009.
24. Gao, Z.; Cecati, C.; Ding, S.X. A Survey of Fault Diagnosis and Fault-Tolerant Techniques—Part I: Fault Diagnosis With Model-Based and Signal-Based Approaches. *IEEE Trans. Ind. Electron.* **2015**, *62*, 3757–3767. [CrossRef]
25. Carvalho, T.P.; Soares, F.A.A.M.N.; Vita, R.; da P. Francisco, R.; Basto, J.P.; Alcalá, S.G.S. A systematic literature review of machine learning methods applied to predictive maintenance. *Comput. Ind. Eng.* **2019**, *137*, 106024. [CrossRef]
26. Zenisek, J.; Holzinger, F.; Affenzeller, M. Machine learning based concept drift detection for predictive maintenance. *Comput. Ind. Eng.* **2019**, *137*, 106031. [CrossRef]
27. Nguyen, K.T.; Medjaher, K. A new dynamic predictive maintenance framework using deep learning for failure prognostics. *Reliab. Eng. Syst. Saf.* **2019**, *188*, 251–262. [CrossRef]
28. Sahal, R.; Breslin, J.G.; Ali, M.I. Big data and stream processing platforms for Industry 4.0 requirements mapping for a predictive maintenance use case. *J. Manuf. Syst.* **2020**, *54*, 138–151. [CrossRef]
29. Hu, J.; Chen, P. Predictive maintenance of systems subject to hard failure based on proportional hazards model. *Reliab. Eng. Syst. Saf.* **2020**, *196*, 106707. [CrossRef]
30. Moro, S.; Laureano, R.; Cortez, P. Using data mining for bank direct marketing: An application of the crisp-dm methodology. In Proceedings of the European Simulation and Modelling Conference-ESM'2011 (EUROSIS-ETI), Guimaraes, Portugal, 24–26 October 2011; pp. 117–121.
31. Recker, J. Opportunities and constraints: The current struggle with BPMN. *Bus. Process. Manag. J.* **2010**, *16*, 181–201. [CrossRef]
32. Völzer, H. An overview of BPMN 2.0 and its potential use. In *International Workshop on Business Process Modeling Notation*; Springer: Berlin/Heidelberg, Germany, 2010; pp. 14–15.

33. Park, G.; Chung, L.; Zhao, L.; Supakkul, S. A goal-oriented big data analytics framework for aligning with business. In Proceedings of the 2017 IEEE Third International Conference on Big Data Computing Service and Applications (BigDataService), San Francisco, CA, USA, 6–9 April 2017; pp. 31–40.
34. Nalchigar, S.; Yu, E. Conceptual modeling for business analytics: A framework and potential benefits. In Proceedings of the 2017 IEEE 19th Conference on Business Informatics (CBI), Thessaloniki, Greece, 24–27 July 2017; Volume 1, pp. 369–378.
35. Abdelsalam, H.M.; Shoaeb, A.R.; Elassal, M.M. Enhancing Decision Model Notation (DMN) for better use in Business Analytics (BA). In *Proceedings of the 10th International Conference on Informatics and Systems*; ACM: New York, NY, USA, 2016; pp. 321–322.
36. García, S.; Luengo, J.; Herrera, F. *Data Preprocessing in Data Mining*; Springer: Berlin/Heidelberg, Germany, 2015.
37. Han, J.; Pei, J.; Kamber, M. *Data Mining: Concepts and Techniques*; Elsevier: Amsterdam, The Netherlands, 2011.
38. Fayyad, U.; Piatetsky-Shapiro, G.; Smyth, P. From data mining to knowledge discovery in databases. *AI Mag.* **1996**, *17*, 37–37.
39. Turban, E.; Sharda, R.; Aronson, J.E.; King, D. *Business Intelligence: A Managerial Approach*; Pearson Prentice Hall: Corydonê, IN, USA, 2008.
40. Elmasri, R.; Navathe, S. *Fundamentals of Database Systems*; Pearson: London, UK, 2017; Volume 7.
41. Abdallah, I.; Dertimanis, V.; Mylonas, H.; Tatsis, K.; Chatzi, E.; Dervili, N.; Worden, K.; Maguire, E. Fault diagnosis of wind turbine structures using decision tree learning algorithms with big data. In *Safety and Reliability–Safe Societies in a Changing World*; CRC Press: Boca Raton, FL, USA, 2018; pp. 3053–3061.
42. Haykin, S.O. *Neural Networks and Learning Machines*, 3rd ed.; Pearson: London, UK, 2008.
43. Grein, H.; Lorenz, M.; Angehrn, R.; Bezinge, A. Inspection periods for Pelton runners. *Water Power Dam Constr.* **1985**, *37*, 49.

Publisher's Note: MDPI stays neutral with regard to jurisdictional claims in published maps and institutional affiliations.

© 2020 by the authors. Licensee MDPI, Basel, Switzerland. This article is an open access article distributed under the terms and conditions of the Creative Commons Attribution (CC BY) license (http://creativecommons.org/licenses/by/4.0/).

Article

An Innovative Technology for Monitoring the Distribution of Abutment Stress in Longwall Mining

Zhibiao Guo [1,2], Weitao Li [1,2,*], Songyang Yin [1,2], Dongshan Yang [1,2] and Zhibo Ma [1,2]

[1] State Key Laboratory for Geomechanics & Deep Underground Engineering,
China University of Mining & Technology, Beijing 100083, China; 108976@cumtb.edu.cn (Z.G.);
sqt1700602045@student.cumtb.edu.cn (S.Y.); zqt1800603070g@student.cumtb.edu.cn (D.Y.);
sqt1700602044@student.cumtb.edu.cn (Z.M.)

[2] School of Mechanics and Civil Engineering, China University of Mining & Technology, Beijing 100083, China

* Correspondence: bqt1900603020@student.cumtb.edu.cn; Tel.: +86-1565-296-5399

Citation: Guo, Z.; Li, W.; Yin, S.; Yang, D.; Ma, Z. An Innovative Technology for Monitoring the Distribution of Abutment Stress in Longwall Mining. *Energies* **2021**, *14*, 475. https://doi.org/10.3390/en14020475

Received: 21 November 2020
Accepted: 12 January 2021
Published: 18 January 2021

Publisher's Note: MDPI stays neutral with regard to jurisdictional claims in published maps and institutional affiliations.

Copyright: © 2021 by the authors. Licensee MDPI, Basel, Switzerland. This article is an open access article distributed under the terms and conditions of the Creative Commons Attribution (CC BY) license (https://creativecommons.org/licenses/by/4.0/).

Abstract: Fracturing roofs to maintain entry (FRME) is a novel longwall mining method, which has been widely used in China, leading a new mining revolution. In order to research the change law of side abutment pressure and movement law of overlying strata when using the FRME, a new abutment pressure monitoring device, namely, the flexible detection unit (FDU), is developed and is applied in the field. The monitoring results show that compared with the head entry (also called the non-splitting entry), the peak value of the lateral abutment pressure in the tail entry (also termed the splitting entry) is reduced by 17.2% on average, and the fluctuation degree becomes smaller. Then, finite difference software FLAC^{3D} is used to simulate the stress change of the solid coal on both sides of the panel. The simulation results show that the side abutment pressure of the tail entry decreases obviously, which is consistent with the measured results. Comprehensive analysis points out that after splitting and cutting the roof, the fissures can change the motion state of the overlying strata, causing the weight of the overburden borne by the solid coal to reduce; therefore, the side abutment pressure is mitigated.

Keywords: fracturing roofs to maintain entry (FRME); field measurement; numerical simulation; side abutment pressure; strata movement

1. Introduction

The technology of gob-side entry retaining (GER) has been widely utilized worldwide since it was put forward in 1950s [1,2]. Compared with traditional mining methods, this technology has many merits, such as reducing the amount of roadway drivage, saving coal resources, alleviating dynamic mining disturbances, and so on [3]. At present, the common GER is to use high water materials, concrete blocks, gangue walls, and other filling bodies to support the roadway roof to isolate the connection between the roadway and the goaf, so that the roadway can be reused [4,5]. However, when the thick coal seam mining or rapid mining is carried out, the demand for filling materials will increase, and the formation speed of the filling body cannot match the speed of mining, so the roof cannot be supported in time. If the early deformation of the gateroad is serious, it will badly affect the use of the gateroad [6]. Based on this, an innovative GER approach is proposed, which can make fully use of the load-bearing capacity of gangue body to reduce periodic weighting load and improve the surrounding rock stress environment [7,8].

Many experts and scholars have conducted research on FRME, obtaining a series of rich results. He et al. [9] invented an energy-absorbing bolt with large elongation and high constant resistance. They introduced its structure and action mechanism in detail, and constructed a constitutive equation to derive the frictional resistance of the bolt during operation. Tao et al. [10] carried out a series of static tension tests on the constant resistance large deformation (CRLD) bolts. The results further indicated that the CRLD bolts had the characteristics of high support resistance, large elongation, absorbing energy, and negative Poisson's ratio effect. Gao et al. [11] used COMSOL software to simulate and investigate bilateral cumulative tensile explosion technology (BCTET); they found that the cracks, created by explosions, could be propagated toward the set direction. However, there were no cracks in the non-set direction. Finally, a complete cutting line was formed between the blasting holes. Hu et al. [12] established a mechanical model for the unilateral crack propagation of the BCTET, and deduced the yield condition of crack formation. Guo et al. [13] implemented a great many axial compression tests on the novel gangue prevention structure in the laboratory, and the results suggested that the torque value of block cable was closely related to the axial force of the gangue prevention structure. Wang et al. [14] built a mechanical model of the retained entry roof according to the energy variational theory, and explored the factors that made the retained entry roof deform. He believed that the rotation of the main roof and the width of the entry had the most obvious influence on the roof deformation, and raised a method to control the roof deformation by designing a reasonable roof splitting height and roadway width. Fan et al. [15] set up a mechanical model of the FRME and studied the vertical stress and displacement of the coal wall under different heights and angles of the roof cutting through UDEC software. Guo et al. [16] simulated the dynamic response of the roof with different roof fracturing angles by FLAC^{3D} for the first time. They considered that the dynamic response of the roof was moderate and the gateway remained stable when the roof splitting angle was 10–20°, and when the angle was 20–30°, the dynamic response increased obviously and the gateway became unstable. Sun and others [17] expounded the principle of the FRME to control rockburst. He believed that the FRME could reduce the vertical stress and stress fluctuation of gateway roof. He et al. [6] investigated the loads monitoring of hydraulic support at different positions on the panel of thick coal seams. The results testified that the loads of hydraulic support near the splitting line could be reduced by approximately 60% compared with that far away from the splitting line, at the same time, periodic weighting intervals of roof increased near the splitting line. The theses [18–20] demonstrated that the FRME could be applied under complex geological conditions.

The above papers discussed the surrounding rock deformation characteristics, engineering technical parameters, key technologies, roof control, and so on through the methods of numerical simulation, theoretical analysis, and field measurement. However, there are no analyses of the overlying strata movement after roof cutting and the changes of the abutment pressure caused by the strata movement. The changes of the abutment stress are the most crucial reason for the large deformation and instability of the entry. It is of great significance to research the changes of abutment stress for further understanding the deformation mechanism of surrounding rock of the FRME.

The purpose of this paper is to compare the difference of lateral abutment pressure between the tail entry and head entry by monitoring the abutment pressure of solid coal on both sides of the working face with self-developed and more reliable FDU, and then the influence of cutting seam on the lateral abutment pressure of solid coal is explored. On the basis of fully considering the reasons for the change of abutment pressure after cutting the roof, the change of overburden movement caused by the slit is analyzed.

At present, there is still no study on the abutment stress of the FRME. Taking the geological conditions of Lvtang Mine as the engineering background, this paper analyzes the side abutment stress of coal mass in the tail roadway and head roadway by self-developed FDU combined with numerical simulation, and explores the changes of abutment stress, so as to reveal the movement laws of overhanging rock.

2. Introduction of the FDU
2.1. Structure and Parameter of the FDU

The FDU consists of flexible shape (thin steel wire and polymer material composition), injection interface, plug, and iron sheet, as shown in Figure 1a. Its main technical specifications are as follows: the measurement range is up to 60 MPa, the length 500 mm, the diameter 45 mm, the accuracy from 0.5 to 1.0%FS, the repeatability from 0.2 to 0.4%FS, and the resolution 0.01%FS. The entity diagram of FDU is shown in Figure 1b.

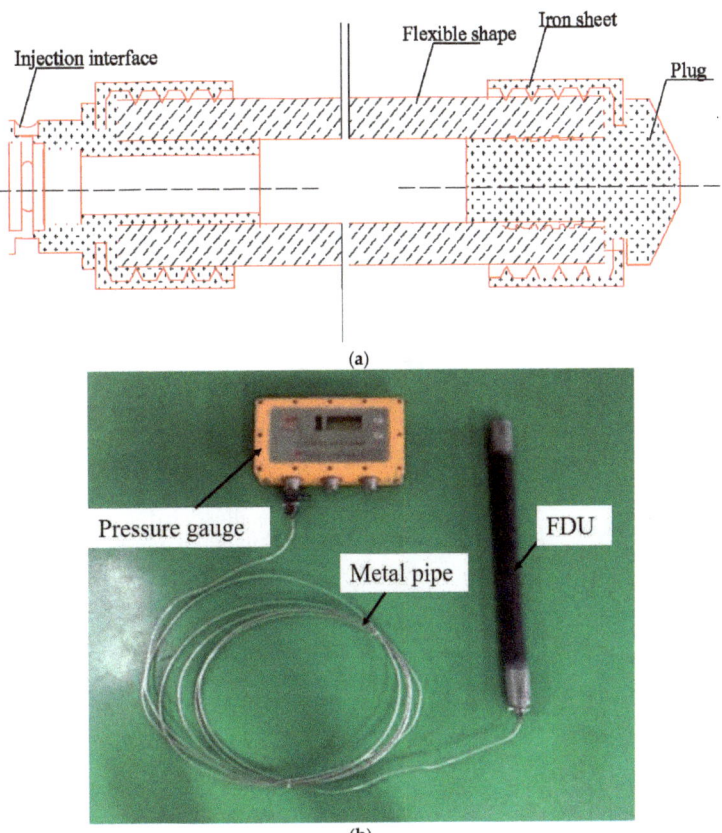

Figure 1. The picture of the flexible detection unit (FDU): (**a**) Interior structural diagram of the FDU. (**b**) Entity graph of the FDU.

2.2. Application Method of the FDU

The installation steps for the FDU are as follows: (1) Use a twist drill rod with a diameter slightly larger than that of the FDU to drill holes of different depth into the solid coal. (2) Connect the hand pump, pressure gauge and metal pipe together through the tee. (3) Fill the manual pump with emulsion and press it until one end of the metal tube flows out of the emulsion to discharge the air inside the metal tube. (4) Fill the emulsion from the injection interface of the FDU to drain the internal air. (5) Connect the metal tubes and FDU. (6) Slowly advance the unit to the bottom of the borehole, as illustrated in Figure 2a. (7) The manual pump continues to press, and this process should ensure that the pressure increases steadily until the pressure gauges read 5.25 MPa and maintain for 30 min. At this time, the units expand to fit the hole wall, as shown in Figure 2b. (8) Relieve the pump pressure and observe the changes of the pressure gauge reading. If the reading cannot be stabilized at the preset initial pressure value, then step 7 should be repeated until the initial pressure reaches a stable level. (9) Debug the transmission substation and the master station to ensure that the pressure gauge data can be transmitted to the ground computer in time and accurately.

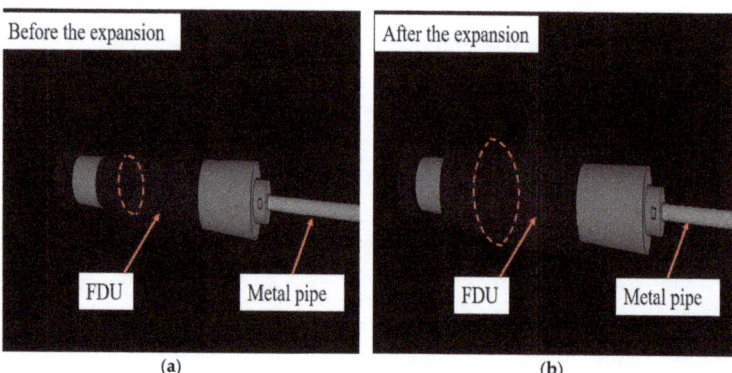

Figure 2. Comparison picture of the FDU before and after applying pressure: (**a**) Before the expansion. (**b**) After the expansion.

2.3. Working Principle of the FDU

At present, it is common that borehole stress meters are made of rigid materials and can only monitor the abutment pressure at a certain point or a certain face. There are no measurement data in the elastic deformation phase of coal caused by the installation clearance of rigid materials, as illustrated in Figure 3a. The objective of the FDU is to monitor the whole changes of abutment pressure in coal. Its working principle is shown in Figure 3b. After the liquid at a certain pressure injected into the FDU, it will expand, which can generate a pre-tightening force to the borehole surroundings. As the stoping face advances, the abutment pressure will move forward, causing the borehole surroundings to deform and break under the influence of dynamic pressure. Therefore, when the FDU is squeezed into different degrees, the internal liquid pressure will change clearly. Those pressure changes will be transmitted to the wireless pressure sensor through metal pipe, and the strain gauge on the elastomer of the sensor will change its value after being pressed, causing the change amount of the electrical signal to amplify. Then, the amplifying signal will be converted into a voltage signal after driven by the sensor. Finally, the CPU will convert the voltage signal into the pressure value and display it on the pressure gauge. Meanwhile, the pressure value will real-timely be transfer to the transmission substation through wireless communication, which will upload to the ground computer via optical cable.

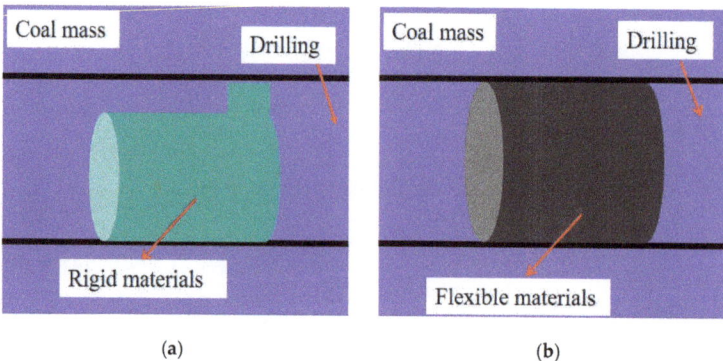

Figure 3. Installation diagram of borehole stress meters with different materials: (**a**) Installation diagram of borehole stress meters with rigid materials. (**b**) Installation diagram of borehole stress meters with flexible materials.

The main structures of the abutment pressure monitoring system are mainly made up of five parts: FDU, pressure gauges, transmission substations, transmission main station, and computer. The working principle of the abutment pressure monitoring system is shown in Figure 4. The FDU, in real-time, can monitor the pressure changes of the surrounding rock in the coal body. The pressure gauge can transmit the pressure value to the transmission substation by wireless signal every 5 min. Each substation can receive the signals of multiple pressure gauges at the same time, and it can transfer the received singles to the main transmission station through the line. The main station can simultaneously process the singles of several substations, and then transmit all the information to the ground transmission interface with the optical fiber. Finally, through the independently developed software system in the computer, the observed data can be displayed in forms of curve and chart. Then, the observed data can be showed to users graphically through the Internet, which is convenient for users to analyze and view them in real-time and remotely.

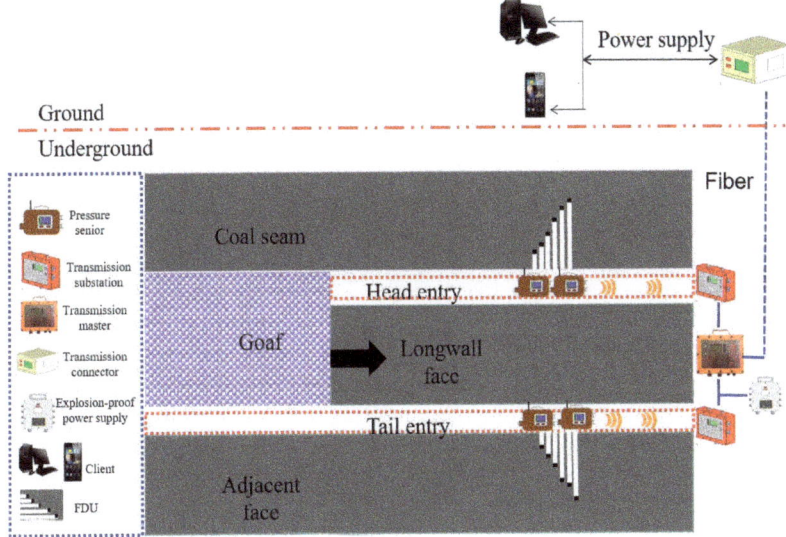

Figure 4. Working principle of the abutment pressure monitoring system.

2.4. Principle of the FRME

The implementation procedure of the FRME can be divided into four parts, which are illustrated in Figure 5. Before the mining of the working face, CRLD anchor cables are constructed in the roadway to strengthen the roof, so as to prevent the disturbance of the roadway roof caused by the subsequent roof pre-split blasting and the roof collapse in the goaf, as shown in Figure 5a. Then, the structure of the blasting holes is implemented on the side of the working face in the tail entry according to the designed height, angle, and distance between the blasting holes. Sequentially putting the cumulative energy explosion tubes [11,19], the emulsified blasting powders, detonators, and the stemming into the blasting holes to form a continuous fracturing line along the axis of the roadway, as shown in Figure 5b. After the mining of the panel, the goaf side of the roadway roof will cave automatically along the splitting face under the action of the mine pressure. Then, the gangue of different size and shape will be formed in the process of roof collapse. Meanwhile, in order to prevent the gangue from rushing into the entry in the process of fall and compaction, U-shaped steels, metal meshes, and single hydraulic pillars beside the entry can be used to block the gangue, as shown in Figure 5c. In this way, the compacted gangue can be used as a side of the entry to continue to serve for the mining of the next panel, as shown in Figure 5d. The three-dimensional schematic diagram of the FRME is shown in Figure 6.

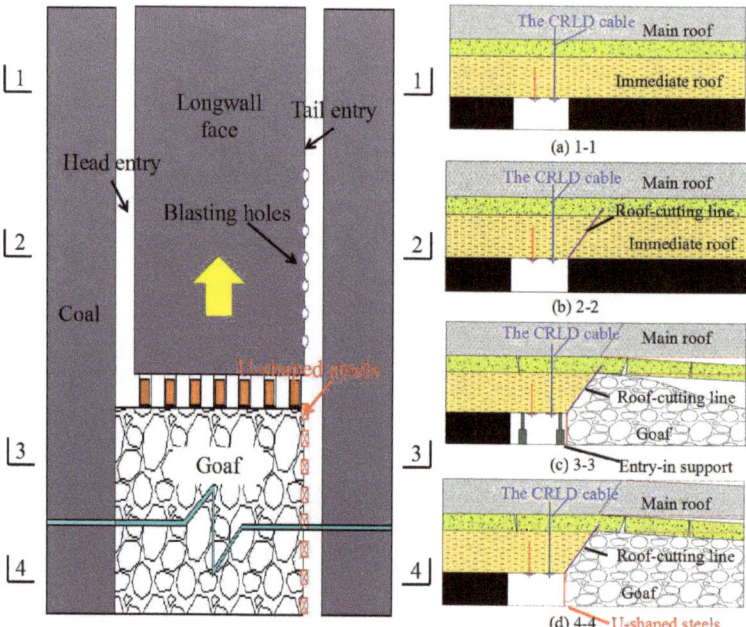

Figure 5. The implementation procedure of the fracturing roofs to maintain entry (FRME): (**a**) The procedure of strengthening the entry roof by constructing the constant resistance large deformation (CRLD) cables. (**b**) The procedure of implementing blasting holes and fracturing the retained entry roof. (**c**) The procedure of installing U-shaped steels and entry-in supports when the coal is mined. (**d**) The procedure of withdrawing the entry-in supports when the retained entry keeps stable.

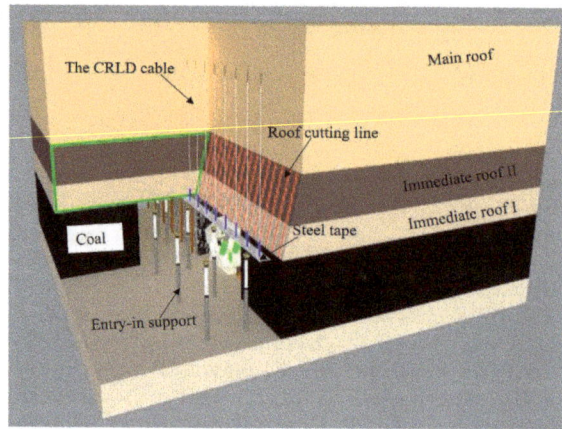

Figure 6. Three-dimensional schematic diagram of the FRME.

3. Methods
3.1. Method of Numerical Analysis
3.1.1. Study Site

Lvtang Coal Mine is located in Bijie area, Guizhou Province, China. This article analyzes the actual engineering geological conditions according to S204 working face of Lvtang Coal Mine. This panel is the first panel in this mining area, and the adjacent working faces are represented by the S205 and S203 panels. The average strike length of S204 panel is 310 m and the dip length is 115 m. The dip angle of coal seam is 3–9°, with an average of 6°. The thickness of coal seam is 0.9–7.55 m, with an average thickness of 3.4 m. The layout of panels is shown in Figure 7. The mine belongs to coal and gas outburst mine. In order to reduce the gas concentration to achieve safe mining, it is necessary to excavate a gas drainage roadway above the working face to extract gas from the coal before mining. It is planned to use FRME in tail entry, and the head entry will naturally fall.

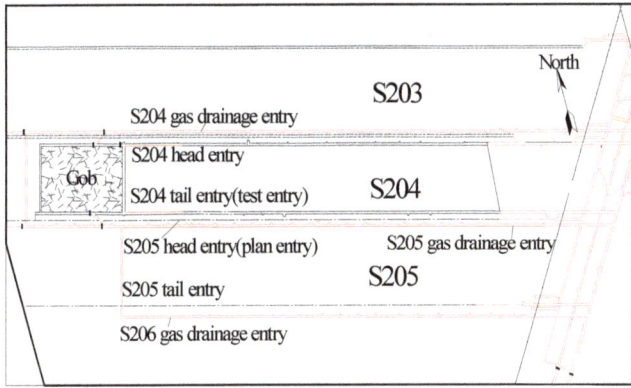

Figure 7. The layout of panels.

The average buried depth of S204 mining panel is 210 m. The geological drilling picture of the S204 panel is shown in Figure 8. The roof strata above the S204 face are mainly composed of silty mudstone and muddy siltstone, and the floor stratum are made up of silty mudstone, coal, and muddy siltstone. It can be seen from the stratigraphic column that the lithology of the roof and the coal seam changes greatly.

Thickness/m	Depth/m	Lithology	Remarks
2.6	194.1	Silty mudstone	
7.3	201.4	Muddy siltstone	Main roof
2.5	203.9	Coal	Immediate roof
3.2	207.1	Silty mudstone	Immediate roof
4.4	211.5	Coal	
2.3	213.8	Silty mudstone	Immediate floor
0.9	214.7	Coal	Immediate floor
4.5	219.2	Muddy siltstone	Main floor

Figure 8. The geological drilling picture of the S204 panel.

3.1.2. Numerical Modal

According to the symmetrical characteristic of the model, in order to shorten the calculation time, the strike length of the model is shortened to become half of the actual engineering geological conditions. The work in [21] also employs the symmetry principle for numerical simulation. At the same time, in order to eliminate the influence of boundary conditions, 60 m boundary coal pillars are added on the left and right sides of the model. This model is divided into 8 layers, and the size (length × width × height) is 244 m × 160 m × 50 m. The Mohr–Coulomb criterion is used in the model. Constraints are imposed on the surrounding and bottom surfaces to restrict its movement. The stress of 5.25 MPa is applied on the upper surface to simulate the weight of the overlying rock. According to the geological situation of S204 coalface in Lvtang Coal Mine, a three-dimensional numerical model is established as shown in Figure 9.

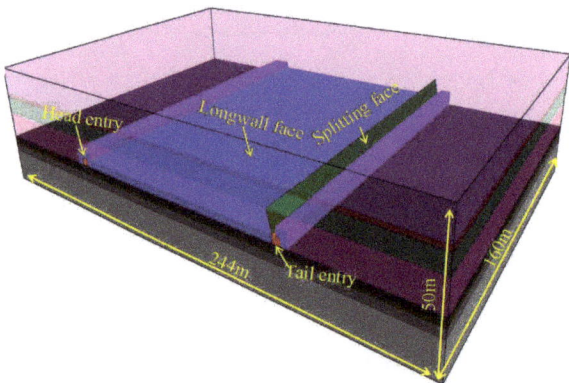

Figure 9. Three-dimensional numerical model of S204 coalface.

The splitting surface is an abstract simulation of the blasting effect. Because the distance between these blast holes is extremely close and they can penetrate each other after blasting, the blast holes and slit between them can be simplified to dispose, which can be regarded as a fissure surface composed of uniform blocks in numerical model. The length of the on-site blast holes is 8 m and the angle is 15°; therefore, the length of the fissure surface is also 8 m, the angle is 15°, and both the width and the diameter of the blast holes are 48 mm. The blasting is simulated by excavating the fissure face.

The mechanical parameters of each rock mass are shown in Table 1. Among them, the parameters of coal body and roof rock are obtained by GSI rock mass classification method on the basis of rock mechanics parameters obtained by laboratory uniaxial compression test and field borehole peep to estimation GSI value. The parameters of floor sandy mudstone are obtained by GSI rock mass classification method based on the measured mechanical parameters of coal mine exploration.

Table 1. Mechanical parameters of rock mass.

Lithology	Density (kg/m^3)	Tension (MPa)	Cohesion (MPa)	Friction (°)	Bulk (GPa)	Shear (GPa)
Coal	1550	2.35	1.45	25.2	1.31	1.44
Muddy siltstone	2240	1.43	3.07	32.0	6.47	4.33
Silty mudstone	2450	3.52	2.18	35.1	4.16	7.4
Splitting face	2046	2.43	2.23	30.7	3.98	4.39

3.2. Method of Field Measurement

In order to discuss and investigate the evolution laws of the side abutment stress in the tail entry and head entry and the influence of the fracture and movement of overlying strata on gateway stability after using the FRME, 12 sets of the FDU were installed in the solid coal of the head entry and tail entry of 100 m in front of the coalface to monitor the changes of coal mass stress, independently. The installation depth of the FDU is different, because the authors of [21–23] found that the load-bearing capacity of coal is related to the distance from the coal wall. The distances between the installation position of the FDU and the gateway surface are 3 m, 5 m, 7 m, 9 m, 11 m, and 13 m, as shown in Figure 10a. According to the actual situation of the mining face, the twist drill pipes with a diameter of 48 mm are selected to drill the holes, which are perpendicular to the coal wall and 1 m away from the gateway floor, as shown in Figure 10b.

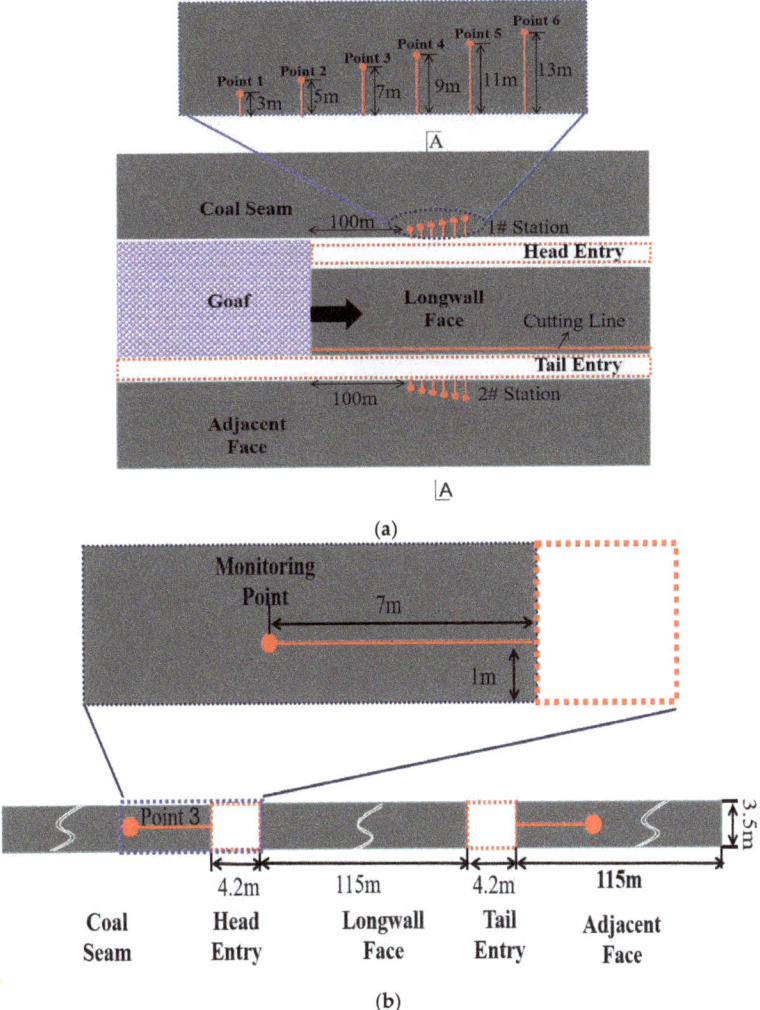

Figure 10. The test site and position of the FDU: (a) Longwall panel layout and the test site of the FDU. (b) A-A cross section in Figure 10a.

4. Data Analysis of the Abutment Stress

4.1. Data Analysis of the Field Measurement

4.1.1. Monitoring Result of the Strike Abutment Stress

Stations 1# and 2# started to be installed at 200 m in front of the working face from 1 August 2019. Due to the need of coal mining and the restriction of construction, the installation was officially completed and connected network single at about 100 m in front of the working face on 16 August. Therefore, the pressure changes of the previous FDU were not recorded in time. The pressure variations were only recorded when the signal was switched on. The unit's pressure had been recorded until 15 September at 100 m behind the working face. The strike abutment pressure monitoring curve of the stations 1# is shown in Figure 11.

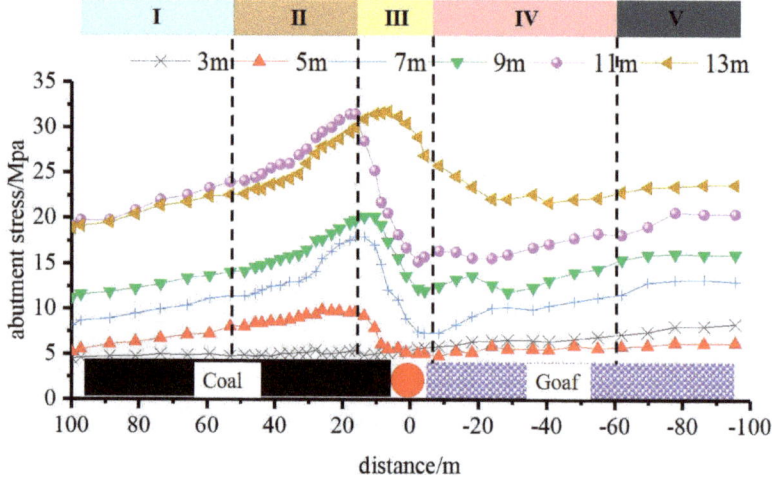

Figure 11. Strike abutment pressure curve of the roof-noncutting entry (head entry) of station 1#.

The abutment pressure at the 3 m position of the station 1# rises the slowest, and the increasing trend is not obvious, which is likely that the coal mass in this range was yielded or even destroyed by the strong abutment pressure, so its bearing capacity is smaller. The variation tendencies of the strike abutment pressure at 5–13 m are the same, showing a state of increasing first, then decreasing and then increasing, and finally stabilizing. However, the speed and amplitude of the strike abutment pressure growth within the range of 100 to 20 m in front of the working face increases in turn with the increase of the coal depth.

About 20 m in front of the panel, the strike abutment stress at 5–13 m decreased rapidly, and the degree of stress fluctuation is large. This is because that as the longwall face approaces the FDU, a concentration area of abutment pressure will be formed ahead of the face, where the abutment pressure will be transmitted to the coal rib through the roof, where the stress concentration zone will be formed, causing the plastic failure of the coal mass. With the advancement of the longwall face, the failure will continue to develop deeper. Finally, a plastic zone with a length of about 20 m is formed on the coal rib, as a result, the carrying capacity of the solid coal is weakened [24]. After the longwall face pushes through the units, the strike abutment stress at 3–13 m grows slowly with the increase of the longwall face distance; in the meantime, the rising trend is almost the same as the amplitude. This is because the weight of the overburden on the longwall face is shifted after the coal seam is mined to the solid coal on both sides of the face and the gangue falling in the goaf, so the solid coal begins to slowly increase in stress. It should be mentioned that the irregular fluctuation of the abutment pressure behind the longwall face belongs to the stress fluctuation that is caused by the periodic collapse of the goaf roof.

The monitored distance of the abutment pressure at 2# station in the tail entry is the same as that of 1# station in the head entry. However, the abutment pressure has changed significantly. Strike abutment pressure curve of station 2# in the tail entry is illustrated in Figure 12.

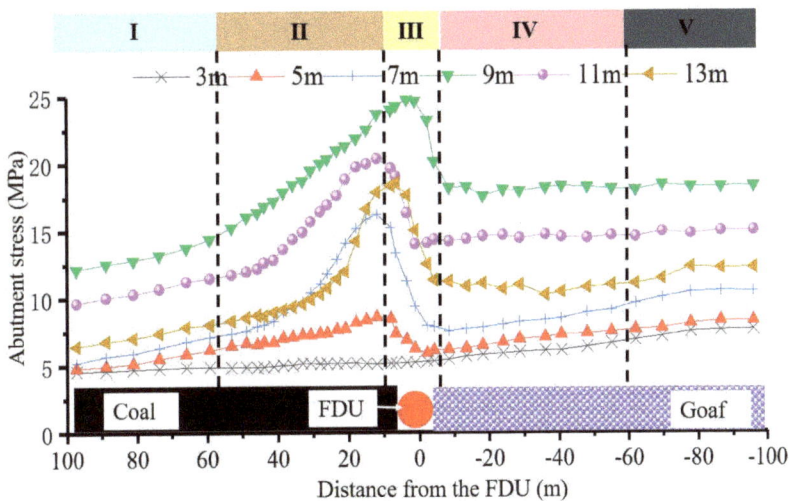

Figure 12. Strike abutment pressure curve of the roof-cutting entry (tail entry) of station 2#.

The change trend of the strike abutment pressure at the 5–13 m measurement points of solid coal in the roof-cutting roadway (tail roadway) is also the same as the roof-noncutting roadway (head roadway), showing a state of increasing first, then decreasing and then increasing, and finally stabilizing. When the FDU is located more than 60 m in front of the working face, the abutment pressure at different measuring points of the 2# station increases slowly, and the curve is relatively stable. This indicates that when the distance of coal body is over 60 m in front of the working face, it is affected slightly by mining pressure. When the FDU is located in the range of 60 to 10 m in front of the working face, the abutment pressure at 5–13 m of station 2# begins to increase rapidly, reaching a maximum value about 10 m in front of the working face. The growth rate of the abutment pressure at 9–11 m is obviously greater than that of other depths, indicating that the coal body in this range is very susceptible to the impact of mining pressure. Moreover, the abutment pressure at 9 m is always greater than that of other depths.

When the FDU is from 10 m in front of the working face to near the working face, the abutment pressure of each measuring point drops rapidly, which is related to the mining of the working face. When the FDU is from near the working face to 60 m behind the working face, the abutment pressure of each measuring point increases slowly. When the lagging face of the FDU exceeds 60 m, the abutment pressure remains stable.

However, we discover that there are several differences in the strike abutment pressure curve of each measuring point between the two stations:

(1) The peak value of strike abutment stress at each measuring point of station 2# has been reduced, with an average diminishment of 17.2%.
(2) The peak point of strike abutment stress at each measuring point of station 2# is closer to the longwall face.
(3) After the stope face pushed pass the units, the abutment pressure at each measuring point of the station 2# increases steadily, unlike the violent fluctuation of the abutment pressure occurs at the measuring point of station 1#, indicating that the periodical pressure of the stope face on the tail roadway weakens.

(4) The abutment pressure at the 9 m measuring point of station 2# is the highest, at the same time, the abutment pressure of each measuring point generally enlarges at first and then decreases as the depth from the coal wall increases.

The variation trend of the strike abutment pressure at each measuring point of station 2# is almost the same as that of station 1#. Therefore, the strike abutment pressure of the solid coal can be divided into 5 regions: slow increasing zone I, sharp increasing zone II, rapid reducing zone III, fluctuation enlarging zone (enlarging zone) IV, and stable zone V.

Slow increasing zone I: in this area, from the beginning position of the abutment pressure rise to 55 m in front of the working face, the stress increases slowly, and the abutment pressure curve is relatively smooth. At this time, the deformations of the entry surroundings are also relatively small, and the influence of the advanced abutment pressure on solid coal is not obvious.

Sharp increasing zone II: abutment pressure from about 55 m to 15 m in front of the face goes up rapidly, and the alteration of the abutment stress curve becomes steep. At this time, the deformations of the roadway surroundings get extremely remarkable, which is obviously affected by the advanced abutment pressure.

Rapid reducing zone III: the stress decreases sharply from about 15 m in front of the panel to near the longwall face. At this time, the deformation and its rate of the roadway surrounding rock is relatively great. The coal body on the side of the solid coal in the entry is plastically damaged, and cracks and holes appear in the internal coal mass. The coal releases stress and the abutment stress start to reduce.

Fluctuation enlarging zone (enlarging zone) IV: this area extends from the vicinity of the longwall face to 60 m behind the working face. The abutment stress shows a state of fluctuation increase. This is due to the roof behind the working face periodically breaks under the action of periodic pressure.

Stability zone V: the stress fluctuation is not obvious in 60 m behind the working face in this area and the curve becomes a stable straight line. It suggests that when the lagging distance of coal face is greater than 60 m, the overlying rock has been stabilized.

4.1.2. Monitoring Result of the Side Abutment Stress

In order to analyze the abutment pressure distribution of the coal mass with different depths at the side of solid coal in the tail entry and head entry and the relationship between the side abutment pressure and the working face distance, the average value of the pressure gauge reading of each unit at 60 m, 40 m, and 20 m in front of and behind the mining panel is taken, respectively, to draw the pressure histograms. Figure 13 shows that the abutment pressure distribution of coal mass with different depths at the side of solid coal in the tail entry and head entry and the relationship between the side abutment pressure and the working face distance.

From Figure 13a,b, we can see that when the stations are in front of the working face, the lateral abutment pressure on both sides of panel increases first then declines as the depth changes. The peak point of the lateral abutment pressure in the tail roadway and head roadway is 9 m and 11 m away from the coal wall, respectively. Therefore, the rising range of lateral abutment pressure in the head entry is larger than that of the tail entry. At the same time, compared with the head entry, the peak value of the lateral abutment pressure is smaller in the tail entry, indicating that roof cutting can play a good effect in stress relieving. The closer the FDU is to the working face, the greater the lateral abutment pressure will become, which suggests that the lateral abutment pressure is in the process of dynamic change and has obvious space-time effect [23].

Figure 13c,d shows that when the measuring stations are behind the coalface, the farther the distance from the same measuring point to the coalface is, the higher the recovery degree of the abutment pressure will become, which is related to the transfer of overburden weight to solid coal on both sides of face after coal seam mining [25]. The lateral abutment pressure of the tail roadway climbs up first and then declines, while the lateral abutment pressure of the head roadway shows an increasing trend which has no obvious regularity. Compared with the head roadway, the lateral abutment pressure of the tail roadway in the back of coalface under the same distance is generally smaller.

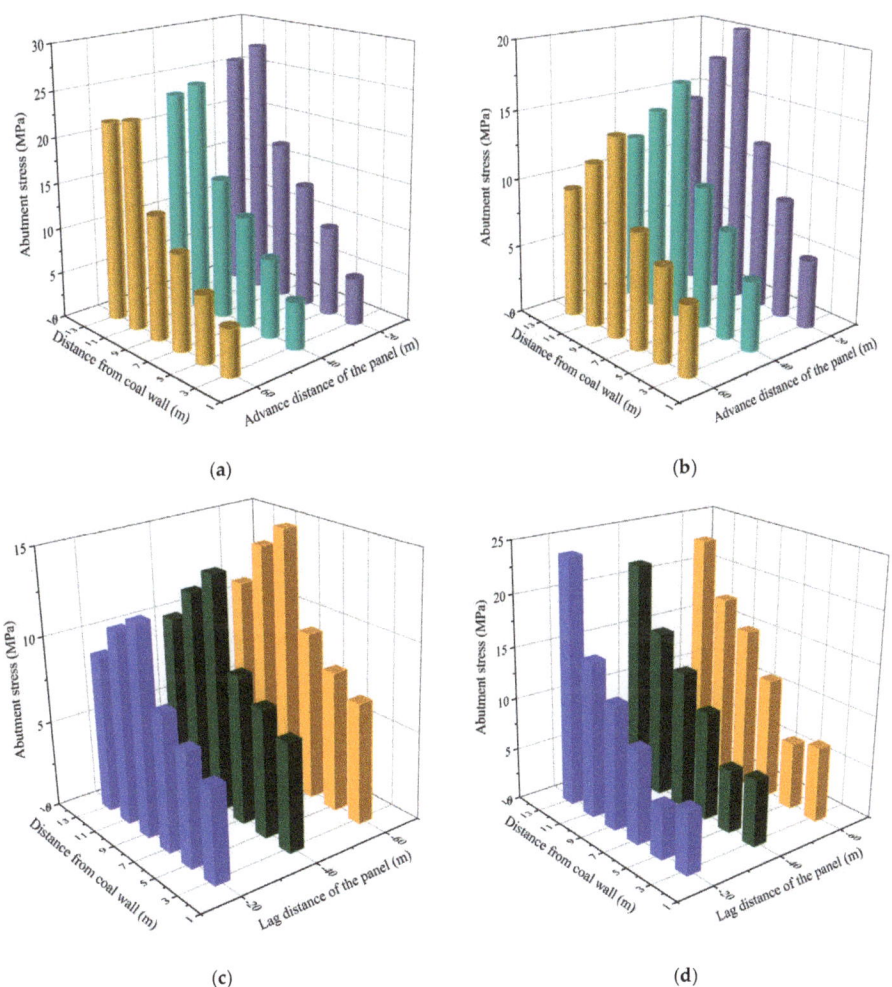

Figure 13. Abutment pressure distribution of coal mass with different depths at the side of solid coal in the tail entry and head entry and the relationship between the side abutment pressure and the working face distance: (**a**) Advanced side abutment pressure in the non-splitting entry (head entry). (**b**) Advanced side abutment pressure in the roof-splitting entry (tail entry). (**c**) Lagged side abutment pressure in the roof-splitting entry (tail entry). (**d**) Lagged side abutment pressure in the non-splitting entry (head entry).

The lateral abutment stress of the tail roadway reaches the maximum at 9 m from the coal wall, and its rising range of 7–9 m from the coal wall is obviously larger than that of 3–7 m in the process of lateral abutment pressure rising. In contrast, in the head roadway, the lateral abutment pressure at a distance of 3 m to 5 m from the coal wall first decreases slightly, then it at a distance of 5 m to 13 m from the coal wall has been increasing, whereas, the increasing rate in this range is not in agreement, which slows down when it is away from the coal wall (5–9 m) and begins to accelerate when it is away from the coal wall (9–13 m).

Variation curve of lateral abutment peak position is shown in Figure 14. We can find that the lateral abutment pressure of the two roadways constantly alters, and the peak position continuously deepens from coal mass. In the end, there will be no change at a certain depth.

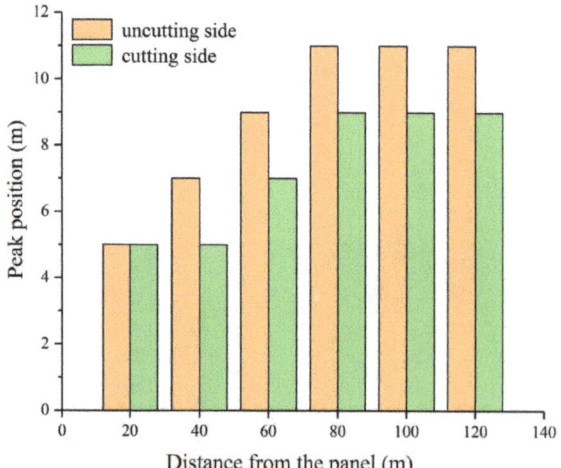

Figure 14. Variation curve of lateral abutment peak position.

Nonetheless, we can also see that there is a significant difference of the lateral abutment pressure in two roadways. The lateral abutment pressure of the head entry has experienced three-step fluctuations to reach stability, while the lateral abutment pressure of the tail roadway goes through two steps to reach a stable state, and a small fluctuation degree is more conducive to maintaining the entry stability, which proves that the slit can change the structure of the roadway roof. As a result, when the technology of the FRME is employed, the solid coal is less affected by the breaking and collapsing gob roof.

4.2. Data Analysis of the Numerical Modal

During the simulated excavation, in order to best meet the reality, we first simulated the excavation of the two entries, then supporting measures of the entries were installed until the calculation reaches the balance, after that the splitting face was mined to simulate blasting. In the end, the simulated exploiting of the mining panel was carried on. The excavation length of the mining panel was 5 m each time, and it was mined a total of 32 times. The cumulative lengths of 40 m and 80 m were selected to research the change laws of side abutment pressure of the FRME.

The three-dimensional cloud maps of the abutment stress distribution in the surrounding rock at the coal face are shown in Figure 15.

From the three-dimensional cloud maps, we can deem that the overall stress will change after the panel is mined. When the roof of mined out area has not completely caved in, the pressure relief area (blue area) is formed. Only if the gob roof collapses fully and caved-rock is compacted by the overlying strata, the stress in the goaf starts to increase slowly. After the mining of the face, the weight of the overhanging rock is supported by the gangue in the goaf, the coal body in front of the panel, and the solid coal on both sides of the roadway, where the stress augments distinctly. When the FRME technology is not used in the tail entry, after 40 m or 80 m excavation of the working face, symmetrical stress concentration areas appear in the solid coal on both sides of the working face (see Figure 15a,b). While, when the tail entry adopts the FRME technology, after the working face is excavated to 40 m or 80 m, due to the blocking effect of the slit, asymmetrical stress concentration areas appear in the solid coal on both sides of the working face (see Figure 15c,d).

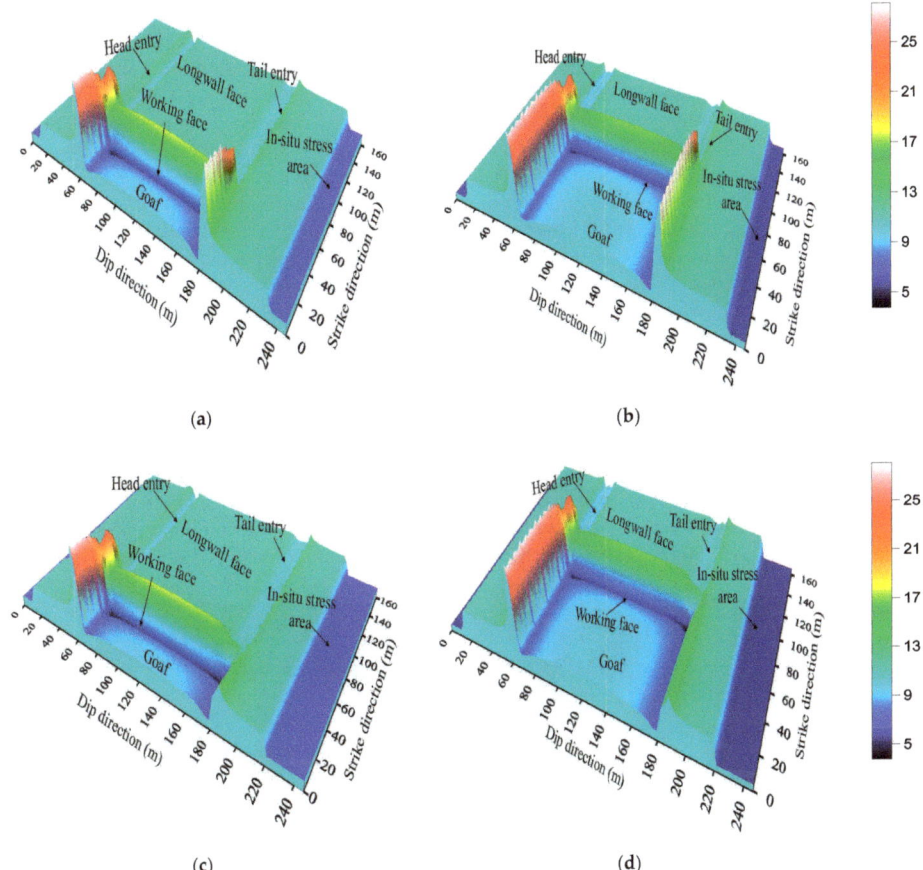

Figure 15. The three-dimensional cloud maps of the abutment stress distribution: (**a**) The stress distribution of 40 m exploitation without roof cutting. (**b**) The stress distribution of 80 m exploitation without roof cutting. (**c**) The stress distribution of 40 m exploitation with roof cutting. (**d**) The stress distribution of 80 m exploitation with roof cutting.

The side abutment pressure of the tail roadway with the roof splitting is significantly lower than that of the head roadway without the roof splitting. The simulation result displays that the peak value of lateral abutment pressure in tail roadway without the roof cutting is around 22.4 MPa. After using the technology of the FRME, the peak value of lateral abutment pressure in tail roadway with the roof cutting is reduced to 18.3 MPa, which is reduced by 18.3%.

Moreover, compared with the average lateral abutment stress in head roadway without roof cutting, the average lateral abutment stress of the tail roadway with roof cutting is also reduced by 18.3%. The technology of the FRME can change the stress state in the surrounding rock and have an excellent pressure relieving effect, which has positive significance to maintain the stability of tail roadway.

After increasing the length of the boundary coal pillar, we can more intuitively observe the influence range of lateral abutment pressure. When the roof is not cut, the lateral abutment pressure in the solid coal of the tail entry returns to the original rock stress at 47 m (see Figure 15a,b). After cutting the roof, the lateral abutment pressure in the solid coal of the tail entry is restored to the original rock stress at 35 m, and the influence range of the lateral abutment pressure is reduced by 25.5% (see Figure 15c,d).

After pre-cracking the roof, the reduction of the lateral abutment pressure of the tail entry is closely related to the slit. The cutting fissure can block the connection between the goaf roof and the entry roof; therefore, the stress of the goaf roof cannot be transmitted to the solid coal of the roadway. In the meantime, the cutting seam can shorten the length of the side roof of the gob-sides in the entry. When the main roof rotates and sinks after the mining of the working face, the deformation degree of extrusion to the roadway roof will be significantly reduced. These are the two main reasons for the decrease of lateral abutment pressure in the tail entry after pre-splitting the roof.

In order to further explain the technical advantages of the FRME, the models with the working face mining to 40 m and 80 m were selected for analysis and sliced along the bottom of the entry to explore the changes in lateral abutment pressure. We can clearly see that when the FRME technology is not used in the tail entry, the lateral abutment pressure presents symmetrical distribution all the time with the advancement of the working face, as shown in Figure 16a,b. When the FRME technology is used in the tail entry, the lateral abutment pressure on both sides of the working face has changed significantly. When the working face advances to 40 m, the stress concentration area on the solid coal of the head entry is closer to the head entry, while the stress concentration on the tail entry side is not obvious, and the abutment pressure is 18.4 MPa, as shown in Figure 16c. When the working face advances to 80 m, the stress concentration area on the solid coal of the head entry tends to be far away from the head entry, and the abutment pressure of the tail entry is about 20 MPa, which is bigger than the mining distance of 40 m, as shown in Figure 16d.

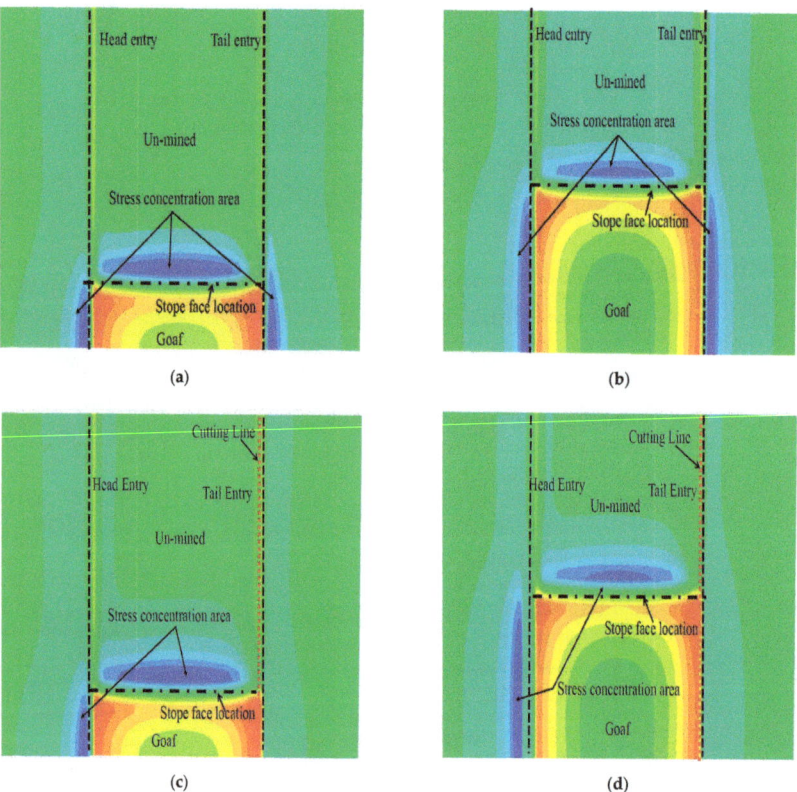

Figure 16. The plane development of the abutment stress distribution: (**a**) The stress distribution of 40 m exploitation without roof cutting. (**b**) The stress distribution of 80 m exploitation without roof cutting. (**c**) The stress distribution of 40 m exploitation with roof cutting. (**d**) The stress distribution of 80 m exploitation with roof cutting.

This phenomenon shows that the lateral abutment pressure increases with the increase in the distance of the lagging working face, which is closely related to the movement of the overburden. The farther the distance from the lagging working face is, the more sufficient the movement of the overburden is and the greater the weight of the overburden carried by the solid coal is, the larger the lateral abutment pressure is.

Figure 17 shows that with the face advancing to 80 m, a plastic failure zone with the width of 11 m and advanced working face of 17 m is formed in the solid coal of the head roadway (see Figure 17a), while a plastic failure zone of 9 m in width and 9.5 m in front of working face is formed in the solid coal of the tail roadway (see Figure 17b). The length and width of the plastic failure zone in the slotted entry is smaller than that in the unslotted entry.

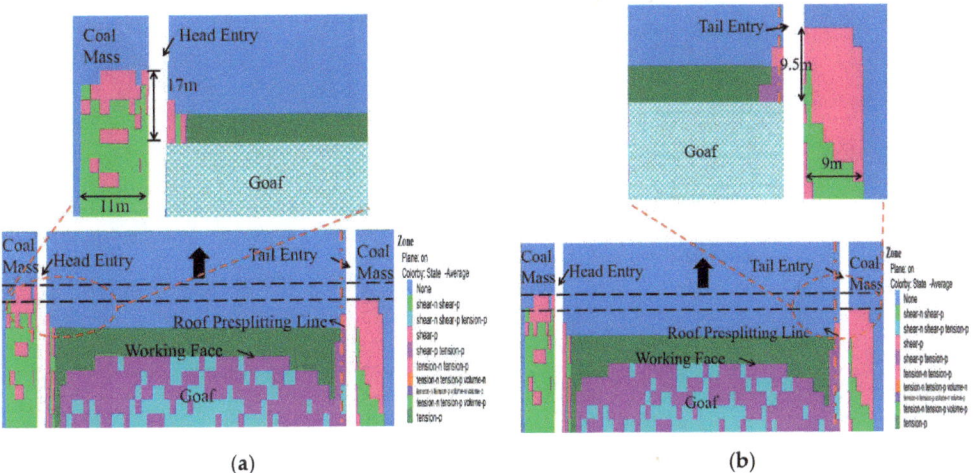

Figure 17. Schematic diagram of plastic zone distribution in roadway: (**a**) Plastic zone of solid coal in the head entry. (**b**) Plastic zone of solid coal in the tail entry.

After pre-splitting and cutting the roof, the influence of coal mining on the solid coal in the tail entry is lessened; that is, the fissure changes the movement state of the overlying rock, so that the weight of the overburden rock supported by the solid coal is reduced. Therefore, the concentration degree of stress is lower, and the impact by upper strata on the coal body becomes smaller. On the other hand, the movement state of the overlying rock on the side of the unslotted head entry has not changed. The weight of the overburden rock born in the solid coal of the head entry is relatively larger, and the concentration degree of stress is higher, which has a greater impact on the coal body.

5. Discussion of Overburden Movement

5.1. Overburden Movement Status in Traditional Coal Pillar Mining

In view of the difference of the abutment pressure at each measuring point between the two stations, we believe that the cutting seam is the main reason for this phenomenon, because the formation of the splitting face can make the roof in the mined-out area collapse more fully, which affects the motion state of the entire coal face roof [26].

As shown in Figure 18, in traditional mining, after the coal seam is mined, the gob roof is difficult to collapse insufficiently. Therefore, the goaf is incompletely filled by the falling gangue. There is large space above the goaf, where the main roof can continue to go down, and when the tensile strength limit is reached, the breakage of the main roof occurs, which generates dynamic pressure impact on the roadway and in turn affects side abutment pressure.

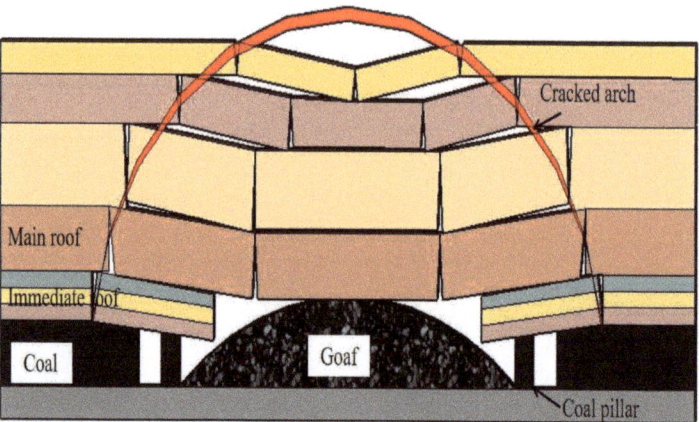

Figure 18. Overburden movement status in traditional coal pillar mining.

In traditional mining, after the coal seam is mined, the gob roof is difficult to collapse insufficiently. Therefore, the goaf is incompletely filled by the falling gangue. There is large space above the goaf where the main roof can continue to go down, and when the tensile strength limit is reached, the breakage of the main roof occurs, which generates dynamic pressure impact on the roadway and in turn affects side abutment pressure. In the meantime, the rotation and subsidence of main roof will squeeze the side roof of the gob-sides, creating a stress concentration zone in the solid coal, and the abutment pressure is further increased. The movement of the rock strata will continue to develop upward. If the upper stratum also fractures, it will once again impact the solid coal of the roadway, causing the weight of the overlying strata borne by the solid coal on both entries will be further rising, while the goaf gangue only bears a small part of the weight of the overlying rock. Therefore, the abutment pressure on the solid coal will increase significantly, and this process continues until the overburden layer only bends and sinks without breaking. The abutment pressure of the solid coal increases, then the destruction degree of the coal body enlarges, creating a large distance between the plastic zone and mining panel. Therefore, the peak point of the abutment pressure is far away from the mining panel. The literature [20,27] believe that the abutment pressure reaches the maximum at the end of plastic failure (the elastic-plastic junction).

5.2. Overburden Movement Status in the FRME

Figure 19 shows that after splitting and cutting the roof, the immediate roof of the goaf in the range of roof-cutting height collapses smoothly under the action of mine pressure and the broken cantilever beam will further fill the gob, which makes the expansion coefficient of gangue augment. The gangue can rapidly connect with the main roof, and it will have a certain bearing capacity to support the main roof after being squeezed by it. Therefore, the space for the main roof to continue sinking is very small, which can prevent the overlying strata from further breaking. Simultaneously, the rotation and subsidence degree of the main roof will be reduced or even disappeared. On the one hand, the weight of the overburden borne by the solid coal is reduced. On the other hand, the extruded gangue has an inclined force on the roof of the retained roadway. As a result, the side abutment pressure of the solid coal must markedly decrease. In addition, the slit can cut off the stress transmission between the entry roof and the goaf roof, and this will avoid the transmission of dynamic loads in the goaf to the solid coal, which is also one of the reasons for the reduction of the side abutment stress. The reduction of abutment pressure will result in the decrease of coal damage degree, and the range of the plastic zone will decrease. Therefore, the peak point of the abutment pressure will be closer to the coal face.

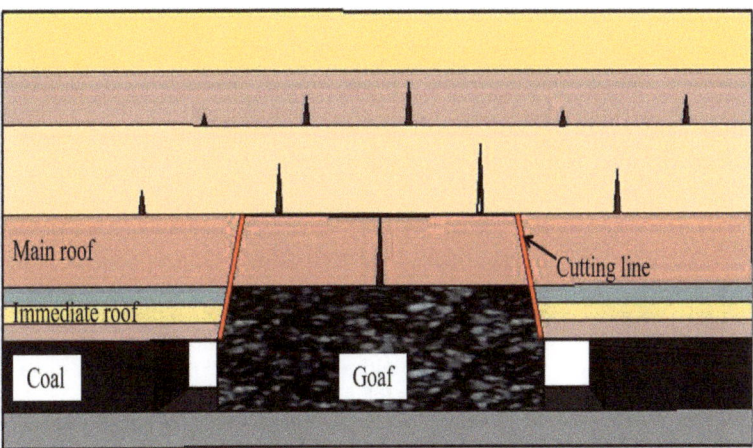

Figure 19. Overburden movement status in the FRME.

The differences in the research on abutment pressure between this paper and the previous papers are shown as follows.

Yan et al. [25] discussed the influence range of lateral abutment pressure in coal pillar under the traditional mining mode through numerical simulation, but did not study the change of abutment pressure when using the FRME. The FRME is an innovative technology for the GER, the study of its lateral abutment pressure can not only fully understand this technology, but also better explain the advantages of the FRME over the traditional mining technology. Zhen et al. [28] compared and analyzed the difference of abutment pressure between traditional mining and the FRME through numerical simulation. However, they did not explore the reasons for this difference in depth. Based on field measurement, this paper considers that the overburden movement is the root cause of the difference in abutment pressure under different mining conditions. The state of overburden movement when using the FRME is described in detail, and the factors of abutment pressure reduction are analyzed from many aspects. Yao et al. [29] discussed the lateral abutment pressure by means of numerical simulation and borehole stress measurement, but did not analyze the lateral abutment pressure in the direction of the coalface strike. On the basis of the FDU field measurement, the abutment pressure in the strike and dip direction of solid coal on the entry under the mining mode of the FRME is researched in detail in this paper, and the strike abutment pressure of the solid coal can be divided into five regions: slow increasing zone, sharp increasing zone, rapid reducing zone, fluctuation enlarging zone (enlarging zone), and stable zone. The differences in abutment pressure on both sides of the working face are compared in detail. Zhang et al. [30] used the vibrating wire stress meters to monitor the advanced abutment pressure of the working face. Because the vibrating wire stress meters are made of rigid materials and cannot be deformed with the change of borehole surrounding rock, they will result in the loss of a large amount of data, which cannot really explain the change of abutment pressure with the advance of the working face. Shen et al. [31] used vibrating wire stress meters to monitor the stress changes of the roadway, so that the stress meters were able to monitor the stress changes parallel to the roadway axis, perpendicular to the roadway axis, and 45°, respectively. Because the direction of the stress meters is difficult to control when they are installed in the borehole and traditional stress meters can only monitor the change of the abutment pressure in a certain direction, they cannot realize the omni-directional abutment pressure monitoring in the borehole, resulting in a large error in the measurement data. In order to overcome the above disadvantages of the traditional borehole stress meters, the FDU has been independently developed to monitor the changes of abutment pressure in coal. When the FDU is used, it can actively apply prestress to the surrounding rock of the borehole after expansion, so that it can fully contact with the surrounding rock and move cooperatively with the surrounding rock, which can monitor the change of abutment pressure in the whole process, and the reliability of measurement data is high.

6. Conclusions

The FRME has broad application prospects. It is necessary to deeply research the variations of the abutment pressure and to reveal the movement laws of the overlying strata when this technology is applied. Because the movement of overburden rock is the fundamental reason for the deformations of the roadway surroundings, we should not focus on the surface problems such as the moving amount of roof and floor, the stress monitoring of anchor cable, hydraulic support pressure, and so on. A clear understanding of the movement laws of overlying rock is of great significance for predicting roadway deformations, coalface pressure, coal mine disasters, and so on. The main conclusions of this paper are as follows.

Through the field applications of the self-developed abutment pressure monitoring equipment, the measured data completely meet the needs for analyzing problems, which explains the reliability and accuracy of the new equipment. In the future, more site monitoring tests and in-depth research about the change laws of abutment pressure are needed.

On-site monitoring data indicate that the side abutment pressure in the entry of roof cutting is different from the entry without roof cutting. In the direction of the coalface strike, the peak value of abutment stress at each measuring point of the entry with roof cutting has been reduced by an average of 17.2%, and the peak point is also closer to the coalface. However, the tendency for variation in the strike abutment pressure of the solid coal in two roadways is almost the same. Therefore, it can be divided into five zones: slow increasing zone, sharp increasing zone, rapid decreasing zone, fluctuation rising zone (rising zone), and stability zone. In the dip direction of the coalface, the peak point position of the side abutment pressure in two gateways is different. The peak point of the side abutment pressure of the roadway with cutting roof is 9 m away from the coal wall, and the peak point of the side abutment pressure of the roadway without cutting roof is 11 m away from the coal wall.

The numerical simulation results show that the lateral abutment pressure of the roadway with cutting roof is significantly reduced. Meanwhile, with the stoping face advancing, the width and length of the plastic zone formed in the solid coal of the roadway with roof cutting are obviously smaller than those of the roadway without roof cutting.

Through the careful analysis of the abutment pressure data of both roadways, combined with the field practice, we believe that the cutting fissure has an obvious effect on the movement of overlying rock. After splitting and cutting the roof, the immediate roof of the goaf in the range of roof-cutting height collapses smoothly under the action of mine pressure and the broken cantilever beam will further fill the gob, which makes the expansion coefficient of gangue augment. The gangue can rapidly connect with the main roof, and it will have a certain bearing capacity to support the main roof after being squeezed by it. Therefore, the space for the main roof to continue sinking is very small, which can prevent the overlying strata from further breakage.

Author Contributions: All the authors contributed to this paper. Z.G. and W.L. discussed and conceived the research. W.L. and D.Y. performed the numerical simulation. W.L. conducted the field test. S.Y. and Z.M. revised the article. All authors have read and agreed to the published version of the manuscript.

Funding: This research received no external funding.

Institutional Review Board Statement: Not applicable.

Informed Consent Statement: Not applicable.

Conflicts of Interest: The authors declare no conflict of interest.

References

1. Wang, Q.; He, M.C.; Yang, J.; Gong, H.K.; Jiang, B.; Yu, H.C. Study of a no-pillar mining technique with automatically formed gob-side entry retaining for longwall mining in coal mines. *Int. J. Rock Mech. Min. Sci.* **2018**, *110*, 1–8. [CrossRef]
2. Zhang, Z.Z.; Bai, J.B.; Chen, Y.; Yan, S. An innovative approach for gob-side entry retaining in highly gassy fully-mechanized longwall top-coal caving. *Int. J. Rock Mech. Min. Sci.* **2015**, *80*, 1–11. [CrossRef]
3. Zhang, N.; Yuan, L.; Han, C.L.; Xue, J.H.; Kan, J.G. Stability and deformation of surrounding rock in pillarless gob-side entry retaining. *Saf. Sci.* **2012**, *50*, 593–599. [CrossRef]
4. Tan, Y.L.; Yu, F.H.; Ning, J.G.; Zhao, T.B. Design and construction of entry retaining wall along a gob side under hard roof stratum. *Int. J. Rock Mech. Min. Sci.* **2015**, *77*, 115–121. [CrossRef]
5. Yang, H.Y.; Cao, S.G.; Wang, S.Q.; Fan, Y.C.; Wang, S.; Chen, X.Z. Adaptation assessment of gob-side entry retaining based on geological factors. *Eng. Geol.* **2016**, *209*, 143–151. [CrossRef]
6. He, M.C.; Gao, Y.B.; Yang, J.; Gong, W.L. An innovative approach for gob-side entry retaining in thick coal seam longwall mining. *Energies* **2017**, *10*, 1785. [CrossRef]
7. He, M.C.; Zhu, G.L.; Guo, Z.B. Longwall mining "cutting cantilever beam theory" and 110 mining method in China—The third mining science innovation. *J. Rock Mech. Geotech.* **2015**, *7*, 483–492. [CrossRef]
8. Gao, Y.B.; Liu, D.Q.; Zhang, X.Y.; He, M.C. Analysis and optimization of entry stability in underground longwall mining. *Sustainability* **2017**, *9*, 2079. [CrossRef]
9. He, M.C.; Gong, W.L.; Wang, J.; Qi, P.; Tao, Z.G.; Du, S.; Peng, Y.Y. Development of a novel energy-absorbing bolt with extraordinarily large elongation and constant resistance. *Int. J. Rock Mech. Min. Sci.* **2014**, *67*, 29–42. [CrossRef]
10. Tao, Z.G.; Zhu, Z.; Han, W.S.; Zhu, C.; Liu, W.F.; Zheng, X.H.; Yin, X.; He, M.C. Static tension test and the finite element analysis of constant resistance and large deformation anchor cable. *Adv. Mech. Eng.* **2018**, *10*. [CrossRef]
11. Gao, Y.B.; Wang, Y.J.; Yang, J.; Zhang, X.Y.; He, M.C. Meso- and macroeffects of roof split blasting on the stability of gateroad surroundings in an innovative nonpillar mining method. *Tunn. Undergr. Space Technol.* **2019**, *90*, 99–118. [CrossRef]
12. Hu, J.Z.; Zhang, X.Y.; Gao, Y.B.; Ma, Z.M.; Xu, X.Z.; Zhang, X.P. Directional presplit blasting in an innovative no-pillar mining approach. *J. Geophys. Eng.* **2019**, *16*, 875–893. [CrossRef]
13. Guo, Z.B.; Wang, Q.; Li, Z.H.; He, M.C.; Ma, Z.B.; Zhong, F.X.; Hu, J. Surrounding rock control of an innovative gob-side entry retaining with energy-absorbing supporting in deep mining. *Int. J. Low-Carbon Technol.* **2019**, *14*, 23–35. [CrossRef]
14. Wang, Y.J.; Gao, Y.B.; Wang, E.Y.; He, M.C.; Yang, J. Roof deformation characteristics and preventive techniques using a novel non-pillar mining method of gob-side entry retaining by roof cutting. *Energies* **2018**, *11*, 627. [CrossRef]
15. Fan, D.Y.; Liu, X.S.; Tan, Y.L.; Song, S.L.; Gu, Q.H.; Yan, L.; Xu, Q. Roof cutting parameters design for gob-side entry in deep coal mine: A case study. *Energies* **2019**, *12*, 2032. [CrossRef]
16. Guo, Z.B.; Zhang, L.; Ma, Z.B.; Zhong, F.X.; Yu, J.C.; Wang, S.M. Numerical investigation of the influence of roof fracturing angle on the stability of gob-side entry subjected to dynamic loading. *Shock Vib.* **2019**, *2019*, 1–13. [CrossRef]
17. Sun, X.M.; Li, G.; Zhao, C.W.; Tang, J.Q.; He, M.C.; Song, P.; Miao, C.Y. Numerical investigation of gob-side entry retaining through precut overhanging hard roof to control rockburst. *Adv. Civ. Eng.* **2018**, *2018*, 1–10. [CrossRef]
18. Ma, Z.M.; Wang, J.; He, M.C.; Gao, Y.B.; Hu, J.Z.; Wang, Q. Key technologies and application test of an innovative noncoal pillar mining approach: A case study. *Energies* **2018**, *11*, 2853. [CrossRef]
19. Hu, J.Z.; He, M.C.; Wang, J.; Ma, Z.M.; Wang, Y.J.; Zhang, X.Y. Key parameters of roof cutting of gob-side entry retaining in a deep inclined thick coal seam with hard roof. *Energies* **2019**, *12*, 934. [CrossRef]
20. Ma, X.G.; He, M.C.; Wang, J.; Gao, Y.B.; Zhu, D.Y.; Liu, Y.X. Mine strata pressure characteristics and mechanisms in gob-side entry retention by roof cutting under medium-thick coal seam and compound roof conditions. *Energies* **2018**, *11*, 2539. [CrossRef]
21. Shabanimashcool, M.; Li, C.C. A numerical study of stress changes in barrier pillars and a border area in a longwall coal mine. *Int. J. Coal Geol.* **2013**, *106*, 39–47. [CrossRef]
22. Cheng, Y.M.; Wang, J.A.; Xie, G.X.; Wei, W.B. Three-dimensional analysis of coal barrier pillars in tailgate area adjacent to the fully mechanized top caving mining face. *Int. J. Rock Mech. Min. Sci.* **2010**, *47*, 1372–1383. [CrossRef]
23. Bai, J.B.; Shen, W.L.; Guo, G.L.; Wang, X.Y.; Yu, Y. Roof deformation, failure characteristics, and preventive techniques of gob-side entry driving heading adjacent to the advancing working face. *Rock Mech. Rock Eng.* **2015**, *48*, 2447–2458. [CrossRef]
24. Suchowerska, A.M.; Merifield, R.S.; Carter, J.P. Vertical stress changes in multi-seam mining under supercritical longwall panels. *Int. J. Rock Mech. Min.* **2013**, *61*, 306–320. [CrossRef]
25. Yan, S.; Bai, J.B.; Wang, X.Y.; Huo, L.J. An innovative approach for gateroad layout in highly gassy longwall top coal caving. *Int. J. Rock Mech. Min.* **2013**, *59*, 33–41. [CrossRef]
26. Liu, H.; Dai, J.; Jiang, J.Q.; Wang, P.; Yang, J.Q. Analysis of overburden structure and pressure-relief effect of hard roof blasting and cutting. *Adv. Civ. Eng.* **2019**, *2019*, 1–14. [CrossRef]
27. Sun, Y.J.; Zuo, J.P.; Karakus, M.; Wang, J.T. Investigation of movement and damage of integral overburden during shallow coal seam mining. *Int. J. Rock Mech. Min.* **2019**, *117*, 63–75. [CrossRef]
28. Zhen, E.; Wang, Y.J.; Yang, J.; He, M.C. Comparison of the macroscopical stress field distribution characteristics between a novel non-pillar mining technique and two other current methods. *Adv. Mech. Eng.* **2019**, *11*, 1–15. [CrossRef]
29. Yao, Q.L.; Zhou, J.; Li, Y.A.; Tan, Y.M.; Jiang, Z.G. Distribution of side abutment stress in roadway subjected to dynamic pressure and its engineering application. *Shock Vib.* **2015**, *2015*, 1–11.

30. Zhang, N.; Zhang, N.C.; Han, C.L. Borehole stress monitoring analysis on advanced abutment pressure induced by longwall mining. *Arab. J. Geosci.* **2014**, *7*, 457–463. [CrossRef]
31. Shen, B.; King, A.; Guo, H. Displacement, stress and seismicity in roadway roofs during mining-induced failure. *Int. J. Rock Mech. Min.* **2008**, *45*, 672–688. [CrossRef]

MDPI
St. Alban-Anlage 66
4052 Basel
Switzerland
Tel. +41 61 683 77 34
Fax +41 61 302 89 18
www.mdpi.com

Energies Editorial Office
E-mail: energies@mdpi.com
www.mdpi.com/journal/energies

www.ingramcontent.com/pod-product-compliance
Lightning Source LLC
LaVergne TN
LVHW070400100526
838202LV00014B/1355